KU-822-026

Rare Prologues
and
Epilogues
1642—1700

EDITED BY
AUTREY NELL
WILEY

KENNIKAT PRESS
Port Washington, N. Y./London

RARE PROLOGUES AND EPILOGUES

First published in 1940
Reissued in 1970 by Kennikat Press
Library of Congress Catalog Card No: 79-113350
ISBN 0-8046-0988-8

Manufactured by Taylor Publishing Company   Dallas, Texas

6002076642

Rare Prologues
and
Epilogues

THE
PROLOGUE
TO HIS
MAJESTY
At the first PLAY, presented at the Cock-pit in
WHITEHALL;

Being part of that Noble Entertainment which Their MAIESTIES received *Novemb.*19.
from his Grace the Duke of ALBEMARLE.

Greatest of Monarchs, welcome to this place
Which Majesty so oft was wont to grace
Before our Exile, to divert the Court,
And ballance weighty Cares with harmless sport.
This truth we can to our advantage say,
They that would have no KING, would have no Play :
The Laurel and the Crown together went,
Had the same Foes, and the same Banishment :
The Ghosts of their great Ancestors they fear'd,
Who by the art of conjuring Poets rear'd,
Our HARRIES & our EDWARDS long since dead
Still on the Stage a march of Glory tread :
Those Monuments of Fame (they thought) would stain
And teach the People to despise their Reign :
Nor durst they look into the Muses Well,
Least the cleer Spring their ugliness should tell ;
Affrighted with the shadow of their Rage,
They broke the Mirror of the times, the Stage ;
The Stage against them still maintain'd the War,
When they debauch'd the Pulpit and the Bar.
Though to be Hypocrites, be our Praise alone,
Tis our peculiar boast that we were none.

What er'e they taught, we practis'd what was true,
And something we had learn'd of honor too,
When by Your Danger, and our Duty prest,
We acted in the Field, and not in Jest ;
Then for the Cause our Tyring-house they sackt,
And silenc't us that they alone might act ;
And (to our shame) most dext'rously they do it,
Out-act the Players, and out-ly the Poet ;
But all the other Arts appear'd so scarce,
Ours were the Moral Lectures, theirs the Farse :
This spacious Land their Theater became,
And they Grave Counsellors, and Lords in Name ;
Which these Mechanicks Personate so ill
That ev'n the Oppressed with contempt they fill,
But when the Lyons dreadful skin they took,
They roar'd so loud that the whole Forrest shook ;
The noise kept all the Neighborhood in awe,
Who thought 'twas the true Lyon by his Pawe.
If feigned Vertue could such Wonders do,
What may we not expect from this that's true !
But this Great Theme must serve another Age,
To fill our Story, and adorne our Stage.

LONDON, Printed for G. Bedell and T. Collins, at the
Middle-Temple Gate in Fleet-street. 1660.

British Museum

THIS WHITEHALL PROLOGUE IS THE EARLIEST
DATED BROADSIDE

ACKNOWLEDGMENTS

The labour of gathering and studying these prologues and epilogues has acquainted me with courtesy that I am pleased to remember here.

To the Right Hon. Lord Balniel I am deeply indebted for the privilege of reprinting Tate's Prologue to King William and Queen Mary from his private library, Bibliotheca Lindesiana. I have also to thank Mr. P. J. Dobell for his generous and prompt attention to my questions regarding rare pieces made available to me from his collection.

Hospitality in libraries it is also a pleasure to acknowledge. The Keeper of Books, Mr. W. A. Marsden, and the Superintendent of the Reading Room, Mr. A. I. Ellis, of the British Museum assisted me in securing the texts of some of my rarest examples. Over several years, especial attention to my inquiries has come from Mr. C. H. Wilkinson, Worcester College, Oxford ; Mr. S. G. Wright, the Bodleian Library; Miss Fannie Ratchford, the Wrenn Library, the University of Texas; Mr. J. A. Petherbridge, the British Museum; and Dr. E. M. Cox, the Garrick Club Library in London. For the privilege of reprinting and reproduction, I am grateful to the Right Hon. Lord Balniel, Mr. P. J. Dobell, the governing body of Christ Church, Oxford, and the authorities of the Bodleian, the British Museum, the Chetham Library in Manchester, the Folger Library, the Harvard College Library, the Henry E. Huntington Library, the National Library of Scotland, the New York Public Library, the Victoria and Albert Museum, the Worcester College Library at Oxford, and the Wrenn Library at the University of Texas.

For permission to use parts of my articles already published, I thank the editors of *Modern Language Notes*, *The Publications of the Modern Language Association*, and *The Review of English Studies*.

vii

PREFACE

The rare prologues and epilogues in this book have been long inaccessible, though their importance is without question. As a *genre* that was necessary to the theatre two hundred and fifty years ago, they have survived after the fashion of other timely writings, being preserved obscurely in tomes of miscellanea, indifferently catalogued, and widely dispersed in the libraries of Great Britain and the United States. They are now brought together for the convenience and information of readers who are interested in the theatre, dramatic history, literature, society, politics, rhetoric, oratory, printers and booksellers, poets, actors, and numerous mirrorings of seventeenth-century taste.

First editions are reprinted with critical addenda, proving authorship and giving brief biographies of the poets, accounts of the speakers, interpretative backgrounds, and variant readings. The information provided therein comes from an examination of more than 1,600 plays, as well as miscellanies, newspapers, manuscripts, and critical discourses leading up to Pope's triumph in the Prologue to *Cato*.

It is the editor's intent to give in their first printing (with spelling, punctuation, and capitalization unchanged, though the type must be modern) and in their original settings the seventeenth-century prologues and epilogues which have survived years of careless indifference since the Restoration. Much wit from the best poets of the age was spent in them; fine art in the speaking of them was required of England's greatest players. They are now collectors' items of price.

In the essays which follow, I am pleased to cite the findings of able scholars and name several whose generous response to inquiries breeds appreciation in the investigator. I am especially grateful to Mr. C. H. Wilkinson, of Worcester College, Oxford, for the unique *Prologue to the Reviv'd Alchemist*, and to Mr. R. B. McKerrow for his study of the printing of this piece. To Professor R. H. Griffith and Professor R. A. Law, of the University of Texas, Professor Hazelton Spencer, of the Johns Hopkins University, and Professor E. H. Wright, of Columbia University, I am much in debt for their critical reading of this book in manuscript and for their friendly advice as scholars many times. Since the beginning of my interest in prologues and epilogues when a fellow of the American Association of University Women, I have known the untiring and most valuable assistance of Professor Griffith, Curator of the Wrenn Library at the University of Texas, where my research in rare editions began.

This work presents material that I collected in part when appointed to a fellowship by the American Council of Learned Societies. I have since continued my research and discovered useful material up to the hour of publication. To the Council for their assistance at the beginning of the study, I express my sincere appreciation. To my sister Margaret for her ever-ready assistance throughout I am always grateful.

AUTREY NELL WILEY.

LONDON, 1939.

CONTENTS

Contents

Contents

Contents

Contents

Contents

Contents

Contents

Contents

Contents

ILLUSTRATIONS

The Earliest Dated Broadside Prologue, Frontispiece

INTRODUCTION

Most of the prologues and epilogues of English drama are semi-oratorical appendages in which the dramatist in the person of the actor stepped out of the ideal world of the stage and spoke directly to an audience. Some, however, are preludes and final pieces framed in the imaginary scenes of a play. Although parasitic in being always created for plays or occasions, they drew so near to independence, to being distinct entities, that as there were elegiac poets, so were there prologue-writing friends. Addresses from the apron were looked upon as species of literary composition, for on numerous occasions even the prologues and epilogues attempted to define themselves. From 1607, when the Induction to Marston's *What You Will* called the prologue an inductive speech, to 1709, when the epilogue to Mrs. Centlivre's *The Busie Body* called epilogues execution speeches, definitions were struck off with some frequency. The prologue was a petition, an organ of censure, an apology or excuse, a satire, a supplicatory address, a grace before a feast, a bill of fare, and a dedication; the epilogue, a plea for pardon, an excuse, an enquiry into censure, a guide to severer judgments, an entreaty for grace, a benediction, a piece of flattery, an arrant bribery, a satire, a petition, a glad flourish, and a swan's note.

To the English playwrights goes the distinction of developing prologues and epilogues that were well-defined types of literary composition, the epilogue of their manufacture being unlike that of any other people. Yet both pieces had their origin in classical antiquity. The prologue, older than the epilogue, is regarded sometimes as a survival of the *proagon* in which Sophocles led on his chorus, the *dithyramb*, the chant of the Hierophant, and the *prologos,* that part of the Greek drama preceding the entrance of the chorus which is probably related to the words spoken by the sacred Herald who proclaimed the coming of the chorus.[1] When of a satiric nature, with a tincture of buffoonery, it had its origin, perhaps, in the Roman *mimus*, a term which designated both the piece and the actor, who, according to Mr. Chambers, performed originally in monologue.[2] The epilogue had a classical source[3] in the moral reflection with which a chorus concluded a Greek play and in the Roman *plaudite*, usually a line requesting applause in the familiar conclusions of Roman comedy: *plausum date, vos plaudite*, and *Spectatores, bene valete, plaudite atque exsurgite*. From the moral reflection of the Greek chorus may very well have come the epilogue that referred to the action of the drama; from the *plaudite*, the epilogue begging approval.

Although deriving from certain forms in classical antiquity, prologues and epilogues in English drama bear the marks of varied influences that played upon these original patterns found in introductions and perorations in the theatre. The priest of the church service acted as a Prologue and was later represented in drama by the Expositor, the Doctor, and the *Baleus Prolocutor*, who prologued plays in a didactic fashion.[4] Some epilogues descended from the *Te Deum* of the religious service and in the sixteenth and early seventeenth centuries shared with the closing prayer for the sovereign. From the *Parade*, or preliminary patter, Mr. Chambers derives the prologue spoken by the author or the presenter of the play,[5] a type which was popular in its varied forms after the Restoration. To the office of the Chorus the prologue sometimes succeeded while retaining its original character:

[1] Gilbert Murray, "An Excursus on the Ritual Forms Preserved in Greek Tragedy," Jane Ellen Harrison, *Themis* (Cambridge: The University Press, 1912), pp. 359–363.

[2] E. K. Chambers, *The Mediæval Stage* (Oxford: The University Press, 1903), I, 5.

[3] W. Davenport Adams, *A Dictionary of the Drama* (London: Chatto & Windus, 1904), I.

[4] E. K. Chambers, *The Elizabethan Stage* (Oxford: The University Press, 1923), II, 148.

[5] *The Mediæval Stage*, I, 85.

. . . in the person of Will Summers which I
have put on to play the Prologue, and meane not
to put off, till the play be done. Ile sit as a Chorus,
and flowte the Actors and him at the end of every
Sceane.[1]

And the Chorus, as in Shakespeare's *Henry the Fifth*, occasionally prologued each of a play's five acts or supplied the
epilogue to such plays as *Henry the Fifth* and *The Knight of the
Burning Pestle*. Seeking other instances of this kind of
absorption which obscured distinctions in form, we observe
that the induction frequently gathered up both the prologue
and the chorus, and the dumb-show had its presenter who
was sometimes identified with the prologue. There was then
a constant play of influences. The prologue, sometimes absorbed
by other forms, also adopted for itself the distinctions of
those same forms that had on another occasion absorbed it.
After 1660, for example, the introductory dialogue, called
the induction in Shakespeare's day, was set before dramas
under the word, *Prologue;* other extraneities—the chorus
and the induction—were seldom revived. Yet after the
Restoration, prologues and epilogues, flexible vehicles of
wit and satire, became the constant aids to almost every
performance in the theatre.

By far the greater number were written in verse, although
prose had a temporary vogue after Lyly and came readily
to the poet's hand when plain prose answered the need
for novelty:

. . . a Prologue in Verse, is as stale as a black
velvet Cloak, and a Bay Garland; therefore you shall
have it plain prose.[2]

Always the poets were aware that a prologue should rime,
but just what verse form best suited the stage-oration was not
early fixed upon. Shakespeare found a source of humour

[1] Thomas Nash, *A pleasant Comedie, called Summers last Will and Testament*
(1600), Prologue.
[2] *The Woman-Hater* (1607), Prologue.

in a reference to the *eight's* and *six's* used in some speeches:

> *Bot* . . . write me a prologue, and let the prologue seem to say, we will do no harm. . . .
> *Quin.* Well, we will have such a prologue, and it shall be written in eight and six.
> *Bot.* No, make it two more; let it be written in eight and eight.[1]

The old tumbling measures, rime royal, and blank verse served with some frequency in the sixteenth century but soon passed into disuse. The sonnet, introducing *The Maid's Metamorphosis* and *Romeo and Juliet*, was not adapted to the manner of stage-oratory; nor was the ode, as used after *The Malcontent.* The ballad, interesting as it was when sung as a prologue to *The Man's the Master*, attained no vogue. New stanzaic forms likewise were invented and discarded. The use of some one kind of verse appears to have been desired, but it was only after 1660 that prologues and epilogues found their characteristic form in the most popular style of the age: iambic-pentameter couplets, with occasional triplets.

I. THE VOGUE OF PROLOGUES AND EPILOGUES

Because prologues and epilogues were ephemeral, it is not possible to state their vogue with the authority of indisputable statistics drawn from playbooks and miscellanies. Many originals no doubt were lost; others were added to dramas that were revived or published by friends of the authors. Editions of plays did not always contain all the prologues and epilogues that were spoken when the plays were presented; and many folio half-sheets giving the texts of popular speeches must have gone into the fire with other papers of only a day's interest.

Before the middle of the sixteenth century one play out of five made use of an introduction or a conclusion or both,

---

[1] *A Midsummer-Night's Dream*, III, i. Professor R. A. Law suggests to me the likelihood of a specific reference to the prologue to Preston's *Cambises.*

which may be termed prologue and epilogue. From 1558 to 1642 the popularity of stage-orations increased, and about forty-eight per cent. of the plays of this period had prologues and epilogues. Of these some—according to my count, sixteen per cent.—had only prologues; eleven per cent. only epilogues. Contemporary allusions show that the vogue during this period was fluctuating. When, at the close of the sixteenth century, a Prologue was used, the speaker had to tell his audience who he was:

> I am a Prologue, should I not tell y(o)u soe
> You would scarce knowe me; tis soe longe agoe
> Since Prologues were in use; men put behinde
> now, that they were wont to put before.
> Thepilogue is in fashion; prologues no more.[1]

Benvolio scoffed at prologues:

> The date is out of such prolixity:
> We'll have no Cupid hoodwink'd with a scarf . . .
> Nor no without-book prologue, faintly spoke
> After the prompter, for our entrance;
> But let them measure us by what they will.[2]

Rosalynd, closing *As You Like It*, conceded that an epilogue was not necessary to a good play, but urged that as to advertise good wine men used good bushes, so good plays proved "the better by the help of good epilogues." Shakespeare accepted the epilogue without repining; but an implication of pleading for favour in prologue and epilogue aroused discontent in Beaumont and Fletcher, who in using them to inveigh against them bore witness to their growing frequency. The prologue to *Nice Valour* told the audience that the poet was reluctant to obey "the late fashion" of addressing them in a couching vein and, aside from this one statement opposing the use of the begging prologue, the speaker introducing the drama

[1] *The Birthe of Hercules* (1610), Prologue. The Malone Society, 1911. The date of composition is before 1600.
[2] *Romeo and Juliet*, I, iv, 3–9.

had nothing to say. Yet it was not merely pride that made the poets scorn a custom encouraging servility. They recognized the absurdity of fooling themselves, or their audiences, into supposing that a Monsieur with a begging knee could wheedle men into applauding a play that had not pleased them:

> Custom, and that a law we must obey,
> In the way of epilogue bids me something say,
> Howe'er to little purpose, since we know,
> If you are pleased, unbegg'd you will bestow
> A gentle censure: on the other side,
> If that this play deserve to be decried
> In your opinions, all that I can say
> Will never turn the stream the other way.[1]

Nevertheless, custom kept the prefatory address alive until a later day when, with renewed vigour of an astonishing nature, the prologue, as well as the epilogue, became an essential of the stage.

As a consequence,˙in 1660, immediately upon the revival of drama, the orator in the long cloak who had prologued plays before 1642 came again. He often put on new habits, and his suit for favour so rapidly consumed the stock of wit that, after hardly more than two years, the poets began to fear a dearth of fancy. For the next forty years, they spent their wit in stage-orations accompanying nine out of every ten plays. Scribblers took up the trade, and many a gallant sought a place in the society of the wits because he had composed a prologue. Rebuking the age after the manner of some great poet like Dryden, and riming on *stage* and *age*, *pit* and *wit*, *raillery* and *gallery*, these first cousins to some Ned Softly spent their little wits so extravagantly that they went into bankruptcy. But, refusing to acknowledge their poverty, they wrote on. Right or wrong, prologues had to be written; epilogues were inevitable.

[1] Massinger, *A Very Woman* (1634), Epilogue. For a similar attitude, see Beaumont and Fletcher, *The Custom of the Country* (Fol., 1647), Epilogue.

II. PROLOGUE-WRITERS

Although the custom of writing prologues and epilogues for other men's plays is essentially a feature of the history of drama after 1660, there were poets who served as makers of stage-orations upon request before the Puritans yielded their power to Charles. As early as 1601 Thomas Dekker, it will be recalled, received ten shillings for a prologue and an epilogue that he wrote for *Penesciones Pillet*.[1] Henslowe recorded two other instances of the custom: Middleton's prologue and epilogue for "the play of bacon" in 1602[2] and Chettle's prologue and epilogue for the Court in the same year.[3] In 1637 Thomas Heywood published thirty-five prologues and epilogues as "Sundry Fancies writ upon severall occasions."[4] In 1646 James Shirley published a volume of poems containing eighteen prologues and epilogues written to plays presented in England and elsewhere, of which several were for plays by other authors. The names of more than sixty poets listed with the prologues and epilogues that they wrote for fellow dramatists' plays, and the miscellanies having prologues and epilogues included in their verse, as indicated in the appendix to this volume, show that seventeenth-century playwrights were aware of the profits that came from having a play cried up by a partial friend:

> And had we made the Prologue wee'd say more.
> That labour he hath sav'd us, cause he wood
> No partial friend should crie it up for good.[5]

In fact, poets of excellence, as well as versifiers, were kept busy at the trade of recommending plays. It was a friendly office to provide a prologue or an epilogue to some ambitious playwright's new exercise, and prologues and epilogues contributed by other hands frequently appeared with the published plays. It is likely that the authorship is usually

[1] *Henslowe's Diary*, ed. W. W. Greg, 1904, p. 153.
[2] *Ibid.*, p. 172.   [3] *Ibid.*, p. 173.
[4] *Pleasant Dialogues and Drammas*, 1637.
[5] Sir Aston Cockain, *Trappolin* (1658), Prologue.

acknowledged in print, if by no more certain description than such accompanying statements as "Written by a Friend," "Written by a Person of Quality," or "Sent by an Unknown Hand." The unfortunate stranger to the Town had to write without the amendments of the witty men; and when he prepared to give his play to the theatre, he had no choice but to write his own prologue and epilogue:

> It is the fate of Strangers to the Town
> To have the Play and Prologue too their own:
> Whilst Writers here for one another sweat,
> Clubbing like Carr-men when a Brother's set.
> Nay, dull insipid Farce you will commend
> For sake of Prologue-writing gifted Friend.[1]

Needless to say, the youthful playwright in his first venture sought anxiously the support of a prologuing friend. Chief among these writers, of course, was Dryden, to whom many applied for prologues and epilogues. Saunders attributed no small part of his play's success to the corrections and the epilogue that it received from Dryden:

> Nevertheless, their perswasions and inducements cou'd not make me Presume, to trust so far to my own small abilities, or to rely so much on my own weak Judgment, as to send it forth into the World, until it had past the Censures of some (I may say) the greatest part of the Witty and Judicious Men of the Town; untill it had receiv'd some Rules for Correction from Mr. Dryden himself, who also was pleas'd to Grace it with an Epilogue, to which it ows no small part of its success.[2]

The numerous prologues and epilogues written by Dryden during a period of thirty-two years testify to the demands that were made upon his genius for writing stage-orations for other men's plays. Ever the master of entertaining his

[1] John Leanerd, *The Counterfeits* (1679), Prologue.
[2] Charles Saunders, *Tamerlane the Great* (1681), Preface.

audience in this mode, he had no cause to fear a rival. Some envy perhaps brewed, for just when he was entering upon a long season in which he was acknowledged the first of poets in the theatre, his prologues and epilogues received a rap in *The Rehearsal*. But contemporary taste relished his novel stage-orations which fitted any play and any part, either the first or the last—a mongrel species of prologue and epilogue in which a sparkling wit enlivened discourses upon such topics as literary criticism and politics. In the opinion of London audiences, no prologue-writer sat near the throne of John Dryden.

The majority of the prologues and epilogues were written by men who knew the playhouse at first hand, and among these playwrights and actors there were some who enjoyed the friendship of the Laureate. The prologue that introduced the play of John Dryden, Junior, *The Husband His Own Cuckold*, was written by Congreve, author of several prologues and epilogues and subject of Dryden's generous prophecy:

> . . . Thou shalt be seen
> (Though with some short parenthesis between,)
> High on the throne of wit, and, seated there,
> Not mine,—that's little,—but thy laurel wear.[1]

The French Huguenot, Motteux, whom Dryden praised as the foreign guest who overmatched the most in an idiom not his own,[2] wrote prologues and epilogues for Ravenscroft, Farquhar, Vanbrugh, and others. Haynes, whose gaiety made him the most popular comedian of his day, wrote comical prologues and epilogues for such men as Powell, Ravenscroft, and Farquhar. To him goes the additional distinction of sometimes speaking his own compositions, as indicated by the appendix to this work and the folio half-sheets reprinted in the following pages. More actor than poet, Haynes referred in 1696 to his occasional ventures into literary crafts:

[1] "Epistle the Twelfth," *The Works of John Dryden*, ed. George Saintsbury (Edinburgh, 1885), XI, 59.
[2] "Epistle the Thirteenth," *The Works of John Dryden*, XI, 67–68.

After so many Years treading the Stage, where
both in my acting and capering Days (to my Vanity
be it spoken) I made no inconsiderable Figure; I
come at last to visit the publick in another of my no
less known Capacities, viz. Poetry; and accordingly
have turn'd this little Off-spring, this natural Brat of
mine, out into the wide World. I confess, indeed,
my Talent this way never made any larger Appearance
before, than a Prologue, a Lampoon, a Sonnet
or Madrigal, or some such shorter Poetical
Fragment . . .[1]

D'Urfey, whom Langbaine described as "a much better
Ballad-maker than Play-wright,"[2] and whom Cibber held
in no high esteem as a writer of stage-orations,[3] wrote
prologues and epilogues, assisting the plays of such playwrights as Shadwell, Powell, and Gould, and publishing a
considerable body in a miscellany, *Pills to Purge Melancholy*.
Addison had recollections of Tom D'Urfey, "the delight
of the most polite companies and conversations":

I myself remember king Charles the Second
leaning on Tom d'Urfey's shoulder more than once,
and humming over a song with him.[4]

The familiar names of still more prologue-writing poets
appear in Appendix B of this work. Among them are actors,
beaux, statesmen, soldiers, noblemen, playwrights who
wrote for fellow playwrights, wits, would-be wits, and
poets who did not concern themselves with the writing of
plays but wrote prologues and epilogues out of friendship
or out of a desire for gain. Prologues and epilogues were
not only the *chefs-d'œuvre* of the wits but also the means of
earning two guineas. Playwrights set much store in them;

[1] Jo Haynes, *A Fatal Mistake* (1696), Preface.
[2] Gerard Langbaine, *An Account of the English Dramatick Poets* (1691),
p. 179.
[3] *An Apology for the life of Mr. Cibber* (1740, 4to), p. 114.
[4] *The Guardian*, May 28, 1713.

and when a poet of merit whom a dramatist engaged to supply a stage-oration deputed another to make one for him, the results sometimes called for an apology like Mrs. Behn's in the Epistle to the Reader, accompanying *The Dutch Lover* (1673):

> . . . Lastly, my Epilogue was promis'd me by a person who had surely made it good, if any, but he failing of his word, deputed one, who has made it as you see, and to make out your penyworth you have it here. The Prologue is by misfortune lost.

III. SPEAKERS OF PROLOGUES AND EPILOGUES

Of the men who spoke prologues and epilogues before the Restoration little is known. Their names are few and sometimes obscure. Before 1600 Nicholas Tooley, Thomas Pope, and Richard Alleyn had probably mastered the prologuing art of Shakespeare's theatre, and by 1620 audiences had listened to Henry Cundall, Richard Burbage, and Thomas Pollard.[1] At a school performance Joseph Beaumont and Nicholas Coleman spoke a prologue and an epilogue in 1626,[2] and one Chaundler, or a candle-maker, got his name written into the margin of Hausted's *The Rival Friends* (1632), acted at Cambridge. Shakerley Marmyon and the Critic had the prologue to Marmyon's *A Fine Companion* (1633). Perhaps the most significant, however, and assuredly the most certain, of the speakers before the closing of the theatres was Ezekiel Fen, who, upon his first acting a man's part had a prologue, written for him by Henry Glapthorne.[3]

Following 1660, the custom of recording the names of speakers under the titles of the published prologues and epilogues was begun. Although never observed consistently, this gesture on the part of playwrights or printers or actors lends invaluable assistance to one who studies the careers

---

[1] For information concerning early actors see Thomas W. Baldwin, *The Organization and Personnel of the Shakespearean Company* (1927).
[2] Appendix C.
[3] *Poems* (1639), p. 28.

of early actors. During the first decade of the Restoration, we know that prologues and epilogues were spoken by Nell Gwinn, Smith, Clun, Betterton, Underhill, Madam Moders, Mrs. Marshall, Lacy, Mohun, Mrs. Knepp, Monmouth, Angel, Harris, Nokes, and Price. Some one hundred and fifteen names were recorded before 1700, and more than four hundred different prologues and epilogues were printed with the names of their speakers.

The best actors were jealous of the prerogative to deliver prologues and epilogues. Colley Cibber, who set great value upon the opportunity to deliver a stage-oration, said that to speak a good prologue well was "one of the hardest Parts, and strongest Proofs of sound Elocution."[1] First among the orators of the theatre were two men and two women: Betterton, Haines, Mrs. Barry, and Mrs. Bracegirdle. With what envy the mere fledglings must have regarded these acknowledged graduates in the art of prologue-speaking! When, in 1695, Cibber wrote his first prologue that was accepted by the players, he offered to give his poem to the theatre upon the condition that he be permitted to speak it. But he asked the impossible:

> . . . This was judg'd as bad as having no Prologue at all! You may imagine how hard I thought it, that they durst not trust my poor poetical Brat to my own care.[2]

Finding, therefore, that his prologue would be given to another, Cibber stood upon terms:

> . . . I insisted that two Guineas should be the Price of my parting with it; which with a Sigh I received, and *Powel* spoke the Prologue: But every Line, that was applauded, went sorely to my Heart, when I reflected, that the same Praise might have been given to my own speaking; nor

[1] *An Apology for the Life of Mr. Colley Cibber* (1740), p. 157.
[2] *Ibid.*, p. 115.

could the success of the Author compensate the
Distress of the Actor.[1]

Some five years after this disappointment, Cibber rejoiced
in a distinct honour. He had been given the epilogue that
Dryden wrote for the presentation of *The Pilgrim* in 1700;
and because the piece was "written so much above the
strain of common authors," he was "not a little pleas'd."[2] Then
Dryden, upon hearing him repeat the epilogue in rehearsal,
made him "a further compliment of trusting" him with the
prologue. This extraordinary distinction astonished the
players and ruffled Wilks:

> . . . This so particular Distinction was look'd
> upon by the Actors, as something too extraordinary.
> But no one was so impatiently ruffled at it, as Wilks,
> who seldom chose soft Words, when he spoke of
> any thing he did not like. The most gentle thing
> he said of it was, That he did not understand such
> Treatment; that, for his part, he look'd upon it as an
> Affront to all the rest of the Company, that there
> should be but One, out of the Whole, judg'd fit
> to speak either a Prologue or an Epilogue.[3]

Cibber did receive an unusual honour in being given both
the prologue and the epilogue. Even the great Betterton
spoke only one stage-oration at a performance.

Of the actors speaking prologues and epilogues from
1660 to 1700, forty-three per cent. were women. In the
first decade of the Restoration three actresses appeared in
the rôle of the orator: Nell Gwinn, Mrs. Marshall, and
Madam Moders. The second decade was most hospitable to
the woman speaker, seeing the début of at least nineteen:
Ariell, Baker, Barry, Betterton, Boutell, Butler, Cook, Cory,
Currer, Davis, Gibbs, Knepp, Knight, P. L., Lee (Lady
Slingsby), Mackarel, Roche, Spencer, and Lady Elizabeth

---

[1] *An Apology for the Life of Mr. Colley Cibber* (1740), p. 114.
[2] *Ibid.*, p. 157.   [3] *Ibid.*, p. 157.

Howard. From 1680 to 1690, only a few new voices were added, one of these being the great Mrs. Bracegirdle, the others of less brilliant fame being Percyval (Mrs. Mountfort), Moyle, and Petty. The last decade of the seventeenth century, like the period from 1670 to 1680, saw at least eighteen additional actresses speaking prologues and epilogues: Allison, Ayliff, Bowman, Bradshaw, Campian, Chock, Hodgson, Howard, Hudson, Lassells, Lindsey, Moor, Perrin, Porter, Prince, Temple, Verbruggen, and Lady Dorothy Burk. Further consideration of the vogue of women in the rôle of stage-orator will be given in the course of this work.[1] A list of all speakers recorded in the publications prior to 1700 is given in Appendix C.

The prologues and epilogues which were published in quarto, folio half-sheet, and folio before 1700 and which are reprinted in this work furnish useful information concerning the leading players and their vogue. Here are the well-known actresses: Mrs. Barry, Mrs. Bracegirdle, Mrs. Butler, Mrs. Cook, Mrs. Cox, Mrs. Croysh's girl, Mrs. Currer, Mrs. Hudson, Mrs. Lindsey, Mrs. Mountfort, Mrs. Moyle, and Lady Slingsby; and the popular actors: Betterton, Goodman, Haynes, Jevon, Lambert, Leigh, Leveridge, Mountfort, Powel, Richards, Smith, and Underhill. The words spoken by these men and women comment at times upon the players and their vicissitudes, and opportunity is here in these texts for some estimate of the kind of speech the audience liked best from a variety of folk: from the gifted artist like Betterton to the frolicker like Haynes.

IV. TYPES OF PROLOGUES AND EPILOGUES

The examples reprinted in this work show that the Restoration had a taste for verses unlike the commonplace prologue, or mere introduction to a drama, and epilogue, or players' leave-taking. The variety after 1660 was as great

1 Parts of these findings are more fully discussed in my "Female Prologues and Epilogues in English Plays," PMLA, XLVIII (Dec., 1933), pp. 1060–1079.

as that to be found in other collections of short poems, and the authors were not constrained to speak merely of the matter within the play's five acts. All the day's interests were theirs to write upon: loyalty, rebellion, church, religion, recantation, playhouses, players, universities, parties, politics, audiences, taste, manners, plays, foreigners, novelties, literature, vacations, poets, women, and many similar topics. With few exceptions, the pieces introduced new plays, a fact indicating perhaps the value placed upon a set of verses which served to placate the hostile critics when a fresh drama or a young playwright was the dish. One example accompanied a revised play, Tate's *A Duke and no Duke*; and three old plays were assisted: *The Alchemist*, *The Northern Lass*, and *The Silent Woman*.

Attention may be called to the outstanding types represented in this work. Something of their history will appear in the introductory essays accompanying the prologues and epilogues reprinted; therefore the discussion at this time may be abbreviated. The prologue and epilogue being treated here for the first time as a literary *genre*, they are classified according to recurring patterns that I have observed during my study of some 1,600 plays. Familiars in this field from the beginning were the begging, the defiant, and the armed prologue and epilogue which appeared frequently. The occasional prologue and epilogue were in demand in all periods, being addresses complimenting Royalty, praising the universities, celebrating the opening of new playhouses or the organization of a new company of actors, and marking the first performance opening a new season or concluding a vacation. Of a still more timely character, prologues and epilogues having a journalistic style flourished after 1660, being chronicles of the times with an editorial tone, hectoring comments upon parties and audiences, critical reviews of events and art in relation to the theatre, and discourses upon recantation. Novel prologues and epilogues, with a long history related later in this book, comprised musical pieces, spectacles, inductions with singing and dancing, dialogues, and animal pieces. Addresses with lineal descent from well-known forms in literature were dialogues, essays, and characters. Among forms adapted to speakers, we note frequent examples of the female, juvenile, and personated prologues and epilogues, each type having an early origin and a long life.

The most significant fact that comes from this study of types is the proof of constant absorption and variation according to the taste of the age. Extremely sensitive to the times, prologues and epilogues actually anticipated journalism, having undertaken many of the functions that were performed by newspapers in the eighteenth century. They were as hospitable to new materials and novelties as a pagan to a new god. When music and dance and spectacle invaded the theatre, they, like their plays, adopted novel modes and in so doing prophesied the next century's apostasy in favour of show and sound. The examples at the end of this book anticipate the theatre in which music had an important place.

V. THE PUBLICATION OF PROLOGUES
AND EPILOGUES

Before 1700, prologues and epilogues were made available to readers in the editions of plays, in miscellanies, and in such separate publications as quartos, folio half-sheets, and folios. The Restoration saw the establishment of the printers' new occupation of turning out prologues and epilogues that might be sold very near the time of their speaking or intended rendering. Only one example, a quarto, bears a date earlier than 1660.[1] Beginning with 1680, the press was busy during ten uninterrupted years with these sheets which were as ephemeral as newsletters. Doubtless, many were lost. Of those surviving, the supply for 1681/2 and 1682 was largest. The present work reprints these rare prologues and epilogues published separately from 1642 to 1700.

Prologues and epilogues given separate publication usually came out as folio half-sheets printed on both sides. The

[1] See Section I of this work.

PROLOGUE

TO THE

REVIV'D

ALCHEMIST.

HE *Alchemist*; Fire,breeding Gold,our *Theme*:
Here muſt no Melancholie be, nor Flegm.
Young *Ben*, not Old, writ this, when in his
Solid in Judgment, and in Wit ſublime.   (Prime,
    The *Siſters*, who at *Theſpian* Springs their Blood
Cool with freſh Streams, All, in a Merry Mood,
Their wat'ry Cups, and Pittances declin'd,
At *Bread-ſtreet's Mer-maid* with our *Poët* din'd:
Where, what they Drank, or who plaid moſt the Rig,
Fame modeſtly conceals : but He grew big
Of this pris'd Iſſue; when a *Jovial* Maid,
His Brows beſprinkling with *Canarie*, ſaid.
    Pregnant by Us, produce no Mortal Birth;
Thy active Soul, quitting the ſordid Earth,
Shall 'mongſt Heav'ns glitt'ring *Hieroglyphicks* trade,
And *Pegaſus*, our winged Sumpter, jade,
Who from *Parnaſſus* never brought to *Greece*,
Nor *Romane* Stage, ſo rare a Maſter-piece.
    This Story, true or falſe, may well be ſpar'd;
The *Actors* are in queſtion, not the *Bard* :
How they ſhall humour their oft-varied Parts,
To get your Money, Company, and Hearts,

Since all Tradition, and like Helps are loſt.
    Reading our Bill new paſted on the Poſt,
Grave Stagers both, one, to the other ſaid,
The ALCHEMIST? What ! are the Fellows mad?
Who ſhall *Doll Common* Act? Their tender Tibs
Have neither Lungs, nor Confidence, nor Ribs.
    Who *Face*, and *Subtle*? Parts, all Air, and Fire :
They, whom the *Authour* did Himſelf inſpire,
Taught, Line by Line, each Tittle, Accent, Word,
Ne're reach'd His Height; all after, more abſurd,
Shadows of fainter Shadows, whereſoe're
A *Fox* he pencil'd, copied out a *Bear*.
    Encouragement for young Beginners ſmall :
Yet howſoe're we'll venture, have at All.
Bold Ignorance (they ſay) falls ſeldome ſhort
In *Camp*, the *Countrey*, *City*, or the *Court*.
    Arm'd with the Influence of your fair Aſpects,
Our Selves we'll conquer, and our own Defects.
A thouſand Eyes dart raies into our Hearts,   (Parts
Would make Stones ſpeak, and Stocks play well their
Some few Malignant Beams we need not fear,
Where ſhines ſuch Glory in ſo bright a Sphere.

THIS IS PROBABLY THE EARLIEST BROADSIDE.*
CERTAINLY, IT IS UNIQUE, THE ONLY COPY BEING IN
THE WORCESTER COLLEGE LIBRARY
*Since it is undated, it is not indisputably earlier than the
Whitehall Prologue of 1660

quarto, the earliest size to be used, appeared twice before the third decade of the Restoration: "The Prologue and Epilogue to a Comedie. Presented, At the Entertainment of the Prince His Highness, by the Schollers of Trinity Colledge in Cambridge," 1642; "The Prologue to Calisto," 1675. Very early, the broadside was adopted; but when both the prologue and the epilogue were published, the folio half-sheet carried printing on both sides. This second form was the established mode from 1681 to 1700. In only a few instances, beginning in 1683, the folio printed on four pages made its appearance.[1]

These separate publications carried the names of twenty-five booksellers and printers who are in Henry R. Plomer's *A Dictionary of the Booksellers and Printers Who Were at Work in England, Scotland, and Ireland*, from 1641 to 1667, and from 1668 to 1725, and three others: Thomas Cross, E. Lucy, and Charles Tebroc.[2] Jacob Tonson's work was by far the most frequent while R. Baldwin, J. Hindmarsh, and J. Nutt stood second, with three publications each. James Calvin, who printed the earliest piece in this work, was apparently known only for his one quarto.[3]

VI. WIT IN ORAL DISCOURSE

There was an eager interest in the perfection of polite conversation during the seventeenth century. Books on eloquence, conversation, jest, wit, and other topics pertaining to the management of the tongue answered the growing demand for ways to make social converse charming and brilliant. Men and women who wished to scintillate conversationally read them and picked up crumbs of eloquence from still other sources, including the playhouses. There, in prologues and epilogues as well as the plays themselves, they found an abundance of repartee. The folio half-sheets

[1] See Sections XX, XXI, and XXXVIII of this book.
[2] See Appendix E.
[3] Henry R. Plomer, *op cit.*, 1641–1667, Calvin.

giving the texts of some of the most popular of these stage-orations were bought, no doubt, by men and women who wished to speak "*a la mode*, and in certain new, and unheard of words,"[1] as writers upon eloquence observed when remarking upon wit that was derived from eloquent extravagance. Prologues and epilogues belong to a history of oral discourse, the conversation of the drawing-room and the orations of the theatre.

Popular interest, then, in well-turned phrases and perfection of style encouraged the publication of such prologues and epilogues as are included in the following pages. To people who grew heated in debate over a metaphor, for example, and who gathered to criticize the latest plays before the echo of the epilogue had died, these sheets were useful. And haste in bringing them out was an essential to their vogue. The silent reading of these pieces after the speaking of them must, however, have cooled the fire in the most enthusiastic if such were men hoping to enjoy the wittiest passages for a second time. For wit has one life, and that the moment when it is 'born, the speaking of it coming pat upon the hour and suddenly fusing two ideas that were until then dissimilar. The surprise pleasing to the mind in that instance cannot be entirely recaptured.

In taking up the best prologues and epilogues of the past, we read how their speakers observed rules of eloquence in their day, soothing and gulling their pliant audiences with artifice, fable, pleasantry, and gravity, or trying to vanquish and humble their stubborn hearers by arguments that were eloquent and imperious, with a violence of figure.[2] The abundance of wit entering into their composition lends a brightness to the style, but a diminished glow, since only by study can we now recreate the situation that made the words witty. The most imaginative reader may come near knowing in reality what pleasure was given by these timely prologues

---

[1] *Entertainments of the Cours* (1658), p. 82.

[2] See the requirements of orators in *Entertainments of the Cours* (1658), p. 91.

and epilogues. Such a first gratification led to their being preserved, for it is the nature of men to pass on to others wit and satire that they have enjoyed:

> A Witty and Satyrical Saying against a Man, or a Work, pleases those that hear it; first, because it is a Witty Saying, and then because it is Satyrical; for Men are naturally better pleased to see others Criticized than to see themselves praised: Such a pleasing saying will not be forgotten, it will be transmitted by one Generation to another, as it appears by the many Witty sayings of the Ancients.[1]

So although custom affected their vogue to a degree, the longevity of prologues and epilogues is due in great part to the timely wit and satire that entered into almost all the prologues and epilogues in the present work. Often, the language was obscene and scurrilous; the satire, offensive. Such was wit in the seventeenth century. These prologues and epilogues are to be looked upon, therefore, as one of our best sources from which we may judge the theatre of Dryden's age, when stage orations were at their best. The seventeenth century admitted that scoffing at serious matters, frolicking, and provoking laughter in an audience were the attributes of a certain type of wit; but it was a second-rate kind:

> . . . And the desire the *Humourist* hath to be some body, and to have a *name* above those of common apprehension, will be sure to actuate the *scoffing vein;* in the exercise of which, if he have *quibbled luckily*, and made folks laugh, he is encouraged to take all such occasions to prove himself a Wit, and to shew he had a pretty way to *play* the *Fool.* And when he hath wanton'd a while, and frolickly toy'd in his *affected merriments,* his *reason* becomes an obedient servant to his *fancy.*[2]

[1] *The Management of the Tongue* (1706), p. 40.
[2] *Saducismus Triumphatus* (1668), p. 4.

xli

Yet prologues and epilogues show the character of Town Wit in their scoffing, self-confidence, quibbling, *à-la-mode* words, novelty, odd metaphors, ridiculous similes, libel, clowning, mimic gesture, extempore variations, and full criticism of the state.

A study of rhetoric in the seventeenth century shows these prologues and epilogues to have accommodated themselves to many of the formalities of oratory. The two chief ornaments of eloquence, amplification and illustration, are here, amplifying through comparison being a highly favoured device in the prologues and epilogues of every age. Here, too, is repetition in its numerous kinds, the variety in type and name being indicated by the following from *The Academie of Eloquence* (1654): *Anadiplosis, Anaphora, Epistrophe, Simploce, Epanados Antimetabole, Agnomination, Epanalepsis,* and *Traducto.* The poets who wrote prologues and epilogues were proficients in the art taught by the treatises on rhetoric in the seventeenth century.

VII. PROLOGUES AND EPILOGUES IN THE
     TRADITION OF THE STAGE

The stage had need of prologues and epilogues. They were serviceable bridges adapting the illusion of the theatre to the audience. Where too great or too little psychical distance handicapped a play, they were links which, if cleverly adjusted, could create conditions in the audience desirable for a satisfactory performance on the stage. A play that the spectators might find so extremely topical that the illusion of art was no longer possible to them was saved from failure in this respect by a prologue and an epilogue increasing psychical distance by such well-known devices as the denial of any relation to contemporary affairs. A very fanciful plot too far removed from the experiences of the audience was brought nearer reality by a familiar prologue and epilogue that drew the spectators into the circle of aesthetic enjoyment. A revived play was given a setting in the new age and interpreted to a strange audience by a new prologue and epilogue. Those orations that served it in its own time could not adjust the new audience to the play. Thus prologues and epilogues were timely, their value being dependent upon the duration of the social conditions which they served. The timeliness that preserved them likewise cast them aside.

For such reasons prologues and epilogues were made and generously used long before aesthetic critics thought of a name for that which separates actual experience from the illusion of art. They show to us now a usefulness which they undoubtedly had in their years of vogue; but theirs was a service which men were not able to define to themselves when, discovering that their plays were no longer dependent upon these brief oratorical aids, they set them aside. Their function was closely related to the uses of the theatre which belonged to aesthetic illusion.

Changes in the theatre affecting this distance between art and actuality lent a vogue to prologues and epilogues after 1660. The Elizabethan playhouse, with its stage surrounded on three sides by the audience, did not keep its imaginary world free of contact with reality. There, no principle of verisimilitude forbade an exchange of confidences between the player and his audience. The soliloquy consulted the pit, and the pit mounted the stage. But as this stage gradually withdrew from its audience, and the ideal world developed behind the frame, the intimacy between actor and spectator lessened. The soliloquy and the aside grew infrequent. The link remaining—a link between the real and the imaginary—was the prologue or epilogue, in which the actor standing on the apron before the frame, outside the ideal regions of the play, spoke directly to his audience, drawing them into his world within the frame by means of a prologue, or driving them out of the unreal into the real by means of an epilogue. If a chief fact in the history of drama is this gradual separation of spectator and player, bringing finally the establishment of an ideal world of the stage never cognizant of the presence of an audience, then a little specu-

xliii

lation indicates the relation of the vogue of prologues and epilogues to the changing theatre. The Elizabethan dramatist had, not only prologues and epilogues, but soliloquies and asides to make sure that the audience followed the action. Prologues and epilogues were therefore not always necessary to the play. After the Restoration the theatre approached verisimilitude, drawing plays away from the audience. But the spectators were not willing to be shut out and left to sit as silent watchers. Descendants of the Elizabethan audience, they demanded recognition. They were a more homogeneous group ; and when they attended their plays, there was an intimacy between them and their players. Their sense of psychical distance, or illusion, was negligible. The most convenient organs for complying with their wishes to be admitted into the illusion of the stage were the prologues and epilogues, links between the real and the unreal.

Eventually, of course, the spectators came to desire that the illusion of the ideal be unbroken. There were complaints in the early years of the eighteenth century against merry epilogues that destroyed the pleasing deceptions of the stage-world. When, in time, the audience at last preferred to sit as lookers-on, inducting themselves into the ideal and taking away with them the illusion of the ideal, then prologues and epilogues had very little excuse for being, so far as dramatic technique is concerned. Tradition, rather than necessity, kept them well into the nineteenth century. Their vogue and their decline are, therefore, another demonstration of the change that crept into the theatre when the players gradually withdrew into their world and left their audiences to the rôle of non-participant spectators.

Such is the office of prologues and epilogues in the history of drama. Studied thoroughly, one of these pieces says more about taste and audiences than any other single poem of forty or fifty lines descending to the present. That which was written for recitation has been preserved out of its oral tradition in books and single sheets, affording us one of the few opportunities for learning something about how players

xliv

spoke these fashionable verses. The italics, for example, are here for more than the printers' extra trouble; they indicate at times the stress that fell upon certain words and phrases when the audience listened to an actor prologuing a play. The dependence of the prologue and epilogue upon their audience was real and essential. Their strength rested in the orator and his response to his audience in gesture, glance, and tone of voice. Listen to one of the few prologues attempted in the cinema to-day, and know then that prologues and epilogues, having at their best an extempore character, though often the products of painstaking revision, must be spoken by an actor in the flesh, standing on the apron of a stage, and divining the taste of a responsive audience.

The / Prologue / and / Epilogue / To /
A   Comedie, / Presented, / At   the
Entertainment   of   the   Prince   His /
Highnesse, by the Schollers of Trinity
Col- / ledge in Cambridge, in March
last, / 1641. / — / By   Francis   Cole. / — /
London: /
Printed for James Calvin, 1642.

4to; 4 leaves, 8 pages.
British Museum.

ABRAHAM COWLEY

Abraham Cowley was born in London in 1618, the seventh
and posthumous child of Thomas Cowley, a stationer. He was
admitted as a king's scholar at Westminster, and he became
a scholar of Trinity College in 1637, B.A. in 1639, minor
fellow in 1640, and M.A. in 1642. Ejected from Cambridge in
1643/4, he retired to Oxford and settled at St. John's College.
In 1646 he followed the queen to France and, being a friend
to the royalists, was employed in various diplomatic services
by the exiled court. On a mission to England in 1656, he was
arrested by mistake for another person but released upon bail
for £1,000. He remained under bail until the Restoration.
On 2 December 1657, by order of the government, he was
created M.D. at Oxford. His retirement to Kent was broken
by a sojourn in France, but he settled at Barn Elms and afterwards (April 1665) in "Porch House" at Chertsey. He died on
28 July 1667 and was buried with great pomp in Westminster
Abbey.

Cowley was highly precocious, and his age considered his

work the model of cultivated poetry. To Dryden his authority was "almost sacred" (*Essay on Heroic Plays*, 1672). Before he became a scholar of Trinity College, he published his *Poetical Blossoms*, 1633, which had a second edition, with *Sylva* added, in 1636, and a third in 1637. *Love's Riddle* appeared in 1638. His Latin comedy, *Naufragium Joculare*, was acted by the members of Trinity College before the University on 2 February 1638 and published soon after. *The Guardian* was performed by the students of Trinity College on 12 March 1641 in honour of Prince Charles, printed in 1650, rewritten in 1658, acted as *Cutter of Coleman Street* at Lincoln's Inn Fields on 16 December 1661, and published in 1663. Among his other publications may be noted *The Mistress*, 1647; *The Four Ages of England* and *A Satyre against Separatists*, 1648; *Poems*, 1656; *Ode upon the Blessed Restoration*, 1660; *Vision, concerning his late pretended Highness, Cromwell the Wicked*, 1661; *A Proposition for the Advancement of Experimental Philosophy*, 1661; *Ode to the Royal Society*, 1661; *Verses upon several Occasions*, 1663. The first collection of his works in one volume folio appeared in 1668, including for the first time *Several Discourses by way of Essays in Prose and Verse*. Cowley's reputation was highest during his lifetime.

COWLEY'S PROLOGUE AND EPILOGUE TO
PRINCE CHARLES

When Prince Charles visited Cambridge in March, 1641, he was entertained at a play acted by the students and written by one of their fellows, Abraham Cowley. Such an occasion called for a prologue and an epilogue. The young playwright supplied both, complimenting the Prince and regretting, at the same time, civil strife and its accompanying indifference to learning. His two occasional pieces were published in quarto in 1642, being probably the first prologue and epilogue to receive separate publication.

Some fifteen years after Charles' visit, Cowley confessed his regret for the "rough drawn" comedy that he wrote in his

Trinity College days,[1] observing that the play was published as *The Guardian* in 1650, but making no mention of the yet-earlier publication of only a part of this college performance, the prologue and epilogue in quarto described at the beginning of this section.

Perhaps this latter publication was unknown to Cowley when he wrote his Preface in 1656, or it may have been one of the pieces which he said were published without his consent and so mangled that he "could neither with honour acknowledge, nor with honesty quite disavow"[2] them. Whatever the reason, Cowley never referred to the quarto printed for James Calvin; and the name of Francis Cole on the title-page prevented Hazlitt, Lowndes, and others from discovering that the text of "The Prologue and Epilogue To A Comedie, Presented at the Entertainment of the Prince His Highnesse" is almost identical with that of the prologue and epilogue to *The Guardian*, published with the play in 1650 and included in the miscellaneous verse of Cowley's collected works. The significant difference between the separate publication in quarto in 1642 and in the prologue and epilogue appearing with the play in 1650 occurs in the prologue after the line, "They'l admit Poesie, which was ever so;" the prologue of 1650 adds two lines:

> Besides, the Muses of late times have bin
> Sanctifi'd by the Verse of Master Prin.

In the various other texts of the prologue published in Cowley's miscellaneous verse in his lifetime and after, these two lines do not occur, the texts following more nearly that of the quarto; neither do they appear in MS. Eg. 2,326 in the British Museum and a manuscript presented to Trinity College, Cambridge, by Mrs. Anne Sadleir, 1669. They do occur, however, in MS. Eg. 2,725, which is apparently a copy of the prologue printed in *The Guardian*.[3]

[1] Preface to *Poems*, 1656. [2] *Ibid.*
[3] Significant variant-readings for the prologue appearing before Cowley's death in 1667 (*The Guardian*, 1650, designated here as G; MS. Eg. 2,725,

3

In summary we may note that the prologue and epilogue to Cowley's "rough drawn" comedy appeared in quarto eight years before the publication of the play, and they were offered to readers under a title-page that carried the words, "By Francis Cole." I have found neither Francis Cole (or Coles) in its variety of spellings nor Francis Gole (or Kole) in the *Alumni Cantabrigienses*, and it seems that Francis Cole never set pen to paper again. Perhaps someone in hot pursuit of Francis Cole may come upon an amusing manuscript in the British Museum, Eg. 2,986, which records the confession of one Francis Cole, who had taken money from another man's chest and spent it in divers ways and places. Singular also is the fact that James Calvin is not known to have owned any other piece, according to *A Dictionary of the Booksellers and Printers, 1641–1667*, by H. R. Plomer. When *The Guardian* was published in 1650, the prologue and epilogue were printed as

Circ. 1650, designated as E; and *Poems*, 1656, designated as P) are the following: l. 2, *so as* (G, P) and *soe as* (E) for *more then;* l. 3, Sr (E) for *Prince, our* (G, E, P) for *the;* l. 9, *yee* (E) and *ye* (P) for *we;* l. 12, *pass too, made* (G, P) and *passe too, made* (E) for *passe, 'twas made;* l. 14, *always* (G, P) and *alwayes* (E) for *ever; Besides, the Muses of late times have bin/Sanctifi'd by the Verse of Master Prin./*(G) inserted after the fourteenth line of the quarto-text; l. 16, *no less their Censure then* (P) for *as much their Censure, as* l. 17, *Prince, does onely* (G, P) and *Prince) doth onely* (E) for *Sir) doth now;* l. 18, *Would* (G, E, P) for *'Twould; yet* (G, E) for *but;* l. 19, *hasty* (E, P) and *hastie* (G) for *hearty;* l. 20, *Ere 'tis* (G, P) and *Ere 'twas* (E) for *Ear't was; 'tis* (G, P) for *t'was;* l. 21, *but duty* (E) for *but our duty;* l. 23, *the* (E) and *our* (G, P) for the misprint, *out;* l. 24, *Acted onely by* (E) *for acted by.*

It is of interest to note also that the manuscript presented to Trinity College by Mrs. Sadleir two years after Cowley's death offers variant-readings which do not correspond to any previous text; l. 7, *may* for *must;* l. 9, *you* for *we;* l. 10, *fell* for *fals;* l. 17, *Sole* for *onely* (G); l. 22, *Ohty* for *I would.*

Notable variant-readings for the epilogue in *The Guardian* (1650) and *Poems* (1656) are l. 1, *is done, great Prince, which* (G) and *great Sir, is done; yet* (P) for *great Sir, is done, it;* l. 2, *your fathers* (G) and *your Fathers* (P) for *your;* l. 3, *and we* (G, P) for *we;* l. 6, *It can* (G, P) for *I, can;* l. 8, *t'has* (P) for *that's;* l. 9, *present* (G), *mortal* (P) for *potent;* l. 10, *It could not die sooner then it was* (G), *Scarce could it Dye more quickly then 'twas* (P) for *Scarce can it dye more quickly then t'was.* The manuscript at Trinity College gives in l. 1, *great prince* for *great Sir,* following the text of P, 1656, and in l. 9, *die* for *fall.*

4

British Museum

THE PROLOGUE SPEAKER
—THE PROLOGUE AND EPILOGUE TO A COMEDIE,
PRESENTED, AT THE ENTERTAINMENT OF THE PRINCE
HIS HIGHNESSE, BY THE SCHOLLERS OF TRINITY COLLEGE
IN CAMBRIDGE, IN MARCH 1641

Cowley's, and they were included in the collected works of Cowley, as we have observed. A manuscript, dated *Circa*. 1650, has the title: "Prologue by A. C. March 22th before Prince Charles" (Eg. 2,725); and another (late seventeenth century, Eg. 2,326) transcribes this prologue among the poems of Cowley. The title to the manuscript at Trinity College leads one to guess that *Cole* was another spelling for *Cowley* : "The Prologue & Epilogue to the Comedy acted before the Prince in Trinity Colledge spoken by the Author Sr Cowley, March; 1642." It is reasonable to think that Cowley did speak his prologue, which apologises for the play in the manner of later prefaces. Hazlitt gives the following note on the quarto, but falls into error:

> Cole (Francis, of Trinity College, Cambridge).— The Prologue and Epilogue to a Comedie, presented at the entertainment of the Prince his Highness, by the Schollars of Trinity College in Cambridge, in March last, 1641. By Francis Cole. London. Printed for James Calvin, 1642, 4to, 4 leaves. With a print of the Author in his theatrical dress on the reverse of the title. At the end is annexed a poem called "The Echo," reprinted in *Restituta*.

Lowndes also refers to the "print of the author." I should be delighted to think that the print on the reverse of the title represents the author in his black coat, but such a happy chance as this seems very slight when one observes that this figure appears with others in the woodcut that was used for the *Canterburie Pilgrimage*, 1641. Both illustrations may be seen in the British Museum: E. 144/9 and Har. 5965. No. 26.[1]

---

[1] The substance of this account first appeared in my note, "The Prologue and Epilogue to the Guardian," *The Review of English Studies*, X (October, 1934), 443–447.

THE PROLOGUE.

Who sayes the Times do Learning disallow?
'Tis false: 'Twas never honoured more then now.
When you appear (great Prince) the Night is done,
You are our Morning Starre; shall be our Sunne.
But our Scean's *London* now, and by the Rout   5
We perish, if the *Round-heads* be about.
For now no Ornament, the head must wear
No Bayes, no Myter, scarce so much as hair.
How can a Play passe safely? when we know
Cheap-side Crosse fals, for making but a show.   10
Our only hope is this, that (it may be)
A Play may passe, 'twas made *ex tempore.*
Though other Arts poor and neglected grow,
They'l admit Poesie, which was ever so.
But we contemn the fury of these dayes,   15
And scorn as much their Censure, as their praise.
Our Muse (blest Sir) doth now on you rely,
'Twould gladly live; but not refuse to die.
Accept our hearty zeal, a thing that's plaid
ear't was a play, and acted ere t'was made: 20
Our Ignorance, but our duty too we show,
I would all ignorant people would do so.
At other times expect our wit or Art,
This Comedy is acted by the heart.

THE EPILOGUE.

The Play great Sir, is done, it needs must fear,
Though you brought all your mercies here:
It may offend your Highnesse, we have now
Three hours done Treason here for ought we know;
But powr your Grace, can above Nature give,   5
I, can give power to make Abortives live.

6

In which if our bold wishes should be crost,
'Tis but the life of one poor week that's lost:
Though it should fall beneath your potent scorn,
Scarce can it dye more quickly then t'was born.   10

The / Prologue / To His / Majesty / At the first Play presented at the Cockpit in / Whitehall, / Being part of that Noble Entertainment which Their Majesties received Novemb. 19. /from his Grace the Duke of Albemarle. /

London, Printed for G. Bedell and T. Collins, at the / Middle-Temple Gate in Fleet-street. 1660.

Folio half-sheet, reverse blank.
Imprint at the bottom of p. 1.
British Museum.

SIR JOHN DENHAM

John Denham, the only son of Sir John Denham (Irish Judge, of Little Horkesley, Essex) by his second wife, Eleanor (daughter of Sir Garrett More, baron Mellefont and Viscount Drogheda), was born in Dublin in 1615, but educated in London. On 18 November 1631 he matriculated at Trinity College, Oxford. He studied law at Lincoln's Inn, but spent much of his time and money at gaming. On 25 June 1634 he married Ann Cotton, by whom he had one son and two daughters. His second wife, whom he married on 25 May 1665, was Margaret, third daughter of Sir William Brooke, K.B. Lady Denham died on 6 January 1666/7 while Denham was convalescent from a fit of madness said to have been brought on by the scandalous conduct of his wife and the Duke of York. Sir John Denham died in March 1668/9 and was buried in Westminster Abbey on 23 March. An accusation of

8

murder brought against him at the time of Lady Denham's death seems to have been unjustified.

Denham supported the king's cause and served his king and queen in their exile. He was made Governor of Farnham Castle, whence he was driven by Sir William Waller on 1 December 1642. He was sent prisoner to London, but allowed to retire to Oxford, where he remained for nearly five years. On 20 July 1651 his estates were sold, and he was penniless. In 1657/8 Cromwell signed a licence authorising him to live at Bury in Suffolk. In 1658/9 he secured a passport to go abroad. Reward came to him after the Restoration in the form of grants and leases. In June 1660 he became Surveyor-general of works, and in 1661 he was made Knight of the Bath. From 1661 until his death, he was M.P. for Old Sarum.

Denham's writings include *The Sophy*, 1642; *Cooper's Hill*, 1642, 1650, 1655; *Cato Major*, 1648; *The Anatomy of Play*, 1651; *The Destruction of Troy*, 1656; Poems in celebration of Monk's efforts issued in single sheets from 1659 to 1667; *Psalms of David*, 1744. Denham contributed to other authors' works. His poems appeared in a collected edition in 1668. A musical elegy on the death of Cowley and *Cooper's Hill* are Denham's best work.

Denham's works have been recently edited by Theodore H. Banks, Jr., in *The Poetical Works of Sir John Denham*, Yale University Press, 1928, containing on pp. 94–95 a reprint of "The Prologue to His Majesty At the first Play presented at the Cock-pit in Whitehall."

FOR THE FIRST PLAY AT THE COCK-PIT
   AFTER THE RESTORATION

On the twenty-ninth of May Charles II entered London's flower-strewn roads. His people's welcome was so magnificent that it set a precedent of luxury to be observed months after by those who were hosts to his Majesty. Among the many obliged to spend in a lavish way were George Monk and John

Denham. Both enjoyed very early the bounty of the new régime, and they united in one expression of homage that is perpetuated by an early, if not the earliest, broadside-publication of lines prefacing a play:

The/Prologue/To His/Majesty/At the first Play presented at the Cock-pit in/Whitehall,/Being part of that Noble Entertainment which Their Majesties received Novemb. 19./from his Grace the Duke of Albemarle.

The men who shared in this entertainment knew their king to be open-handed among his favourites. General Monk welcomed Charles at Dover on 25 May 1660 with fit show of humility and devotion, and, having received for this the embrace and kiss of his master, was knighted the next day at Canterbury, invested with the order of the Garter, and made master of the horse. On July 7 he became Baron Monck of Potheridge, Beauchamp, Teyes, Earl of Torrington, and Duke of Albemarle, with a pension of seven hundred pounds a year and the estate of New Hall in Essex. On November 19 he honoured his king and queen with a Noble Entertainment, which included a play, *The Silent Woman*, at the Cock-pit in Whitehall. For this first dramatic presentation at court, a prologue was necessary; and John Denham, who had been made Surveyor-General of Works in June as a reward for his loyalty to the Stuarts, and who was, according to John Evelyn, a better poet than architect, appears to have written the lines reprinted here, welcoming the "Greatest of Monarchs" upon his return from exile.[1]

[1] Though "The Prologue To His Majesty At the first Play presented at the Cock-pit in Whitehall" is assigned to Sir William Davenant in *Bibliotheca Lindesiana*, item 816, other references give the piece to Sir John Denham. See Wood, *Athenae Oxoniensis*, 1721, II, 424; Langbaine, *Dramatick Poets*, interleaved with MS. notes by Oldys and others (Bodleian, Malone. 129), p. 127; Theodore H. Banks, Jr., *The Poetical Works of Sir John Denham*, Yale University, 1928, pp. 94–95; Eleanore Boswell, *The Restoration Court Stage*, Harvard University, 1932, p. 15, with a reference to Pepys, 20 Nov. Hist. MSS. V, 200.

THE
PROLOGUE
TO HIS
MAJESTY
At the first PLAY presented at the Cock-pit in
WHITEHALL,

Being part of that Noble Entertainment which Their
Majesties received *Novemb.* 19. from his Grace the Duke of
ALBEMARLE.

Greatest of Monarchs, welcome to this place
Which Majesty so oft was wont to grace
Before our Exile, to divert the Court,
And ballance weighty Cares with harmless sport
This truth we can to our advantage say,   5
They that would have no *KING*, would have no Play:
The *Laurel* and the *Crown* together went,
Had the same *Foes*, and the same *Banishment*:
The Ghosts of their[1] great Ancestors they fear'd,
Who by the art of conjuring Poets rear'd,   10
Our *HARRIES* and our *EDWARDS* long since dead
Still on the Stage a march of Glory tread:
Those Monuments of Fame (They thought) would stain
And teach the People to despise their Reign:
Nor durst they look into the Muses Well,   15
Least the cleer Spring their ugliness should tell;
Affrighted with the shadow of their Rage,
They broke the Mirror of the times, the Stage;
The Stage against them still maintain'd the War,
When they debauch'd the *Pulpit* and the *Bar*,   20
Though to be *Hypocrites*, be our Praise alone,
'Tis our peculiar boast that we were none.'
What er'e they taught, we practis'd what was true,
And something we had learn'd of honor too,

---

[1] Crossed out and changed to "your" in a manuscript hand.

11

When by Your Danger, and our Duty prest, 25
We acted in the Field, and not in Jest;
Then for the *Cause* our Tyring-house they sack't,
And silenc't us that they alone might act;
And (to our shame) most dext'rously they do it,
Out-act the Players, and out-ly the Poet; 30
But all the other Arts appear'd so scarce,
Ours were the *Moral Lectures*, theirs the Farse:
This spacious Land their Theater became,
And they *Grave Counsellors*, and *Lords* in Name;
Which these Mechanicks Personate so ill 35
That ev'n the Oppressed with contempt they fill,
But when the Lyons dreadful skin they took,
They roar'd so loud that the whole Forrest shook;
The noise kept all the Neighborhood in awe,
Who thought 'twas the true Lyon by his Pawe. 40
If feigned Vertue could such Wonders do,
What may we not expect from this that's true!
But this Great Theme must serve another Age,
To fill our Story, and adorne our Stage.

London, Printed for *G. Bedell* and *T. Collins*, at the *Middle-Temple Gate* in *Fleet-street*. 1660.

Prologue / To The / Reviv'd / Alchemist.

Folio half-sheet, reverse blank.
Worcester College Library, Oxford.

A UNIQUE PROLOGUE TO A REVIVAL

Of all the rare prologues and epilogues reproduced in these pages, this from the Worcester College Library is perhaps the most interesting: a broadside bound with other pieces of 1660 and entitled "Prologue to the Reviv'd Alchemist." In two columns printed on one side of the leaf, an unnamed author speaks like a very early voice in the theatre of the Restoration:

> Young Ben, not Old, writ this, when in his Prime,
> Solid in Judgment, and in Wit sublime.
>
> . . . .
>
> The Actors are in question, not the Bard:
> How they shall humour their oft-varied Parts,
> To get your Money, Company, and Hearts,
> Since all Tradition, and like Helps are lost.

Who this poet is remains a question. In an essay, "Worcester College Library," *Oxford Bibliographical Society Proceedings & Papers*, I, iv, pp. 263–320, Mr. C. H. Wilkinson, of Worcester College, suggests three names: Killigrew, Shirley, and—the most probable—Sir William Davenant. He tells me, however, that there is no external evidence to support his suggestion. So, thus far, with only internal evidence at hand, and with a fresh reading of prologues and epilogues in *Madagascar, with other Poems* (1672) and *Poems on Several Occasions* (1672), we may suspect an echo of Davenant's sentiment, as Mr. J. Q. Adams pointed out when I showed the Prologue to him:

13

A Unique Prologue

They, whom the Authour did Himself inspire,
Taught, Line by Line, each Tittle, Accent, Word,
Ne're reach'd His Height; all after, more absurd,
Shadows of fainter Shadows, wheresoe're
A Fox he pencil'd, copied out a Bear.

Mr. R. G. Noyes, speaking from his study of Jonson on the
Restoration stage, and citing performances of *The Alchemist*
at Gibbon's Tennis Court on 22 June, 14 August, 16 December,
1661, and sometime in 1662 (Dr. Edward Browne's memorandum book, B.M. MS. Sloane 1,900), says it would be
strange if Davenant wrote the prologue for Killigrew's actors.
Of course, we do not overlook the claims of Shirley, for in his
Poems (1646), ii, 36–37, appears "A Prologue to the
Alchimist," acted in Ireland, showing a poet's deep respect
for the genius of Ben Jonson.

This prologue is especially interesting to the student of
drama for the light that it may cast upon theatrical affairs of
1660: the vogue of Jonson's comedies, the playhouse, and the
players. Obviously, dating the piece is of no little importance.
It is bound among others of 1660, but need not be assuredly
of that year. Mr. Noyes dates it about 1660; and Mr.
McKerrow, who has kindly studied the text for me, says there
is very little in it by which one can fix the year of publication,
though the date will fall between 1650 and 1670. There is a
reference to the familiar custom of posting play-bills, and
there is a comment upon the actors' lack of experience:

Reading our Bill new pasted on the Post,
Grave Stagers both, one, to the other said,
The Alchemist? What! are the Fellows mad?
Who shall Doll Common Act? Their tender Tibs
Have neither Lungs, nor Confidence, nor Ribs.

This latter evidence indicates that the comedy had not been
presented for a long time, and the prologue reprinted here
may have been for a performance prior to the earliest which
we have record of (that of 22 June, 1661, Gibbon's Tennis

Court, occupied by Killigrew's company). If the "young Beginners" were from the Nursery, then (as Professor Hazelton Spencer, of Johns Hopkins, has suggested to me) the unique broadside-prologue in the Worcester College Library at Oxford is very significant in theatrical tradition.

PROLOGUE
TO THE
REVIV'D
ALCHEMIST.

The *Alchemist;* Fire, breeding Gold, our *Theme:*
Here must no Melancholic be, nor Flegm.
Young *Ben*, not Old, writ this, when in his Prime,
Solid in Judgment, and in Wit sublime.
    The *Sisters*, who at *Thespian* Springs their Blood   5
Cool with fresh Streams, All, in a Merry Mood,
Their wat'ry Cups, and Pittances declin'd,
At *Bread-street's Mer-maid* with our *Poët* din'd:
Where, what they Drank, or who plaid most the Rig,
Fame modestly conceals: but He grew big   10
Of this pris'd Issue; when a *Jovial* Maid,
His Brows besprinkling with *Canarie*, said.
    Pregnant by Us, produce no Mortal Birth;
Thy active Soul, quitting the sordid Earth,
Shall 'mongst Heav'ns glitt'ring *Hieroglyphicks* trade,   15
And *Pegasus*, our winged Sumpter, jade,
Who from *Parnassus* never brought to *Greece*,
Nor *Romane* Stage, so rare a Master-piece.
    This Story, true or false, may well be spar'd;
The *Actors* are in question, not the *Bard:*   20
How they shall humour their oft-varied Parts,
To get your Money, Company, and Hearts,
Since all Tradition, and like Helps are lost.
    Reading our Bill new pasted on the Post,
Grave Stagers both, one, to the other said,   25
The Alchemist? What! are the Fellows mad?
Who shall *Doll Common* Act? Their tender Tibs
Have neither Lungs, nor Confidence, nor Ribs.
    Who *Face*, and *Subtle?* Parts, all Air, and Fire:
They, whom the *Authour* did Himself inspire,   30
Taught, Line by Line, each Tittle, Accent, Word,

A Unique Prologue

Ne're reach'd His Height; all after, more absurd,
Shadows of fainter Shadows, wheresoe're
A *Fox* he pencil'd, copied out a *Bear*.
   Encouragement for young Beginners small: 35
Yet howsoe're we'll venture; have at All.
Bold Ignorance (they say) falls seldome short
In *Camp*, the *Countrey*, *City*, or the *Court*.
   Arm'd with the Influence of your fair Aspects,
Our Selves we'll conquer, and our own Defects,   40
A thousand Eyes dart raies into our Hearts,
Would make Stones speak, and Stocks play well their
     Parts:
Some few Malignant Beams we need not fear,
Where shines such Glory in so bright a Sphere.

The / Prologue / To / Calistho, / With
The / Chorus's / Between   The / Acts. /
—/ Orn. /—/ London, / Printed in the
Year MDCLXXV.

4to; 12 leaves, 24 pages.
British Museum.

JOHN CROWNE

Little starch Johnny Crowne, of stiff and prim cravat, was the
son of William Crowne, gentleman, who emigrated to Nova
Scotia with his family and on 10 August 1656 received a large
tract of territory from Oliver Cromwell. After the Restoration
the French took his lands, and his title was not upheld by the
authorities. John Crowne came to England early in the
reign of Charles II and devoted his time mainly to drama,
though his early work was a romance, *Pandion and
Amphigenia*, 1665, fancied, he said, when he was scarce twenty.
In 1673 he joined Dryden and Shadwell in writing *Notes and
Observations on the Empress of Morocco*. For the theatres he wrote
Juliana, 1671; *The History of Charles the Eighth of France*, 1672;
Andromache, 1675; *Calisto*, 1675; *The Countrey Wit*, 1675;
The Destruction of Jerusalem, Two Parts, 1677; *The Ambitious
Statesman*, 1679; *The Misery of Civil War*, 1680; *Henry the
Sixth*, 1681; *Thyestes*, 1681; *City Politiques*, 1683; *Sir Courtly
Nice*, 1685; *Darius King of Persia*, 1688; *The English Frier*,
1690; *Regulus*, 1694; *The Married Beau*, 1694; *Caligula*, 1698.
Crowne is also the author of *Daeneids*, a poem, published in
1692, and songs set by Henry Purcell and published in
Motteux's *Gentleman's Journal*, 1691/2. According to A. H.
White, *John Crowne, His Life and Dramatic Works*, 1922, the
dates of Crowne's birth and death are 1640 and 1712.

18

John Crowne

The second quarto in this collection is Crowne's Prologue to *Calisto*, entered in the Term Catalogue, 19 June 1675, price 6d. This piece, with scene, song, and dance, occupies a significant place in the development of English prologues and serves as a text for comment upon those playhouse adornments which were to insinuate themselves into drama and sometimes usurp the traditional actors' prerogatives.

The King's carpenter, Richard Rider, provided Crowne's play at Whitehall with a "Prospect of Somersett house & ye Thames," topped by clouds, and a Temple of Fame with lights behind varnished silk. In truth, be it to his credit, in part, that perhaps the most elaborate production at Whitehall during the Restoration began when the red, white, and blue curtains were drawn and Moll Davis, as the River Thames in the present prologue, showed her charming self affrighted at the sound of lamenting voices. Before 1674/5, the year that saw the first performance of *Calisto*, English drama had had some acquaintance with prologues and epilogues that charmed the senses thus. There were precedents for their break-away: native, in the prologues and epilogues to masques; foreign, in the prologues to certain plays by Corneille, Molière, and Quinault, in the *récits* to ballets, and in the prologues to Italian operas. Look, for instance, at *Le Ballet Royal de la Nuit* (1653), or the prologues to *Andromède* (1650), *La Comédie sans comédie* (1654), *La Toison d'or* (1660), *Psyché* (1671), and *Fêtes de l'Amour de Bacchus* (1672) for extraordinary effects sought in the preludes used by theatres across the Channel. The playhouse of the past gave English examples, though in their use of spectacle, scenes, and machines the English were most often merely learners indebted not only to their own countrymen in masques, but also to proficient foreign artists who created such *pièces de machine* as we find on the French and Italian stages. Before Crowne's elaborate experiment, we may note a chorus prologue to Robert Greene's *Alphonsus King of Aragon* (c. 1589, pr. 1599), the

19

prologue and epilogue to Daniel's *The Vision of the Twelve Goddesses* (1604), and the prologue to Heywood's *Loves Mistresses* (1640). But after 1670 we find our playwrights, at court and away, composing prologues and epilogues more and more after the fashion of the French while the sturdy prefatory speech that was accustomed to prologue a play was replaced by a novelty that carried a strong suspicion of Gallic, more than English, pattern.

In England we may note some prologues and epilogues with scenes that were either inorganic, exerting no notable influence upon the content of the prologue, or dramatic, having some marked effect upon the content and often modifying the pattern of the address. Had the experiments in scenes ended with setting prologues and epilogues in a background consisting of a cloud, from which Cupid descended to address an audience, or several planets in a Heaven, to which the stage-orator pointed, there would have been nothing noteworthy in the history of prologues and epilogues as regards their adoption of scenery. The most interesting example before Crowne's is Cartwright's *The Royal Slave*, presented at Oxford on 30 April 1636, before the King and Queen, with exotic scenes for the prologue and epilogue. Even then perspective and costume pleased the Royal Presence, if Wood tells a true story in his *History and Antiquities of the University of Oxford*, II, 407–414, for the Queen's desire to see Cartwright's play acted again by her players necessitated the removal of clothes and perspectives by wagon to Hampton Court, with a request by the Chancellor at Oxford that the clothes and stage not "come into the hands and use of the common Players." So, with no little care, the private theatres guarded their properties. Eventually the common players did have their own scenery and elegance, as we may note in the prologue to *The Indian Queen*, with both scene and musical accompaniment, when presented at the Theatre Royal in January, 1663/4; and in Duffett's burlesque prologue and epilogue to *The Empress of Morocco*, with scenes, machines, and songs, when performed at Drury Lane, *c.* December, 1673. Looking forward from the year of Crowne's magnificent entertainment at Whitehall and observing the public theatres after Dryden and Howard began the fashion of decorating the prologue there, we discover that although play-bills announced complete acts sometimes as prologues, there were no inspired imitators who could make spectacle or mere scene in prologues and epilogues more than a novelty in a London playhouse.

Before Crowne gave his Prologue an orchestra and singers, music for prologues and epilogues had been introduced in accompaniments, preludes, and interludes; and vocal pro-logues and epilogues had likewise occurred, some early examples being the famous jig-song epilogue to *Twelfth Night*, a prologue that was sung by Pan and a Nymph in praise of the King and Queen when Davenant's *The Faithful Shepherdess* was performed at Somerset House on Twelfth Night, 1663, and an epilogue sung by Harris and Sandford, to the delight of Pepys, at the presentation of Davenant's *The Man's the Master*, March, 1667/8. Accompaniments, preludes, and interludes were used in the prologues to Marston's *Sophonisba* (1606), Holyday's *Technogamia* (1618), Davenant's *The First Day's Entertainment at Rutland House* (1657), Dryden and Howard's *The Indian Queen* (*Four New Plays*, 1665), and Dryden's *Secret Love* (1668). Musical prologues and epilogues, though note-worthy as early as 1663, were not in their greatest vogue when Crowne's *Calisto* was performed; their period of popularity came after 1697, when they were used with comedies most frequently, though also with tragedies, operas, pastorals, and masques.

Although the tripping stage-orator did not win a remarkable vogue in prologues and epilogues, dancers did have some place in these parts of a performance. It will be recalled that in the sixteenth century Bottom, concluding his play, asked the audience: "Will it please you to see the Epilogue, or to heare a Bergomask dance, betweene two of our company?' Theseus answered: "No Epilogue, I pray you; for your play needs no excuse. . . . But come, your Bergomasks, let your Epilogue alone." Apparently, however, even in Shakespeare's day some audiences accepted both, for we know a new type of epilogue at the close of Shakespeare's *Henry the Fourth*, the second part, in which a dancer speaks and dances. Before the Restoration, in fact, the epilogue adopted the dance, but after 1660 the prologue likewise took it up, making use of devices like those in vogue during the seventeenth century in France. Excepting the use of Jevon and Haynes, we may say the majority of the prologues in English drama employed not one dancer, but groups, those examples preceding Crowne's *Calisto* being notably *The Ungrateful Favourite* (1664) and Edward Howard's *The Womens Conquest* (1671).

Interesting information concerning Crowne's *Calisto* may be found in Miss Eleanore Boswell's *The Restoration Court Stage*, published by the Harvard University Press in 1932. There the reader will find the names of such well-known actors and actresses as Moll Davis, Mary Knight, Charlotte Butler, and Charles Hart listed among the performers in *The Prologue to Calisto*, 1675.

Miss Boswell says the Lord Chamberlain sent a warrant to the Master of the Great Wardrobe, two days before the performance, to provide souvenir copies, and she thinks the printed book provided for by this warrant may have contained the prologue and the *intermedii*. She says this was privately printed, and it is her belief that the printer, having printed a large surplus, later put the pieces on the market, the Lord Chamberlain's warrant being his substitute for licence and entry in the Stationers' Register. Whatever the full history of the quarto may be, we do know from the Term Catalogue that in 1675 for sixpence one might read and picture for oneself the most elaborate prologue ever invented for the stage in Whitehall.

PROLOGUE.

The curtain is drawn up, and there appears a Nymph leaning on an Urne, representing the River Thames, attended by two Nymphs, representing Peace and Plenty: Near her are the four Parts of the World seeming to make offerings to Her: On the opening of the Scene, lamenting voices are heard on both sides of the Theatre, at which, the Nymph of the River seems affrightned.

Voices within. *Fly, Fly, Help, Oh! Help or we dye.*
Tha.   What mournful cries are these on ev'ry side!
The Winds waft nothing to this Island o're
But the complainings of some Neighbr'ing Shore,
And all the Ecchoes are in groans employ'd.   5
The fair *Augusta too, I weeping see,   *London
Though none so fair, so rich, so great   anciently so
    as She;   called.
Alas! my Fears encrease:
You gentle Nymphs of Plenty and of Peace,
    Shall now go seek some other Shore.   10
And you that with your Presents wait,
    Shall bring your gifts no more.
Plen.   I to no other Dwelling will betake,
Pea.   Thy beautious Streams I never will forsake,
Euro.   And we our Presents still will make.   15
Om.   We our presents still will make.
Ple.   Thy stores with all my Plenty shall be fill'd.
Pea.   My Halcion on thy Banks her Nest shall build.
Eur.   Thou shalt in all my noblest Arts be skill'd.
Asi.   My Jewels shall adorn no Brow but Thine.   20
Amer.   Thy Lovers in my Gold shall shine.
Afri.   Thou for thy Slaves, shalt have these Scorched
    Sons of mine.
Pea.
Plen.   } Thy beautious streams we never will forsake.

23

Euro.
Asi.
Afr.   } And we our presents still will make.
Amer.

Om.   We our presents still will make.   25
Pea.   What should so much Beauty fear,
        Round this Isle the Heavens appear
        Like your own streams, all undisturb'd and clear:
Tha.   These beautious Nymphs unfrightned too,
        Not minding what on other Shores they do,   30
        Their innocent delights pursue.
Pea.   See, They (void of grief or fear)
        Come to entertain you here.

        Enter Nymphs, who Dance, and go off.

Tha.   Oh! now my Spirits I recover,
        I've wak'd the *Genius* of this Isle, my War-like
            Lover.   35
        Enter the Genius of England.

Gen.   What cries are these disturb my pleasing Rest?
Tha.   'Tis I, (my Love) 'tis I, thy ayde request.
Gen.   Is it my Nymph, what dost thou fear?
Tha.   Does not my Love sad cries around him hear?
Gen.   Wilt thou thy fear at every shriek proclaim?   40
Tha.   Am I alone to blame?
        Do you not see *Augusta*, rich and fair,
        (Though to her Lap, I all my Treasure bear)
        Will for no comfort stay her Tears?
        Augusta is inclin'd to fears.   45
        Be she full, or be she wayning,
        Still *Augusta* is complaining.
        Give her all you can to ease Her,
        You shall never, never please Her.
Gen.   These fears do not belong to Her nor You;   50
        Europe only should lament,
        The Nymphs of his fair Continent.

        Some Gyants now pursue.

24

But this sweet Isle no Monster can invade.
Tha. Oh send those poor distressed Nymphs some Aid.
Eur. From the mild power of this happy place.   55
 Who is inclin'd,
To make the World as peaceful as his mind,
 They have already gain'd the grace:
Two Heroes of his own coelestial Race
Are sent; the one to Triumph o're the Seas,   60
And all the watery Divinities.
The other, Monsters of the Land to quell,
 And make the Nymphs in safety dwell.
Gen. The first, in War has all perfections gain'd,
That can by humane nature be attain'd: 65
The second promises, to be
All that in the first we see.
Eur. *Mars* to the first does all his glory lend:
The second Beauty, Youth, and Love attend.
Gen. Both in high perfections shine: 70
Valour, Glory, race Divine:
Wait a while, and you shall see
Both return with Victory.
Pea. Hark, hark; the Triumph's near,
And see! they both already crown'd appear.   75

 Enter One crown'd with a Naval Crown, attended
 by Sea-gods and Tritons.

Rejoyce you watry Deities:
The mighty Monsters of the Seas,
 This valiant Prince has slain.
The God of this fair Isle shall now,
Command (as all his Right allow)   80
 The Empire of the Mayne.

 Enter one Crown'd with a Mural Crown, attended
 by Warriours.

Ye Gods and Nymphs of Plains and Groves;
Of Springs and Streams, enjoy your Loves:
This youthful *Hero* has subdu'd,

25

The Satyrs now of ev'ry Wood: 85
Has kill'd or ta'n e'm all for Slaves,
And chac'd the Gyants from their Caves.
Cho. of all.   Let us both their praises sing,
     Whilst we both in Triumph bring,
         Let us all contend to grace e'm   90
     With our loud, and joyfull'st thanks,
     Whilst upon the flow'ry banks,
         Of this beautious Nymph we place e'm.

    Two Entries are Danc'd: One of Sea-gods and the
      other of Warriours.

Gen.   Now welcom Heroes to my blest abode,
      And to my Nymph belov'd by ev'ry God.   95
Tha.   Welcom to my Love and me,
      Now we all shall happy be.
Cho.   Now we all shall happy be.

    A Temple of Fame appears.

Ple.   Now you whose valour gives the World repose,
      See what Fame on you bestows.   100
      Her shining Temple shall preserve your names,
      And thence her Trumpet your renown proclaims.
Gen.   To our Divinity now let us go,
      And at his Feet your Crown and Trophies throw.
Eur.   I will my thanks in Offerings proclaim.   105
Asi.   I'le lend you Spice.
Amer.   I Gold.
Afr.   And I the same.
Tha.   I'le be your Guide.
      My streams beneath his Palace slide.   110
        There it is not far before you,
         Pleasure, Arts, Religion, Glory,
      Warm'd by his propitious Smile,
      Flourish there, and bless this Isle.
Gen.   But stay! what wonder does my spirit seize?   115
      See! here are both the great Divinities.   *Turning to*
                                           the King
                                           and Queen.

Tha. The God and Goddess too of this bless'd Isle!
　　Chast Beauty in her aspect shines,
　　　And Love in his does smile.
Gen. Quickly (*Heroes*) as 'tis meet,　　　　　　　　120
　　Throw your Trophies at their Feet.
　　　Fall down, and adore e'm.
　　Whilst with speed we hither call,
　　The Gods of neighbr'ing Groves, and all
　　　Their Nymphs to dance before e'm.　　　　　125

　　Enter Rural Gods and Nymphs, and Dance.

When the Prologue is done, and all gone off the Stage,
Enter Two, who sing this Song.

Now for the Play, the Prologue is done,
The Dancing is o're, and the Singers are gone.
The Ladies so fine, and so fair it surpasses,
Are dress'd, and have all tak'n leave of their glasses.
Where are the Slaves should make ready the Stage?　　130
Here, here are the slaves should make ready the Stage.

An Entry of Carpenters.

The Song to the Minouet, Danced in the Prologue, to be sung by
Shepheards.

Happy we Swaines, who are young and have leisure,
　　And but the wit our advantage to know.
We do not need either Fortune or Treasure,
　　Love and Delight with the youthful will go.　　135
Coyest of Nymphs may be won to the pleasure,
　　By Shepheards who love, and have youth to bestow.
Then whilst we are young, let's to pleasure betake us,
　　Each Swain with his Nymph, and each Nymph with
　　　her Swain
Embrace, and be happy as Loving can make us,　　140
　　And so make the most of our youth that we can.

The / Prologue / To / Pastor Fido. /
Spoken by Mr. Edward Lambert.

Folio half-sheet, reverse blank.
Bodleian Library.

ELKANAH SETTLE

Elkanah Settle, son of Josias Settle, was born on 1 February at Dunstable and baptised on 9 February 1647/8. On 13 July 1666 he matriculated from Trinity College, Oxford, but left without a degree. He then went to London, where he entered upon a literary career, assisted by Rochester. His first play, *Cambyses*, was acted probably in January 1670/1; and his second, *The Empress of Morocco*, was performed at Dorset Garden in July 1673 and at Whitehall, where prologues were spoken by Rochester and Mulgrave. *The Empress of Morocco* is said to be the first play ever published with engravings. On 28 February 1673/4 Settle married Mary Warner.

Settle's differences with Dryden began when *The Empress of Morocco* won recognition. With Crowne and Shadwell, Dryden wrote *Notes and Observations on the Empress of Morocco*; and Settle answered in *Notes and Observations on the Empress of Morocco Revised* (1674). Dryden described Settle as Doeg in *Absalom and Achitophel* (1682); then Settle wrote a whig reply, *Absalom Senior* (1682). Dryden continued his references to Settle in several plays, and Settle concluded with *Reflections on several of Mr. Dryden's Plays* (1687).

Settle entered politics, writing in support of both parties, assisting the Whigs, shifting to the Tories, then returning to the Whigs. Among his political writings are his *Character of a Popish Successor* (1681), *A Narrative of the Popish Plot* (1683), *A Panegyrick on Sir George Jefferies* (1683), and *Heroick Poem* on the coronation of James II.

28

Elkanah Settle

After 1688 Settle wrote drolls, ballads, and such other bits as the market absorbed. He was made city poet in 1691. Triumphs of London (1691), four pageants with the same title (1692–1695), and Glory's Resurrection (1698) belong to this final period of his literary career. In 1718 he entered the Charterhouse, through the influence of friends who knew his distress, and died there on 12 February 1723/4.

Settle's dramatic works, with date of performance and date of publication in parentheses, are Cambyses (c. Jan. 1670/1, 1671), The Empress of Morocco (July 1673, 1673), Love and Revenge (Nov. 1674, 1675), The Conquest of China (May 1675, 1676), Ibrahim (c. June 1676, 1677), Pastor Fido (c. Dec. 1676, 1677), Fatal Love (c. Sept. 1680, 1680), The Female Prelate (c. Sept. 1679, 1680), The Heir of Morocco (c. March 1682, 1682), Distress'd Innocence (c. Oct. 1690, 1691), The Fairy-Queen (April 1692, 1692), The New Athenian Comedy (unacted, 1693), The Ambitious Slave (Feb. 1693/4, 1694), Philaster (c. Dec. 1695, 1695), The World in the Moon (May 1697, 1697), The Virgin Prophetess (1701), The Siege of Troy (unacted, 1707), The City-Ramble (August 1711, 1711), The Lady's Triumph (1718).

THE PROLOGUE TO PASTOR FIDO

On the following broadside prologue to Pastor Fido in the Bodleian Library [Wood 416 (132)] there is a manuscript note by Wood, assigning the piece to Elkanah Settle, 1677. Pastor Fido, a free handling of Fanshawe's translation of Guarini's Il Pastor Fido, was first acted at Dorset Garden in 1676 and printed in quarto in 1677, with a prologue which speaks of "Renown'd Guarini's sacred dust," but is unlike the example reprinted here with a reference to "fam'd Guarini's sacred Dust."

For the first time in this collection of rare stage-orations the speaker's name is given, though designating the actor who spoke a prologue or an epilogue became a frequent practice later. Edward Lambert, who repeated this prologue to Pastor

29

Fido, is not named among the *dramatis personæ* by Genest.[1] He is to be ranked with others who assisted Settle's plays and lent especial lustre to the art of compliment and harangue: Lady Elizabeth Howard, Mrs. Knight, Mrs. Lee, Mrs. Rogers, Miss Dennis Chock, Horden, and Betterton.

[1] *Some Account of the English Stage*, I, 196-197.

THE
PROLOGUE
TO
PASTOR FIDO.
Spoken by Mr. *Edward Lambert.*

Preface and *Prologue,* are such *modish* Toys,
Books ar'nt without *this,* nor without *that* Plays.
Welcome, *Gallants!* and *Ladies* of the *May,* ⎫
You shall be *courted modishly* to day, ⎬
Because *without you,* there had been *no Play.* ⎭   5
As to our Play's *Original;* we'l first
Do right to fam'd Guarini's sacred Dust,
It's *learn'd* Author. Nor let it be *decry'd,*
'Cause *All's Italian, Nothing's Frenchifi'd.*
For, Plays (you know) like *Cloaths* submit *to Mode,*   10
And that's but *dull,* that keeps the *common Road.*
We caren't for that—for *here,* Sirs! nought you'l have,
But what is *Noble, Sage, Wise, Solid, Grave.*
Stern CATO *a Spectator* might be here,
And *modest* Virgins may *Unmaskt* appear.   15
You've *Comedy* in it's *most ancient* dress,
As when *of old, Carted* through *Villages.*
Here's then *no place,* for th' *Sparks* and th' *Blades*
 o' th' Times,
(Vallueing themselves upon *their Garb, their Crimes*)
Who scoff at *us poor Bumkins:* whole defence   20
Is our *simplicity,* our *Innocence.*
To please *such Fopps* (for *mortally* we *hate* 'um)
Wee'l ne're *attempt.*————————
 In short, you've here, *the Passions rudely* drest
To *act* their *parts,* if *Fear* balks not *the rest.*   25
Here's *coy* Love, *flattring* Hope; *cold* Desperation,
Enliv'ning Joys, *fawning* Dissimulation,
Pleasing Revenge, *easy* Credulity,
Fondness, Moroseness, *Rage,* and *Cruelty*

Charm'd into *Pity*.—Here are *Love's* Fatigues   30
It's Toyls: and *Lover's* Wit, Councels, Intrigues.
And if *All this* won't *take*, stop here—for not
(As I'me a *Sinner*) *one word* of the *Plot*.
For, since 'tis at *your choice*, to *clap* or *hiss*, ⎫
Expect *the rest*: if *well*, we do in *This*   ⎬   35
Your *patience* crave; *pardon* in what's *amiss*. ⎭

The End.

The Epilogue./Writ by/Mr. Drey-/
den, Spoke/before His/Majesty/at
Oxford,/March 19./1680./
London, Printed for Rich. Royston.

Folio half-sheet, reverse blank.
Imprint at bottom of p. 1.
Bodleian Library.

The/Epilogue/Spoken to the King
at the opening the/Play-House at
Oxford on Saturday last./Being March
the Nineteenth 1681.

Folio half-sheet, reverse blank.
No imprint.
Christ Church Library.

JOHN DRYDEN

John Dryden was born at Aldwinkle All Saints, Northamptonshire, 9 (?) August 1631. His father, Erasmus Dryden, was
the third son of Sir Erasmus Dryden, bart., of Canons Ashby,
Northamptonshire; and his mother, Mary Pickering, was the
daughter of Henry Pickering, rector of Aldwinkle.

Beginning his learning at Tichmarsh, Dryden was admitted
to a scholarship at Westminster and elected to a scholarship
at Trinity College, Cambridge, admitted 11 May, matriculated
6 July 1650. After receiving his B.A. in 1654, he went to
London, where he began his literary career with *Heroic
Stanzas* (1659) on the death of Cromwell, 3 September 1658.
His *Astrea Redux* (1660) celebrated the return of Charles II,
and a *Panegyric* (1661) honoured the king's coronation. On

26 November 1662 he was elected a member of the Royal Society, and on 1 December 1663 he married Lady Elizabeth Howard.

With his brother-in-law, Sir Robert Howard, Dryden wrote *The Indian Queen*, which was acted at the Theatre Royal in 1662 and published in *Four New Plays* (1665). Until his death in 1700 Dryden wrote frequently for the stage and held first place among the playwrights of the Restoration. His dramatic works, with the date of performance and the date of publication, are *The Wild Gallant* (Feb. 1662/3, 1669), *The Rival Ladies* (*c.* June 1664, 1664), *The Indian Emperour* (*c.* April 1665, 1667), *Secret Love* (March 1666/7, 1668), *Sr Martin Mar-all* (August 1667, 1668), *An Evening's Love* (June 1668, 1671), *Tyrannick Love* (*c.* April 1669, 1670), *The Conquest of Granada* (Part I *c.* Dec. 1670, Part II Jan. 1670/1; 1672), *Marriage A-la-Mode* (*c.* May 1672, 1673), *The Assignation* (*c.* Nov. 1672, 1673), *Amboyna* (*c.* June 1673, 1673), *Aureng-Zebe* (Nov. 1675, 1676), *The State of Innocence* (unacted, 1677), *All for Love* (Dec. 1677, 1678), *The Kind Keeper* (March 1677/8, 1680), *Oedipus* (*c.* Jan. 1678/9 1679), *Troilus and Cressida* (*c.* April 1679, 1679), *The Spanish Fryar* (March 1679/80, 1681), *The Duke of Guise* (Nov. 1682, 1683), *Albion and Albanius* (June 1685, 1685), *Don Sebastian* (Dec. 1689, 1690), *Amphitryon* (April 1690, 1690), *King Arthur* (*c.* May 1691, 1691), *Cleomenes* (April 1692, 1692), *Love Triumphant* (*c.* Dec. 1693, 1694), *Secular Masque: The Pilgrim* (1700). Dryden was also the greatest writer of prologues and epilogues in his day, being much sought after by young aspirants to theatrical success. Some ninety-five pieces are now assigned to him. His reputation was at its height in 1682. He was distinguished at the same time as a satirist, poet, critic, and translator. In addition to many small pieces which appeared in such various collections as the *Covent Garden Drollery* (1672), *New Court Songs and Poems* (1672), and *Miscellany Poems* (1684, 1685, 1693, 1694), his most significant works are *Annus Mirabilis*, 1667; *Essay on Dramatic Poesy*, 1668; *Defence*, 1668; *Absalom and Achitophel*, 1681; *The Medal*, 1682; *Mac Flecknoe*, 1682; *Absalom and Achitophel*, II (with

Nahum Tate), 1682; *Religio Laici,* 1682; *Threnodia,* 1685; *The Hind and the Panther,* 1687; *Britannia Rediviva,* 1688; *Eleonora,* 1692; *Juvenal and Persius,* 1693; *Alexander's Feast,* 1697; *Virgil,* 1697; *Fables,* 1700. His essays and prefaces to his plays and translations exerted a vigorous influence upon prose style. Examples of his prose not already listed may be found in his *Life of Plutarch,* 1683; *Defence of Papers written by the late King,* 1686; *Tr. Bouhours' life of Xavier,* 1688; *Preface to Walsh's Dialogue concerning Women,* 1691; Character of St. Evremont, prefixed to St. Evremont's *Miscellaneous Essays,* 1692; Character of Polybius, prefixed to a tr. by Sir Henry Sheere, 1693; Prose tr. of Dufresnoy's *Art of Painting,* 1695.

In 1668 the M.A. was conferred upon Dryden by the Archbishop of Canterbury. In 1668 he was made Poet Laureate and Historiographer, with a salary of £200 and a butt of canary wine. Though the salary was ill paid, an addition of £100 was made before 1679. On 17 December 1683 he became collector of customs in the port of London. He lost all his offices, however, with the Revolution of 1688. He died on 1 May 1700 at his house in Gerrard Street and was buried in the Poets' Corner of Westminster Abbey. In drama, prose, and poetry John Dryden was the leading literary man of his age.

In *The Works of John Dryden,* ed. Sir Walter Scott and George Saintsbury, 1885, Vol. X, and in the Oxford Standard Authors Series, *The Poems of John Dryden,* ed. John Sargeaunt, 1929, Dryden's prologues and epilogues in considerable number may be found. The rare epilogue reprinted in the following section, however, is included in neither; see the introductory essay concerning this item.

THE RAREST OF DRYDEN'S BROADSIDES

To-day's collector of Dryden's prologues and epilogues must have a purse of ten-pound-notes, for dealers quote high prices when they sell these folio half-sheets. Among Dryden's rarest is the epilogue reprinted here, the Britwell Court copy having been sold in 1927 for £340. Mr. W. G. Hiscock, who has recently studied this perhaps earliest of Dryden's folio half-sheets, calls attention to the fact that the London edition says: "Spoke before His Majesty at Oxford," whereas one that he discovered in the Christ Church Library a few years ago is headed: "Spoken to the King at the opening of the Play-House."

Though this broadside epilogue was published with these plain words in 1680/81, "Writ by Mr. Dreyden," it was not three decades before a version of the piece came out in Tom Brown's *Works* (1708), III, 96. Being one of only two stage-orations in this volume, Dryden's lines, under the title "The Epilogue," followed a "Prologue to a Musick Speech had in the Theatre in Oxford." The epilogue printed in Brown's *Works* is as follows:

> As from a darkned Room, some Optick Glass
> Transmits the distant Species as they pass;
> The Worlds large Landskip is from far descry'd,
> And Men contracted on the Paper glide.
>   Thus crowded *Oxford* represents Mankind,
> And in these Walls *Great Britain* seems confin'd:
> *Oxford* is now the publick Theatre,
> And you both Audience and Actors are;
> The gazing World on the new Scene attend,
> Admire the Turns, and wish a prosperous end.
> *Oxford*, the Seat of Peace, the quiet Cell,
> Where Arts, remov'd from noisy Business, dwell;
> Should calm your Minds, unite the jarring parts,
> And with a kind Contagion seize your Hearts.
> O! may its Genius like soft Musick move,
> And tune you all to Concord and to Love;
> Our Acts, which has in Tempest long been tost,
> Could never rest on so secure a Coast.
> From hence you may look back on civil Rage,
> And view the Ruins of the former Age:
> Here a new World its Glories may unfold,
> And here be sav'd the Remnant of the old:

But while your Thoughts on Publick Cares are bent,
Past Ills to heal, and future to prevent.
Some vacant Hours allow to your Delight, ⎤
Mirth is the pleasing Business of the Night, ⎬
The King's Prerogative, the Subject's Right. ⎦
Where all your Hours to sullen Cares confin'd,
The Body would be weary'd by the Mind;
'Tis Wisdom's part, betwixt Extreams to steer,
Be Gods in Senate, but be Mortals here.

The London edition of the broadside was first reprinted in *The London Mercury*, March 1930, by Mr. R. G. Ham; and a limited edition of 250 copies of the Epilogue "Spoken to the King at the opening of the Play-House" was brought out by Mr. Hiscock in 1932: *John Dryden. Epilogue. 19 March 1681*, printed by John Johnson at the Clarendon Press. Mr. Hiscock thinks this epilogue, which he discovered in the library of Christ Church at Oxford, may be Dryden's first broadside, and he says that from an examination of Oxford printing in 1681 we may believe that it was printed by L. Lichfield, jun., at Oxford. The text is reprinted in this book, with the kind permission of the Governing Body of Christ Church.

1680 was a hard year for the Theatre Royal, and, as Professor Allardyce Nicoll's quotations from the Lord Chamberlain's department[1] indicate, it saw His Majesty's Comedians repairing some of their late misfortunes by furnishing the University "as much divertisement as theire vacancie from theire studies" would allow. Dryden was then well acquainted with the skills of prologue and epilogue writing. He was, in fact, the poet most likely to be sought out when the players needed an epilogue for their performance of Saunders' *Tamerlaine* at Oxford for the Oxford Parliament, 21–8 March 1681.[2] He wrote for performances there at least seven years before the Miscellany of 1684 gathered up most of the Oxford pieces.

[1] *A History of Restoration Drama* (Cambridge University Press, 1928), pp. 295–296.

[2] Hugh Macdonald, *John Dryden* (Oxford Press, 1939), pp. 139–140.

Writ by
Mr. *Drey-
den*, Spoke
before His
MAJESTY
at *Oxford,*
March 19.

THE EPILOGUE.

1680. As from a darkned Room some Optick Glass
Transmits the distant Species as they pass,
The Worlds large Landskip is from far descry'd,
And men contracted on the Paper glide:
Thus crowded Oxford represents Mankind, 5
And in these Walls Great Britain seems confin'd;
Oxford is now the Publick Theatre,
And you both Audience are and Actors here:
The gazing World on the New Scene attend,
Admire the Turnes, and with a prosperous end, 10
This place the Seat of Peace; the quiet Cell,
Where Arts remov'd from noisy bus'ness dwell,
Should calm your Wills, Unite the Jarring parts,
And with a kind Contagion seize your hearts.
Oh! may its Genius like soft Musick move, 15
And Tune you all to Concord and to Love:
Our Ark that hath in Tempest long been tost,
Could never Land on so secure a Coast.
From hence you may look back on Civil rage,
And view the Ruins of the former Age: 20
Here a New World its Glories may unfold,
And here be Sav'd the Remnants of the Old.
But while your Day-sun publick thoughts are bent
Past ills to heal, and Future to prevent,
Some vacant hours allow to your delight; } 25
Mirth is the pleasing bus'ness of the night,
The King's Prerogative, The Peoples Right:
Were all your hours to Sullen Cares confin'd,
The body would be Jaded by the mind.
'Tis Wisdom's part betwixt Extremes to steer, 30
Be Gods in Senates, but be Mortals here.

London, Printed for *Rich. Royston.*

38

John Dryden

The
EPILOGUE

Spoken to the King at the opening the PLÁY-House at
Oxford on Saturday last. Being *March* the Nineteenth 1681.

As from a darkn'd Roome some Optick glass
Transmits the distant Species as they pass;
The worlds large Landschape is from far descry'd,
And men contracted on the Paper glide;
Thus crowded Oxford represents Mankind,
And in these Walls *Great Brittain* seems Confin'd.
Oxford is now the publick *Theatre;*
And you both Audience are, and Actors here.
The gazing World on the New Scene attend,
Admire the turns, and wish a prosp'rous end.
This Place the seat of Peace, the quiet Cell
Where Arts remov'd from noisy buisness dwell,
Shou'd calm your Wills, unite the jarring parts,
And with a kind Contagion seize your hearts:
Oh! may its Genius, 'like soft Musick move,
And tune you all to Concord and to Love.
Our Ark that has in Tempests long been tost,
Cou'd never land on so secure a Coast.
From hence you may look back on Civil Rage,
And view the ruines of the former Age.
Here a New World its glories may unfold,
And here be sav'd the remnants of the Old.
But while your daies on publick thoughts are bent
Past ills to heal, and future to prevent;
Some vacant houres allow to your delight, ⎤
Mirth is the pleasing buisness of the Night, ⎬
The Kings Prerogative, the Peoples right. ⎦
Were all your houres to sullen cares confind,
The Body wou'd be Jaded by the Mind.
'Tis Wisdoms part betwixt extreams to Steer:
Be Gods in Senates, but be Mortals here.

FINIS.

39

A Prologue spoken at Mithridates King of/Pontus, the First Play Acted at the Theatre/Royal this Year, 1681./ Epilogue./ London, Printed for J. Sturton.

Folio half-sheet; printed on both sides.
Imprint at bottom of p. 2.
British Museum.

For the biographical sketch of the probable author, John Dryden, see pp. 33–35.

FOR THE FIRST PLAY AT THE THEATRE ROYAL IN 1681

When fashionable Londoners returned from their four months' vacation,[1] the Theatre Royal opened with Lee's *Mithridates*, for which there were a new prologue of welcome and a new dialogue-epilogue. Dryden may have written both poems for this occasion since, as Mr. R. G. Ham observes, the manuscript notations by Luttrell on the half-sheet in the Huntington Library assign the two to him.[2] Saintsbury, breaking away from the example of Christie and including the epilogue in *The Works of Dryden* (1885),[3] points out that

[1] Mr. R. G. Ham, *Otway and Lee* (Yale University Press, 1931), n. 2, p. 236, says Collier, in his MS. *History of the Restoration Stage* (Harvard Library), p. 227, states that he owns the original manuscripts of these poems and that he finds in them mention of two months instead of four.

[2] *Otway and Lee*, p. 236.

[3] Variant readings indicate differences mainly in spelling, punctuation, number, and tense that set Saintsbury's version apart from the present and original text. Two variants of slightly more interest are in line 14 with *perk* instead of the original *pearch't* and in line 40 with *sense* instead of the original *sex*. See Vol. X, pp. 351–353.

for the first time this epilogue is received into Dryden's poems, "though it be granted that it is in a very rough condition." For several plays by Lee, Dryden contributed prologues and epilogues, beginning with an epilogue to *Mithridates* when it was performed in Drury Lane, probably in March, 1677/8, and continuing with a prologue to *Cæsar Borgia* at Dorset Garden in 1679, a prologue to *Sophonisba* when the players acted at Oxford in 1680, the prologue and epilogue to *The Princess of Cleve* at Dorset Garden in 1681, and the epilogue to *Constantine the Great* at Drury Lane in 1683.

We have reproduced here a very early epilogue that has the tone of a playhouse-commentary. After 1660 the habit of commenting upon the frills that were invading the theatre won upon prologues and epilogues with so stubborn a force that stage-orations became intelligencers of the theatre, recording opinions that remind us now of the persistent journalist's complaints. In no other place did actors and authors so frequently announce their views in explanations, justifications, and protests. Pleading for relief from the variety entertainments that invaded their plays, they were thus beforehand with judgments which the critics liked to be the first to retail outside the theatre. In such manner prologues and epilogues were admirable organs by which poets stole the critics' thunder.

The first twenty-one lines of this epilogue were spoken by the "best actor and the greatest rogue"[1] in King Charles's day, Cardell Goodman—Scum Goodman to those who disliked him. Born a gentleman, but inclined to the stage, Goodman was an actor with a past that careened toward a maze of error. Defacing a portrait of the Duke of Monmouth; basking in the favour of the Duchess of Cleveland, to whom he paid extravagantly amorous attention; sinking to the lowest depths as a criminal who plotted murder; terrorizing the roads as a highwayman; suffering imprisonment in Newgate and the Bastille,[2] the actor who concluded the first play at the theatre Royal in

---

[1] Dr. Doran's *Annals of the English Stage* (1888), I, 101.
[2] F. Dorothy Senior, *The Life and Times of Colley Cibber*, p. 22.

41

1681 was often "Scum" rather than a frequent and valuable stage-orator. He was with Powel, Harris, Adams, Lyddal, Kew, and others in the epilogue to Duffett's *The Empress of Morocco* in 1673, taking the part of Thunder; and he spoke the prologue to Lee's *Constantine the Great* at Drury Lane in 1683. Sharing his lines in the epilogue to *Mithridates* with Mrs. Cox, he introduced a female orator, the first in this collection of epilogue-rarities.

Mrs. Cox was presented as the "Toy" that Goodman hoped might "save the falling Stage." By 1681 a woman speaking an epilogue was hardly a novelty, for since 1660 female prologues and epilogues had appeared yearly.[1] During a twenty-one year-period, 1667 to 1688, to which, of course, this epilogue by Goodman and Mrs. Cox belongs, I have found at least seventy-five plays presented with female prologues and epilogues. Most often it was the epilogue that fell to the woman's care, for young girls and coquettes in a play's leave-taking were an especially popular amusement in the playhouse filled with ogling beaux. Hear Mrs. Cox's words in this half-sheet, and know the ways of the so-called female epilogue who no longer begged of her audience: "Pray, think no worse of me for my petticoat."

[1] See the Introduction to this work, pp. xxxv–xxxvi.

A PROLOGUE spoken at MITHRIDATES King of
PONTUS, the First Play Acted at the THEATRE ROYAL
this Year, 1681.

After a four Months Fast we hope at length
Your queasie Stomachs have recover'd strength
That You can taste a Play (your old coarse Messe)
As honest and as plain as an Addresse.
And therefore Welcome from your several Parts,   5
You that have gain'd kind Country Wenches Hearts:
Have watch'd returning Milk-maids in the Dark,
And sinn'd against the Pales of every Park.
Welcom fair Ladies of unblemish'd Faith,
That left Town Bagnio's for the fruitful Bath;   10
For when the Season's Hot, and Lover's there,
The Waters never fail to get an Heir.
Welcom kind Men that did your Wives attend,
And Welcom He that was the Husbands Friend,
Who holding Chat did silently Encroach,   15
With Treacherous Hand to grabble in the Coach.
Hail you New-Market Brothers of the Switch   ⎫
That leap left Strumpets, full of Pox and Itch, ⎬
A leap more dangerous than the Devil's Ditch. ⎭
Last Welcom you who never did appear;   20
Gave out i' th' Country, but lay fluxing here.
Now Crawl abroad with Stick, lean-chapt and thin,
And Fair as Lady that hath new lain in;
This Winter let us reckon you our own,
For all Wise Men will let the State alone: 25
The Plot's remov'd, a Witness of Renown
Has lodg'd it safe, at t'other End o'th' Town,
And that it ne're may fail, some pious Whore ⎫
Has cast her Mite, and fairly at his Dore   ⎬
Laid two small squalling Evidences more;   ⎭   30
Which well instructed, if we take their words,

43

In time may grow to hang two Popish Lords;
Heav'n Grant the Babes may Live, for Faith there's
    need,
Swearers fall off so fast, if none succeed
The Land's in danger quite to loose the breed.   35
Unless you break an Act, which were a Sin,
And for recruit let Irish Cattle in.
Well; after all 'twere better to Compound,
Then let the foolish Frolick still go round,
Both sides have lost and by my Computation   40
None but Jack Ketch has gained in the Nation.

EPILOGUE.

Pox on this Play-house, 'tis an old tir'd Jade,
'Twill do no longer, we must force a Trade;
What if we all turn Witness of the Plot?
That's overstockt, there's nothing to be got.
Shall we take Orders? That will Parts require,   5
And Colledges give no Degrees for Hire,
Would *Salamancha* was a little nigher.
Will nothing do? Oh now 'tis found I hope;
Have not you seen the Dancing of the Rope?
When *Andrew's* Wit was clean run off the
    Score,   10
And *Jacob's* Cap'ring Tricks could do no more,
A Damsel does to the Ladders Top advance
And with two heavy Buckets drags a Dance;
The Yawning Crowd pearch't up to see the
    sight,
And slav'r'd at the Mouth for vast Delight: 15
Oh Friends there's nothing to Enchant the
    Mind,
Nothing like that sweet Sex to draw Mankind:
The Foundred Horse that switching will not stir,
Trots to the Mare, afore without a Spur.

Faith I'le go scoure the Scene-room and
  Engage   20
Some Toy within to save the falling Stage.

                                   Exit.

       Re-Enters with Mrs. Cox.

Who have we here again, what Nymphs i' th'
  Stocks?
Your most Obedient Servant, sweet Madam Cox.
You'd best be Coy, and Blush for a pretence,
For Shame say something in your own Defence. 25

Mrs. *Cox,*   What shall I say? I have been hence so long
I've e'ne almost forgot my Mother Tongue;
If I can Act I wish I were ten Fathom
Beneath————————————

M. *Goodman.* —Oh Lord, Pray, no swearing, Madam;
Mrs. *Cox,*   Why Sir, If I had sworn, to save the Nation 30
I could find out some Mental Reservation.
Well in plain Termes, Gallants, without a
  Shamm,
Will you be pleas'd to take me as I am.
Quite out of Countenance, with a down cast
  look,
Just like a Truant that returnes to Book: 35
Yet I'me not old, but if I were this place
Ne're wanted Art to peice a ruin'd Face.
When Grey-Beards Govern'd I forsook the
  Stage,
You know 'tis piteous work to Act with Age;
Though there's no sex amongst these
  Beardless Boys,   40
There's what we Women love, that's Mirth
  & Noise,
These young Beginners may grow up in time,
And the Devil's in't if I'me past my Prime.

London, *Printed for* J. Sturton.

A / Prologue / To a New Play, called /
The Royallist. / The Epilogue, spoken
by Mr. Underhill.

Folio half-sheet; printed on both sides.
British Museum.

THOMAS D'URFEY

Thomas D'Urfey was born at Exeter in 1653. He was handsome and of such good humour that he was a favourite of both king and court. Listed in the order of their performance, with date of acting and date of publication in parentheses, D'Urfey's dramatic works are *The Siege of Memphis* (*c.* Sept. 1676, 1676), *Madam Fickle* (Nov. 1676, 1677), *The Fool Turn'd Critick* (Nov. 1676, 1678), *A Fond Husband* (May 1676, 1677), *Trick for Trick* (*c.* March 1677/8, 1678), *Squire Oldsapp* (*c.* June 1678, 1679), *The Virtuous Wife* (*c.* Sept. 1679, 1680), *Sir Barnaby Whigg* (*c.* Sept. 1681, 1681), *The Royalist* (Jan. 1681/2, 1682), *The Injured Princess* (*c.* March 1681/2, 1682), *A Common-Wealth of Women* (*c.* Sept. 1685, 1686), *The Banditti* (Feb. 1685/6, 1686), *A Fool's Preferment* (*c.* April 1688, 1688), *Bussy D'Ambois* (*c.* March 1690/1, 1691), *Love for Money* (*c.* Dec. 1689, 1691), *The Marriage-Hater Match'd* (Jan. 1691/2, 1692), *The Richmond Heiress* (*c.* Feb. 1692/3, 1693), *The Comical History of Don Quixote* (*c.* May 1694, 1694), *The Comical History of Don Quixote*, II (*c.* May 1694, 1694), *The Comical History of Don Quixote*, III (*c.* Nov. 1695, 1696), *The Intrigues of Versailles* (*c.* Feb. 1696/7, 1697), *Cinthia and Endimion* (*c.* Sept. 1697, 1697), *The Campaigners* (*c.* Nov. 1698, 1698), *The Famous History of the Rise and Fall of Massaniello*, Two Parts (*c.* May 1699, 1700), *The Bath* (*c.* July 1701, 1701), *The Old Mode & the New* (Feb. 1703, 1704), *Wonders in the Sun*

46

Thomas D'Urfey

(April 1706, 1706), *The Modern Prophets* (May 1709, 1709), *New Opera's, with Comical Stories* (1721), *The English Stage Italianiz'd* (1727). His poems were in great demand, and he wrote numerous prologues, epilogues, and songs which appeared in the editions of the plays that they accompanied and in *Wit and Mirth* (1684, 1699, 1700, 1706, 1710, 1719, 1720). He also wrote *Tales, Tragical and Comical*, 1704, and *Tales, Moral and Comical*, 1706. Courtiers saw Charles II leaning familiarly on D'Urfey's shoulder, holding a corner of the sheet of music from which D'Urfey was singing, "Remember, ye Whigs, what was formerly done." Thomas D'Urfey died on 26 February 1723 and was buried at St. James's Church, Piccadilly.

D'URFEY'S TORY PROLOGUE AND EPILOGUE

When D'Urfey's prologue and epilogue to *The Royalist* broke out against the Whigs in January, 1681/2, England's acquaintance with the terms *Whigs* and *Tories* was at least two years old, for the *Oxford English Dictionary* gives 1679 as the likely date for the naming of these two parties. By 1681 both words had entered into the vocabulary of prologue- and epilogue-speakers. It is then, perhaps, only interesting to think that the half-sheet entered here may be the earliest bold party-organ out of the theatre, belonging to the paper-scuffle that occupied the next few years. Avowedly Tory, it may have been printed apart from its play to be sold where friends and enemies of the party devoured and scrapped partisan words like D'Urfey's.

Both the prologue and the epilogue were printed with the play in 1682, with very slight change in text. In the prologue, line 3 has *State* where the earlier text has *Fate;* line 6 has *Brumigham's* instead of the earlier *Brimigham's;* line 39 has *That* instead of *This;* line 40 has *Then* instead of *And;* and line 41 introduces the word *To* and gives *Exemplar* instead of *Examples.* In the epilogue, line 20, *row'zd up* occurs instead of *raised.*

47

A manuscript note in the play that I have seen in the Library of Congress names Smith the speaker of the prologue; but the epilogue is printed with the statement that it was spoken by Underhill, as is also shown in the original publication which is reproduced here. So Smith, perhaps, and Underhill, with certainty, spoke these lines in Dorset Garden in January, 1681/2. Of Smith's position in playhouse-affairs we have already spoken, and the reader may turn to the prologue for Otway's *Venice Preserved* if he wishes to renew acquaintance with William Smith. Cave Underhill shows his comic face for the first time in this collection of rare pieces sold by the booksellers, but he is a veteran of the theatre, having already to his credit twenty years of truly comic playing and thirty years waiting. During that half-century England did not see a Gravedigger in *Hamlet* surpassing his. Underhill is said to have never understood his vogue, and it seems that the poets may have caused him to confess his lack of understanding in order that they might win through him more laughter from the audience that was looking at broad-faced, flat-nosed, wide-mouthed, and thick-lipped Cave Underhill while he seriously pondered the first lines of his epilogue:

> What in my face cou'd this strange Scribler see,
> (Uds Heart) to make an Evidence of me?

Apollo's Feast (1703) contains an epilogue spoken by Underhill in Puritanical habit at the New Theatre, and the second volume of D'Urfey's *Wit and Mirth* (1719) offers a prologue recited by Underhill. The face and the voice of Comical Cave prologued Otway's *Titus and Berenice*, performed in Dorset Garden probably in December, 1676; but the epilogue was his more frequent vehicle, as may be seen by his lines spoken at the end of Cowley's *Cutter of Coleman Street* (L.I.F. Dec. 16, 1661), Shakespeare's *Twelfth Night* (L.I.F. May 28, 1663), Dryden's *Troilus and Cressida* (D.G. April, 1679), D'Urfey's *The Royalist* (D.G. Jan., 1681/2), and (with Bowen and Gypsey) Motteux's *Love's a Jest* (L.I.F. *c.* Sept., 1696). The Poets who wrote his prologues and epilogues may have found in him what *The Tatler* described on May 21, 1709:

> . . . There is certainly nature excellently repre-
> sented in his manner of action; in which he ever
> avoided the general fault of players, of doing too
> much. It must be confessed, he has not the merit of
> some ingenious persons now on the stage, of adding
> to his authors; for the actors were so dull in the last
> age, that many of them have gone out of the world,
> without having ever spoke one word of their own in
> the theatre. Poor Cave is a part fit for a man who has
> one foot in the grave, viz. a gravedigger. All
> Admirers of true comedy, it is hoped, will have the
> gratitude to be present on the last day of his acting,
> who, if he does not happen to please them, will have
> it even then to say, that it is his first offence.

An "ultra Tory," he is named in Dr. Doran's *Annals of the Stage*[1] as one "addicted in coffee-houses to drink the Duke of York's health more heartily than that of his brother, the King." In such loyal mood, no doubt, he spoke the lines reprinted here.

[1] Ed. Robert W. Lowe, 1888, I, 140.

A
PROLOGUE
To a New PLAY, called
THE ROYALLIST.

How! the House full! and at a *Royal Play!*
That's strange! I never hop'd to see this day.
But sure this must some change of Fate fore-tell;
For th' Pit (methinks) looks like a *Commonweal;*
Where Monarch Wit's bafl'd by ev'ry Drudge,   5
And each pert Railing *Brimigham's* a Judge.
But know, ye Criticks of unequal Pride, ⎫
The Dice now give kind chances on our side; ⎬
Tories are upmost, and the *Whigs* defy'd. ⎭
Your *Factious Juries* and *Associations* ⎫ 10
Must never think to ruine twice Three Nations; ⎬
No, there's one 'bove you has too long had Patience. ⎭
Changing of sides is now not counted strange;
Some for *Religion*, some for *Faction* change:
And (lest Examples should be too remote,) ⎫ 15
A *Rev'rend Clergy-man* of famous note ⎬
Hath chang'd his *Cassock* for a *Campaign-Coat;* ⎭
Amongst the Saints doth most devoutly *Stickle*,
And holy Bag-pipe Squeals in *Conventicle.*
Another sort there are that rore and rant;   20
Are *Loyal;* but all other Vertues want:
Ask their Religion, they cry, *What a Pox,*
Damn me ye Dog, I'm stanch, I'm Orthodox.
These are as bad as t'other ev'ry way,
And much unlike my part I act to day;   25
A *Royallist* by *Nature*, not by *Art,*
That loves his Prince and Countrey at his Heart;
Addresses loves, to all Mankind is civil;
But hates *Petitions* as he hates the Devil;
Perfect in Honour, constant to his Friend;   30
And only hath one fault, is wondrous kind.
Yet who here would refuse a kind Intrigue;
Faith none who does it is a Rigling *Whig.*
This is his Character, and is't not pity

But such as he bore Office in the City?⁣ 35
How would all honest Hearts their Fates esteem,
Were all our Common-Council-men like him?
How glad to be preserv'd from Factious Furies,
If such as he was Fore-man of the Juries.
This point once gain'd, Sedition would want force,⁣ 40
And equal Justice take its proper Course;
Hang up all those for an Examples show,
That have deserv'd it Twenty years ago.

The Epilogue, spoken by Mr. Underhill.

What in my face cou'd this strange Scribler see,
(Uds Heart) to make an *Evidence* of me?
That never cou'd agree with *Ignoramus,*
But for a *Tender Conscience* have been famous.
For who of these among you here that have⁣ 5
Not in your Rambles heard of *Tory Cave;*
Who rores in Coffee-house, and wasts his Wealth,
Toping the Gentleman in *Scotland's* Health.
This part should have been given some hardy Fool,
That had more sense for Int'rest than his Soul.⁣ 10
I never had the knack of Truth-denying, ⎫
Loving Sedition, Loyalty defying; ⎬
Nor could I take Ten Pound a week for Lying. ⎭
But since 'tis so, I must intreat the pity
Of you our (never failing) Friends i'th' City.⁣ 15
For though I was not e're brought up to th' Trade,
Like Setting-Dog I may with Art be made.
In time such wholsom Documents receive:
Uds Zooks, who knows but I may stand for *Shrieve?*
And faith, that thought hath raised my ambition:⁣ 20
Well, Sirs, give me but House-room, and Provision;
Cry up the *Play*, and always let me find
My Benefactors Bountiful and Kind;
Then, if you want a Swinger at a word,
Zounds I'le swear for you through a two-inch-Board.⁣ 25

FINIS.

Prologue. / By Mr. Otway to his Play call'd Venice preserv'd, or the Plot/discover'd. Acted at His Royal Highness the Duke of / Yorks Theatre, the 9th of February, 1681. / Epilogue. / London, Printed for A. Green. 1681.

Folio half-sheet; printed on both sides.
Imprint at bottom of p. 2.
British Museum.

Prologue / To a New Play, called / Venice Preserv'd ; / or / The Plot Discover'd. / At the Duke's Theatre ; Spoken by Mr. Smith. / Epilogue / To the Same. / Spoken by Mr. Betterton. / London, Printed for A. Banks. 1682.

Folio half-sheet; printed on both sides.
Imprint at bottom of p. 2.
British Museum.

THOMAS OTWAY

Thomas Otway, born on 3 March 1651/2 at Milland in Sussex, was the only son of Humphrey Otway, curate of Trotton. He was educated at Winchester College and at Christ Church,

Oxford, which he entered as a commoner on 27 May 1669. In the autumn of 1672 he left the University without a degree and went to London.

Failing in his first attempt to act in Mrs. Behn's *The Forc'd Marriage* (December 1670), Otway turned to writing plays, *Alcibiades* (1675) being performed in September 1675; *Don Carlos* (1676), in June 1676; *Titus and Berenice* (1677), in *c.* December 1676; *Friendship in Fashion* (1678), in April 1678; *The History and Fall of Caius Marius* (1680), in *c.* September 1679; *The Orphan* (1680), in *c.* March 1680; *The Souldiers Fortune* (1681), in March 1679/80; *Venice Preserv'd* (1682), in February 1681/2; *The Atheist* (1684), in *c.* September 1683.

Mrs. Barry's indifference to his love for her made Otway desperate. He enlisted in the army and went to Holland in 1678. On 10 February 1678 he received a commission as ensign, and on 1 November he became a lieutenant. Late in 1679 he returned to London, where he resumed his writing. *The Orphan* (1680) showed that his literary powers had matured, and *Venice Preserv'd* (1682) proved his ability in poetic tragedy. In addition to his dramas, Otway wrote prologues and epilogues for himself and for other authors, notably Mrs. Behn (prologue to *The City Heiress*) and Lee (prologue to *Constantine the Great*). He wrote the English rendering of Ovid's *Epistle of Phaedra to Hippolytus* (1680) and *The Poet's Complaint of his Muse* (1680). His verses prefaced Creech's translation of Lucretius (1682), and a few of his poems were included in Tonson's *Miscellany Poems* (1684). Otway died in April 1685 and was buried on 16 April in the churchyard of St. Clement Danes. The first collected edition of his plays appeared in 1713.

An excellent edition of Otway's works is *The Works of Thomas Otway*, ed. J. C. Ghosh, Oxford: The Clarendon Press, 1932, in two volumes.

VENICE PRESERV'D

Hoping that 1681/2 would see him no longer in the rear

of fortune, Otway dedicated *Venice Preserved* to the Duchess of Portsmouth:

> . . . Forgive me then, Madam, if (as a poor peasant once made a present of an apple to an Emperor) I bring this small tribute, the humble growth of my little garden, and lay it at your feet. . . . Your noble pity and compassion found me, where I was far cast backward from my blessing; down in the rear of Fortune, called me up, placed me in the shine, and I have felt its comfort. You have in that restored me to my native right, for a steady faith, and loyalty to my Prince, was all the inheritance my father left me, and however hardly my fortune deal with me, 'tis what I prize so well that I ne're pawned it yet, and hope I ne're shall part with it.

For his loyalty and for his play, Otway had his reward in the day's applause. He was then first among the playwrights of his age, and his genius had come to assist at the triumphal rise of Tory principles. For the first production of his great tragedy, he had timely words in the prologue and epilogue, which are extant in two folio half-sheets, one being printed for A. Green, 1681, with the title:

> Prologue./By Mr. Otway to his Play call'd Venice preserv'd, or the Plot/discover'd. Acted at his Royal Highness the Duke of/Yorks Theatre, the 9th of February, 1681./(Epilogue, *verso*).

and another being printed for A. Banks, 1682, with a different title:

> Prologue/To a New Play, called/Venice Preserv'd;/or/The Plot Discover'd./At the Duke's Theatre; Spoken by Mr. Smith./
>
> Epilogue/To the Same./Spoken by Mr. Betterton./ (*verso*).

A comparison of the two texts shows the variations to be mainly in an occasional word of minor importance and in punctuation, capitalization, and spelling. The lines of the prologue showing more significant differences are the ninth:

"But 'tis he says, to Reason plain, and Sence;"
(A. Green, 1681)
"But is to each man's reason plain and sense;"
(A. Banks, 1682)

and the thirtieth:

"Thanks Heav'n, for all his Age, he's hang'd at last."
(A. Green, 1681)
"In spight of Age, thanks Heav'n he's Hang'd at last."
(A. Banks, 1682)

The same may be said of the epilogue, the notable differences occurring in line 2, with *done* (1681) replaced by *ended* (1682); line 7, *bad me boldly say* (1681), *boldly bad me say* (1682); line 14, *Scoules* (1681), *Frowns* (1682); line 22, *A general sign all Blockheads have no* (1681), *Or general Pique, that Blockheads have to* (1682); line 23, *Nothing doth Damn his Pen, when* (1681), *Nothing shall daunt his Pen when* (1682); and lines 28 and 29 (1681), which are reversed in the text of 1682. Both folio half-sheets vary from the texts printed with the play in 1682, the chief variants aside from spelling, punctuation, and capitalization being these with Q designating the play:

Title of folio half-sheet (1682) alone names the speaker, Smith:
The Prologue: l. 1, *Unsettled* (1681), *unsettled* (1682), *distracted* (Q 1682); l. 3, *we know not* (1681, 1682), *I know not* (Q 1682); l. 4, *began* (1681), *begin* (1682, Q 1682); l. 5, *makes* (1681), *made* (1682, Q 1682); l. 11, *and Sense by* (1681), *by Sense and* (1682, Q 1682); l. 16, *Or Spanish* (1681, Q 1682), *Of Spanish* (1682); l. 20, *Ribs* (1681), *Limbs* (1682, Q 1682); Q 1682 lacks a couplet:

Thomas Otway

He has no Truths of such a Monstrous Stature
And some believe there are none such in Nature.
(1681)

Here are no Truths of such a Monstrous stature,
And some believe there are none such in Nature.
(1682)

l. 23 (folio) or l. 21 (Q), *But* (1681, 1682), *Yet*
(Q 1682); l. 24 or l. 22, *Yet* (1681), *But* (1682,
Q 1682), *Man* (1681), *Men* (1682), *man* (Q 1682);
l. 29 or l. 27, *And* (1681, 1682), *Till* (Q 1682);
l. 30 or l. 28, *Thanks Heav'n, for all his Age, he's*
(1681), *In spight of Age, thanks heav'n he's* (1682),
In spight of Age (thanks Heaven) is (Q 1682); l. 31 or l.
29, *there's* (1681), *here's* (1682), *is* (Q 1682); l. 32
or l. 30, *greater* (1681), *higher* (1682, Q 1682); l. 34
or l. 32, *all London* (1681, Q 1682), *in London*
(1682); l. 36 or l. 34, *Oh* (1681, Q 1682), *Ah*
(1682).

The Epilogue: Title of folio half-sheet (1682)
alone names the speaker, Betterton; l. 2, *done, pray
give* (1681), *ended, give* (1682), *ended pass* (Q 1682);
l. 11, *Courage* (1681, 1682), *Spirit* (Q 1682); l. 14,
Scoules (1681), *scowles* (Q 1682), *Frowns* (1682);
l. 22, *A general sign* (1681), *Or general Pique, that*
(1682), *Or general Pique all* (Q 1682), *no* (1681),
to (1682, Q 1682); l. 23, *doth Damn* (1681), *shall
daunt* (1682, Q 1682), *doth* (1681, 1682), *does*
(Q 1682); l. 24, *of* (1681), *at* (1682, Q 1682);
l. 26, *the* (1682), *their* (1681, Q 1682); l. 27,
whil'st (1681), *while* (1682, Q 1682); l. 28, *Fame*
(1681), *Name* (1682, l. 29, Q 1682); l. 31, *dread*
(1681), *Read* (1682), *reade* (Q 1682); l. 32, *Martyrs*
(1681), *Martyr* (1682), *Martyr's* (Q 1682); l. 33,
retain (1681, Q 1682), *maintain* (1682). The
edition of the play adds the note for ll. 27–28: *The
Rascal that cut the Duke of York's picture.*

In both prologue and epilogue there are allusions to persons, events, and conditions contemporary with the play's performance. Manifestly, the two are to be taken as early and significant examples of the newly conceived stage-oration which commented upon the day's affairs so faithfully that it seemed a prologue- or epilogue-journal. Thus the theatre made adjustment to the times, answering the new interests of its audience, particularly an avidity for news, which Dryden mentioned in his prologue to Lee's *Cæsar Borgia* in 1679, and which Shadwell satirized during the same year in a prologue to *The Woman-Captain*. The playhouse was then England's weather-glass.

Before the words reprinted here were spoken, prologues and epilogues had said not a little about the plotting times. The epilogue to Shadwell's *A True Widow* began with lines alluding to the unsettled state of affairs at home.[1] Mrs. Behn's *The Feign'd Curtizans* was presented with a prologue that referred to suspicions and jealousies that employed the busy, fearful town. In fact, England's nerves were unstrung while guards, watches, and similar aids to security lent atmosphere that fathered prologues and epilogues like Otway's. In 1679, probably in September, Lee's *Cæsar Borgia* was presented with an epilogue referring to the popish excitement and to Father Lewis, who was lately executed at Usk. Scarcely a month intervened between the deed and the allusion in this

---

[1] Mr. Albert S. Borgman says the play was produced sometime between Oct. 17, 1678, the day on which the body of Sir Edmundbury Godfrey was found, and Feb. 16, 1678/9, the date of the dedication, and he concludes that the epilogue referred to the panic that followed the murder (*Thomas Shadwell*, New York: The New York University Press, 1928, p. 32, note). Mr. Allardyce Nicoll says Shadwell's play was performed about March, 1677/8 (*A History of Restoration Drama*, p. 373). If the epilogue, which appears in the copy of the play for 1679, was spoken at the first presentation, as was the custom, then the "troubled Times" in March, 1677/8, were not occasioned by either the discovery of a conspiracy by Titus Oates, in the latter part of September, 1678 (Luttrell, *A Brief Historical Relation of State Affairs*, Oxford: At the University Press, 1857, I, 1), or the strange death of Sir Edmundbury Godfrey, whose body was found on Oct. 17, 1678 (Luttrell, I, 1).

instance, so eager was the public for comment upon its distress. During the same year Bedloe's *The Excommunicated Prince*, a Popish Plot in a Play, was published with a prologue referring to the Pope and priests. In March, 1679/80, Dryden's *The Spanish Fryar* was presented with an epilogue, written by a friend, ridiculing the priests. Probably in March, 1679/80, Crowne's *The Misery of Civil-War*, which was reissued in 1681 as *Henry the Sixth, The Second Part*, was performed with a prologue and an epilogue referring to the religious disputes of the day. Crowne likewise attacked the Papists in the prologue and epilogue to *Thyestes*, which was performed probably in March, 1680/1. In 1681, probably in September, Crowne's *Henry the Sixth, The First Part*, was presented with a prologue promising that the play contained "A little Vinegar against the Pope," and an epilogue referring to the confusion that had come in politics as a result of the Popish agitation.[1] Another play of about the same date, D'Urfey's *Sir Barnaby Whigg*, was presented with a prologue, commenting upon the plotting age; and near the close of 1681 Dryden's prologue to Banks's *The Unhappy Favourite* referred to the troubled state. In February, 1681/2, the prologue to Otway's *Venice Preserved* took note of the "distracted times."

References to contemporary personages occurred in prologues and epilogues with the greatest rarity before 1660;[2]

[1] The play was opposed, says Gerald Langbaine, *The English Dramatick Poets* (1691), p. 96, by the Popish faction who, through powers at court, had the play suppressed. By the rest of the audience the play was well received.

[2] The reader may note one of the few instances of a reference of this type in the sixteenth century in the prologue that Machiavel spoke to Marlowe's *The Jew of Malta*:

> Albeit the world thinks Machiavel is dead,
> Yet was his soul flown beyond the Alps;
> And now the Guise is dead, is come from France,
> To view this land, and frolic with his friends.

The Duke of Guise was assassinated in 1588. See *The Jew of Malta*, c. 1589, E. K. Chambers, *The Elizabethan Stage*, III, 424–425.

but with the rise of newspapers and the enjoyment of greater freedom of expression in the playhouse, personal references and allusions entered into the oratory of the theatre. Kings, queens, dukes, duchesses, commanders of military and naval forces, statesmen, poets, and men of humbler note woke sometimes to find themselves praised or cursed in couplets prologuing or ending a play. Such was the experience of Shaftesbury, Oates, Mother Creswell, Scroop, Sir Thomas Armstrong, Dryden, the Duke of York, and the picture-mangler when Smith and Betterton spoke Otway's prologue and epilogue to *Venice Preserved*.

Fortunate, indeed, the play that was introduced and closed by the best actors in a playhouse! On at least two different occasions before Otway's tragedy was thus blessed, Smith and Betterton spoke for the same play. Betterton repeating the prologue, Smith speaking the epilogue—these two gifted actors appeared for Tuke's *The Adventures of Five Hours* and Etherege's *The Man of Mode*. For the third time, this pair— already entering upon their life-long friendship without a break—came to recite for Otway's *Venice Preserved*, Smith taking the prologue, Betterton the epilogue. William Smith, the original Pierre of *Venice Preserved*, was almost Betterton's rival at this time. Though beginning work as a barrister, he had turned to the stage and had become an actor of social position and histrionic power. No less than ten prologues and seven epilogues fell to him before 1683, and we deduce there-from a surmise that William Smith,[1] of commanding figure, was looked upon as one of the best prologue-speakers in his time. To him were assigned lines by Dryden, and he spoke before the King and Queen. He was then more than Betterton's equal, if the number of prologues and epilogues entrusted to an actor be evidence of skill; for Betterton, to whom the years ahead were to give the highest acclaim ever granted an actor, had spoken seven prologues and two epilogues by 1683,

[1] For all prologues and epilogues spoken before 1700, see William Smith, Appendix C.

though the future held many more for him.[1] His strong, full, and articulate voice was well fitted to the prologue- and epilogue-style; for, according to Anthony Aston, it tuned to an artful climax that commanded "universal attention even from the *fops* and orange girls." As we read the numerous prologues and epilogues spoken by this Roscius of England's theatre, we think ourselves into seeing him even now—the ruddy, sanguine Betterton, his left hand lodged in his breast between his coat and waistcoat, his right free for rare but just interpreting gestures, his low voice rising to a magnificent climax. "The best actor in the world," said Pepys;[2] and on May 28, 1663, he made this memorandum: "never to think enough of Betterton."

[1] Betterton's seventeenth-century pieces are named in Appendix C. Beginning with 1700, he was given these: Prologues to Rowe's *The Ambitious Step-Mother* (L.I.F., the old theatre, *c.* Dec. 1700), Prologue by Falstaff, acted by Betterton (mentioned by Prior in a letter to Abraham Stanyan, Jan. 8, 1700, Bickley's *Life of Prior*, p. 110), Gildon's *Love's Victim* (L.I.F., the old theatre, *c.* April 1701), Trapp's prologue to the University of Oxford, July 5, 1703, Rowe's *The Fair Penitent* (prologue designed for Betterton, L.I.F., the old theatre, *c.* May 1703), Boyle's *As You Find It* (L.I.F., the old theatre, April 1703), Trapp's *Abra-Mule* (L.I.F., the old theatre, Jan. 1703/4), Dennis' *Liberty Asserted* (L.I.F., the old theatre, Feb. 1703/4), Rowe's *The Biter* (L.I.F., the old theatre, *c.* Dec. 1704), Centlivre's *The Gamester* (L.I.F., the old theatre, *c.* Jan. 1704/5), Shakespeare's *Henry the Eighth* (the prologue designed to be spoken, printed in *The Diverting Post*, Dec. 9–16, 1704), Rowe's *Ulysses* (Haymarket, once the Queen's Theatre, Nov. 1705), Centlivre's *The Platonick Lady* (Haymarket, once the Queen's Theatre, Nov. 1706), Rowe's *The Royal Convert* (Haymarket, once the Queen's Theatre, Nov. 1707). He spoke epilogues to Porter's *The Villain* (L.I.F. Oct. 1662), Otway's *Venice Preserved* (D.G. Feb. 1681/2), Behn's *The Luckey Chance* (D.L. *c.* April 1686), Dogget's *The Country Wake* (L.I.F. *c.* May 1696), Manley's *Almyna* (Haymarket, once the Queen's Theatre, Dec. 1706).

[2] Nov. 4, 1661.

PROLOGUE.

By Mr. *Otway* to his *Play* call'd *Venice preserv'd*, or the *Plot discover'd*. Acted at his Royal Highness the Duke of YORKS THEATER, the 9th of *February*, 1681.

In these *Unsetled Times*, when each Man dreads,
The *Bloody Stratagems* of Buisy Heads;
When we have fear'd three years we know not what,
Till *Witnesses* began to dye oth' *Rot;*
What makes our Poet meddle with a Plot?   5
   Was't that he fancy'd for the very sake,
And name of Plot, his trifling Play might take?
For there's not in't one Inch-board *Evidence*,
But 'tis he says, to Reason plain, and Sence;
And that he thinks a plentiful Defence.   10
   Were *Truth* and *Sence* by *Reason* to be Try'd,
Sure all our *Swearers* might be laid aside.
No, of such *Tools* our Author has no need;
To make his *Plot*, or make his *Play* succeed.
He of *Black-Bills* has no prodigious Tales,   15
Or *Spanish-Pilgrims* throw'n a Shore in *Wales*.
Here's not one *Murder'd-Magistrate* at least,
Kept Rank like Venson, for a City-Feast;
Grown four days stiff, the better to prepare,
And fit his pliant Ribs, to Ride in Chair: 20
He has no Truths of such a Monstrous Stature,
And some believe there are none such in Nature.
But here's an Army rais'd, tho under Ground;
Yet no Man seen, nor one Commission found!
Here is a *Traytor too, that's very old*,   25
Turbulent, subtle, Mischievous and bold;
Bloody, Revengful, and to Crown his Part;
Loves Fumbling with a Wench, with all his heart.
And after having many Changes past,
Thanks Heav'n, for all his Age, he's hang'd at last.   30
Next, there's a *Senator* that keeps a Whore;

In *Venice* none a greater Office bore.
To Lewdness every night, the Letcher ran,
Show me all *London*, such another Man;
Match him at *Mother-Creswells* if you can.   35
  Oh *Poland! Poland!* had it been thy lot,
T'have heard in time of this *Venetian-Plot;*
Thou surely chosen hadst, one King from thence,
And honour'd them, as thou hast *England* since.

EPILOGUE.

The Text is done, and now for *Application*,
And when that's done, pray give your *Approbation*.
Tho' the Conspiracy's prevented here,
Methinks I see another hatching there.
And there's a certain Faction feign would sway,   5
If they had strength enough, and dam this Play;
But this the Author bad me boldly say,
If any take his plainness in ill part,
He's glad on't, from the bottom of his heart.
Poets in honour of the truth should write,   10
With the same Courage, brave Men for it Fight.
And tho against, him causless hatred rise,
And daily where he goes, of late he spies;
The Scoules of sullen and Revengeful Eyes.
'Tis what he knows with much contempt to bear,   15
And serves a Cause too good to let him fear.
He fears no Poison from an *incens'd Drab*,
No *Ruffians Five-foot-Sword*, nor *Raskal's Stabb;*
Nor any other Snares of Mischief laid,
Not a *Rose-Ally, Cudgel, Ambuscaid*   20
From any private Cause, where Malice Reigns;
A general sign all *Blockheads* have no Brains.
  Nothing doth Damn his Pen, when Truth doth call,
No not the *Picture-Mangler of Guild-Hall;*
The *Rebel-Tribe*, of which, that *Vermin's* one,   25

Have now set forward, and their Course begun.
And whil'st *that Princes Figure* they deface,
As they before had Massacred his Fame;
Durst their base Fears, but look him in the Face,
They'd use his Person, as th'have us'd his Fame.   30
A Face in which, such Lineaments they dread,
Of that great Martyrs, whose rich Blood they shed.
That their Rebellous Hate they still retain,
And in his Son wou'd Murder him again
With Indignation then, let each brave Heart,   35
Rouze and unite, to take his injur'd part.
Till Royal Love and Goodness call him home,
And Songs of Triumph meet him as he come.
Till Heav'n his Honour, and our Peace Restore,
And Villains never wrong his Virtue more.   40

LONDON, Printed for *A. Green*. 1681.

PROLOGUE
To a New PLAY, called
VENICE PRESERV'D;
or
The PLOT Discover'd.
At the Duke's Theatre; Spoken by Mr. Smith.

In these unsettl'd Times, when each man dreads
The Bloudy Stratagems of buisy Heads,
When we have fear'd three years I know not what, ⎫
Till Witnesses begin to die o'th' Rot,   ⎬
What made our Poets meddle with a *Plot?*   ⎭   5
Was't that he fanci'd, for the very sake
And name of *PLOT*, his trifling *Play* might take?
For there's not in't *one Inch-board-Evidence;* ⎫
But is to each man's reason plain and sense; ⎬
And that he thinks a plausible defence.   ⎭ 10
Were *Truth* by Sense and Reason to be try'd,
Sure all our *Swearers* might be laid aside.
No, of such Tools our Author has no need,
To make his *Plot*, or make his *Play* succeed.
He of *Black-Bills* has no prodigious Tales,   15
Of *Spanish-Pilgrims* thrown ashoar in *Wales.*
Her's not one murder'd Magistrate at least,
Kept rank, like Ven'son, for a City-Feast;
Grown four days stiff, the better to prepare
And fit his plyant Limbs to ride in *Chair.*   20
Here are no Truths of such a Monstrous stature,
And some believe there are none such in Nature.
But here's an *Army* rais'd, though *under ground,*
Yet *no Men seen, nor one Commission found.*
Here is a Traitor too, that's very old,   25
Turbulent, subtle, mischeivous and bold,
Bloudy, Revengeful; and to Crown his Part,
Loves fumbling with a Wench with all his heart
And after having many Changes past,

64

In spight of Age, thanks Heav'n he's Hang'd at last.　30
Next, here's a Senator that keeps a Whore;
In *Venice* none a higher Office bore:
To Lewdness every night the Leacher ran:
Shew me in *London* such another man:
Match him at Mother *Creswels* if you can:　　35
Ah *Poland, Poland*, had it been thy Lot
T'have heard in time of this *Venetian-Plot*,
Thou surely chosen hadst one *Plot* from thence,
And honour'd Them, as thou hast *England* since.

EPILOGUE
To the Same.
Spoken by Mr. BETTERTON.

The Text is done, and now for Application:
And when that's ended, give your Approbation.
Tho the Conspiracy's prevented Here,
Methinks I see another Hatching There.
And there's a certain Faction fain would sway,　　5
If they had strength enough, and damn this Play;
But this the Author boldly bad me say.
If any take his Plainness in ill part,
He's glad on't from the bottom of his Heart.
Poets in Honour of the Truth should Write,　　10
With the same Courage Brave Men for it Fight.
And tho' against him causeless Hatred rise,
And daily where he goes of late he spies
The Frowns of sullen and revengeful Eyes.
'Tis what he knows, with much contempt, to bear,　15
And serves a Cause too good to let him fear.
He fears no Poyson from an incens'd Drab,
No Ruffians five foot Sword, nor Rascals Stab;
Nor any other Snares of Mischief, laid,
Not a *Rose-Ally* Cudgel, Ambuscade.　　20
From any private Cause where Malice Reigns,

Or general Pique, that Blockheads have to Brains.
Nothing shall daunt his Pen when Truth doth call,
No, not the Picture-Mangler at *Guild-Hall.*
The Rebel Tribe (of which that Vermin's one)   25
Have now set forward, and the Course begun.
And while that Prince's Figure they deface,
Durst their base Fears but look Him in the Face,
As they before had Massacred His Name,
They'd use His Person as they've us'd his Fame.   30
A Face, in which such Lineaments they Read,
Of that Great Martyr, whose Rich Blood they Shed,
That their Rebellious Hate they still maintain,
And, in his Son, would Murder Him again.
With Indignation then let each Brave Heart,   35
Rowze and Unite to take His Injur'd Part,
Till Royal Love and Goodness call Him Home,
And Songs of Triumph meet Him as He come.
Till Heaven His Honour and His Peace Restore,
And Villains never wrong His Vertue more.   40

London, Printed for *A. Banks.* 1682.

A/Prologue/Written by Mr. Dryden, to a New Play,/call'd, The Loyal Brother, &c./ The Epilogue by the same Hand ;/ Spoken by Mrs. Sarah Cook./ London, Printed for J. Tonson.

Folio half-sheet; printed on both sides.
Imprint at bottom of p. 2.
British Museum.

For the biographical sketch of the author, John Dryden, see pp. 33–35.

THE PRICE OF A PROLOGUE

For the new playwright of the seventeenth and eighteenth centuries nothing tempered the chill of a first performance so effectively as a prologue or an epilogue by a seasoned writer. Among the poets who recommended other men's plays, Dryden stood pre-eminent. He was a prologuing poet for some thirty-two years; and before he wrote the lines reprinted below, he had become so sure a master of this type of writing that he wrote yearly for plays performed by the King's and Duke's players.

There is a story about the amount that Dryden charged for his pieces, and report says the prologue and epilogue reproduced here were the first to come at a higher price. They were written for *The Loyal Brother*, a drama by a virgin playwright, Thomas Southerne, who is said to have told something of his early purchases from Dryden to Alexander Pope and his listener, Warburton. At any rate, both wrote of Dryden's bargain with Southerne, Warburton saying in *The Works of Alexander Pope* (1751), VI, 82, that Dryden wrote a prologue and an epilogue for four guineas until probably 1682, when he charged Southerne six, remarking at the time: "Not, young man, out of disrespect to you, but the players have had my goods too cheap." It is on the authority, then, of Warburton that tradition assigns the distinction of raising the price of the Laureate's prologues to Southerne, on whose birthday Pope wrote:

> May Tom, whom heav'n sent down to raise
> The price of prologues and of plays,
> Be ev'ry birth-day more a winner.[1]

Malone repeats Warburton's story, but makes an observation which indicates that, as in most matters that descend by way of oral testimony, there are other versions to be reckoned with:

> . . . In the Life of Southerne, however, pub-
> lished shortly afterwards by Shiels and the younger
> Cibber, on the testimony of a gentleman who had
> been personally acquainted with that poet, the sums
> are said to have been *five* and *ten* guineas; and Dr.
> Johnson with more probability supposes, that
> Dryden's original price of a Prologue was *two*
> guineas, and that from Southerne he demanded
> three; so difficult is it to elicit truth from any
> traditional tale.[2]

Some thirteen years after Southerne paid Dryden for the prologue and epilogue here before us, Colley Cibber "insisted

---

[1] *The Works of Alexander Pope*, ed. Whitwell Elwin and W. John Courthope (London, 1882), IV, 496-497.

[2] Edmond Malone, *The Critical and Miscellaneous Works of John Dryden*, I, 456.

that two Guineas should be the Price"[1] of the first prologue that he ever made public.[2]

From the folio half-sheet prologue and epilogue to Southerne's *The Loyal Brother*, printed for Jacob Tonson, we get more information than from the quarto copy of the play. The texts show no remarkable variation; but whereas the copy of the play fails to name either the author of the prologue and epilogue or the speaker of the epilogue, both are given in the separate printing.

Saying more than a little about faction and lashing the Whigs severely, Dryden provided Southerne with a prologue and an epilogue that were timely when *The Loyal Brother* was acted at Drury Lane (c. March 1681/2) and adequate for separate publication. He did not forget, at the same time, to write in the interest of the Virgin Poet in the epilogue, which was spoken by Mrs. Cooke, whose name appears twice in this collection of rare epilogues. Sarah Cooke was no novice in her rôle at this time.[3] In 1682 Dryden's lines were given to her again, the play being *The Duke of Guise*; and in 1684 Dryden's pen served Southerne once more in the prologue to *The Disappointment.*

[1] *An Apology for the Life of Mr. Colley Cibber* (1740), 4to, p. 114.

[2] In this matter of prices the evidence is scant, and for the period before the Restoration we have only several entries in Henslowe's Diary : 1591–1609. Before summarizing these facts, we remind ourselves that the first entry is a forgery: *Henslowe's Diary*, ed. Walter W. Greg (London: A. H. Bullen, 1904), p. xxxix. The other entries pass as genuine in Mr. Greg's edition: ten shillings to Dekker for a prologue and an epilogue to a play, "ponesciones pillet" (p. 153); five shillings to Middleton for a prologue and an epilogue to be spoken at Court when the "plays of bacon" was presented (p. 172); five shillings to Chettle for a prologue and an epilogue to be used at Court (p. 173).

[3] Appendix C.

A
PROLOGUE
Written by Mr. Dryden, *to a New Play,*
call'd, The Loyal Brother, &c.

Poets, like Lawfull Monarchs, rul'd the Stage,
Till Criticks, like Damn'd Whiggs, debauch'd our Age.
Mark how they jump: Criticks wou'd regulate
Our Theatres, and Whiggs reform our State:
Both pretend love, and both (Plague rot 'em) hate. 5
The Critick humbly seems Advice to bring,
The fawning Whigg Petitions to the King:
But ones advice into a Satyr slides;
T'others Petition a Remonstrance hides.
These will no Taxes give, and those no Pence: 10
Criticks wou'd starve the Poet, Whiggs the Prince.
The Critick all our troops of friends discards;
Just so the Whigg wou'd fain pull down the Guards.
Guards are illegal, that drive foes away,
As watchfull Shepherds, that fright beasts of prey. 15
Kings, who Disband such needless Aids as these,
Are safe—as long as e're their Subjects please.
And that wou'd be till next Queen *Besses* night:
Which thus, grave penny Chroniclers endite.
Sir Edmond-berry, first, in wofull wise, 20
Leads up the show, and Milks their Maudlin eyes.
There's not a Butcher's Wife but Dribs her part,
And pities the poor Pageant from her heart;
Who, to provoke revenge, rides round the fire,
And, with a civil congee, does retire. 25
But guiltless blood to ground must never fall:
There's *Antichrist* behind, to pay for all.
The Punk of *Babylon* in Pomp appears,
A lewd Old Gentleman of Seventy years.
Whose Age in vain our Mercy wou'd implore; 30
For few take pity on an Old-cast Whore.

The Devil, who brought him to the shame, takes part; ⎫
Sits cheek by jowl, in black, to cheer his heart: ⎬
Like Theef and Parson in a *Tyburn*-Cart.   ⎭
The word is giv'n; and with a loud Huzzaw   35
The Miter'd Moppet from his Chair they draw:
On the slain Corps contending Nations fall;
Alas, what's one poor Pope among 'em all!
He burns; now all true hearts your Triumphs ring;
And next (for fashion) cry, *God save the King.*   40
A needful Cry in midst of such Alarms:
When Forty thousand Men are up in Arms.
But after he's once sav'd, to make amends,   ⎫
In each succeeding Health they Damn his Friends: ⎬
So God begins, but still the Devil ends.   ⎭ 45
What if some one inspir'd with Zeal, shou'd call,
Come let's go cry, God save him at *White Hall?*
His best friends wou'd not like this over-care:
Or think him e're the safer for that pray'r.
Five Praying Saints are by an Act allow'd: 50
But not the whole Church-Militant, in crowd.
Yet, should heav'n all the true Petitions drain ⎫
Of *Presbyterians*, who wou'd Kings maintain; ⎬
Of Forty thousand, five wou'd scarce remain.   ⎭

The EPILOGUE *by the same Hand;*
Spoken by Mrs. Sarah Cook.

A Virgin Poet was serv'd up to day;
Who till this hour, ne're cackled for a Play:
He's neither yet a Whigg nor Tory-Boy;
But, like a Girl, whom several wou'd enjoy,   ⎫
Begs leave to make the best of his own natural Toy. ⎭ 5
Were I to play my callow Author's game,
The King's House wou'd instruct me, by the Name:
There's Loyalty to one: I wish no more:
A Commonwealth sounds like a Common Whore.

Let Husband or Gallant be what they will,   10
One part of Woman is true Tory still.
If any Factious spirit shou'd rebell,
Our Sex, with ease, can every rising quell.
Then, as you hope we shou'd your failings hide,
An honest Jury for our play provide: 15
Whiggs, at their Poets never take offence;
They save dull Culpritts who have Murther'd Sense:
Tho Nonsense is a nauseous heavy Mass,
The Vehicle call'd Faction makes it pass.
Faction in Play's the Commonwealths man's bribe: 20
The leaden farthing of the Canting Tribe:
Though void in payment Laws and Statutes make it,
The Neighbourhood, that knows the Man, will take it.
'Tis Faction buys the Votes of half the Pit;
Theirs is the Pention-Parliament of wit.   25
In City-Clubs their venom let 'em vent;
For there 'tis safe, in its own Element:
Here, where their madness can have no pretence,
Let 'em forget themselves an hour in sense.
In one poor Isle, why shou'd two Factions be? ⎤   30
Small diffrence in your Vices I can see;   ⎬
In Drink and Drabs both sides too well agree. ⎦
Wou'd there were more Preferments in the Land;
If Places fell, the party cou'd not stand.
Of this damn'd grievance ev'ry Whigg complains;   35
They grunt like Hogs, till they have got their Grains.
Mean time you see what Trade our Plots advance,
We send each year good Money into *France*:
And they, that know what Merchandise we need,
Send o're true Protestants, to mend our breed.   40

FINIS.

London, Printed for *J. Tonson*.

The/Prologue/To the City Heiress,/ Or, Sir Timothy Treatall./—/Written by Tho. Otway. Spoken by Mrs. Barry./ Epilogue./—/Written by a Person of Quality. Spoken by Mrs. Butler./ London, Printed for J. Tonson, at the Judge's Head in Chancery-lane, 1682.

Folio half-sheet; printed on both sides.
Imprint at bottom of p. 2.
British Museum.

For the biographical sketch of the prologue-writer, Thomas Otway, see pp. 52–53.

THE FEMALE PROLOGUE AND EPILOGUE

With the opportunity again at hand in March, 1681/2, the successful author of *Venice Preserved* wrote for the Tories and mocked the Whigs for their fears of the Papists. His lines, serving as the prologue to Mrs. Behn's *The City Heiress*, were spoken by the original Monimia of *The Orphan*, Mrs. Barry, who already owed Otway a life-long debt of gratitude for his creation of this part to which she was able to bring an interpretation that made her the greatest actress of her time. In such circumstances as these accompanying the first per-formance of *The City Heiress*, Mrs. Behn was the most for-tunate author, for the prelude to her drama was written by a playwright in the day's highest favour and spoken by an actress who was then two years without a rival. Ill luck had lately been hers in *Like Father like Son*, and Shadwell noted the fact when he mocked Otway for writing the prologue reprinted here:

> Poetess *Afra* though she's damn'd to day
> To morrow will put up another Play;
> And Ot—y must be Pimp to set her off,
> Lest the enraged Bully scoul and scoff,
> And hiss, and laugh, and give not such applause
> To th' *City-heresie* as the *good old Cause*.[1]

Beginning in 1678, prologues and epilogues helped in no small way to acquaint playhouse-audiences with the full, clear, and strong voice of their gracefully majestic Mrs. Elizabeth Barry. In fact, the theatre gave to Davenant's pupil, whom Rochester allegedly made an actress, an average of three epilogues to every prologue.[2] Three of the pieces that she spoke are included in my collection of rare publications, those coming after 1681/2, the date for *The City Heiress*, being the following:

> Epilogue by a Person of Quality. Spoken by Mrs. Barrey.
> Printed for Charles Tebroc.
> *Folio half-sheet, epilogue, recto.*
> *British Museum and the Bodleian.*

---

[1] *The Tory Poets* (1682), p. 8. See comments, by R. G. Ham, *Otway and Lee*, Yale University Press, 1931, p. 202; and by J. C. Ghosh, *The Works of Thomas Otway*, Clarendon Press, 1932, I, 34. Mr. Ghosh gives three lines from this same source that are parodies of lines 36, 41, and 42 of Otway's prologue to *The City Heiress*:

> To part with stolen half-Crown for—no jest;
> *Sham treats you may have paid for o're and o're,*
> *But who e're paid for a Sham-Play before?*
> (*The Tory Poets*, 1682)
> To part with zealous Guinny for—no feast.
> Sham-Plots you may have paid for o'er and o'er;
> But who e'er paid for a Sham-Treat before?
> (Otway's prologue, *The City Heiress*, 1682)

[2] Appendix C.

74

Epilogue/Spoken by Mrs. Barry,/April the 7th, 1709./At a Representation of/Love for Love:/For/ The Benefit of Mr. Betterton/at His leaving the Stage./—/—/London,/Printed for E. Sanger at the Post-House at the/Middle Temple-Gate, and E. Curll at the Peacock without Temple-Bar, 1709./ Price 2d./

Octavo.

British Museum.

Of all her numerous epilogues, the one most often printed is the piece described in the foregoing title; it was included in *A Collection of Original Poems* (1714)[1] and *Poems on Several Occasions* (1714)[2] not long after her death on 7 November 1713. A merry epilogue of her rendering is in a collection of poems in manuscript in the British Museum (Ad. MS. 29,310, pp. 11–12)—fifty-five lines of wit and banter, taking pecks at the French, the Dutch, and John Bull. The majority of her pieces are to be found, however, in the plays for which they were written; and the list given in Appendix C is culled from such play-books, as well as miscellanies, manuscripts, and ephemerae of the class reprinted in this book.

In the epilogue to *The City Heiress*[3] likewise it was "women to the women." Mrs. Behn's play ended, as it began, in the care of the theatre's almost indispensable "she"—the woman orator known sometimes as the prologue in petticoats, the

---

[1] "Epilogue Spoken by Mrs. Barry, April the 7th, 1709. At a Representation of *Love for Love*;" A/Collection/of Original/Poems,/Translations, and Imitations,/By/Mr. Prior, Mr. Rowe, Dr. Swift,/and other Eminent Hands. /—/Ornament/—/London:/Printed for E. Curll, at the Dial and Bible/ against St. Dunstan's Church in Fleetstreet, 1714./; p.3. See, also, *The Life of Mr. Thomas Betterton* (1710).

[2] "Epilogue Spoken by Mrs. Barry, At the Theatre Royal in Drury Lane, April the 7th, 1709. At her Playing in *Love for Love* with Mrs. Bracegirdle, for the Benefit of Mr. Betterton;" Poems/on/Several Occasions./—/By N. Rowe, Esq;/—/Ornament/London:/Printed for E. Curll at the Dial and Bible against/St. Dunstan's Church in Fleet-street. 1714/; pp. 32–35.

[3] The text of the prologue and epilogue published in the play in 1682 shows no notable variation from that of the folio half-sheet.

she-epilogue, the female prologue and epilogue. This time Mrs. Charlotte Butler (or Botelar) was the epilogue in petticoats, the mistress of amiability, whose sweet voice and gentle manner assisted the lines now left us to read as we choose, mindful of the Person of Quality who wrote them and of the actress who lent herself to humour in a gay, lively, and alluring manner.[1]

[1] Appendix C.

THE
PROLOGUE
To the CITY HEIRESS,
Or, Sir TIMOTHY TREATALL.

Written by Tho. Otway. *Spoken by Mrs.*
Barry.

How vain have prov'd the Labours of the Stage,
In striving to reclaim a vitious Age!
Poets may write the mischief to impeach,
You care as little what the Poets teach,
As you regard at Church what Parsons preach.　　5
But where such Follies and such vices reign,
What honest Pen has patience to refrain?
At Church, in Pews, ye most devoutly snore,
And here, got dully drunk, ye come to roar;
Ye go to Church to gloat, and Ogle there,　　10
And come to meet more lewd convenient here:
With equal zeal ye honour either place
And run so very evenly your Race,
Y'improve in Wit just as you do in Grace.
It must be so, some Daemon has possest　　15
Our Land, and we have never since been blest.
Y'have seen it all, or heard of its Renown,
In a reverend shape it stalk'd about the Town,
Six Yeomen tall attending on its frown.
Sometimes with humble note and zealous lore,　　20
'Twou'd play the apostolick function o'er.
But, Heav'n have mercy on us when it swore.
When e'er it swore, to prove the Oaths were true,
Out of its mouth at Random Halters flew
Round some unwary neck, by Magick thrown,　　25
Though still the cunning Devil sav'd its own;
For when the Inchantment could no longer last,
The subtile Pug, most dexterously uncast,

77

Left awfull form for one more seeming pious,
And in a moment vary'd to defy us: } 30
From silken Doctor, home-spun *Ananias*
Left the lewd Court, and did in City fix,
Where still by its old arts it plays new tricks, }
And fills the heads of Fools with Politicks.
This Daemon lately drew in many a guest, 35
To part with zealous Guinny for—no feast.
Who, but the most incorrigible Fops,
For ever doom'd in dismal Cells, call'd Shops,
To cheat and damn themselves to get their livings,
Who'd lay sweet Money out in Sham-Tanksgivings? 40
Sham-Plots you may have paid for o'er and o'er;
But who e'er paid for a Sham-Treat before?
Had you not better sent your Offerings all,
Hither to us, than Sequestrators hall?
I being your Steward, Justice had been done ye; 45
I cou'd have entertain'd you worth your Money.

EPILOGUE.

Written by a Person of Quality. Spoken by Mrs. Butler.

My Part, I fear, will take with but a few,
A Rich young Heiress to her first Love true!
'Tis damn'd unnatural, and past enduring,
Against the fundamental Laws of Whoring.
Marrying's the Mask, which Modesty assures, 5
Helps to get new, and covers old Amours;
And Husband sounds so dull to a Town Bride,
You now a-days condemn him e'r he's try'd;
E'r in his office he's confirm'd Possessor,
Like Trincaloes you choose him a Successor, 10
In the gay spring of Love, when free from doubts,
With early shoots his Velvet Forehead sprouts.
Like a poor Parson bound to hard Indentures,

You make him pay his First-fruits e'r he enters.
But for short Carnivals of stoln good Cheer,   15
You're after forc'd to keep Lent all the Year;
Till brought at last to starving Nun's condition,
You break into our Quarters for Provision:
Invade Fop-Corner with your glaring Beauties,
And tice our Loyal Subjects from their Duties.   20
Pray, Ladies, Leave that Province to our care,   ⎫
A Fool is the Fee-simple of a Player,   ⎬
In which we Women claim a double share.   ⎭
In other things the Men are Rulers made;
But catching Woodcocks is our proper Trade.   25
If by Stage-Fops they a poor Living get,   ⎫
We can grow rich, thanks to our Mother Wit,   ⎬
By the more natural Block-heads in the Pit.   ⎭
Take then the Wits, and all their useless Prattles.
But as for Fools, they are our Goods and Chattels,   30
Return, Ingrates, to your first Haunt the Stage,
We've taught your Youth, and help'd your feeble Age.
What is't you see in Quality we want,   ⎫
What can they give you which we cannot grant?   ⎬
We have their price, their Frolicks and their paint. ⎭ 35
We feel the same Youth dancing in our Blood;
Our dress as gay—All underneath as good.
Most men have found us, hitherto more true,   ⎫
And, if we're not abus'd by some of you,   ⎬
We're full as fair—perhaps as wholesome too.   ⎭ 40
But if at best our hopefull Sport and Trade is,
And nothing now will serve you but great Ladies;
May question'd Marriages your Fortune be,
And Lawyers drain your Pockets more than we:
May Judges puzzle a clear Case with Laws,   45
And Musquetoons at last decide the Cause.

FINIS.

London, Printed for *J. Tonson*, at the *Judge's Head* in *Chancery-lane*, 1682.

A Prologue by Mr. Settle to his/
New Play, called The Emperor of
Morocco, with the Life / of Gayland.
Acted at the Theatre Royal, the 11th.
of/March, 1682./
The Epilogue Spoken by Mrs.
Coysh's/Girl, as Cupid./
London:/Printed for A. Banks.

Folio half-sheet; printed on both sides.
Imprint at bottom of p. 2.
National Library of Scotland.

For a biographical sketch of the author, Elkanah Settle,
see pp. 28–29.

THE POLITICAL PROLOGUE AND EPILOGUE

With the separate publication of his prologue and epilogue
to The Heir of Morocco[1] in 1682, Settle entered the political
parties' paper-scuffle at a time when the theatre took a lively
interest in state affairs. In 1682, anonymously, he answered
Dryden's attack upon the Whigs in Absalom and Achitophel,
1681, with Absalom Senior; but his anger also muttered and
snarled in his prologue to The Heir of Morocco, printed
in folio half-sheet as "A Prologue by Mr. Settle to
his New Play, called The Emperor of Morocco, with the life of
Gayland. Acted at the Theatre Royal, the 11th. of March, 1682."
If this piece was circulated among Dryden's enemies, it gave

[1] No notable variations from the text of the folio half-sheet occur in the
edition of the play.

80

the Whigs a delicious relish, on the like of which more than a few gormandized.

Looking beyond this prologue through a very brief period, however, we find Settle recanting and announcing himself a Tory[1] while a voice from an enemy speaks in *Remarks upon E. Settle's Narrative* (1683):

> And is E. Settle turned Recanter! nay then, there may be some hopes of the conversion of the Devil and all his Angels. But his own fellow Poets will not believe it; they, in their *Prologues*, say he has only turn'd *Cat in Pan*.

In short, the charge against Settle is that greed and desire for money made him write for the Whigs, this prologue not excepted. His recantation made strange reading of these Whiggish lines.

Settle's epilogue belongs to a small class that may be termed juvenile and personated. Some value was set upon youthful speakers very early—before the Commonwealth, in fact, for Thomas Heywood's *Pleasant Dialogues and Drammas* (1637) contains the following interesting lines for a "little Richard" who spoke both prologue and epilogue:

> *A young witty Lad playing the part of Richard the third: at the Red Bull: the Author because hee was interested in the Play to incourage him, wrot him this Prologue and Epilogue. The Boy the Speaker.*

> If any wonder by what magick charme,
> *Richard* the third is shrunke up like his arme:
> And where in fulnesse you expected him,
> You see me onely crawling, like a limme
> Or piece of that knowne fabrick, and no more,
> (When he so often hath beene view'd before.)
> Let all such know: a Rundlet ne're so small
> Is call'd a vessell: being a Tunne; that's all.

[1] For Settle's part in the political disputes of his time, see F. C. Brown, *Elkanah Settle*, University of Chicago Press, 1910, pp. 21–26, 67–70.

Hee's tearm'd a man, that showes a dwarfish thing,
No more's the Guard, or Porter to the King.
So Pictures in small compasse I have seene
Drawne to the life, as neare, as those have beene
Ten times their bignesse: Christenmas loaves are bread,
Larze folio Sheets which Printers over-looke,
And cast in small, to make a pocket booke?
So *Richard* is transform'd: if this disguise
Show me so small a letter for your eyes,
You cannot in this letter read me plaine,
Hee'l next appeare, in texted hand againe.

The Epilogue.

Great I confesse your patience hath now beene,
To see a little *Richard :* who can win,
Or praise, or credit? eye, or thinke to excell,
By doing after what was done so well?
It was not my ambition to compare,
No envie, or detraction: such things are
In men of more growne livers, greater spleene,
But in such lads as I am, seldome seene.
 I doe, but like a child, who sees one swim,
And (glad to learne) will venter after him
Though he be soundly duckt for't, or to tell
My mind more plainely, one that faine would spell,
In hope to read more perfect: all the gaines
I expect for these unprofitable paines,
Is, that you would at parting from this place
Doe but unto my littlenesse that grace
To spie my worth, as I have seene dimme eyes
To looke through spectacles, or perspectives,
 That in your gracious view I may appeare,
 Of small, more great; of coming far off, neare.[1]

Children were given prologues and epilogues more fre-

---

[1] Thomas Heywood, *Pleasant Dialogues and Drammas* (1637), pp. 247–248.

quently after 1660. At the Duke's Theatre in March, 1663/4, there was a little girl whom Pepys applauded, because she acted prettily in Carlell's *Heraclius* and spoke the epilogue "most admirably." These little people, usually named merely "Boy" and "Girl" in the play-bills and editions of the dramas, were novelties in the theatre when Mrs. Coysh's Girl spoke Settle's epilogue, and we must look to the nineties of the seventeenth century and to the early decades of the eighteenth century for evidence of a certain vogue enjoyed by the children, the youngest being four years old. Little Miss Dennis Chock at six charmed her audience with lines that are typical of the verse written for child actors in this period;[1] and at seven she spoke bold words, shameful, in fact, for even the author who was this time reckless, witty Jo Haynes.[2] To such pieces the lines reprinted from Settle's broadside offer a refreshing contrast.

For *The Heir of Morocco* Mrs. Coysh's Girl assumed one of the very familiar rôles among the personated epilogues—the rôle of Cupid. We have only to turn through the early miscellanies to discover how conventional Settle's choice here really is. The masque, for instance, would have gone limping, without such a crutch as Venus' son supplied. But the words that this Cupid in Settle's epilogue speaks are new: they are the flippant, bold, begging, daring words of the young actress's older sisters who knew the ways of beaux and fops.

[1] See pieces that little Miss Chock spoke as epilogues to Powell's *Bonduca* (1696) and Settle's *The World in the Moon* (1697).
[2] Epilogue to Powell's *The Cornish Comedy*, 1696.

A Prologue by Mr. *Settle* to his
New Play, called *The Emperor of* Morocco, with the Life of
Gayland. Acted at the *Theatre Royal*, the 11th. of *March*, 1682.

How finely would the Sparks be catch'd to Day,
Should a Whig-Poet write a Tory-Play?
And you, possess'd with Rage before, should send
Your random Shot abroad, and maul a Friend:
For you, we find, too often, hiss or clap   5
Just as you live, speak, think, and fight, by hap.
And Poets, we all know, can Change, like you,
And are alone to their own Intrest true:
Can Write against all sense, nay even their own;
The Vehicle, call'd Pension, makes it down.   10
No fear of Cudgels, where there's hope of Bread:
A well-fill'd Panch forgets a Broken Head.
But our dull Fop on every side is damn'd:
He has his Play with Love and Honour cram'd.
Rot your Old-fashion'd Hew in Romance,   15
Who in a Lady's Quarrel breaks a Launce.
Give us the Modish Feat of Honour done,
With Eighteen well-chew'd Bullets in one Gun.
Charg'd but with Eighteen Bullets, did I say,
Damn it, if that won't do, we'll bring one day,   20
Queen Besses Pocket Pistol into play.
Give us Heroick Worthies of Renown,
With a revenging Rival's Mortal Frown,
Not by dividing Oceans kept asunder,
Whilst angry Spark comes on, like Jove, with Thunder, 25
Gives out in Harlem Gazet, Blood and Wounds
In Foreign Fray, to sculk on English Ground,
And scorning Duels, a poor Prize at L'Sharps
He only fights for Fame in Counterscarps.
Do not you follow his Revenge and Fury,   30
Be you those tender hearted Things, his Jury.
Give us Old-Baily Mercy for our Play:

84

Ah no! no Pray'rs nor Bribes your Hearts can sway,
Your cruel Talents lye the other way.
　Criticks   35
Are Polish Bullies, fire and lightning all,
The Blunderbuss goes off, and where you hit you maul.

　　　The Epilogue Spoken by Mrs. *Coysh's*
　　　　　　Girl, as *Cupid*.

Ladies, the Poet knew no better way,
Than to send me to Prattle for his Play;
I am your Cupid, and you cannot sure
Drive such a small, young Begger from your dore:
Do you be but as kind, as you are fair,   5
And by my Quiver, Bow and Darts, I swear,
The little Tiny God, whose help you want,
Shall hear your Pray'rs, and all your Wishes grant;
The Country Lady shall come up to Town,
And shine, in her old Coach, and her new Gown;   10
The City Wife shall leave her poor Tom Farthing,
And take a harmless Walk to Covent Garden;
Those very Eyes shall still look young and gay,
That Conquer'd on the Coronation-day;
And you, the brighter Beauties of the Court,   15
You who the World undo, but Stage support,
You shall subdue all hearts, while I sit still;
I'll break my Bow, and leave your Eyes to kill;
Nay the Court-Star, your Beauties to advance,
Has left her Darling Sphear, to set in France.   20

　　　　　　　Finis.

LONDON: Printed for A. Banks.

Prologue to a New Play, called Anna/Bullen, Acted at the Duke's House./ Epilogue to the same./ London : Printed for Allen Banks. 1682.

Folio half-sheet; printed on both sides.
Imprint at bottom of p. 2.
Chetham Library, Manchester.

JOHN BANKS*

Little is known about the life of John Banks, who was born about 1650, and who wrote plays as late as 1695. Banks was bred to the law. He was a member of the society of the New Inn. In 1677 he saw his first play performed, *The Rival Kings*, which was published during the same year. The *Destruction of Troy*, acted probably in November 1678, appeared in print in 1679. Other dramatic works, with date of acting and date of publication, are *The Unhappy Favourite: or the Earl of Essex* (c. Sept. 1681, 1682), *Vertue Betray'd: or Anna Bullen* (c. April 1682, 1682), *The Island Queens: or, The Death of Mary, Queen of Scotland* (unacted, 1684), *The Innocent Usurper; or, The Death of the Lady Jane Gray* (unacted, 1694), *Cyrus the Great; or, The Tragedy of Love* (c. April 1695, 1696), and a new edition of *The Island Queens* titled *The Albion Queens* (1704). John Banks is said to have been buried at St. James's, Westminster.

* Although the folio half-sheet makes no statement to indicate that the prologue and epilogue were not written by the author of *Vertue Betray'd*, John Banks, the quarto-edition of the play states that the prologue was written by a "Person of Quality." The epilogue passes in both instances as Banks's.

86

John Banks

The prologue and epilogue to a "New Play called Anna Bullen, acted at the Duke's House," published as a folio half-sheet in 1682, appear in John Banks's *Vertue Betray'd: or, Anna Bullen* (1682) with textual differences, lines 23 and 24 of the prologue in folio half-sheet being omitted in the edition of the play, and lines 5 and 6 in the epilogue printed with the play being omitted in the epilogue published in folio half-sheet. Other variants to be noted in particular are these:

Prologue:[1] The author named in the play is a "Person of Quality;" l. 2, *to each* (F), *ev'ry* (Q); l. 10, *the* (F), *our* (Q); l. 15, *me a Pit of Drinkers* (F), *us a Pit of Drunkards* (Q); l. 18, *their Life's* (F), *there lives* (Q); l. 21, *this* (F), *a* (Q); ll. 23 and 24 (F) omitted in Q; l. 27 (F), *In Gods Name let each man keep to's own Vocation*, l. 25 (Q), *A Gods name, let each keep to his Vocation;* l. 30 (F), *Fears he's not safe, if but one side's his Friend*, l. 28 (Q), *'Tis not enough if but One Side's his Friend;* l. 31 (F), *to all*, l. 29 (Q), *you all.*

Epilogue: L. 1, *Opinions* (F), *Opinion* (Q); l. 3, *his* (F), *our* (Q); F lacks ll. 5 and 6 of Q; l. 6 (F), *vast*, l. 8 (Q), *large;* l. 9 (F), *what is worse*, l. 11 (Q), *what's more strange:* l. 12 (F), *who*, l. 14 (Q), *that;* l. 14 (F), *And get your Money, which was all their aim*, l. 16 (Q), *Who have your Money, that was all their Ayme;* l. 15 (F), *the*, l. 17 (Q), *their;* l. 19 (F), *With Faction guilt, or fac'd with Loyalty*, l. 21 (Q), *with Faction fac'd, and guilt with Loyalty;* l. 21 (F), *forget*, l. 23 (Q), *neglect;* l. 22 (F), *who ventures*, l. 24 (Q), *that ventur'd;* l. 25 (F), *for*, l. 27 (Q), *in;* l. 31 (F), *give*, l. 33 (Q), *make;* ll. 34, 35, 36 (F):

---

[1] The folio half-sheet is F; the play, Q.

Then more we hope will run to such a Sight,
Than would to see 500 Monsters fight,
Or hear our stubborn Captain's last Good Night.

ll. 36, 37, 38 (Q):

And that five hundred Monsters are to fight,
Then more will run to see so strange a sight,
Than the Morocco, or the Muscovite.

Both the prologue and the epilogue are commentaries upon the times, but they differ from the majority of pieces in this class in their denunciation of stage-politics. *Vertue Betray'd* was Banks's historical drama which, despite its kinship to heroic tragedy, reflected tendencies toward the school of pathos that gained vogue after 1682. The prologue and epilogue reprinted here introduced what Mr. Nicoll calls the first of the "she tragedies" made popular after 1700.

Prologue to a New Play, called Anna
Bullen, *Acted at the Duke's House.*

To all Impartial Judges in the Pit,
And to each beautious Patroness of Wit,
I'm sent to plead the *Poet's* Cause, and say,
There's not one slander in his Modest Play.
He brings before your eyes a modern Story,   5
Yet meddles not with either *Whig* or *Tory.*
Was't not enough (vain men, of either side)
Two Roses once the Nation did divide?
But must it be in danger now agen,
Betwixt the *Scarlet*, and *Green-Ribbon-men?* 10
Who made this diff'rence were not *Englands* Friends;
Be not their Tools, to serve their Plotting Ends.
Damn the State-Fop, who here his Zeal discovers, ⎤
And o'r the Stage like our Ill Genius hovers: ⎬
Give me a Pit of Drinkers, and of Lovers: ⎦ 15
Good Sanguine men, who mind no State-Affair,
But bid a base World of it self take care.
We hope their Life's not so abhorr'd a thing,
But loves his Countrey, and would serve his King
But, in your Parties why should we engage, ⎤ 20
Or meddle with the *Plots* of this mad Age? ⎬
We lose enough by those upon the Stage.   ⎦
Again bring your ill Nature, your false Wit,
Your noisie Mirth, your fighting in the Pit.
Welcom masque Teazer, peevish Gamester, Huffer, 25
All Fools; but Politicians we can suffer
In Gods Name let each man keep to's own Vocation,
Our Trade is to mend you, and not the Nation.
Besides, our Author has this further end, ⎤
Fears he's not safe, if but one side's his Friend. ⎬ 30
He needs to all, his weakness to defend.   ⎦
And, to oblige you to't, hopes he has shown,
No Countrey has men braver than your own.

His Heroes all to *England* are confin'd:
To your own Fathers sure you will be kind.   35
He brings no Foreigners to move your pity,
But sends them to a *Jury of the City*:

EPILOGUE *to the same.*

Well, Sirs, your kind Opinions now, I pray
Of this our neither *Whig* nor *Tory* Play:
To blow such Coals his conscious Muse denies;
Wit (Sacred Wit) such Subjects shou'd despise:
To abuse one Party with a Cursed Play,   5
And bribe the other for a vast *Third Day*.
Like *Gladiators* then you strait resort,
And crowd to make your *Nero*-Faction sport.
But, what is worse, that men of sense should do it,
For worrying one another, pay the *Poet*:   10
So Butchers at a baiting take delight
For him who keeps the Bears to roar and fight;
Both friends and foes such Authors make their Game,
And get your Money, which was all their aim:
No matter for the *Play*, nor for the *Wit*,   15
The better *Farce* is acted in the *Pit*.
Both Parties to be cheated well agree,   ⎫
And swallow any Non-sence, so it be   ⎬
With *Faction* guilt, or fac'd with *Loyalty*.   ⎭
Here's such a Rout with *Whigging* and with *Torying*,   20
That you forget your dear lov'd Sin of *Whoring*
The Vizard Masque, who ventures her half Crown,
Finding no hopes but here to be undone:
Like a cast Mistress, past her dear Delight,
Turns Godly strait, and goes to Church for spite;   25
And does not doubt, since you are grown so fickle,
to find more Cullies in a *Conventicle*.
We on the Stage stand still, and are content
To see you act what we should represent.

You use us like the Women that you wooe,   30
You give us Sport, and pay us for it too.
Well, we're resolved in our next *Play-Bill*
To print at large a Tryal of your Skill;
Then more we hope will run to such a Sight,   ⎫
Than would to see 500 Monsters fight,   ⎬   35
Or hear our stubborn Captain's last *Good Night.* ⎭

London : Printed for *Allen Banks.* 1682.

A/Prologue/By Mrs. Behn to her
New Play,/called/Like Father, like
Son,/or the/Mistaken Brothers,/
Spoken by Mrs. Butler./
Epilogue spoken by Mr. Gevan./
London, Printed for J. V. 1682.

Folio half-sheet; printed on both sides.
Imprint at bottom of p. 2.
Chetham Library, Manchester.

APHRA BEHN

Aphra Johnson, daughter of John Johnson, a barber, was baptised on 10 July 1640 at Wye in Kent. She spent her childhood in the West Indies but returned to England probably in 1658. She married a city merchant named Behn but was a widow before 1666. During the Dutch war she was sent to Antwerp to work as a spy.

The first woman in England to make a living by writing, Mrs. Behn wrote plays, stories, poems, and numerous prose pamphlets. Her plays, with date of performance and date of publication in parentheses, are *The Forc'd Marriage* (Dec. 1670, 1671), *The Amorous Prince* (c. May 1671, 1671), *The Dutch Lover* (Feb. 1672/3, 1673), *Abdelazer* (c. April 1676, 1677), *The Town Fopp* (c. Sept. 1676, 1677), *The Debauchee* (c. Feb. 1676/7, 1677), *The Rover* (March 1676/7, 1677), *Sir Patient Fancy* (Jan. 1677/8, 1678), *The Feign'd Curtizans* (c. March 1678/9, 1679), *The Young King* (c. June 1679, 1683), *The Second Part of the Rover* (Feb. or April 1680, 1681), *The Roundheads* (c. Dec. 1681, 1682), *The City Heiress* (c. March 1681/2, 1682), *The False Count* (c. Sept. 1682, 1682), *The Luckey Chance*

Aphra Behn

(c. April 1686, 1687), *The Emperor of the Moon* (c. March 1686/7, 1687), *The Widdow Ranter* (c. Nov. 1689, 1690), *The Younger Brother* (c. Dec. 1696, 1696). Her verse is in *Poems* (1684), Charles Gildon's *Poetical Remains* (1698), and numerous occasional odes in pamphlet form. Her fiction is illustrated by *The Adventures of the Black Lady* (1684), *La Montre* (1686), *Lycidus* (1688), *The Lucky Mistake* (1689). In 1698 her histories and novels were collected, *Oroonoko* and several less significant works being included; and in 1702 her plays were collected.

In April 1689 Aphra Behn died and was buried in Westminster Abbey. *The Widdow Ranter* (1690) and *The Younger Brother* (1696) were acted and published posthumously.

THE PROLOGUE AND EPILOGUE TO
LIKE FATHER, LIKE SON

The only parts of Mrs. Behn's unsuccessful *Like Father, like Son* ever to be published were the prologue and epilogue printed in folio half-sheet in 1682 and reprinted here. According to the title, Mrs. Charlotte Butler (sometimes Botelar) spoke the twenty-six lines of party prattle introducing the drama. This was the first prologue entrusted to her alone, though she had appeared in the rôle of Plenty, acting with a great many others, in the elaborate prologue to Crowne's *Calisto* in 1675. During some sixteen years Mrs. Butler spoke prologues and epilogues,[1] and four broadsides in this collection carry her name:

A/Prologue/By Mrs. Behn to her New Play,/ Called/Like Father, like Son,/or the/Mistaken Brothers,/Spoken by Mrs. Butler./ London, Printed for J.V. 1682.

Epilogue. (to The City Heiress)/—/Written by a Person of Quality. Spoken by Mrs. Butler./—/ London, Printed for J. Tonson, at the Judge's Head in Chancery-lane, 1682.

[1] Appendix C.

Prologue to Romulus,/Spoken by Mrs. Butler,/—/
Written by Mrs. Behn./—/
London: Printed by Nath. Thompson, 1682.
Epilogue./Spoken by Mrs. Butler./
Printed for C. Corbet at the Oxford-Arms in
Warwick-lane. 1684.

One of her epilogues is included in *Poems on Affairs of State*,
Part III (1698), pp. 189–190: "Epilogue. By Mrs. Butler—
Spoken immediately after the others running out."

> Poor Madam *Butler*, too, are you defeated,
> You never were before so basely Cheated.

Besides these words concerning our prologue-speaker's part
in the drama, Jevon, speaking the epilogue, had much to say
in disavowal of the play's relation to contemporary politics
and as much to give in jest to his fellow actors. The last of
these, he called on to the stage, requesting that he speak lines
for the play:

> Here's Blundering *Richards* is my Huffing Esquire,
> Damn me, the best in England's for't, d'e hear.
> Is that your Cue come nearer, Faith thy Face
> Has features not unlike Joe Hains's Grace.
> Impudence assist thee, and boldly try
> To speak for us, and for the Comedy.

Richards, whose epilogue written by a Person of Quality
for *The Constant Nymph* (1678) brought him out saying, "Gad
Gentlemen, I know not what to say," found his tongue this
time for two lines:

> I'le do't Gallants, I'le Justify this Play;
> 'Od Zoons 'tis Good, and if you lik'd you may.

Acknowledged to be not only hilarious but unreliably wilful,
Jevon, who spoke all the epilogue except these last lines, may
have taken liberties with both the author and the audience
while preparing to call Richards. On another occasion when,

as Lycurgus, he had to "fall on his sword," he put it flat on the stage and, "falling over it, 'died,' according to the direction of the acting copy."[1] He had a way of enlivening the wit of prologues and epilogues, the example reprinted being probably his first. In those which followed, he sometimes sang a snatch of song or danced, for the ex-dancing master in him showed in epilogue-novelties. Midway in his career as a speaker, he introduced his own drama, *The Devil of a Wife*, with the announcement:

"My Name's Mr. Jevon, I'm known far and near,"
then turned gay:

Catcalls well tun'd might do well in Opera's,
They serve for Hoboys to fill up a Chorus,
Or in a French Love Song, observe you now,
A Cadmeus Pur Qua, Pur Qua, Meme vou. (Sings)
Begar Monsieur it be De pretty Whyne,
Ki La D'ance De Mineway, Oh it be very fine.[2] (Dances.

Four of the rare broadsides included in this collection carry the name of Thomas Jevon (or Gevan).[3]

G. Thorn-Drury included the Prologue and Epilogue to Mrs. Behn's *Like Father, like Son* in his *A Little Ark* (1921), pp. 43–45, with the following note, which refers to the copy reprinted in this collection:

Although there is, apparently, another copy of it in the Chetham Collection, it has altogether escaped notice. Students of the stage-history of the period were aware that Mrs. Behn had written an Epilogue for what was thought to have been a revival of Randolph's "Jealous Lovers," in 1682. The leaf,

[1] Dr. Doran's *Annals of the English Stage*, ed. R. W. Lowe, 1888, I, 143.
[2] Jevon took his tune out of a popular song in Quinault's *Cadmus et Hermione*. See Sec. XLI, the introductory essay, in the present work. The *"Mineway"* is probably the French *menuet*.
[3] See the reprints in this work, Sec. XIV (Epilogue), Sec. XXIV (Epilogue), Sec. XXIX (Prologue), Sec. XXXIV (Epilogue).

now reproduced, shows that it was an alteration, under a new title, supplies the names of some of the actors, and also enables us to date the performance with some approach to exactness.

Compare the epilogue with the epilogue to *The Jealous Lovers* (1682), reprinted from *Miscellany, Being a Collection of Poems By several Hands* (1685), p. 263, in *A Little Ark*, p. 46. G. Thorn-Drury's collection of seventeenth-century verse, *A Little Ark*, was published as a limited edition of twenty copies by P. J. and A. E. Dobell, 8 Bruton Street, W., London, in 1921.

A
PROLOGUE
By Mrs. *Behn* to her New PLAY,
called
Like Father, like Son,
or the
Mistaken Brothers,
Spoken by Mrs. *Butler*.

Lord what a House is here, how Thin 'tis grown!
As Church 'ere Conventicling was put down:
Since all the Brave are to *Newmarket* gone!
Declining States-men are abandon'd too,
Who scarce a Heartless *Whigg* will Visit now: 5
Who once had Crowds of Mutineers in Fashion,
Fine drawn in Cullys of th' *Association*:
Sparks, Justices and Jurymen by Dozens,
Whom his perverted late betrays and Cozens.
But change of Scene, having unvail'd their Cheats,   10
Pensive State Puss alone, Majestick Sits;
Purr's on his pointless Mischiefs, tho' in vain;
Verses are all the Darlings of his Brain.
So we who having Plotted long to please,
With new Parts, new Cloathes, new Face, new Dress;   15
To draw in all the yielding Hearts o' th' Town,
His Highness comes and all our Hopes are gone.
Ah Fickle Youth, what lasting Joys have we,
When Beauty thus is left for Loyalty;
I would to Heaven ye had been all *Whiggs* for me: 20
Whilst Honest *Tory* Fools abroad do Roame,
Whigg Lovers Slay and Plot, and Love at Home.
Nay one Advantage greater far than this,
The Party helps to keep their Mistresses.
The Devils it't if I'm not Fine and Vain,   25
Whom publick Bank Contribute to Maintain.

97

Aphra Behn

Epilogue spoken by Mr. Gevan.

And now *Messiers*, what do you say,
Unto our Modern Conscientious Play?
Nor *Whigg*, nor *Tory* here can take Offence,
It Libels neither Patriot, Peer nor Prince.
Nor Sheriff, nor Burgess, nor the Reverend Gown;   } 5
Faith Here's no Scandal worth Eight Hundred Pound,   }
Our Damage is at most but Half a Crown.   }
Only this Difference you must allow,   }
That you receive th' Affront and pay us too;   }
Would some Body had manag'd matters so.   }   10
Here's no Reflection on Damn'd Witnesses,   }
We Scorn such out of Fashion things as these,   }
They fail to be Belov'd, and fail to Please.   }
No *Salamanchian* Doctorship's Abus'd,
Nor a Malitious State'man here Accus'd.   15
Tho' here are Fools of every Fashion,
Except State Fools, the Fools of Reformation.
And these Originals decline so fast,
We shall have none to Copy by at last.
There's *Joe* and *Jack* a pair of Whining Fools   20
And *Leigh*, and I, Dull, Lavish, Creeping Tools. (Pointing at
                                                    Mr. Williams,
                                                    Mr. Wiltshire.

Bowman's for Mischief all, and carry's on   }
With Faun and Sneer as Gilting *Whigg* has done,   }
But like theirs too, his Projects are o'r thrown.   }
Sweet Mistriss *Corall* here has lost her Lover,   25
Pshaw *English* or *Irish* ground shall find another.
Poor Madam *Butler* too, are you defeated,   To
You never were before so basely Cheated.   Mrs. Butler
Here Mistris *Betty*, Hah! she's grown a very Woman, 30
Thou'st got me Child, better me than no man.
Here's Blundering *Richards* is my Huffing Esquire,
Damn me, the best in *England's* for't, d'e hear.
Is that your Cue come nearer, Faith thy Face

Has Features not unlike *Joe Hains's* Grace.
Impudence assist thee, and boldly try   35
To speak for us, and for the Comedy.

Mr. Richards Speaks.

I'le do't Gallants, I'le Justify this Play;
'Od Zoons 'tis Good, and if you lik'd you may.

London, Printed for *J. V.* 1682.

Prologue/To His Royal Highness,/ Upon His first appearance at the Duke's Theatre/since his Return from Scotland./—/Written by Mr. Dryden. Spoken by Mr. Smith./—/ London, Printed for J. Tonson.

Folio half-sheet, reverse blank.
Imprint at bottom of p. 1.
British Museum.

For the biographical sketch of the author, John Dryden, see pp. 33–35

The / Epilogue. / Written by Mr. Otway to his Play call'd Ve-/nice Preserv'd, or a Plot Discover'd; spo-/ken upon his Royal Highness the Duke of York's/coming to the Theatre, Friday, April 21./1682./ Printed for Joseph Hindmarsh at the Black Bull in Cornhill, 1682.

Folio half-sheet; printed on both sides.
Imprint at bottom of p. 2.
British Museum and Mr. P. J. Dobell's collection.

For the biographical sketch of the author, Thomas Otway, see pp. 52–53.

HONOURING THE DUKE OF YORK
UPON HIS RETURN

The Tory party and Dryden assisted *Venice Preserv'd* in a swift rise to fame while Otway, taking the tide at its flood, wrote epilogues for special performances that began with prologues by a far better hand. Seemingly, a Tory victory announced itself with an assured flourish when Otway's plotting tragedy was acted again, and we find the Duke of York, returning in March 1682 from Scotland, honoured upon his first appearance at the theatre with a special performance of *Venice Preserv'd*, which began with a prologue written by Dryden and spoken by Smith, and ended with an epilogue by the newly acclaimed playwright himself, Thomas Otway.

In the rare broadside prologue, printed for Jacob Tonson, William Smith, the first actor who spoke a prologue to *Venice Preserv'd*, appeared again, repeating lines by Dryden. He was the original Pierre returning on this gay twenty-first of April to bend his knee to the rejoicing Tories and the Duke of York attending the play after celebrations in the Merchant Taylors Hall.

The play being ended, Otway's epilogue blessed the name of the "injur'd Prince" in words that Tories might joy to hear, or read years after in a folio half-sheet printed for Joseph Hindmarsh in 1682. The earliest advertisement of a prologue and an epilogue that I have noted in the newspapers of the seventeenth century recommended these two pieces to men of "Sense and Loyalty":

> Mr. Drydens Prologue, and Mr. Otways Epilogue to Venice Preserv'd, Spoken by Mr. Smith, and Mr. Betterton, upon his Royal Highness the Duke of Yorks Coming to the Theatre. Recommended to All men of Sense and Loyalty.[1]

[1] *The Observator*, April 27, 1682.

PROLOGUE
To His ROYAL HIGHNESS,
Upon His first appearance at the DUKE'S THEATRE
since his Return from SCOTLAND.
Written by Mr. Dryden. *Spoken by Mr.* Smith.

In those cold Regions which no Summers chear,
When brooding darkness covers half the year,
To hollow Caves the shivering Natives go;
Bears range abroad, and hunt in tracks of Snow:
But when the tedious Twilight wears away,   5
And Stars grow paler at th' approach of Day,
The longing Crowds to frozen Mountains run,
Happy who first can see the glimmering Sun!
The surly Salvage Off-spring disappear;
And curse the bright Successour of the Year.   10
Yet, though rough Bears in Covert seek defence,
White Foxes stay, with seeming Innocence:
That crafty kind with day-light can dispense.
Still we are throng'd so full with *Reynard's* race,
That Loyal Subjects scarce can find a place: 15
Thus modest Truth is cast behind the Crowd:
Truth speaks too Low; Hypocrisie too Loud.
Let 'em be first, to flatter in success;
Duty can stay; but Guilt has need to press.
Once, when true Zeal the Sons of God did call,   20
To make their solemn show at Heaven's *White-hall,*
The fawning Devil appear'd among the rest,
And made as good a Courtier as the best.
The Friends of *Job,* who rail'd at him before,
Came Cap in hand when he had three times more.   25
Yet, late Repentance may, perhaps, be true;
Kings can forgive if Rebels can but sue:
A Tyrant's Pow'r in rigour is exprest:
The Father yearns in the true Prince's Breast.
We grant an Ore'grown Whig no grace can mend;   30

But most are Babes, that know not they offend.
The Crowd, to restless motion still enclin'd,
Are Clouds, that rack according to the Wind.
Driv'n by their Chiefs they storms of Hail-stones pour:
Then mourn, and soften to a silent showre.   35
O welcome to this much offending Land
The Prince that brings forgiveness in his hand!
Thus Angels on glad Messages appear:
Their first Salute commands us not to fear:
Thus Heav'n, that cou'd constrain us to obey, ⎤   40
(With rev'rence if we might presume to say,) ⎬
Seems to relax the rights of Sov'reign sway: ⎦
Permits to Man the choice of Good and Ill;
And makes us Happy by our own Free-will.

London, Printed for *J. Tonson.*

THE
EPILOGUE.

Written by Mr. Otway *to his Play call'd* Venice Preserv'd,
or a Plot Discover'd; *spoken upon his Royal Highness the Duke
of* York's *coming to the* Theatre, *Friday,* April 21. 1682.

When too much Plenty, Luxury, and Ease,
Had surfeited this Isle to a Disease;
When noisome Blaines did its best parts ore-spread,
And on the rest their dire Infection shed;
Our *Great Physician*, who the Nature knew ⎤   5
Of the Distemper, and from whence it grew, ⎬
Fix't for Three Kingdoms quiet (Sir) on You: ⎦
He cast his searching Eyes o're all the Frame,
And finding whence before one *sickness* came,
How once before our *Mischiefs* foster'd were,   10
Knew well *Your Vertue*, and apply'd You there:
Where so Your Goodness, so Your Justice sway'd,
You but appear'd, and the *wild Plague* was stay'd.

When, from the filthy Dunghil-faction bred,
New-form'd Rebellion durst rear up its head, } 15
Answer me all: who struck the Monster dead?
　See, see, the injur'd Prince, and bless his Name,
Think on the *Martyr* from whose Loynes he came:
Think on the Blood was shed for you before,
And Curse the *Paricides* that thirst for more.　20
His Foes are yours, then of their *Wiles* beware:
Lay, lay him in your Hearts, and guard him there;
Where let his Wrongs your Zeal for him Improve;
He wears a Sword will justifie your Love.
With Blood still ready for your good t'expend,　25
And has a Heart that *ne're forgot* his friend.
　His *Duteous Loyalty* before you lay,
And learn of him, *unmurm'ring* to obey.
Think what he'as born, your Quiet to restore;
Repent your madness and *rebell* no more.　30
　No more let *Bout'feu's* hope to lead *Petitions*,
Scriv'ners to be Treas'rures; *Pedlars*, Polititians;
Nor ev'ry *fool*, whose Wife has *tript* at Court,
Pluck up a spirit, and turn *Rebell* for't.
　In Lands where Cuckolds multiply like ours,　35
What Prince can be too Jealous of their powers,
Or can too often think himself alarm'd?
They're male contents that ev'ry where go arm'd:
And when the *horned Herd's* together got,
Nothing portends a Commonwealth like *that*.　40
　Cast, cast your Idols off, your Gods of wood,
Er'e yet *Philistins* fatten with your blood:
Renounce your Priests of *Baal* with *Amen-faces*,
Your *Wapping* Feasts, and your *Mile-End* High-places.
　Nail all your *Medals* on the Gallows Post,　45
In recompence th' *Original* was lost:
At these, illustrious Repentance pay,
In his kind hands your humble Offrings lay:
Let Royal Pardon be by him implor'd,
Th' *Attoning* Brother of your *Anger'd* Lord:　50

He only brings a *Medicine* fit to aswage
A peoples *folly*, and rowz'd Monarch's *rage;*
An *Infant Prince* yet lab'ring in the womb,
Fated with wond'rous happiness to come,
He goes to fetch the mighty blessing home: 55
Send all your *wishes* with him let the Ayre
With gentle breezes waft it safely here,
The Seas, like *what* they'l carry, *calm* and *fair:*
Let the *Illustrious Mother* touch our Land
Mildly, as hereafter may her Son Command;   60
While our glad Monarch welcomes her to shoar,
With kind assurance; she shall part *no more.*
   Be the *Majestick Babe* then smiling born,
And all good signs of Fate his Birth adorn,
So live and grow, a constant pledg to stand   65
Of Cæsar's *Love* to 'an *obedient* Land.

Printed for Joseph Hindmarsh *at the* Black Bull *in* Cornhill, 1682.

Prologue / To / The Dutchess, / On Her Return from / Scotland. / — / Written by Mr. Dryden. / — / Printed for Jacob Tonson at the Judge's Head in / Chancery-lane near Fleetstreet. 1682.

Folio half-sheet; printed on both sides.
Imprint at bottom of p. 2.
British Museum.

For the biographical sketch of the author, John Dryden, see pp. 33–35.

Epilogue / To / Her Royal Highness, / On Her Return from / Scotland. / — / Written by Mr. Otway. / — / Printed for Jacob Tonson, at the Judge's Head in Chancery-lane, 1682.

Folio half-sheet, reverse blank.
Imprint at bottom of p. 1.
The Henry E. Huntington Library.

For the biographical sketch of the author, Thomas Otway, see pp. 52–53.

TO THE DUCHESS OF YORK UPON HER RETURN FROM SCOTLAND

Dryden's prologue and Otway's epilogue celebrating the Duke of York's first visit to the theatre after his return from Scotland were not six weeks old when the Duchess, returning on 27 May from Scotland, occasioned the writing of similar congratulatory pieces by the same two poets and the presentation of *Venice Preserv'd*, which had welcomed her husband. It was then nine years since James had persuaded his brother Charles to defy the Houses of Parliament and give him his consent to marry the Catholic princess Mary of Modena. As the Duchess of York attending a play given in her honour on 31 May 1682, she heard herself honoured in Dryden's lines as "The Peoples Wonder, and the Poets Theam;" and while the future waited in her to conclude the chapter on the Stuarts in England, she listened to Otway's epilogue, concluding:

> Time have a Care; bring safe the hour of joy
> When some blest Tongue proclaims a Royal Boy:
> And when 'tis born, let Nature's hand be strong;
> Bless him with days of strength and make 'em long;
> Till charg'd with honors we behold him stand,
> Three Kingdoms Banners waiting his Command,
> His Father's Conquering Sword within his Hand:
> Then th' English Lions in the Air advance,
> And with them roaring Musick to the Dance,
> Carry a *Quo Warranto* into France.

In May, the month of Otway's writing, six years later the birth of a royal son brought political change that the loyal poet Otway never dreamed of while his *Venice Preserv'd* celebrated Tory victories.

PROLOGUE
To
The Dutchess,
On Her Return from
SCOTLAND.
Written by Mr. Dryden.

When Factious Rage to cruel Exile, drove
The Queen of Beauty, and the Court of Love;
The Muses Droop'd, with their forsaken Arts,
And the sad *Cupids* broke their useless Darts.
Our fruitfull Plains to Wilds and Desarts turn'd,   5
Like *Edens* Face when banish'd Man it mourn'd:
Love was no more when Loyalty was gone,
The great Supporter of his Awfull Throne.
Love cou'd no longer after Beauty stay,
But wander'd Northward to the verge of day,   10
As if the Sun and He had lost their way.
But now th' Illustrious Nymph return'd again,
Brings every Grace triumphant in her Train:
The wondring *Nereids*, though they rais'd no storm,
Foreslow'd her passage to behold her form: 15
Some cry'd a *Venus*, some a *Thetis* past:
But this was not so fair, nor that so chast.
Far from her sight flew Faction, Strife and Pride:
And Envy did but look on her, and dy'd.
What e'er we suffer'd from our sullen Fate,   20
Her sight is purchas'd at an easy rate:
Three gloomy Years against this day were set:
But this one mighty Sum has clear'd the Debt.
Like *Joseph's* Dream, but with a better doom;
The Famine past, the Plenty still to come.   25
For Her the weeping Heav'ns become serene,
For Her the Ground is clad in cheerfull green:
For Her the Nightingales are taught to sing,
And Nature has for her delay'd the Spring.

John Dryden

The Muse resumes her long-forgotten Lays,⠀⠀⠀⠀⠀⠀⠀⠀30
And Love, restor'd, his Ancient Realm surveys;
Recalls our Beauties, and revives our Plays.
His Wast Dominions peoples once again,
And from Her presence dates his Second Reign.
But awfull Charms on her fair Forehead sit,⠀⠀⠀⠀⠀35
Dispensing what she never will admit.
Pleasing, yet cold, like *Cynthia's* silver Beam,
The Peoples Wonder, and the Poets Theam.
Distemper'd Zeal, Sedition, canker'd Hate,
No more shall vex the Church, and tear the State;⠀⠀40
No more shall Faction civil Discords move,
Or onely discords of too tender love:
Discord like that of Musicks various parts,
Discord that makes the harmony of Hearts,
Discord that onely this dispute shall bring,⠀⠀⠀⠀45
Who best shall love the Duke, and serve the King.

FINIS.

Printed for *Jacob Tonson* at the *Judge's Head* in *Chancery-lane* near *Fleetstreet*.
1682.

EPILOGUE
To
Her Royal Highness,
On Her RETURN from
SCOTLAND.
Written by Mr. Otway.

All you, who this Day's Jubilee attend,
And every Loyal Muses Loyal Friend;
That come to treat your longing wishes here,
Turn your desiring Eyes and feast 'em, there.
Thus falling on your Knees with me implore,⠀⠀⠀⠀5
May this poor Land ne'er lose that Presence more:

John Dryden

But if there any in this Circle be,
That come so curst to envy what they see:
From the vain Fool that would be great too soon,
To the dull knave that writ the last Lampoon!　　10
Let such, as Victims to that Beautie's Fame,
Hang their vile blasted Heads, and Dye with shame.
Our mighty Blessing is at last return'd,
The joy arriv'd for which so long we mourn'd:
From whom our present peace we' expect increas't,　15
And all our future Generations blest:
Time have a Care: bring safe the hour of joy
When some blest Tongue proclaims a Royal Boy:
And when 'tis born, let Nature's hand be strong;
Bless him with days of strength and make 'em long;　20
Till charg'd with honors we behold him stand,
Three Kingdoms Banners waiting his Command,
His Father's Conquering Sword within his Hand:
Then th' English Lions in the Air advance,
And with them roaring Musick to the Dance,　　25
Carry a *Quo Warranto* into *France*.

Printed for *J. Tonson*, at the *Judge's Head* in *Chancery-lane*, 1682.

To the/Duke/On His/Return./—/
Written by Nat. Lee./—/
Printed for J. Tonson, at the Judge's
Head in Chancery-lane, 1682.

Folio half-sheet; printed on both sides.
Imprint at bottom of p. 2.
The Folger Library.

NATHANIEL LEE

Nathaniel Lee, said to have been the third son of Richard
Lee, D.D., was probably born in 1653. He was educated at
Westminster school and Trinity College, Cambridge, being
admitted at Trinity on 7 July 1665 and graduated B.A. in
January 1667/8. While at Cambridge, he contributed an ode
to *Threnodia*, by Cambridge students, on the death of George
Monck, duke of Albemarle.

Lee attempted acting but failed because of nervousness.
He turned then to writing tragedies with considerable success.
Before March 1676/7, the year in which his *The Rival Queens*
made his reputation as playwright secure, he had written *The
Tragedy of Nero* (1675), acted in May 1674: *Sophonisba* (1676),
acted in April 1675; and *Gloriana* (1676), acted in January
1675/6. His subsequent productions were *Mithridates* (1678),
acted *c*. March 1677/8 ; *Cæsar Borgia* (1680), acted *c*. Sept.
1679; *Theodosius* (1680), acted *c*. Sept. 1680; *Lucius Junius
Brutus* (1681), acted in Dec. 1680; *The Princess of Cleve* (1689),
acted in 1681; *Constantine the Great* (1684), acted *c*. Dec.
1683; and *The Massacre of Paris* (1690), acted in October 1689.
Lee worked also with Dryden in *Oedipus* (1679) and *The Duke
of Guise* (1683), and Dryden favoured him with several
prologues and epilogues: Prologue to the University of Oxford

Nathaniel Lee

at the acting of *Sophonisba*, Epilogue for *Mithridates*, and Prologue for *Cæsar Borgia*.

Lee's mind failed at the close of 1684; and on 11 November 1684 he was placed in Bethlehem Hospital, where he remained five years. After his release from the Hospital, he received a pension of ten pounds from the company at the Theatre Royal. On 6 May 1692 he was buried in the parish church of St. Clement Danes. A collected edition of his works appeared in 1713.

LINES TO THE DUKE OF YORK

Though Lee's folio half-sheet, "To the Duke On His Return," is not entitled *Prologue*, it is included in this volume as an occasional and timely address in the playhouse. A note on the sheet in the Folger Library states that the lines were spoken at the King's theatre. Luttrell had it by May 29, 1682, the date on the copy in the Huntington Library. It is an impassioned expression of loyalty, praising both the Duke and the Duchess, whom Dryden and Otway honoured in prologues and epilogues at the same time. Though probably second only to Dryden as a man of influence in literary matters of his day, Lee did not practise the art of prologue writing with any frequency. The address reprinted here reveals him in a rare mood, which the author of a life-sketch in the *Dictionary of National Biography* thinks was Lee's attempt to remove a bad impression created by his *Brutus* in December 1680.

To the
Duke
On His
Return.
Written by Nat. Lee.

Come then at last, while anxious Nations weep,
Three Kingdoms stak't! too pretious for the deep.
Too pretious sure, for when the Trump of fame
Did with a direfull sound your Wrack proclaim,
Your danger and your doubtfull safety shown,   5
It dampt the Genius, and it Shook the Throne.
Your Helm may now the Sea-born Goddess take,
And soft *Favonius* safe your passage make.
Strong, and auspicious, bee the Stars that reign,
The day you launch, and *Nereus* sweep the Main.   10
Neptune aloft, scour all the Storms before,
And following *Tritons*, wind you to the Shore;
While on the Beach, like Billows of the Land,
In bending Crowds the Loyal English stand:
Come then, thô late, your right receive at last;   15
Which Heaven preserv'd, in spite of Fortunes blast,
Accept those hearts, that Offer on the Strand;
The better half of this divided Land.
Venting their honest Souls in tears of Joy,
They rave, and beg you wou'd their lives employ,   20
Shouting your sacred name, they drive the air,
And fill your Canvas Wings with gales of prayer.
Come then I hear three Nations shout agen,
And, next our *Charles*, in every bosome reign;
Heaven's darling Charge, the care of regal stars,   25
Pledge of our Peace, and Triumph of our Wars.
Heav'n eccho's Come, but come not Sir alone,
Bring the bright pregnant Blessing of the Throne.
And if in Poets charms be force or skill,
We charge you, O ye Waves, and Winds be still,   30

Soft as a sailing Goddess bring her home,
With the expected Prince that loads her Womb,
Joy of this Age and Heir of that to come.
Next her the Virgin Princess shines from far,
Aurora that, and this the Morning Star.   35
Hail then, all hail, they land in *Charle's* Armes,
While his large Breast, the Nations Angel warms.
Tears from his Cheeks with manly mildness roul,
Then dearly grasps the treasure of his Soul:
Hangs on his Neck, and feeds upon his form,   40
Calls him his Calm, after a tedious Storm.
O Brother! He cou'd say no more, and then,
With heaving Passion clasp'd him close again.
How oft he cry'd have I thy absence mourn'd,
But 'tis enough Thou art at last return'd: 45
Said I return'd! O never more to part,
Nor draw the vital warmth from *Charles* his heart.
Once more, O Heav'n, I shall this Vertue prove,
His Council, Conduct, and unshaken Love.
My People too at last their Errour see,   50
And make their Sovereign blest in loving Thee.
Not but there is a stiff-neck'd-harden'd Crew
That give not *Cæsar*, no nor God his due.
Reprobate Traytors, Tyrants of their Own,
Yet Grudge to see their Monarch in his Throne.   55
Their stubborn Souls with brass Rebellion barr'd,
Desert the Laws, and Crimes with Treason guard.
  Whom I—but there he stop'd, and cry'd 'tis past,
Pity's no more, this warning be their last;
Then sighing said, my Soul's dear purchas'd rest,   60
Welcome, Oh welcome, to my longing Brest:
Why should I waste a tear while thou art by,
To all extreams of Friendship let us fly,
Didain the factious Crowd that wou'd rebell
And mourn the Men that durst in death-excell, } 65
Their Fates were Glorious since for thee they fell. }
And as a Prince has right his Arms to weil'd,

When stubborn Rebels force him to the Field;
So for the Loyal, who their Lives lay down,
He dares to Hazard both his Life and Crown.	70

Finis.

Printed for *J. Tonson*, at the *Judge's Head* in *Chancery-lane*, 1682.

The / Prologue / Spoken by Mr. Powel. / at Oxford, July the tenth. 1682./
The / Epilogue / Spoken by Mrs. Moyle./at Oxford July the 18th. 1682.

Folio half-sheet; printed on both sides.
No imprint.
The National Library of Scotland.

UNIVERSITY PROLOGUES AND EPILOGUES

Having come now to the last University broadside of the seventeenth century to be reprinted in this collection, we may summarize with an eye on the years before and after 1682, the date of Powell's prologue and Mrs. Moyle's epilogue to an Oxford audience. The prologues and epilogues spoken at Oxford are far more numerous than those spoken at Cambridge, although it appears that Trinity College, Cambridge, heard the first prologue and epilogue ever printed in quarto apart from the play that they accompanied:

> The/Prologue/and/Epilogue/To/A Comedie,/Presented,/At the Entertainment of the Prince His/ Highnesse, by the Schollers of Trinity Col-/ledge in Cambridge, in March last,/1641./—/By Francis Cole./—London:/Printed for James Calvin, 1642.

Nearly forty years later came the first of the University broadsides, Dryden's epilogue written for a performance at Oxford, March 19 1680/1, and extant in two versions which may be seen in the Bodleian and the Christ Church Library, Oxford. The addresses of the quarto and the broadsides were for performances honouring a royal visitor; and though spoken at Cambridge and Oxford, respectively, they addressed the dis-

tinguished presence, not the University. The quarto, further-
more, was written by a student for a student-performance.

University addresses, spoken by visiting players, praised
Oxford; and the best-known writer of lines in this category
was John Dryden, who wrote early but after Shadwell and
Settle had tried their skill. "The Prologue to Cambyses at
Oxford 1672. Spoken by Betterton in a riding habit," first
printed by Mr. W. J. Lawrence in 1930 from a manuscript in
the Bodleian,[1] places Settle before Dryden by one year. A
line in Settle's prologue speaks of the players' "tributary
thanks for your last Act;" so this newly discovered prologue
belongs to a second visit or a second performance, which Mr.
Lawrence thinks occurred in 1671. Mr. Lawrence's suggestion
is that "A Prologue at Oxford" in *A Collection of Poems written
upon several Occasions by Several Persons* (1673) was for an opening
performance that was followed by Settle's *Cambyses.* This
earlier prologue, beginning:

> Your most obliging kindness one year shown
> A second time has brought your Servants down
> From the tumultuous and unlearned town,

appears to be a variant of "The Prologue to the Oxford
Schollers at the Act there, 1671," beginning:

> Gentlemen,
> Your civil kindness last year shown
> A second time hath brought your Creatures down
> From the unlearned and Tumultuous Town,

and closing with the appending initials "T.S."[2] This manuscript
prologue, says Mr. Lawrence, was written at folio 176,
preceding the one offering Settle's prologue to *Cambyses;* and
this piece is a slight variant of one erroneously endorsed "Mr.
Dryden's 2nd Prologue for ye Players at Oxford."[3] In the

---

[1] "Oxford Restoration Prologues," *The Times Literary Supplement,* Jan. 16,
1930, p. 43.

[2] Bodleian, *Eng. Poet. E 4.*

[3] The text of this piece from *Poet.* 19, in the Bodleian, is given by
Mr. Lawrence in his "Oxford Restoration Prologues."

British Museum, I have found a manuscript like the prologue
to *Cambyses*, discovered by Mr. Lawrence in the Bodleian,
under the title, "A Prologue spoken to ye University: by ye
Dukes House";[1] and with it appears "An Epilogue to ye
University at ye same time," which I believe has never been
included in a collection of University addresses, and which I
print here:

> Learning in its long progress from ye East
> Did visit many countryes like a Guest,
> From Syria it to fertile Egypt ran
> From Persia to ye wilder Indian,
> The Magi and the fam'd Gymnosophist
> Welcom'd almighty learning as it past
> To haughty Greece, from thence to prouder Rome,
> At last it staid at Oxon as its home
> Wn ye great conquering Cæsar first came here,
> Not any mark of learning did appear
> But wt on ev'ry naked Pict was seen,
> And painted on his hierogliphick skin:
> But since she grew majestically great
> Wn she made Oxon her imperiall seat,
> The loyall Oxon, that has still withstood
> And still made head gainst ye rebellious flood,
> Oxford yt does, & will forever stand
> Th' only untam'ed City in ye Land
> Tis hither from all parts ye afflicted flye
> For Oxon is ye nations Sanctuary.
> Wn pious Charles too sensibly did feel
> The pride & ins'lence of pretended Zeal,
> Wn many Cityes did his hopes defeat,
> He found in Oxon a secure retreat,
> Then was ye pen, & peacefull Gown layd by,

---

[1] British Museum, Ad. MS. 14,047. The variant readings are not
numerous: l. 3 in the B.M. has *favour* instead of *power;* l. 5, *Tis* instead of
It's; l. 30, *Wee have ye confidence* instead of *That we have confidence;* l. 32, *has*
instead of *hath.* Other differences—punctuation, spelling and capitalization—
are negligible. "Elkanah Settle" is not at the end of the B.M. MS.

And ev'ry one to dreadfull armes did fly.
Tis doubtfull wch more honour did afford
Their conquering pens, or their victorious sword;
This from the world did gain them high esteem
That they did not leave him, but he them.
Tis here our Princes have been still secure
Against ye rage of pestilence & war;
Tis here ye sacred Muses have been free,
Wn all ye Nation was in slavery.
They like ye Summer by their rage & spight
Eclypst, but could not be extinguisht quite:
That of wch learned Johnson did complain,
And often wisht to see, but wisht in vain,
Fate has bestow'd on us: he wisht to see
A learned, a selected company
To sit in judgemt on ye playes he writ
And give em ye imortall stamp of witt.
In London noe such Auditors appear,
Nor can they be seen any where, but here.
Tis true, wee have great witts, great Judges there,
But wt they but pretend to be, you are.
You Plaudits where they are deserv'd bestow,
Where you find weaknesses, you pardon too.
This makes us with an awfull rev'rence stand,
And not your praise, but pardon Srs demand.
Since yn you still were mercifull & good,
Accept what wee have done, for wt we should
Since to divert you was our sole intent
Pray Srs think that well done, wch was well meant.[1]

With this epilogue, then, we have three University pieces
for 1671 before Dryden's prologues which came in 1673 and
1674, and which appear in the same British Museum Manuscript (Ad. MS. 14,047) on pages 119, 118, 117: "A Prologue
to ye University by ye Kings House," which is "Prologue, to
the University of Oxon. Spoken by Mr. Hart, at the Acting

[1] British Museum. Ad. MS. 14,047.

of the Silent Woman, written by Mr. Dryden" in *Miscellany Poems* (1684), and "Another Prologue: by ye Kings House," which is "Prologue, to the University of Oxford, 1674. Spoken by Mr. Hart. Written by Mr. Dryden" in *Miscellany Poems* (1684). With this second prologue there is a manuscript epilogue entitled "An Epilogue to ye University at ye same time," which is in *Miscellany Poems* (1684) as "Epilogue, Spoken by Mrs. Boutell. Written by Mr. Dryden." *Miscellany Poems* (1684) contains an epilogue spoken at Oxford as a companion piece to the first prologue, 1673, at the acting of the *Silent Woman*: "Epilogue, Spoken by the same. Written by Mr. Dryden."

In 1673 the ablest composer of lines for University audiences wrote his first address to Oxford—a prologue spoken by Hart when the *Silent Woman* was acted there. He wrote an epilogue for the same occasion, and in the next year Oxford heard another of his prologues spoken by Hart and another of his epilogues rendered by Mrs. Boutell or Mrs. Marshall, both names having been recorded in *Miscellany Poems* (1684), pp. 269–271, 275–277. An "Epilogue to the University of Oxford, 1677, by Mr. Jo. Haynes," copied into G. Thorn-Drury's *Note Book* in the Bodleian, was in a seventeenth-century manuscript announced for sale in *The Oldenburgh House Bulletin*, No. 3, at Dobell's Antiquarian Bookstore in Tunbridge Wells, April 1935. Dryden's composition of University pieces continued after 1674, examples in addition to the four already named being printed in *Miscellany Poems* (1684):

Prologue to thè University of Oxford.
    First line: Discord, and Plots which have
        undone our Age.
Prologue to the University of Oxford: By Mr. Dryden.
    First line: Tho' Actors cannot much of learning
        boast.
Epilogue to Oxford: Spoken by Mrs. Marshall, Writ by Mr. Dryden.

University Prologues and Epilogues

First line: Thespis, the first Professor of our Art.[1]

There was also, of course, the rarest of his epilogues: "The Epilogue. Writ by Mr. Dreyden, Spoke before His Majesty at Oxford, March 19, 1680," which was published as a folio half-sheet. And in *The Works of John Dryden*, ed. Scott (revised by Saintsbury, 1885), X, 356–357, there is a prologue to the University of Oxford, *c.* 1680/81, beginning "The famed Italian Muse, whose rhymes advance."

Though not the first to address Oxford in prologues and epilogues, Dryden knew the art of compliment so well that he had sometimes to wonder at the success of his lines. To Rochester, for instance, Malone says he wrote once:

> Your lordship will judge how easy 'tis to pass anything upon an university, and how gross flattery the learned will endure.[2]

Concerning these flattering addresses to Oxford, Dryden's critics have been more gracious in their opinions. Saintsbury said of them:

> . . . It has been mentioned that Dryden speaks slightingly of these University prologues, but they are among his best pieces of the class, and are for the most part entirely free from the ribaldry with which he was but too often wont to alloy them.[3]

Taking as a good example the Prologue to the University of

1 Miscellany Poems./Containing a New/Translation/of/Virgil's Eclogues,/ Ovid's Love Elegies,/Odes of Horace,/And Other Authors;/With Several/ Original Poems./—By the most Eminent Hands./—/two lines of Latin/—/ London,/Printed for Jacob Tonson, at the Judges-head in/Chancery-Lane near Fleet-street, 1684./; pp. 271–278. The first four pieces in this volume, appearing on pp. 263–271, were named in the discussion of Dryden's prologues and epilogues for 1673 and 1674.

2 *Dryden's Prose Works*, I, ii, 13.

3 See the comments upon Dryden's prologues and epilogues in G. Saintsbury, *Dryden*, New York and London: Harper & Brothers, 1902, pp. 63–65.

Oxford, beginning "Tho' actors cannot much of Learning boast," he named the piece "the most famous prologue to the University of Oxford" and added:

> . . . This is the prologue in which the poet at once displays his exquisite capacity for flattery, his command over versification, and his singular antipathy to his own Alma Mater. . . .

Among other prologues and epilogues spoken at Oxford or Cambridge during the seventeenth and early eighteenth centuries, we may note the following:

> Epilogue to Lee's *Sophonisba* spoken by Sophonisba at its first playing at Oxford, 1680.
> First line: To this learn'd Audience gladly we submit.
> The Prologue Spoken by Mr. Powel. at Oxford, July the Tenth. 1682.
> First line: By a dissenting Play-house frantick rage.
> The Epilogue Spoken by Mrs. Moyle. at Oxford July the 18th. 1682.
> First line: As some kind Sister, who ith' Fields does take.[1]

> A Long Prologue, To a Short Play. Spoken By a Woman at Oxford, Drest like a Sea Officer.
> First line: With Monmouth Cap, and Cutlace by my side.[2]
> An Epilogue Spoken to the University of Oxon. By Mrs. Cook.
> First Line: In these our Pious times, when writing Plays.[3]

[1] The epilogue, and the prologue above, are printed in broadside. Copies are in the National Library of Scotland and in the Huntington Library.
[2] *Poems on Affairs of State*, Part III, 1698, pp. 58–62.
[3] *Ibid.*, Part III, pp. 173–176.

Prologue spoken before the University of Oxford, 1683.

> First line: When Greece o'rewhelm'd in the wide Deluge lay.

Epilogue.

> First line: Not with more grief the Whiggish herd beheld.[1]

Prologue Spoken to the Ladies before the Musick Act, at the Publick Commencement at Cambridge, On Tuesday the 5th, of July. 1698. Written by Mr. Blomer.

> First line: Thus long our Learned Arts have rul'd the Day.[2]

Epilogue By the same Hand.

> First line: Dread Criticks! We have nothing more to plead.[3]

The Strowlers Prologue at Cambridge.

> First line: In early Days cre Prologues did begin.[4]

A long Prologue to a short, and an ill-Acted Play, spoken by a Woman at Oxford; in the Year, 1691.

> First line: With Monmouth's Cock, and Cutlace by my Side.[5]

A Prologue To the University of Oxford, Spoken

---

[1] Epilogue, and Prologue above, in *A Collection of Miscellany Poems, Letters*, &c. By Mr. Brown, &c., 1699, pp. 61–65.

[2] *A New Miscellany of Original Poems, On Several Occasions.* Written by the E of D. Sir Charles Sidley, Sir Fleetw. Shepheard, Mr. Wolelly, Mr. Granvill, Mr. Dryden, Mr. Stepney, Mr. Rowe. And several other Eminent Hands. Never before Printed, 1701, pp. 183–187.

[3] *Ibid.*, pp. 187–191.   [4] *Ibid.*, pp. 248–251.

[5] *A Pacquet from Parnassus*, Vol. I. No. 1. 1702, with this note appended: "To this, we beseech yee Gentlemen, let us add, That tho' the Play was ill-acted, yet the Gentlewoman spoke the Prologue well; and some People desire no other Immortality then Paper Eternity, and 'tis fit the Lady should have her Deserts." Compare this with "A Long Prologue, To a Short Play. Spoken By a Woman at Oxford, Drest like a Sea Officer" in *Poems on Affairs of State*, Part III, 1698, pp. 58–62, an earlier version.

by Mr. Betterton, on Monday, July the 5th, 1703.
First line: Once more our London Muses pleas'd
repair.[1]

Prologue spoken to the University. By Mr.
Mumford, 1687.
First line: What? Tho Commissions open'd in a
Day.
Epilogue by Mrs. Mumford.
First line: Since Acts of late are out of Fashion
grown.[2]

Prologue To The University of Oxford. Written
by Mr. Steel, and Spoken by Mr. Wilks. 1706.
First line: As wandring Streams by secret Force
return.[3]

Prologue to a Musick Speech had in the Theatre in
Oxford.
First line: Well! for a careful provident Bawd,
say I.
The Epilogue.
First line: As from a darkned Room, some
Optick Glass.[4]

[1] Folio half-sheet, verso blank: A/Prologue/To The/University of Oxford./ Spoken by Mr. Betterton. In a manuscript note (B.M. 1347.m.38) are authorship and date: "Dr. Trapp. July 5. 1703." A similar broadside will be presented to the Bodleian Library in June, 1940, by the Friends of the Bodleian. The text, with minor variations in spelling, capitalization, and punctuation, appears in a quarto in the British Museum: A/Prefatory/ Prologue,/By way of Introduction,/To one Spoken by Mr. Betterton/at Oxford, on Monday/the 5th of July./Spoken by Mr. Mills at the/Theatre-Royal in Drury-Lane,/on Friday the 16th of July,/1703./The/Epilogue,/ By way of Answer,/To the foregoing/Prologue,/Spoken by Mr. Mills. Genest says these pieces were spoken on July 16, 1703, at the *Fool's Preferment* (II, 275).

[2] Epilogue, and Prologue above, in *Apollo's Feast: or, Wits Entertainment*, 1703, pp. 136–137.

[3] Folio half-sheet. The Chetham Library. Announced in *The Daily Courant*, July 4, 1706 (No. 1317). Included in *The Muses Mercury*, Sept., 1707 (No. 9), p. 208.

[4] Epilogue, and Prologue above, in *The Third Volume of the Works of Mr.*

The Prologue to the University of Oxford.
Written by Mr. Tickell. Spoken by Mr. Cibber.
1713.
>   First line: What Kings henceforth shall Reign,
>   what States be free.[1]

As University addresses in folio half-sheet, therefore, the prologue and epilogue reprinted here interest the student of seventeenth-century poetry and drama. There is more than an echo of playhouse anxieties in the lines that Powell spoke, and the coquetry of Mrs. Moyle's epilogue is heavily embossed with flattery that mocks the London spark. The year of unrest, of course, is 1682. The appearance of George Powell as an actor in 1687 clouds Powell records, for the better-known son's parts are not always designated by the words "the younger." We do know, however, that the elder Powell, who was Hecate in the epilogue to Duffett's *The Empress of Morocco* in December 1673, and who spoke the epilogue to Leanerd's *The Rambling Justice* in March 1677/8, is the speaker named in this piece. He is probably "Poel," who is named the speaker of a prologue to *The Indian Emperor*, published in Duffett's *New Poems* in 1676.

Thomas Brown, 1708, pp. 94–96. The epilogue, however, is Dryden's rarest, which is reprinted from the folio half-sheet in the Bodleian in my collection here, pp. 38–39.
1 Folio half-sheet. The Worcester College Library.

Prologue
Spoken by Mr. Powel.
at Oxford, July *the Tenth.* 1682.

By a dissenting Play-house frantick rage,
We the poor remnant of a ruin'd Stage,
Must call the very Storm that wrack't us kind,
Since we this safe, and pleasant harbour find:
So shipwrack't Passengers, if they espy   5
Any kind remnant of the Ship that's nigh,
Embrace with thanks the charitable Oar
That Fate prepar'd, and make towards the Shore.
    Our tribe infected with the City fits
Was setting up a Common-wealth of wits,   10
And still (to make the parallel more true)
Was falling out, and without reason too:
Mov'd by these broils, which rais'd us still more high,
We made at last a real Tragedy.
Old Relique's of th' infection still we bear,   15
For each man here is turn'd Petitioner.
And to your kindness, for the double recruit
Of Wit and Fortune, makes his humble Suit.
    Faith 'twas high time to leave the noisy Town,
When what scarce made a show was pulling down.   20
When Our gay Ribbons, and such useless things,
Were all condemn'd to make new Bible Strings.
Our short-Jump Canters stifly have defy'd
All Rhymes, since *David's* good Burlesquers dy'd; ⎫
Have all things else but State-lampoons decry'd. ⎬ 25
Good Poems they like Holy-water fear,
Because there seem's some kind of concord there.
    Here *Genuine* peace do's ev'ry breast inspire,
And to a general calmness all conspire.
Rebellion, which is there the onely Prize   30
By which the canting, hot-brain'd *Zealots* rise,

In this fair Paradise dare's not show her face,
As if some flameing Cherub kept the place.
So when the Plague Our Climate did infest,
And with new-heats the late burnt Town posses't;   35
The fearful Steams (that lodg'd ith' circling Air)
Kept out of sight, and durst not enter here.

Finis.

The
Epilogue
Spoken by Mrs. Moyle.
at Oxford July *the 18th.* 1682.

As some kind Sister, who ith' Fields does take
A turn or two for contemplations sake,
If she by chance some Brother spy's a stray,
Leaves her grave looks, and throws her Book a way,
Kindly reparing to the Hedg that's next   5
They clear the point, and there Act out the Text:
So I who thought; when leaving you, t' have made
A Zealous Sister of the canting Trade;
Now find my fainting Piety retires,
Your charming looks have kindled new desires: } 10
Alass! my heat of Zeal now yields to stranger fires. }
You take our hearts, altho you spread no Snare,
Without a combat still you conquer here:
Nature untaught by Mimick Art's disguise,
Lets your Peculiar Charms obtaine the Prize.   15
    Our *London* Sparks far diff'rent methods make,
But all their mighty doings will not take,
With one poor word as great a coyl they raise,
As your Town-Brutes about the Town-Clerks place.
By sensless Oaths they think kind Love t'inspire,   20
But that great Blustring quite puts out the fire:
And tho they still new Protestations bring,

These t'us they keep, just as their Vows to th' King.
With the same Speeches still their flame they show:
Set forms (alass)! they no where else allow.   25
And yet in this we must their kindness own,
They'd have our Smocks up, though your Surplice down.
  The same damn'd Stamp your Whiggish Townsmen
    bear,
But chiefly that dull slow Machen the—
Poor sinner he'd not the Abhorrence sign,   ⎤ 30
Tho all to this Association joyn,   ⎬
In cheating you they joyntly all combine.   ⎦
  In vain by fruitless means you Scholars try
E're to reform this Heath'nish Progeny.
The Dull unmoulded ore will nere refine,
'Tis hard to change conspiring Heaven's design: 35
Do what you will, the Brutes will leave (you'l see)
At once their Dullness, and Disloyalty.

Finis.

Prologue to Romulus,/Spoken by Mrs. Butler. / — / Written by Mrs. Behn./—/ Epilogue to the Same,/Spoken by the Lady Slingsby./ London : Printed by Nath. Thompson, 1682.

Folio half-sheet; printed on both sides.
Imprint at bottom of p. 2.
British Museum.

For the biographical sketch of the author, Mrs. Aphra Behn, see pp. 92–93.

THE FORBIDDEN EPILOGUE

Since party addresses occur not at all infrequently in this volume, by 1682 the words *Tory* and *Whig* bring on reader's apathy unless the prologues and epilogues naming these contentious factions have flung their speakers and authors into some picturesque difficulties. Viewed in this light, the separate publication of Mrs. Behn's prologue and epilogue to *Romulus*, reprinted here, is more than a party sheet. It must be read with a note in the *True Protestant Mercury*,[1] which indicates that in the epilogue both Mrs. Behn and the actress who spoke her lines offended persons of quality and caused the Lord Chamberlain to order both in custody:

> Thurs. last being acted Play calld the *Tragedy of Romulus* at the Dukes Theatre and the *Epilogue* spoken by the Lady Slingsby, and written by Mrs. Behn

[1] No. 168, Sat. Aug. 12–Wed. Aug. 16, 1682.

which reflected on the D. of Monmouth, the Lord Chamberlain has ordered them both in custody to answer that affront for the same:

Whether Lady Mary Slingsby, who spoke Mrs. Behn's epilogue, was made to feel very keenly the shame of her political error, history does not say. She withdrew from the stage three years later, having appeared in addresses as Lady Slingsby at least twice in 1682: Epilogue to *Romulus* in August[1] and Prologue to *Mr. Turbulent*,[2] probably in January. All other addresses assigned to her preceded this date and were recorded as spoken by Mrs. Mary Lee: epilogues to Settle's *Love and Revenge*, acted in 1674, Otway's *Alcibiades* and (with Smith) Settle's *The Conquest of China* in 1675, D'Urfey's *Madam Fickle* and Otway's *Titus and Berenice* and *The Cheats of Scapin* in 1676; and the prologue to *The Constant Nymph* in 1677. Genest (I, III), relying upon Downes, says she was probably Mrs. Dixon, later Mrs. Aldridge, then Mrs. Lee (wife of Anthony Leigh), and finally Lady Mary Slingsby. At her death in 1694, she was buried in old St. Pancras churchyard as "Dame Mary Slingsby, Widow."[3]

The speaker of Mrs. Behn's prologue, Mrs. Butler, we have already met in these pages,[4] and this is not her first association with Mrs. Behn in the theatre. She delivered the prologue to Mrs. Behn's *Like Father, like Son* in the same year.

[1] The broadside prologue and epilogue to *Romulus* in the Huntington Library bears a manuscript note: "8 July 1682," and one in the Folger Library says "9 August 1682." If the play was acted "Thurs. last," as stated in the *True Protestant Mercury*, Sat. Aug. 12—Wed. Aug. 16, 1682, then the broadside prologue and epilogue would seem to have been printed and circulated before the performance of the play—if the MS. note indicates the date of purchase. The date on the Folger copy seems to be nearer to the date of performance since "Thurs. last" was August 10. In the *Loyal Impartial Mercury*, No. 46, Nov. 17, 1682, an advertisement states that *Romulus and Hersilia* will be published in November.
[2] Reissued as *The Factious Citizen*, 1685.
[3] Dr. Doran's *Annals of the English Stage*, ed. Robert W. Lowe (1888), I, 148.
[4] See pp. 76, 94, and Appendix C.

Occasionally, though often not without some difficulty, the so-called Preaching Sisters turned to politics. Lady Desbro, speaking the epilogue to Mrs. Behn's *The Round-Heads* in 1681, flayed the "pious cheats" who descended from the founders of the Commonwealth. Mrs. Bowman, dressed as Victory, spoke an epilogue in 1705, praising "great Anne's Arms"[1] and the victories of Marlborough. Such sentiments, appropriate to 1705, were quite otherwise, however, six years later, as Mrs. Centlivre discovered in January, 1711/12, when she thought to have Mrs. Oldfield speak an epilogue concluding with a tribute to Marlborough.[2] The first night, the play had to come off without the epilogue for a reason which Mrs. Centlivre stated in the Preface to *The Perplex'd Lovers*:

> . . . It seems the Epilogue design'd would not pass; therefore the Managers of the Theatre did not think it safe to speak it, without I cou'd get it licens'd, which I cou'd not do that Night, with all the Interest I could make.

At an hour when the Commons were accusing Marlborough, and the Queen was listening to their charges, parties formed against the epilogue because it was reported to be notoriously whiggish. The times were not then kind to the female politician of the stage; and Mrs. Oldfield was forced to heed the threats of the opposing party that demanded her silence. As early examples of the female prologue and epilogue with a political turn, then, Mrs. Behn's lines printed in folio half-sheet are reprinted here.

[1] William Mountfort, *Zelmane* (1705), Epilogue.
[2] *The Perplex'd Lovers* (1712), Preface.

PROLOGUE to ROMULUS,
Spoken by Mrs. Butler.
Written by Mrs. Behn.

How we shall please ye now I cannot say;
But Sirs, 'Faith here is *News from Rome* to day;
Yet know withal, we've no such Packets here,
As you read once a Week from Monkey *CARE*.
But 'stead of that Lewd Stuff (that clogs the Nation)   5
Plain Love and Honour; (tho quite out of Fashion;)
Ours is a Virgin Rome, long, long, before
Pious Geneva Rhetorick call'd her Whore;
For be it known to their Eternal Shames,
Those Saints were always good at calling Names: 10
Of *Scarlet Whores* let 'em their Wills devise,
But lete 'm raise no other *Scarlet Lies;*
Lies that advance the *Good Old Cause*, and bring
Into Contempt the Prelates with the KING.
Why shou'd the *Rebel Party* be affraid?   15
They're *Ratts* and *Weazles* gnaw the *Lyon's* Beard;
And then in Ignoramus Holes they think,
Like other Vermin, to lie close, and stink.
What have ye got ye *Conscientious Knaves*,
With all your *Fancy'd Power*, and *Bully Braves?*   20
With all your *standing to't;* your *Zealous Furies;*
Your *Lawless Tongues*, and *Arbitrary Juries?*
Your *Burlesque Oaths*, when one *Green-Ribbon-Brother*
In Conscience will be *Perjur'd* for another?
Your Plots, *Cabals;* Your *Treats, Association,*   25
Ye shame, Ye very Nusance of the Nation,
What have ye got but one poor Word? Such Tools
Were *Knaves* before; to which you've added *Fools.*
    Now I dare swear, some of you *Whigsters* say,
Come on, now for a swinging Tory Play.   30
But, Noble *Whigs*, pray let not those *Fears* start ye,
Nor fright hence any of the *Sham Sheriffs Party;*

For, if you'l take my censure of the story,
It is as harmless as e're came before ye,
And writ before the times of *Whig* and *Tory*.   35

EPILOGUE to the Same,
Spoken by the Lady Slingsby.

Fair Ladies, pity an unhappy Maid,
By Fortune, and by faithless Love betray'd.
Innocent once.—I scarce knew how to sin,
Till that unlucky Devil entring in,
Did all my Honour, all my Faith undo: 5
Love! like *Ambition*, makes us Rebels too:
And of all Treasons, mine was most accurst;
Rebelling 'gainst a King and Father first.
A Sin, which Heav'n nor Man can e're forgive;
Nor could I *Act* it with the face to live.   10
My Dagger did my Honours cause redress;
But Oh! my blushing Ghost must needs confess,
Had my young Charming Lover faithful been,
I fear I'd dy'd with unrepented Sin.
Theres nothing can my Reputation save   15
With all the *True*, the *Loyal* and the *Brave;*
Not my Remorse, or Death, can expiate
With them a Treason 'gainst the KING and *State*.
Some Love-sick Maid perhaps, now I am gone,
(Raging with Love, and by that Love undone,)   20
May form some little *Argument* for me,
T'excuse m'*Ingratitude* and *Treachery*.
Some of the Sparks too, that infect the Pit,
(Whose Honesty is equal to their Wit,
And think *Rebellion* but a petty Crime,   25
Can turn to all sides Int'rest does incline,)
May cry '*I gad I think the Wench is wise;*
'*Had it prov'd Lucky, 'twas the way to rise.*
'*She had a* Roman *Spirit, that disdains*

Aphra Behn

'*Dull Loyalty, and the Yoke of Sovereigns.*　　　　　30
'*A Pox of Fathers, and Reproach to come;*
'*She was the first and Noblest* Whig *of* Rome.
But may that Ghost in quiet never rest,
Who thinks it self with Traytors Praises blest.

London: Printed by *Nath. Thompson,* 1682.

Prologue./To The/King and Queen,/
At The/Opening/of/Their Theatre./
—/Spoken by Mr. Batterton: Written
by Mr. Dryden./—/
Epilogue./—/Spoken by Mr. Smith:
Written by the same Authour./—/
London,/Printed for Jacob Tonson,
at the Judge's Head in/Chancery-lane.
1683.

Folio; printed on four pages.
Imprint at bottom of p. 4.
British Museum.

For the biographical sketch of the author, John Dryden,
see pp. 33–35.

THE OCCASIONAL PROLOGUE
AND EPILOGUE

With the union of the King's and Duke's players accom-
plished, the King and Queen attended the opening of their
playhouse on November 16, 1682, and heard the addresses,
which are reprinted here from a very rare folio. Dryden, their
ablest celebrant, composed a prologue of triplets for this
occasion, departing a little from customary paths, and filed
his couplets into an epilogue of far-from-humble appeal.
His words were spoken by Betterton and Smith, distinguished
playhouse orators who are already well known in these
pages.[1]

[1] Betterton, pp. 59–60, 124; Smith, pp. 59, 101.

John Dryden

Doubly occasional, the prologue and epilogue celebrated an event in the history of playhouses, as well as a royal visit. Comments contributory to theatrical chronicles, including even the physical details of the playhouses themselves, are familiar matter in prologues and epilogues from the time when Shakespeare said:

> . . . Can this Cockpit hold
> The vasty fields of France? Or may we cram
> Within the wooden O the very casques
> That did affright the air at Agincourt?[1]

A list of pieces annotating playhouse history is almost without end, and even the prologues and epilogues that were written for special occasions in the progress of the theatre survive in considerable number in the plays, miscellanies, and broadsides of the seventeenth and eighteenth centuries. In this group occur addresses written for opening performances, removals to other houses, re-openings, players' unions, and similar events in stage-history.[2]

---

[1] Prologue to *Henry the Fifth*.

[2] Though very infrequently printed with the plays, some examples may be noted in a prologue to the city, "Newly after the Removal of the Dukes Company from Lincoln-Inn-fields to their new Theatre, near Salisbury Court," printed with Wycherley's *Gentleman Dancing-Master* (1673), a prologue spoken at the Theatre in Lincolns-Inn-Fields published in Pordage's *Herod and Mariamne* (1674), and the occasional addresses on the opening of the New House, published in Congreve's *Love for Love* (1695). As would be expected, the greatest number of prologues and epilogues of an occasional nature appeared in miscellanies; as for example: "A Prologue spoken upon removing of the late Fortune Players to the Bull," J. Tatham's *The Fancies Theatre*, 1640; "A Prologue spoken at the Cock-pit, at the coming of the Red-Bull Players thither," J. Tatham's *Ostella*, 1650; "A Prologue for a Company of Players leaving London for York, upon their first appearance," "Epilogue," "Prologue to Henry the third of France at the Royal Theatre. By Hart. 1678," "Epilogue (by a Woman) to the same Play, soon after the Royal Theatre was fir'd. 1678," Thomas Shipman's *Carolina*, 1683; "Prologue Spoken the first day of the King's House Acting after the Fire. Writ by Mr. Dryden," "Prologue for the Women, when they Acted at the Old Theatre in Lincolns-

John Dryden

Of the distinct types of prologues and epilogues that recur in the latter part of the seventeenth century, those eulogizing and flattering members of the royal family are the oldest and most conventional. A century and more had taught both king and spectator to look for them; and the playhouse, in its typical compliance with custom, did not disappoint this expectation. The habit of patronage in the Renaissance, as

inn-Fields. Written by Mr. Dryden," "A Prologue spoken at the Opening of the New House, Mar. 26, 1674. Written by Mr. Dryden," "An Epilogue for the Kings House. Written by Mr. Dryden," *Miscellany Poems*, 1684; "A Prologue Spoken at the Opening of the Duke's New Play-House," by Etherege, *A Collection of Poems*, 1701; "A Prologue on the propos'd Union of the Two Houses," Farquhar's *Love and Business: In a Collection of Occasionary Verse*, 1702; "An Epilogue," spoken by Underhill at the New Theatre in Puritanical habit, *Apollo's Feast*, 1703; "A Prologue to the Corinthian Queen," "A Prologue spoke by Mr. Betterton at the New Theatre in Little Lincolns-Inn-Fields," "An Epilogue for the Theatre Royal," Nos. 4, 5, 34, respectively, *The Diverting Post*, 1704–1705; "Prologue Spoken at the Opening of the Queen's Theatre in the Hay-Market," by Dr. Garth, "Prologue spoken at Her Majesty's Theatre in the Hay-market, on Saturday, the 8th of November, by I. B. Esq;" by Cibber, Nos. 2 and 10, respectively, *The Muses Mercury*, 1707; "Spoken upon his Royal Highness the Duke of York coming to the Theatre, Friday, April 21, 1682," "Spoken to Her Royal Highness on Her Return from Scotland, In the Year 1682," *The Works of Mr. Thomas Otway*, 1712; "A Prologue, at the Opening of the Play-house, Spoken by Young Powell," *Wit and Mirth: or Pills to Purge Melancholy*, 1719; "Prologue in a Halter. Design'd to have been Spoke by Penkeman, at the first opening his New Theatre in Richmond," "A Prologue, Spoke by Mr. Pinkeman at his Theatre at Richmond, with an Ass standing by him: To a Play bespoke by the Prince," *The Second Part of Penkethman's Jests*, 1721. Prologues and epilogues given separate publication are "The Prologue to His Majesty at the first Play presented at the Cock-pit in Whitehall," 1660; "A Prologue spoken at Mithridates King of Pontus, the First Play Acted at the Theatre Royal this Year, 1681;" Epilogue to the same; Prologue and Epilogue to the King and Queen at the Opening of Their Theatre, 1683; "Prologue Spoken at the First Opening of the Queen's New Theatre, in the Hay-Market," 1705; "The Opening Prologue Paraphras'd in a Familiar Stile, for the better Conception of the True Meaning, and for the Particular Use of Mr. Jer. Collier," 1705; "The Prologue at the Opening of the Theatre Royal, the Day after His Majesty's Publick Entry," 1714; "Prologue and Epilogue, Spoken at the Opening of the Theatre in Drury-Lane 1747."

well as the desire for praise in the sovereign's bosom, taught players to speak lines from the poets whose words delighted Eliza and their James. The most considerable body of eulogistic prologues and epilogues comes from the time of Elizabeth, James I, and Charles I;[1] and the poets who wrote most frequently in this mood are Lyly, Thomas Heywood, and Ben Jonson. It seems that Heywood saw his ink hardly dry on one panegyric sheet before he was composing another, for almost seventy per cent. of the speeches included in his *Pleasant Dialogues* (1637) addressed the Royal Presence. Elizabeth was accustomed to the humble, kneeling prologue in such fashion as this:

> As wretches in a storme (expecting day)
> With trembling hands and eyes cast up to heaven,
> Make Prayers the anchor of their conquerd hopes,
> So we (deere Goddesse) wonder of all eyes,
> Your meanest vassalls (through mistrust and feare,
> To sinke into the bottome of disgrace,

---

[1] See, for example, the following, listed with dates of printing as given in Chambers' *The Elizabethan Stage*, IV, pp. 379–397, and in the original editions of the plays: 1584, Prologue to Lyly's *Sapho and Phao*, Epilogue to his *Campaspe*; 1587 (8), Epilogue to T. Hughes' *The Misfortunes of Arthur*; 1591, Prologue and Epilogue to Lyly's *Endymion*, Epilogue to *Tancred and Gismunda*; 1592, Prologue to Lyly's *Gallathea*, Prologue to his *Midas*; 1598, Prologue to *A Most Pleasant Comedy of Mucedorus*; 1600, Prologue to Dekker's *The Shoemaker's Holiday*, Epilogue to Jonson's *Every Man out of his Humour*; 1607, Epilogue to *The Christmas Prince*; 1615, Prologue and Epilogue to Tomkins' *Albumazar*; 1621, Prologue and Epilogue to *The Masque of Metamorphosed Gipsies*; 1629, Prologue to Beaumont and Fletcher's *The Faithful Shepherdess*; 1630, Prologues to *Ignoramus*; 1631, Prologue and Epilogue to Jonson's *Bartholomew Fair*; 1632, Prologue to Massinger's *The Emperor of the East*, Prologue to Hausted's *Rivall Friends*; 1633, Prologue and Epilogue to Marlowe's *The Jew of Malta*; 1636, Prologue to Heywood's *Love's Mistress*; 1638, Prologue and Epilogue to Suckling's *Aglaura*; 1639, Prologue and Epilogue to Mayne's *The City Match*, Prologue and Epilogue to Cartwright's *The Royal Slave*; 1640, Prologue and Epilogue to Habington's *The Queen of Aragon*, Prologue to Jonson's *Staple of News*; 1642, Prologue and Epilogue to Cowley's *The Guardian* published separately; 1649, Epilogue to Wase's *Electra*.

By our imperfit pastimes) prostrate thus
On bended knees, our sailes of hope do strike.[1]

James heard himself acclaimed "Great Prince and mighty Monarch" in slightly less extravagant language; and Charles, with his Queen, could, after delay, come eventually to Cambridge and hear a refreshing prologue of welcome like this from Hausted:[2]

Most sacred Majesties, if yee doe wonder
To be saluted by an aged Prologue,
Know that upon these temples I doe weare
An Embleme of our Mothers fate, who since
Shee has in expectation of your presence
Numbred the tedious moments, is growne old:
For each expecting minute that has pass'd
Has seem'd an hower, and every hower a yeare.
But will ye see what power yee retaine?
Wee by your presence are made young againe.[3] *He pulls off his head of haire and beard.*

When Charles II returned the players to their stage, prologues and epilogues of homage were again the order of the day. Thomas Jordan published several in his *Royal Arbor* (1664), a new edition of *A Rosary of Rarities* and *A Nursery of Novelties;* and it seems that he was the most frequent eulogist in this particular realm before the genius of the age, John Dryden, came to comment upon all momentous occasions. Prologues and epilogues honouring the king and members of the royal family were spoken before Charles II, James II, William and Mary, and Queen Anne with the familiar sixteenth-century tone appreciably changed, as the examples in this volume

[1] "The Prologue as it was pronounced before the Queenes Majestie," Dekker's *The Shoemakers Holiday. or The Gentle Craft*, N.D.

[2] By the prologue to Hausted's play, *The Rivall Friends*, in the British Museum, there is a MS. notation: "Mr. Chaundler."

[3] "Prologue. Upon occasion of their Majesties comming being deferr'd," Hausted's *The Rivall Friends*, 1632.

indicate. The means of circulating words of praise had improved, and prologues and epilogues to the Royal Presence were printed not only in playbooks[1] and miscellanies,[2] but in quartos and folios entirely apart from the plays.[3] Thus they

[1] See, for example: Prologue and Epilogue, R. Lower's *The Amorous Fantasme*, 1661; Prologue, Jordan's *The Tricks of Youth*, 1663; Epilogue, Cowley's *Cutter of Coleman-Street*, 1663; Prologue and Epilogue, Stapylton's *The Slighted Maid*, 1663; Prologue and Epilogue, Tuke's *The Adventures of Five Hours*, 1663; Prologue, Shadwell's *Epsom Wells*, 1673; Two prologues to Settle's *The Empress of Morocco*, 1673; Epilogue, Crowne's *Calisto*, 1675; Prologue by D'Urfey, to Settle's *Ibrahim*, 1676, printed in *Wit and Mirth* (1719), II, 339; Prologue, by Dryden, to Banks' *The Unhappy Favourite*, 1682; Epilogue, Waller's *The Maid's Tragedy*, altered, 1690; Prologue, by Motteux, to Ravenscroft's *The Anatomist*, 1697.

[2] Approximately one seventh of the miscellanies containing prologues and epilogues published from 1637 to 1719, included addresses to the Royal Presence. Out of more than a century of publications in this category, see especially: some twenty-three speeches in Thomas Heywood's *Pleasant Dialogues*, 1637; "A Prologue to the King," "Epilogue to the King," "A Prologue to the King, August 16. 1660," Thomas Jordan's *Royal Arbor*, 1664 (a new edition of *A Rosary of Rarities* and *A Nursery of Novelties*); "Epilogue to the King at Whitehall," Davenant's *Poems on Several Occasions* in *Works*, 1673; "A Prologue By way of Satyr, spoke before King Charles II. at New Market," D'Urfey's *New Poems*, 1690; "Prologue To The Queen. Upon Her Majesty's coming to see the Old Batchelour. By Mr. Congreve," *The Annual Miscellany*, 1694; "A Prologue Spoken at the Court at Whitehall, Before K. Charles II. By the Lady Elizabeth Howard," Rochester's *Poems*, (&c.) *On Several Occasions*, 1696; "Epilogue to the Ladies, spoke by Mr. Wilks at the Musick-Meeting in Drury-Lane, where the English woman sings. Written by Mr. Manwaring upon the occasion of their both singing before the Queen and King of Spain at Windsor," "Prologue, spoken at Court before the Queen, on her Majesty's Birth-Day. 1703/4," *Poems on Affairs of State*, III, 1704; "A Prologue Spoken at Court, before the Queen, On Her Majesty's Birth-Day, M.DCC.IV" (Same as Prologue for the Queen's birthday listed from *Poems on Affairs of State*, 1704), *Poems on Several Occasions*, 1707; "Spoken upon his Royal Highness the Duke of York Coming to the Theatre," "Spoken to Her Royal Highness on Her Return from Scotland," *The Works of Mr. Thomas Otway*, 1712; "A Prologue to the King at the Masque at Court," "A Prologue, Made to Entertain her Royal Highness, at her coming to the Play, call'd, Ibrahim 13, Emperor of the Turks," D'Urfey's *Wit and Mirth*, II, 1719.

[3] "The Prologue and Epilogue to a Comedie, Presented, at the Entertainment of the Prince His Highness, by the Schollers of Trinity Colledge in

came to be enjoyed again by those who were pleased to hear them in the theatre, read by others, who took their pleasures from printed leaves in coffee-houses and libraries, and abandoned to the fate of news-sheets and similar 'ephemerae that did not come into the hands of men like Luttrell and Wood. The earliest of these rare prologues and epilogues greeted the "Prince His Highnesse" and appeared in quarto, 1642; the first broadside prologue bearing a date was addressed to His Majesty, 1660; and Dryden's earliest broadside was an epilogue spoken before His Majesty at Oxford, 1680. The king inspired the words of some of the rarest prologues and epilogues; and the subject, as well as the occasion, being royal, somebody with foresight caused the addresses to be printed as they descend to us here.

Cambridge," 1642; "The Prologue to His Majesty at the first Play presented at the Cock-pit in Whitehall," 1660; "The Epilogue. Writ by Mr. Dreyden, Spoke before His Majesty at Oxford," 1680; "Epilogue. Written by Mr. Otway to his Play call'd Venice Preserv'd, or a Plot Discover'd; spoken upon his Royal Highness the Duke of York's coming to the Theatre, Friday, April 21, 1682"; "Prologue To His Royal Highness, Upon His first appearance at the Duke's Theatre since his Return from Scotland," 1682; "Prologue to The Dutchess, On Her Return from Scotland," 1682; Epilogue to Her Royal Highness, On Her Return from Scotland," 1682; "To the Duke on His Return," 1682; "Prologue. To the King and Queen, At the Opening of Their Theatre," 1683, and Epilogue for the same occasion; "The Prologue (sic) To King William and Queen Mary, At a Play Acted before Their Majesties at Whitehall," 1689; "Prologue Spoken At Court Before the Queen, On her Majesty's Birth-day, 1703–4," 1704; "Prologue To The Court; On the Queen's Birth-day, 1704," 1705; "A Prologue For the 4th of November, 1711. Being the Anniversary for the Birth-day of the Late K. William, of Glorious and Immortal Memory," 1711; "The Prologue at the Opening of the Theatre-Royal, the Day after His Majesty's Publick Entry," 1714; "A New Prologue, On the Anniversary of his Majesty K. George," 1725; "A Prologue for His Majesty's Birth-Day, May 28, 1725."

PROLOGUE.
To The
King and Queen,
At The
Opening
of
Their THEATRE.

Spoken by Mr. *Batterton:* Written by Mr. *Dryden.*

Since Faction ebbs, and Rogues grow out of Fashion,
Their penny-Scribes take care t'inform the Nation,
How well men thrive in this or that Plantation.

How *Pensilvania's* Air agrees with Quakers,
And *Carolina's* with Associators: 5
Both e'en   *   good for Madmen and for Traitors.

Truth is, our Land with Saints is so run o'er,
And every Age produces such a store,
That now there's no need of two *New-Englands* more.

What's this, you'll say, to Us and our Vocation?   10
Onely thus much, that we have left our Station,
And made this Theatre our new Plantation.

The Factious Natives never cou'd agree;
But aiming, as they call'd it, to be Free,
Those Play-house Whiggs set up for Property.   15

Some say they no Obedience paid of late;
But wou'd new Fears and Jealousies create;
Till topsy-turvy they had turn'd the State.

---

* Blotted. Other texts give *too.*

Plain Sense, without the Talent of Foretelling,
Might guess 'twou'd end in down-right knocks and
    quelling: 20
For seldome comes there better of Rebelling.

When Men will, needlesly, their Freedom barter
For Lawless Pow'r, sometimes they catch a Tartar:
(There's a damn'd word that rhimes to this call'd
    Charter.)

But, since the Victory with Us remains,   25
You shall be call'd to Twelve in all our Gains:
(If you'll not think us sawcy for our pains.)

Old Men shall have good old Plays to delight 'em:
And you, fair Ladys and Gallants that slight 'em,
We'll treat with good new Plays; if our new Wits   30
    can write 'em.

We'll take no blundring Verse, no fustian Tumour,
No dribling Love, from this or that Presumer:
No Dull fat Fool shamm'd on the Stage for humour.

For, faith, some of 'em such vile stuff have made,
As none but Fools or Fairies ever Play'd;   35
But 'twas, as Shopmen say, to force a Trade.

We've giv'n you Tragedies, all Sense defying:
And singing men, in wofull Metre dying;
This 'tis when heavy Lubbers will be flying.

All these disasters we well hope to weather;   40
We bring you none of our old Lumber hether:
Whigg Poets and Whigg Sheriffs may hang together.

John Dryden

EPILOGUE.

Spoken by Mr. *Smith*: Written by the same Authour.

New Ministers, when first they get in place
Must have a care to Please; and that's our Case:
Some Laws for publick Welfare we design,
If You, the Power supreme, will please to joyn:
There are a sort of Pratlers in the Pit,   5
Who either have, or who pretend to Wit:
These noisie Sirs so loud their Parts rehearse,
That oft the Play is silenc'd by the Farce:
Let such be dumb, this Penalty to shun,
Each to be thought my Lady's Eldest Son.   10
But stay: methinks some Vizard Masque I see,
Cast out her Lure from the mid Gallery:
About her all the flutt'ring Sparks are rang'd;
The Noise continues though the Scene is chang'd:
Now growling, sputtring, wauling, such a clutter,   15
'Tis just like Puss defendant in a Gutter:
Fine Love no doubt, but e'er two days are o'er ye,
The Surgeon will be told a wofull story.
Let Vizard Masque her naked Face expose,
On pein of being thought to want a Nose: 20
Then for your Lacqueys, and your Train beside,
(By what e'er Name or Title dignify'd)
They roar so loud, you'd think behind the Stairs
Tom Dove, and all the Brotherhood of Bears:
They're grown a Nuisance, beyond all Disasters,   25
We've none so great but their unpaying Masters.
We beg you, Sirs, to beg your Men, that they
Wou'd please to give you leave to hear the Play.
Next, in the Play-house spare your pretious Lives;
Think, like good Christians, on your Bearns and Wives: 30
Think on your Souls; but by your lugging forth,
It seems you know how little they are Worth:
If none of these will move the Warlike Mind,
Think on the helpless Whore you leave behind!

We beg you last, our Scene-room to forbear, 35
And leave our Goods and Chattels to our Care:
Alas, our Women are but washy Toys,
And wholly taken up in Stage employs:
Poor willing Tits they are: but yet I doubt
This double Duty soon will wear 'em out. 40
Then you are watcht besides, with jealous care;
What if my Lady's Page should find you there?
My Lady knows t'a tittle what there's in ye;
No passing your guilt Shilling for a Guiney.
Thus, Gentlemen, we have summ'd up in short, 45
Our Grievances, from Country, Town and Court:
Which humbly we submit to your good pleasure;
But first vote Money, then Redress at leasure.

FINIS.

LONDON,
Printed for *Jacob Tonson*, at the *Judge's Head* in *Chancery-lane*. 1683.

Prologue,/To The/Duke of Guise./
—/Written by Mr. Dryden : Spoken
by Mr. Smith./—/
Epilogue./—/Written by the same
Authour : Spoken by Mrs. Cooke./
Another/Epilogue/Intended to have
been Spoken to the / Play, before it
was forbidden, / last Summer. / — /
Written by Mr. Dryden./—/
London,/Printed for Jacob Tonson,
at the Judge's Head in Chancery-lane.
1683.

Folio ; printed on four pages.
Imprint at bottom of p. 4.
British Museum.

For the biographical sketch of the author, John Dryden,
see pp. 33–35.

TIMELY PROLOGUES AND EPILOGUES

The Green-Ribbon Men and the Scarlet, as well as the
Protestants and Papists, clogged prologues and epilogues of the
seventeenth century with party wrangle, for the theatre then
was as truly the nation's hour-glass as the newspaper was
years after. While London had an ear, as well as an eye, for
news and the debate of public opinion, poets like Dryden and
actors like Betterton and Smith supplied the playhouses with

couplets about the day's absorbing interests.[1] Nobody knew better than Dryden the demands that such a rage as this made upon those who had to comply with popular taste; and we find the First Poet of the age writing an epilogue in 1681 for Banks's *The Unhappy Favourite* with these words upon the appetite for sensational, scandalous, and tattling news:

> 'Tis not our Want of Wit that keeps us poor,
> For then the Printers Press would suffer more:
> Their Pamphleteers their Venom daily spit.
> They thrive by Treason, and we starve by Wit:
> Confess the Truth, which of you has not laid
> Four Farthings out, to buy the Hatfield Maid?
> Or, what is duller yet, and more does spite us,
> Democritus his Wars with Heraclitus?
> These are the Authors that have run us down,
> And exercise your Criticks of the Town;
> Yet these are Pearls to your lampooning Rhimes,
> Y'abuse your selves more dully than the Times.
> Scandal, the Glory of the English Nation,
> Is worn to Rags, and scribbl'd out of Fashion.

Nevertheless, Dryden's name is writ large in any account of prologues and epilogues that served the interest of party.

With *The Duke of Guise*, which was intended for July 18, but which was withheld until the end of November to find a more favourable political season, Dryden supported the Tories, writing and publishing a prologue, an epilogue, and another epilogue intended for the play before it was forbidden during the summer of 1682. These three pieces, reprinted

---

[1] For prologues and epilogues dealing with political and religious topics, see the essay introducing lines for *Venice Preserved*, pp. 53–60, and such examples as the following, listed according to the date of performance: 1681—Prologue to D'Urfey's *Sir Barnaby Whigg*, Prologue and Epilogue to Mrs. Behn's *The Round-Heads*, Epilogue to Lee's *The Princess of Cleve;* 1681/2—Prologue and Epilogue to Southerne's *The Loyal Brother;* 1682— Prologue and Epilogue to Banks's *Vertue Betray'd;* 1682/3—Prologue to Crowne's *City Politiques;* 1683—Epilogues to Lee's *Constantine the Great* and Otway's *The Atheist.*

here, were not without significance in the whiggish atmosphere; and Dryden had to write a *Vindication* on their account and that of the play, denying that he caused Lee to enter the party struggle.

Dryden's "Prologue, to the Duke of Guise," with two epilogues, was published in folio in 1683[1] and is now a rarity. Copies are in the Brindley Collection of the British Museum, Sir Walter Scott's Library at Abbotsford, the late T. J. Wise's Library in London, the Wrenn Library of the University of Texas, and the Huntington Library in California.[2]

[1] The prologue and the first epilogue are reprinted in the play (1683), with no significant textual differences. See *The London Mercury*, July 28–Aug. 1, 1682, p. 2.

[2] The copy in the Huntington Library has a MS. note, indicating the performance of the play to have been "Nov. 30" and the date for the purchase of the folio "4 Dec. 1682."

PROLOGUE,
To The
Duke of GUISE.
Written by Mr. *Dryden:* Spoken by Mr. *Smith.**

Our Play's a Parallel: The Holy League
Begot our Cov'nant: Guisards got the Whigg:
Whate'er our hot-brain'd Sheriffs did advance,
Was, like our Fashions, first produc'd in *France:*
And, when worn out, well scourg'd, and banish'd   5
    there,
Sent over, like their godly Beggars here.
Cou'd the same Trick, twice play'd, our Nation gull?
It looks as if the Devil were grown dull;
Or serv'd us up, in scorn, his broken Meat,
And thought we were not worth a better Cheat.   10
The fulsome Cov'nant, one wou'd think in reason,
Had giv'n us all our Bellys-full of Treason:
And yet, the Name but chang'd, our nasty Nation
Chaws its own Excrement, th'Association.
'Tis true we have not learn'd their pois'ning way,   15
For that's a mode but newly come in play;
Besides, your Drug's uncertain to prevail;   ⎫
But your true Protestant can never fail,   ⎬
With that compendious Instrument, a Flail.   ⎭
Go on; and bite, ev'n though the Hook lies bare;   20
Twice in one Age expell the lawfull Heir:
Once more decide Religion by the Sword;
And purchase for us a new Tyrant Lord.
Pray for your King; but yet your Purses spare;
Make him not two-Pence richer by your Prayer.   25
To show you love him much, chastise him more;
And make him very Great, and very Poor.
Push him to Wars, but still no Pence advance;

* For Smith's prologues and epilogues refer to Appendix C.

149

John Dryden

Let him lose *England* to recover *France*.
Cry Freedom up with Popular noisy Votes: 30
And get enough to cut each others Throats,
Lop all the Rights that fence your Monarch's Throne;
For fear of too much Pow'r, pray leave him none.
A noise was made of Arbitrary Sway;
But in Revenge, you Whiggs, have found a way,   35
An Arbitrary Duty now to pay.
Let his own Servants turn, to save their stake;
Glean from his plenty, and his wants forsake.
But let some *Judas* near his Person stay,
To swallow the last Sop, and then betray.   40
Make *London* independant of the Crown:
A Realm apart; the Kingdom of the Town.
Let *Ignoramus* Juries find no Traitors:
And *Ignoramus* Poets scribble Satyres.
And, that your meaning none may fail to scan,   45
Doe, what in Coffee-houses you began;
Pull down the Master, and Set up the Man.

EPILOGUE.
Written by the same Authour: Spoken by Mrs. *Cooke.**

Much Time and Trouble this poor Play has cost;
And, faith, I doubted once the Cause was lost.
Yet no one Man was meant; nor Great nor Small;
Our Poets, like frank Gamesters, threw at all.   5
They took no single Aim :————
But, like bold Boys, true to their Prince and hearty,
Huzza'd, and fir'd Broad-sides at the whole Party.
Duells are Crimes; but when the Cause is right,
In Battel, every Man is bound to fight.
For what shou'd hinder Me to sell my Skin   10
Dear as I cou'd, if once my hand were in?
Se defendendo never was a Sin.

* For Mrs. Cooke's prologues and epilogues refer to Appendix C.

'Tis a fine World, my Masters, right or wrong,
The Whiggs must talk, and Tories hold their tongue.
They must doe all they can——   15
But We, forsooth, must bear a Christian mind;
And fight, like Boys, with one Hand ty'd behind;
Nay, and when one Boy's down, 'twere wondrous wise,
To cry, Box fair, and give him time to rise.
When Fortune favours, none but Fools will dally: ⎤ 20
Wou'd any of you Sparks, if *Nan* or *Mally*   ⎬
Tipt you th'inviting Wink, stand shall I, shall I? ⎦
A *Trimmer* cry'd, (that heard me tell this Story)
Fie, Mistress *Cooke!* faith you're too rank a Tory!
Wish not Whiggs hang'd, but pity their hard Cases;   25
You Women love to see Men make wry Faces.
Pray, Sir, said I, don't think me such a *Jew;*
I say no more, but give the Dev'l his due.
Lenitives, says he; suit best with our Condition.
Jack Ketch, says I, 's an excellent Physician.   30
I love no Bloud——. Nor I, Sir, as I breath;
But hanging is a fine dry kind of Death.
We *Trimmers* are for holding all things even:
Yes — just like him that hung 'twixt Hell and Heaven.
Have we not had Mens Lives enow already?   35
Yes sure: — but you're for holding all things steddy;
Now since the Weight hangs all on one side, Brother,
You *Trimmers* shou'd, to poize it, hang on t'other.
Damn'd Neuters, in theri middle way of steering,
Are neither Fish, nor Flesh, nor good Red-Herring: 40
Not Whiggs, nor Tories they; nor this, nor that;
Not Birds, nor Beasts; but just a kind of Bat:
A Twilight Animal; true to neither Cause,
With Tory Wings, but Whiggish Teeth and Claws.

John Dryden

Another
EPILOGUE
Intended to have been Spoken to the
P L A Y, before it was forbidden,
last Summer.
Written by Mr. *Dryden*.

Two Houses joyn'd, two Poets to a Play? }
You noisy Whiggs will sure be pleas'd to day; }
It looks so like two Shrieves the City way. }
But since our Discords and Divisions cease,
You, Bilbo Gallants, learn to keep the Peace: 5
Make here no Tilts: let our Poor Stage alone; }
Or if a decent Murther must be done, }
Pray take a Civil turn to *Marybone*. }
If not, I swear we'll pull up all our Benches;
Not for your sakes, but for our Orange-Wenches: 10
For you thrust wide sometimes; and many a Spark,
That misses one, can hit the other Mark.
This makes our Boxes full; for Men of Sense
Pay their four Shillings in their own defence:
That safe behind the Ladies they may stay;   15
Peep o'er the Fan, and Judg the bloudy Fray.
But other Foes give Beauty worse alarms;
The *Posse Poetarum's* up in Arms:
No Womans Fame their Libells has escap'd;
Their Ink runs Venome, and their Pense are Clap'd.   20
When Sighs and Pray'rs their Ladies cannot move,
They Rail, write Treason, and turn Whiggs to love.
Nay, and I fear they worse Designs advance,
There's a damn'd Love-trick new brought o'er from
     France,
We charm in vain, and dress, and keep a Pother,   25
While those false Rogues are Ogling one another.
All Sins besides, admit some expiation;
But this against our Sex is plain Damnation.
They joyn for Libells too, these Women-haters;

152

And as they club for Love, they club for Satyrs: 30
The best on't is they hurt not: for they wear
Stings in their Tayls; their onely Venom's there.
'Tis true, some Shot at first the Ladies hit,
Which able Markesmen made and Men of Wit:
But now the Fools give fire, whose Bounce is louder; 35
And yet, like mere Train-bands, they shoot but Powder.
Libells, like Plots, sweep all in their first Fury;
Then dwindle like an *Ignoramus* Jury:
Thus Age begins with Towzing and with Tumbling;
But Grunts, and Groans, and ends at last in Fumbling. 40

FINIS.

Newly Printed, The Prologue and Epilogue to the King and Queen, at the Opening of their Theatre.

Religio Laici, or a Lay-man's Faith. A Poem. Both Written by Mr. *Dryden*.

LONDON,

Printed for *Jacob Tonson*, at the *Judge's Head* in *Chancery-lane*. 1683.

A/Lenten Prologue/Refus'd by the/ Players.

Folio half-sheet; printed on both sides.
No imprint.
Wrenn Library, University of Texas.

THOMAS SHADWELL

Thomas Shadwell, son of John Shadwell of the parish of Broomhill, Norfolk, was born at Broomhill House in the parish of Weeting in 1640 or 1642. He was educated at home for five years and at the school of Bury St. Edmunds for one year. On 17 Dec. 1656 he was admitted a pensioner to Caius College, Cambridge, but left without a degree. He then entered the Middle Temple, travelled abroad, and wrote.

Although Dryden wrote a prologue for Shadwell's *A True Widow* (1679), strife arose between the two in 1682. Shadwell's *Medal of John Bayes* referred to Dryden's *Medal*, and Shadwell's *Epistle to the Tories* libelled Dryden, who had his revenge in *MacFlecknoe* and *Absalom and Achitophel, II.* In 1683 Shadwell and Thomas Hunt attacked Dryden in *Some Reflections upon the Pretended Parallel in the play called the Duke of Guise*, which Dryden answered in his *Vindication of the Duke of Guise*. In 1685 Shadwell was attacked in the *Laurel*. In 1687 Shadwell replied to *MacFlecknoe* in a translation, *The Tenth Satire of Juvenal*, by Henry Higden. In 1688 he succeeded Dryden as Poet Laureate and Historiographer Royal. He died on 19 Nov. 1692 and was buried at Chelsea on 24 Nov.

Shadwell was outstanding as a dramatist who continued the Jonsonian tradition. His wife was an actress, and one of his daughters, Anne, was Mrs. Oldfield. Shadwell's plays with the date of performance and the date of publication in parentheses, are *The Sullen Lovers* (May 1668, 1668), *The Royal Shepherdess* (Feb. 1668/9, 1669), *The Humorists* (c. Dec. 1670,

1671), *The Miser* (Jan. 1671/2, 1672), *Epsom Wells* (Dec. 1672, 1673), *The Tempest* (April 1674, 1674), *Psyche* (Feb. 1674/5, 1675), *The Libertine* (June 1675, 1676), *The Virtuoso* (May 1676, 1676), *The History of Timon of Athens* (c. Jan. 1677/8, 1678), *A True Widow* (c. March 1677/8, 1679), *The Woman-Captain* (c. Sept. 1679, 1680), *The Lancashire Witches* (c. Sept. 1681, 1682), *The Squire of Alsatia* (May 1688, 1688), *Bury Fair* (c. April 1689, 1689), *The Amorous Bigotte* (c. March 1689/90, 1690), *The Scowers* (c. Dec. 1690, 1691), *The Volunteers* (Nov. 1692, 1693).

Shadwell's occasional verse, in addition to that already mentioned, included *A Lenten Prologue, A Congratulatory Poem on His Highness the Prince of Orange's coming into England* (1689), *A Congratulatory Poem to the Most Illustrious Queen Mary* (1689), *Ode to the King on his Return from Ireland* (1690), *Ode on the Anniversary of the King's Birth* (1690), *Votum Perenne* (1692). Other poems were published in Gildon's *Poetical Remains* (1698) and Nichols's *Select Collection of Poems*, V, 298–301.

INTENDED PIECES

Prologues and epilogues in English drama were written, of course, to be spoken in the theatre; but, for a variety of reasons, some failed to attain this end. Political opposition silenced a few. Refusals from playwrights, players, and playhouses took their toll. In the final reckoning, there must have been many that fell on stony ground, for a considerable number of intended-but-never-spoken addresses survive in printed matter. Their captions are sometimes variable, and it is possible that the so-called designed and intended pieces were occasionally spoken since we do find a few published in some books as "rejected" and in others as "spoken."

Circumstances of various kinds brought prologues and epilogues into the printers' hands. Run off in the regular way in folio, quarto, octavo, or sixtcenmo, they were usually displayed by their publishers under captions in which such terms as "spoken" and "to be spoken" indicated that they were genuine stage-orations. Other addresses, however, which were not delivered were printed so that their forbidden or neglected messages might be read. The prologue and epilogue described as "Design'd to be spoken" or "Intended to have been spoken" may have attracted the attention of some curious readers, but the mystery of a piece only designed or intended must have faded into the light of common day when some publisher brought out a prologue "Refus'd" or "Rejected." In this latter class "A Lenten Prologue Refus'd by the Players," published in folio half-sheet without the name of the author, without the name of the printer or publisher, and without the place and date of publication, proves a rare piece indeed.[1]

Although even the nineteenth-century prologue or epilogue that failed to find a speaker sometimes found a publisher and came out in a separate publication,[2] three centuries lend very few examples in this rarest mode of publication:

A/Lenten Prologue/Refus'd by the/Players.
Folio half-sheet.

Another/Epilogue/Intended to have been Spoken to the/Play, before it was forbidden,/last Summer./ Written by Mr. Dryden./

London,/Printed for Jacob Tonson, at the Judge's Head in Chancery-lane. 1683.
Folio containing the prologue and another epilogue to *The Duke of Guise.*

A/Prologue,/Sent to Mr. Row,/ To his new Play, call'd The Fair Pe-/nitent. Design'd to be Spoken by Mr. Betterton; refus'd.
Quarto.

The/Prologue and Epilogue/To the Last/New Play of the Albion Queens, or, the/Death of Mary

---

[1] This folio half-sheet in the British Museum will be reprinted below.
[2] See, for example, "The Rejected Prologue," by W. H., 1872.

Queen of Scotland./Printed as they were written, but not permitted to be spoken./ Sold by J. Nutt, near Stationers-Hall. 1704. *Quarto.*

The/Rejected Prologue./By/W. H./ Melbourne:/Clarson, Massina, & Co., Printers./ 72 Little Collins Street East./1872. *Sixteenmo.*

Disappointed poets had also, of course, the miscellanies into which they might thrust a piece never spoken. *Sylvae: or, the Second Part of Poetical Miscellanies* (1685) carried a prologue intended for *A Duke and No Duke*.[1] Robert Gould's prologue designed for his own play, *The Rival Sisters*, had to be content with a mere printing in his *Poems* (1689).[2] Perhaps, Mountfort never put on the "long Presbyterian Cloak" intended for him in D'Urfey's *New Poems* (1690); and Haynes probably made no second recantation in Turkish garb, the lines which he should have spoken being printed as one of three intended pieces in the same volume.[3] Garth's "Prologue designed for Tamerlane, but never spoke" was published in *A Pacquet from Parnassus* (1702)[4] and in *Poems on Affairs of State* (1703)[5]; the same appeared in January, 1707, in *The Muses Mercury* as "A Prologue Spoken at a Representation of Tamerlane. Written by Dr. G—th"[6]; and, with some difference in text, it was printed in *A Compleat Key to the Seventh Edition of the Dispensary* (1714) under the caption: "A Prologue Designed for Tamerlane Spoke on the Irish Theatre by Mr. Moore. Written by Dr. Garth."[7] A prologue that was designed for Mr. Betterton's rendering and sent to Mr. Rowe for his *Fair Penitent* met refusal but found a place in *Poems on Affairs of State* (1704)[8] after having been published in

---

[1] P. 162.
[2] Pp. 53–54. Another edition of 1709 gives the prologue on pp. 66–67.
[3] See D'Urfey's *New Poems* (1690), pp. 112–115; 204–207.
[4] Vol. I, No. 2.   [5] Pp. 312–313.   [6] Pp. 5–6.
[7] Pp. 31–33.   [8] Pp. 417–420.

quarto in 1704. Most interesting among all forbidden pieces, however, is Dryden's "Prologue to the Opera of the *Prophetess*," which was published in *The Muses Mercury* (1707) with this informing note:

This Prologue was forbidden to be spoken the second Night of the Representation of the *Prophetess*. Mr. *Shadwell* was the occasion of its being taken notice of by the Ministry in the last Reign: He happen'd to be at the House on the first Night, and taking the beginning of the Prologue to have a *double Meaning*, and that Meaning to reflect on the *Revolution*, he told a Gentleman, *He would immediately put a stop to it*. When that Gentleman ask'd, Why he wou'd do the Author such a Disservice? He said, *Because while Mr. Dryden was Poet Laureat, he wou'd never let any Play of his be Acted*. Mr. *Shadwell* informing the Secretary of State of it, and representing it in its worst Colours, the Prologue was never Spoken afterwards, and is not Printed in Mr. *Dryden's* Works, or his Miscellanies. Whatever was the meaning of the Author then, had he liv'd to have seen the Happy Effects of the Revolution in Her present Majesty's Triumphant Reign, he wou'd have blush'd at his Poor Politicks, and Vain Malice. Tho' we say this with some warmth, we wou'd not be understood to mean any thing derogatory to Mr. *Dryden's* Merit; to which, as a Poet, we pay as much deference as any one, and think the *British* Muse indebted to him for his admirable Versification, as much as to all the Writers who went before him. Indeed, he has so refin'd our Numbers, that he has taught all who follow him, to do better in that kind, than those who were famous for their Excellence in it in the last Century.[1]

It is evident that books of verse offered the poets a good

[1] *The Muses Mercury* (1707), pp. 4–5.

chance to salvage their "intended" prologues and epilogues. The list runs on, and the reader who looks further will find such examples as Lord Lansdowne's Epilogue designed for *The British Enchanters* printed in his *Poems upon Several Occasions* (1712); an Epilogue to *The Way of the World*, "Design'd to have been spoken by Mrs. Cross," published with *A Poem on the Drawing Room*, by T. B. Gent., 1716; "An Epilogue, Design'd to be spoke" for *The Beaux Stratagem* (1736) in the second volume of *The Works of the late Ingenious Mr. George Farquhar;* "Prologue in a Halter. Design'd to have been Spoke by Penkeman, at the first opening his New Theatre in Richmond" in *The Second Part of Penkethman's Jests* (1721); "Epilogue to Jane Shore. Design'd for Mrs. Oldfield" in *Miscellaneous Poems and Translations*, by several Hands, 1722; and "An Epilogue, Design'd to be spoken by Mrs. Woffington, in the Character of a Volunteer" printed in *A Banquet of the Muses* (1746).

In the quartos of plays likewise we find prologues and epilogues that were intended for a performance but were never spoken. Examples here, as in the miscellanies, are much more frequent in the eighteenth century than in the seventeenth.[1] In Corey's *The Metamorphosis* (1704) is Charles Johnson's prologue designed for Mrs. Verbruggen; in Swinny's *The Quacks* (1705), an epilogue "forbid to be spoke." Thomas Baker's epilogue designed to be repeated by Mrs. Bracegirdle at Mrs. Centlivre's *The Platonick Lady* arrived too late but was published with the play in 1707. An epilogue intended for Mrs. Oldfield came out in Mrs. Centlivre's *The Perplex'd Lovers* (1712). For the person who "should have play'd Joan to Cloudy" there was an epilogue designed and then printed in *The Mohocks* (1712). A prologue by an unknown hand was published with *Lady Jane Gray* (1715). In each instance the playbook carried the spoken pieces as well as the belated.

Chief perhaps among all rejected prologues surviving in

---

[1] See Duffett's *The Amorous Old Woman* (1674), with a prologue intended but not spoken; Walker's *Love without Interest* (1699), with a prologue designed to have been spoken by Powell.

separate publication is "A Lenten Prologue refus'd by the Players." The Reverend Montague Summers says it may be ascribed to Shadwell and reprints one text in his edition of Shadwell's works.[1] Thomas Shadwell did not make the writing of prologues and epilogues his absorbing occupation. His name appears with an epilogue spoken by Mrs. Barry in Maidwell's *The Loving Enemies* (1680) and an epilogue spoken by Mrs. Bracegirdle in Brady's *The Rape* (1690); but he appears to have written stage-orations almost always for his own plays.

From internal evidence we know that the Lenten Prologue was written after the publication of Dryden's *The Medal* in March 1681/2, as Mr. Summers points out in his Introduction to *The Complete Works of Thomas Shadwell*.[2] In fact, Mr. Summers says it appeared almost immediately afterwards; but in his *The Restoration Theatre*, p. 179, he mentions the date, 11th April, 1683. The prologue was published in *A Third Collection of Poems . . . against Popery* (1689)[3] with a date in the title: "A Lenten Prologue Refus'd by the Players. 1682;" and like designation occurs in *The Muses Farewell to Popery* (1690, second edition), pp. 163–166, *State Poems* (1697), pp. 154–156, and *Poems on Affairs of State*, Part II (1697), pp. 163–166. Mr. Summers reprints the prologue in *The Complete Works* with a similar caption,[4] but he says in his notes[5] that the text is from the "original broadside 1682." His text varies from that of the folio half-sheet which I reprint here.

---

[1] *The Complete Works of Thomas Shadwell* (London: The Fortune Press, 1927), I, clxxxi; II, 242–244.
[2] Vol. I, p. clxxxi.
[3] Pp. 26–27.
[4] Vol. V, pp. 242–244.
[5] Vol. V, p. 409.

A
Lenten Prologue
Refus'd by the
PLAYERS.

Our Prologue-Wit grows flat: the Nap's worn off;
And howsoe're We turn, and trim the Stuff,
The Gloss is gone, that look'd at first so gaudy;
'Tis now no Jest to hear young Girls talk Baudy.
But Plots, and Parties give new matter birth;   5
And State Distractions serve you here for mirth!
At *England's* cost Poets now purchase Fame ⎤
While factious Heats destroy us, without Shame ⎬
These wanton Neroes fiddle to the Flame. ⎦
The Stage, like old Rump-Pulpits, is become   10
The Scene of News, a furious Party's Drum.
Here Poets beat their brains for Volunteers,
And take fast hold of Asses by their Ears.
Their jingling Rhime for Reason here you swallow;
Like *Orpheus* Musick it makes Beasts to follow.   15
What an enlightning Grace is want of Bread?
How it can change a Libeller's Heart, and clear a
        Laureats Head!
Open his eyes till the mad Prophet see   Medal
Plots working in a future power to be   P. 14
Traitors unform'd to his *Second Sight* are clear; ⎤   20
And Squadroms here, and Squadrons there appear; ⎬
Rebellion is the *Burden* of the *Seer*. ⎦
To Bayes in Vision were of late reveal'd
Whigg-Armies, that at Knights-bridge lay   (Rehearsal
        conceal'd.   Com. p. 31.
And though no mortal eye could see't before   25
The Battaile was just entring at the Door!   (Rehearsally
A dangerous *Association*—sign'd by None!   Comedy p. 52
The Joyner's Plot to seize the King alone!

161

Stephen with *Colledge* made this Dire compact; ⎫
The watchful *Irish* took 'em in the Fact— ⎬ 30
Of riding arm'd! Oh Traiterous *Overt* Act! ⎭
With each of 'em an ancient Pistol sided;
Against the Statute in that Case provided.
But why was such an Host of Swearers prest?
Their succour was ill Husbandry at best. 35
Bayes's crown'd Muse, by Sovereign Right of Satyre,
Without desert, can dubb a man a Traitor.
And Toryes, without troubling Law, or Reason,
By loyal Instinct can find Plots and Treason.
But here's our Comfort, though they never scan 40
The merits of the Cause, but of the Man,
Our gracious Statesmen vow not to forsake
Law—that is made by Judges whom they Make.
Behind the Curtain, by Court-Wires, with ease
They turn those Plyant Puppets as they please. 45
With frequent Parliaments our hopes they feed,
Such shall be sure to meet—but when there's Need.
When a sick State, and sinking Church call for 'em,
Then 'tis our Tories most of all abhor 'em.
Then Pray'r, that Christian Weapon of defence, ⎫ 50
Gratefull to Heaven, at Court is an Offence, ⎬
If it dare speak th' untamper'd Nations sence. ⎭
Nay Paper's Tumult, when our Senates cease;
And some Men's Names alone can break the Peace.
Petitioning disturbs the Kingdom's Quiet; 55
As choosing honest Sheriffs makes a Ryott.
To punish Rascals, and bring *France* to Reason, ⎫
Is to be hot, and press things out of Season; ⎬
And to damn Popery is *Irish* Treason. ⎭
To love the King, and Knaves about him hate, 60
Is a Fanatick Plot against the State.
To Skreen his Person from a Popish Gun
Has all the mischief in't of *Forty One*.
To save our Faith and keep our Freedom's Charter,
Is once again to make a Royal Martyr. 65

This Logick is of Tories deep inditing
The very best they have—but Oaths, and Fighting.
Let 'em then chime it on, if 'twill oblige yee,
And *Roger* vapour o're us in *Effigie*.
Let 'em in Ballads give their folly Vent,   70
And sing up Nonsence to their Hearts content.
If for the King (as All's pretended) they
May here drink Healths, and curse, sure We may pray.
Heaven once more keep him then for *Healing Ends*
Safe from old Foes—but most from his new Friends! 75
Such Protestants as propp a *Popish* Cause,
And loyal men, that break all Bound of Laws!
Whose Pride is with his Servants Salaries fed,
And when they've scarce left him a Crust of Bread,
Their corrupt Fathers foreigne Steps to follow,   80
Cheat even of scraps, and that last Sopp would swallow.
French Fetters may this Isle no more endure;
Spite of *Rome's* Arts stand *England's* Church secure,
Not from such Brothers as desire to mend it,
But false Sons, who designing worse to rend it   } 85
With leud *Lives*, and no-*Fortunes* would defend it.

Finis.

The / Prologue and Epilogue / To
The / City Politicks. / The Prologue
spoken by Mr. Smith. /
The Epilogue spoken by Mr. Lee
in the Character/of Bartaline the Old
Lawyer. /
London : Printed for Tho. Benskins
in St. Brides Churchyard, 1683.

Folio half-sheet; printed on both sides.
Imprint at bottom of p. 2.
The Henry E. Huntington Library.

For the biographical sketch of the author, John Crowne,
see p. 18.

THE PROLOGUE AND EPILOGUE TO
THE CITY POLITICKS

Crowne's *The City Politicks*, attacking Shaftesbury, was licensed
on 15 June 1682, as a "new Comedy,"[1] but on 26 June the Lord
Chamberlain banned the play in an order to Betterton:

> Whereas I did signifie His Ma^{tes} pleasure in my
> Order dated ye 15th of June instant that a New Play
> of M^r. Crownes called (blank) should be lycensed &
> Acted at His Royall Highnesse Theatre I doe now
> againe signifie His Ma^{tes} pleasure that you forbeare
> acting ye said play vntill further Order.[2]

[1] L. C. 5/144, p. 247. Allardyce Nicoll, *A History of Restoration
Drama* (1928), n. 1, p. 259.
[2] Nicoll, *loc. cit.*

Almost six months passed before it was permitted, the "further order" giving leave to act coming on 18 December 1682. Mr. Nicoll thinks *The City Politicks* was not performed before the opening of the new year. It was printed for R. Bentley and Joseph Hindmarsh in 1683, with a prologue and an epilogue showing no significant textual variations from the prologue and epilogue printed in folio half-sheet for Thomas Benskins in 1683. A date in manuscript, "20 Jan. 168$\frac{3}{2}$," appears on a copy of the prologue and epilogue in folio half-sheet in the Huntington Library.

Like their play, Crowne's prologue and epilogue are political, and they belong to a group of stage-orations that were journalistic in their conception. The prologue, in the usual mode, was spoken by William Smith, whose position as a stage-orator has been described[1]. The epilogue, in a style less frequently adopted, began with prose dialogue recited by two gentlemen and Anthony Lee (or Leigh) in the character of an old lawyer, Bartoline, and concluded with a conventional address in heroic couplets which Leigh spoke in the manner of a counsellor. The prologues and epilogues recited by Leigh are not numerous,[2] but assignments of this kind fell to him during some thirty years.

[1] See pp. 59, 101, 146.
[2] Appendix C.

The
Prologue and Epilogue
To The
City POLITICKS.

The PROLOGUE spoken by Mr. *SMITH*.

Good Heaven be thank'd, the frenzy of the Nation
Begins to cure, and Wit to grow in fashion:
Long the Two Theatres did proudly jarr,
And for chief sway, like two Republicks Warr;
When of the sudden a devouring Host   5
Of dreadful Knights, (I say not of the Post)
But strange tongue Warriors over-run the Town,
And blew the Stage, almost the Kingdom down.
And with the Stage the Poets must expire,
For Bells will melt, if Steeples be on Fire;   10
Then Coffee-houses Theatres were grown,   ⎫
Where Zealots acted in a furious tone   ⎬
Oliver's Porter, Damming *Babylon*.   ⎭
But they more Mad; for he in his worst Fit
Was ne're so Mad as to talk *TREASON* yet.   15
'Tis strange those Men should wish the *POPE* such evil,
Who are so kind to the *POPE'S* Friend, the *DEVIL!*
They Drink, they Whore, and at there Rulers Rant,
And all is well in a True *PROTESTANT*.
Those follies have the Nation long employ'd,   20
Almost all the *POETS* Trade destroy'd.
That they may justly seek Reprizals now,
And Board those Pirates which brought them so low,
Seize on that Ware by which some Men by stealth,
Promote the Traffick of a Common-wealth: 25
Ware some believe by Priests and Jesuits Spunn,
They Weave the Cloath, *FANATICKS* put it on.
But some will say, a *POET* mend the Age!
In these high matters how dare they engage?
Why, *SIRS*, a Poets Reformation scorn;   30

Since the Reformers now all Poets turn?
And by their awkward jangling Rhimes proclaim,
Like Bells rung backward, that the Towns on Flame?
The City Whiggs such cursed Poets chuse,
For that alone they should their *CHARTER* lose.   35
He is a wretched Coxcomb, who believes
Muses, like *JURIES*, will be pack'd by *SHERIFFS*.
But their ill Palate no fine dressing needs,   ⎫
All stuff that any Whiggish fancy breeds,   ⎬
They swallow down, and live like Ducks on Weeds. ⎭ 40
These things give all the Nations round delight,
Sure at our Fools to laugh we have most right.
Let's not our mirth to foraign Kingdoms send,
But here the growth of our own Country spend.
Heaven knows what sums the *CAUSE* has cost this
      Town!   45
Here you may have it all for Half-a-Crown.

The E P I L O G U E spoken by Mr. L E E in the Character
      of *Bartaline* the Old Lawyer.

Enter a Gentleman to Bartaline.

   1. *Gent.* Sir, I come to you from certain worthy
Gentlemen the world is pleased to call *Whiggs*.
   Bar. Whiggs? Sir, they are the Props and Pillars of
the Nation.
   1. *Gent.* Sir, There is a Poet has been so bold as
to write a Play against 'em, in which several of 'em
think themselves abused; now, Sir, they desire to
know if they have not an *Action of Slander* against the
Poet?
   Bar. Ay, ay, Sir, he's a Rascal.
   1. *Gent.* And may not have considerable dammages?
   Bar. Oh! very considerable—
   1. *Gent.* Here are Two Pieces.

Bar. Two Pieces—? pretty indifferent dammages—I believe they may have some Dammages.

1. *Gent.* Here's one great person thinks himself much abus'd, and has sent you 20 Pieces.

Bar. Sir, he shall have great Dammages, he shall trounce the Poet, a Rascal to abuse great persons.

1. *Gent.* I'le tell him.——*Ex.*

Enter a second Gent.

2. Sir, I come to you from a person that wants your Councel, but he is a swingeing *Tory.*

Bar. Well, he's ne're the worse man, provided he has a swingeing Purse.

2. Sir, he has writ a Play against Faction, and some *Whiggs* think themselves hit home in it, and they are bringing *Actions of Slander* against him to punish him.

Bar. Sir, if he has hit the *Whiggs* home he is a good Marks-man, for now they are all upon the Wing.

2. Sir, he desires to know whether there lies an *Action of Slander* against him or no? and so, whether he had best compound the business in time, or go through with it?

Bar. Oh! let him go through with it.

2. And you will assist him?

Bar. Ay, ay, in private.

2. But he has no Money, he must Sue in *Forma Pauperis.*

Bar. Forma Pauperis? Oh! damn'd Rogue, does he abuse great men and has he no Money? Tell him I have consider'd it, and I won't defend a slanderous Rascal in abusing honest men.

2. You said you would help him through with it.

Bar. Ay, through the Pillory. A Rascal without Money abuse great men, and then Sue in *Forma Pauperis!*—Come the Court is sat.—I must Plead for the Plaintiff.

You Learned, Reverend Judges in this place,

John Crowne

I come to Plead here in a weighty Case;
And I beseech you quickly make an end on't,
The *WHIGGS* are Plaintiffs, *POET* is Defendant.
I'me for the Plaintiffs, they have Coyn good store;   5
Poets are in the wrong, because they're poor.
And I ne're mind a Cause but as I'me Feed,
Like Quacks, we Cure no Man that will not bleed.
WHIGGS are my Clyents; And, my Lords, I say,
They have been scandaliz'd in a damn'd Play,   10
Which those good men for busy Fops does jear,
Who vigilant for Church and State appear.
What if such men should have no wit at all?
Pray did not Geese once save the Capital?
But say these honest men be in the wrong,   15
Railing does to no private men belong;
Boldly to Rail is one of the chief spriggs
Of the Prerogative of Prince of Whiggs;
TITUS the first, who did that Power attain,
—I take it—*Anno primo*—of his Reign—   20
From *WHIGGS*, to whom by Custome it belongs,
WHIGGS are all Freeholders of their Tongues,
And Pens too.—
I'le prove it out of *Janeway's* Reports,
And the Decrees of sev'ral Coffee-Courts.   25
The *POET* has no title then to rail,
Let him be seiz'd, nor let Wit be his Bayl.
Wit is a Tory, ne're with us would joyn,
Wit never help'd the Whiggs to write one Line.
'T has been accus'd, and in our Writings sought;   30
But still the Coroner *Non inventus* brought.
But Learned Judges, I leave all to you,
If you're for *TORIES*, I will be so too.
Noint Witches, they will fly, though ne're so old;
I'le be as nimble too, noint me with Gold: 35
I'le quickly to the Tory party skip,
Greaze my Fist well, I'le let our Faction slip.   FINIS.

LONDON : Printed for *Tho. Benskins* in St. *Brides Church yard*, 1683.

Prologue to Dame Dobson the
Cunning Woman./Spoken by Mrs.
Currer./
Epilogue to the Same !/Spoken by
Mr. Jevorn./
London : Printed for Jo. Hind-
marsh, Bookseller to his Royal
Highness, at the/Black Bull in Corn-
hil, 1683.

Folio half-sheet; printed on both sides.
Imprint at bottom of p. 2.
British Museum.

EDWARD RAVENSCROFT

Edward Ravenscroft was descended from an ancient family
once located in Flintshire. In 1671 he was a member of the
Middle Temple, and in July 1672 his first play, *The Citizen
turn'd Gentleman*, was performed at Dorset Garden. For
twenty-five years he occupied himself with play-writing, his
dramas being *The Citizen turn'd Gentleman* (1672), reissued
as *Mamamouchi* in 1675; *The Careless Lovers* (1673), acted in
March 1672/3; *The Wrangling Lovers* (1677), acted c. Sept.
1676; *Scaramouch a Philosopher*, etc. (1677), acted in May
1677; *King Edgar and Alfreda* (1677), acted c. Dec. 1677;
The English Lawyer (1678), acted c. Dec. 1677; *The London
Cuckolds* (1682), acted in Nov. 1681; *Dame Dobson* (1684),
acted c. Sept. 1683; *Titus Andronicus* (1687), acted c. April
1686; *The Canterbury Guests* (1695), acted in Sept. 1694;
The Anatomist (1697), acted c. March 1697; *The Italian*

Husband (1698), acted in 1697. Ravenscroft had no close rival among his contemporaries in farce. It was his habit to borrow materials freely, but he adapted his borrowings with skill. In addition to his plays, he wrote prologues and epilogues, several of his epilogues being composed for fellow dramatists. His quarrel with Dryden, which attracted considerable attention, began with the original prologue to *Mamamouchi* (1671, 1675), which referred to Dryden's plays of "rhyme and noise." Dryden answered in the prologues to *Marriage A-la-Mode* (1673) and *The Assignation* (1673). Ravenscroft continued the quarrel in the prologue to *The Careless Lovers* (1673).

BRIEF CHRONICLES OF THE PLAYHOUSE

Before Jeremy Collier attacked the immorality of the stage, literary criticism, even more than moral philosophy, had efficaciously rebuked the corrupt playhouse of the Restoration, and the prologue reprinted here is an interesting comment from the theatre upon this changing taste of the eighties. Zeal for reform was already burning in the English bosom. Criticism, according to Spingarn, "was evolving a theory of poetry in which obscenity could find no place."[1]

More than a passing interest attaches itself, therefore, to Ravenscroft's unwilling right-about-face described in the lines spoken by Mrs. Currer. In November 1681 in *The London Cuckolds* he had given his audience a taste of the vulgar and immoral, but a little less than two years made a change in the people for whom he wrote. He had to give them *Dame Dobson* in 1683, putting Mrs. Currer "quite out of heart" because she had no smutty jests in all the play:

> His *London Cuckolds* did afford you sport.
> That pleas'd the Town, and did divert the Court.
> But 'cause some squeamish Females of renown
> Made visits with design to cry it down,

[1] *Critical Essays of the Seventeenth Century*, ed. J. E. Spingarn, (by permission of the Clarendon Press, Oxford) I, lxxxiv.

He swore in's Rage he would their humors fit,
And write the next without one word of Wit,
    No Line in this will tempt your minds to Evil,
It's true, 'tis dull, but then 'tis civil.
No double sense shall now your thoughts beguile,
Make Lady Blush, nor Ogling Gallant Smile.[1]

Saucy Mrs. Currer had spoken a prologue to *The Counterfeit Bridegroom* in 1677, an epilogue to D'Urfey's *Squire Oldsapp* in 1678, a prologue to Mrs. Behn's *The Feign'd Curtizans* in 1678/9, an epilogue to Tate's *The Loyal General* in 1679, and an epilogue with other players for Ravenscroft's *The London Cuckolds* in 1681, before she came to make her bright appearance in this prologue to *Dame Dobson*, commenting upon the taste of the day in a tone which years after would seem editorial to ears acquainted with newspapers. That is, as a matter of fact, the way of many prologues and epilogues in this period; they are brief editorial comments to be spoken to folk whose avidity for news gave rise to journalism.

Choosing a personal point of view, likewise, Jevon surveyed the scene with fervour, spicing his critical epilogue with the humour that we have already learned to expect in his rôles.[2] But after noting the indisputable fact that his lines rebuke the times, we may look at the style of the exposition for something distinctly interesting to those readers who watch for the interplay of literary forms. The character-essay of the seventeenth century has entered into this epilogue, in the passage on the critic, as it entered into a goodly number, uniting timely comment with type-portraiture.

Characters of critics appeared occasionally in prologues and epilogues before 1660. In the epilogue to *Wily Beguilde* a brief character of the censurer appeared:

But if there be, (as tis no doubt there is)
In all this round some Cinique censurers,
Whose onely skill consists in finding faults,

---

[1] From the Prologue to *Dame Dobson*, folio half-sheet, 1683.
[2] For Jevon, see pp. 94–95 and Appendix C.

That have like Midas mightie Asses eares,
Quicke iudgements that will strike at everie stale,
And perhaps such as can make a large discourse
Out of Scoggins iests, or the hundred merrie tales.[1]

At the beginning of the seventeenth century, the gallant who censured a play with as much assurance as he judged the cut of a beard provoked comment which showed the influence of the character-manner:

> . . . As some one ciuet-wit among you, that knowes no other learning than the price of setten and vellets; nor other perfection, then the wearing of a neat sute; and yet will censure as desperately as the most profess'd critique in the house: presuming, his clothes should beare him out in't.[2]

After Jonson, the benches and three-footed stools came more and more to serve as jury chairs; and, as critics of a severe nature, beaux and gallants provoked comment in prologues and epilogues. After 1660 no less than fifty-six per cent. of the characterizations in prologues and epilogues referred to the dress of the man of fashion, forty-two per cent. to his conduct. In fact, during the years in which poets were frequently practising the art of character-writing prologues and epilogues commented upon the critics, their prerogative to rail[3] and their habit of entering into cabals.[4]

---

[1] *Wily Beguilde* (1606), Printed for the Malone Society (London: The Oxford University Press, 1912), Epilogue.

[2] Ben Jonson, *Cynthia's Revels* (1616), Induction: The Third Child's speech.

[3] See for example, Lee's *Lucius Junius Brutus* (1681), Prologue; D'Urfey's *A Common-Wealth of Women* (1686), Prologue: Mountfort's *The Injur'd Lovers* (1688), Prologue; The Earl of Orrery's *Herod the Great* (1694), Epilogue; Congreve's *The Way of the World* (1700), Epilogue; Trapp's *Abra-Mule* (1704), Prologue; D'Urfey's *The Modern Prophets* (1709), Preface; Charles Johnson's *The Generous Husband* (1711), Prologue.

[4] See, for example, Dryden's *Sir Martin Mar-all* (1668), Epilogue; D'Urfey's *The Richmond Heiress* (1692), Prologue.

To this hostile crew, the poets made reply in defiant and threatening verse:

> For if you dare but Whisper one false Note
> Here in the House, or passing to take Boat
> Good faith I'll mow you off with my short sword,[1]

and Jo Haynes did really come on the stage, not with Davenant's sword, but with a Western Scythe in his hand when he spoke the prologue to D'Urfey's *A Common-Wealth of Women* (*1686*):

> From the West, as Champion in defence of Wit,
> I come, to mow you Critticks of the Pit.

Occasionally, some poets were moved to write several lines portraying these fault-finding grievances of the playhouses, and in such passages I have found a few characters, such as we have in the epilogue to *Dame Dobson*. A single metaphor, like the epigrams in Francis Meres' *Wits Recreations*,[2] portrayed the critics in the epilogue to Tate's *Cuckolds-Haven*, presented in May, 1685:

> But Criticks are a sort of Country-men,
> Their Valour of the true Militia-Strein;
> Who from the fighting Foe, like Lightning fled,
> But come like Thunder back, to Maul the Dead.[3]

In the prologue to D'Urfey's *The Common-Wealth of Women*, presented in the same year, probably in September, a character of critics appeared, illustrating the portrait that introduced occasional metaphors and similes to heighten the satire; and again, in part illustrative of the conceited style, the epilogue to Congreve's *The Mourning Bride* (1697) sketched the critics. Several other prologues and epilogues remarked upon the

---

[1] Sir William Davenant, *News from Plimouth*, Epilogue, *Works* (1673).
[2] See, for example, Francis Meres, *Wits Commonwealth* (1640), 40. Man:
    Man's like the earth, his hair like grasse is grown,
    His veins the rivers are, his heart the stone.
[3] Nahum Tate, *Cuckolds-Haven* (1685), Epilogue.

critical wit and reflected the influence of the character-sketch in their methods, but the passages were not, strictly speaking, *characters* because of their failure to attain totality of impression or form.

Ravenscroft sometimes furnished other dramatists' plays with epilogues. His friend, Mrs. Aphra Behn, received such assistance for her *Debauchee* (1677) and her *Town-Fopp* (1677). Bancroft's first play, *The Tragedy of Sertorius* (1679), had an epilogue by Ravenscroft, and Whitaker's only drama, *The Conspiracy* (1680), closed with one of Ravenscroft's epilogues. These contributions to fellow playwrights' undertakings preceded the prologue and epilogue to *Dame Dobson*, reprinted here from the folio half-sheet of 1683.[1]

[1] No significant textual differences occur in the prologue and epilogue printed with the play in 1684.

Prologue to *Dame Dobson* the *Cunning Woman*.
Spoken by Mrs. Currer.

Gallants, I vow I am quite out of heart,
I've not one smutty Jest in all my part.
Here's not one Scene of tickling Rallery;
There we quite lose the Pit and Gallery.
   His *London Cuckolds* did afford you sport.   5
That pleas'd the Town, and did divert the Court.
But 'cause some squeamish Females of renown
Made visits with design to cry it down,
He swore in's Rage he would their humors fit,
And write the next without one word of Wit.   10
   No Line in this will tempt your minds to Evil,
It's true, 'tis dull, but then 'tis very civil.
No double sense shall now your thoughts beguile,
Make Lady Blush, nor Ogling Gallant Smile.
   But mark the Fate of this mis-judging Fool!   15
A Bawdy Play was never counted Dull,
Nor modest Comedy e're pleas'd you much,
'Tis relish'd like good Manners 'mongst the *Dutch*.
In you, Chast Ladies, then we hope to day,
This is the Poets *Recantation* Play   20
Come often to't that he at length may see
'Tis more than a pretended Modesty:
Stick by him now, for if he finds you falter,
He quickly will his way of writing alter;
And every Play shall send you blushing home,   25
For, tho you rail, yet then we're sure you'll come.
Thus Brides are Coy and Bashful the first night,
But us'd to't once, are mad for their delight.
Do not the *Whiggish* Nature then pursue,
Lest like *Whig-Writer*, he desert you too.   30
Whig-Poet when he can no longer Thrive,
Turns *Cat in Pan* and writes his *Narrative*.
No *Irish* Witness sooner shall recant,
Nor oftner play the *Devil* or the *Saint*.

Edward Ravenscroft

Epilogue to the Same!
Spoken by Mr. Jevorn.

Tho I am no great Conjurer you see
Nor deal in Devil or Astrology,
Yet from your Physnomies I shrewdly guess
The Poet stole the *French Divineress*
But let not that, pray, put you in a passion,   5
Kidnapping has of late been much in fashion.
If Alderman did *Spirit* men away,
Why may not Poets then Kidnap a Play?
Poets are Planters, Stage is their Plantation,
But tho they are for Trade and Propagation,   } 10
Yet don't like *Thievish Whiggs* Rob their own Nation. }

   But, Fellow Citizens, beware Entrapping,
For, whilst y'are busie sending Folks to *Wapping*, }
'Ygad your Wives e'ne go abroad *Kidnapping*. }
Tending to this, of late I heard such stories,   15
That I for safety Marry'd 'mongst the Tories.
And see from City Prigg I am become
A *Beau Garcon*, a man of th' *Sword: rare Thumb!*
Jerné I am all *Tory* now, *par ma foy*
I hate a *Whigg:* I'm *l'Officiere du Roy*.   20
And now I bid defiance to the City,
Nor *Whig*, nor *Critick* shall from me have pitty.
And as in Valour, I in Wit am grown,
Then to 'em *Gillet;* let 'em know their own.

   You *Whigs*, but *Criticks* are amongst the *Cits*   25
And *Criticks* are meer *Whigs* amongst the *Wits*.
Thro your cross Nature you'l no mercy show,
But would the *Monarchy* of *Wit* o're throw;
And *Criticks* here with the same spirit stickle
For *Liberty*, as Whigs in *Conventicle*   30
'Gainst *Sheriffs* and *Poets* equally you Baul,
You Riot in a *Play-House*, they't *Guild-Hall*.

   But Noise, you see, and Faction often fails,
Law is our Shield against your *Prot'stant Flails*

Law and large *Fines* may send you all to Jails.. 35
And if you *Criticks* here are troublesome
I'l *Diametrically* upon you come,
And maul you with my Charm, *Firm*, *Close*, *Standfast*
  Thumb!
  Then there's your Wheadling Critick, seems a Friend,
Commends by halves, and with a *But* i'th' end, 40
Has sly reserves which still to Faction tend.
They praise a Play, and on the Poet fleer,
But, his back turn'd, loll out their tongue and Jeer.
Thus amongst *Wits*, as *Whiggs* too, these are Trimmers,
They'r like a sort of *Half Crowns* we call Swimmers. 45
Broad to the Eye, but though the Stamp seems fair
Weigh 'em they're light, and damn'd *mixt Metal* are.
These blame the *City*, but uphold their *Charter*, ⎫
They Rail at *Treason*, but give Traitors Quarter, ⎬
And when a *Rebel's* hang'd, they stile him Martyr. ⎭ 50
For *Perjur'd Villains* they wou'd have *Reprieve*
And to *False Witnesses* can *Pensions* give,
Yet won't allow a *Mayor* may choose his Sheriff.
They cry, to Magistrates we'l give all Honor:
But let's have *Law :*—Then Holloo—take him *Coroner.* 55
  But, Friends, don't think that you shall longer Sham us,
Or that we'll Bugbear'd be by your Mandamus;
You see *Dame Dobsons* Devil long was famous,
But fail'd at last: so will your *Ignoramus.*

London : Printed for *Jo. Hindmarsh*, Bookseller to his Royal Highness, at the Black Bull in *Cornhil*, 1683.

The/Prologue and Epilogue,/To The Last New Play ;/Constantine the Great./—/Prologue.   Spoken by Mr. Goodman :/
Epilogue./Spoken by Mrs. Cook,/ Printed for C. Tebroc, 1683.

Folio half-sheet; printed on both sides.
Imprint at bottom of p. 2.
Chetham Library, Manchester.

A True Coppy/Of The/Epilogue/ To/Constantine the Great./That which was first Published being false printed/ and surreptitious./—/Written by Mr. Dryden./—/
London, Printed for J. Tonson, at the Judge's Head in Chancery-lane, 1684.

Folio half-sheet; reverse blank.
Imprint at bottom of p. 1.
Mr. P. J. Dobell's private collection.

Opinion differs concerning the authorship of the prologue. For the biographical sketch of Thomas Otway, see pp. 52–53; for Nathaniel Lee, pp. 111–112.

For the biographical sketch of the author of the epilogue, John Dryden, see pp. 33–35.

THE PROLOGUE AND EPILOGUE TO
CONSTANTINE THE GREAT

The broadside prologue and epilogue to Lee's *Constantine the Great* has not passed without scholars' notice. Mr. R. G. Ham[1] and Mr. J. C. Ghosh,[2] in particular, have spoken out of their full knowledge of the works of Otway and Lee. The prologue they are inclined to give to Otway, Mr. Ghosh calling attention to the fact that it was included by Tonson in his edition of Otway's collected works in 1712 but attributed to Lee by Richard Wellington in his publication of Lee's collected works in 1713, and Mr. Ham finding it "tragically in keeping with the lives of both poets." Uncertainty in this matter of attribution arises out of the fact that the prologue and epilogue were published in broadside in 1683, without mention of authorship, and printed in the first quarto edition of *Constantine the Great* in 1684, without indication that Lee was not their maker. Usually, as Mr. Ghosh says, when a poet other than the playwright wrote a prologue or an epilogue for a drama, his name appeared with his lines. The absence of a name would imply that the author of the play wrote his own prologue and epilogue; therefore, the omission of names in the broadside before us clouds the records.

I may cite from my study of prologues and epilogues some practices in publication which will throw light upon our question. Sometimes a prologue or an epilogue written by a playwright for his own play does not carry his name when published in broadside. See, for example, "The Prologue to Pastor Fido," with no author named, though a manuscript note "Written by Elkanah Settle 1677" appears on the folio half-sheet in the Bodleian; and turn to the Prologue and Epilogue to D'Urfey's *The Royalist*, published in broadside, without naming D'Urfey. *Venice Preserved* shows two practices.

---

[1] *Otway and Lee*, pp. 208–209.

[2] A letter to *The Times Literary Supplement*, 14 March, 1926; *The Works of Thomas Otway*, I, 65.

The first broadside, printed for A. Green, 1681, names Otway the author of the prologue to his own work:

> Prologue./By Mr. *Otway* to his *Play* call'd *Venice preserv'd*, or the *Plot/discover'd*. . . .

But the second broadside, printed for A. Banks, 1682, omits Otway's name:

> Prologue/To a New Play, called/Venice Preserv'd;/or/The Plot/Discover'd. . . .

We see that when a playwright is the author of the prologue and epilogue to his own play, his name does sometimes appear in the broadside; as for example, in "A Prologue by Mr. *Settle* to his New Play, called *The Emperor of Morocco*" and in "A Prologue By Mrs. *Behn* to her New Play, called *Like Father, like Son*." As a further contribution to this matter, I may call attention to a fact which I have stated in this book and which shows an earlier play of Lee's to offer a problem of somewhat similar nature, *Mithridates*. A prologue and an epilogue written for a performance of this play in 1681 were printed in broadside without the name of the poet who wrote them, but a manuscript note by Luttrell on the broadside in the Huntington Library assigns both poems to Dryden. In fact, Dryden's property in prologues and epilogues is still without a clear title, and the intricacies of publication involved in broadsides, playbooks, and miscellanies puzzle often, as the reader will see in the discussion of Dryden's Prologue to Mrs. Behn's *The Widow Ranter*.

The epilogue of the folio half-sheet published by Tebroc in 1683 was "false printed and surreptitious." A true version was published by Tonson in 1684:

> A True Coppy/Of The/Epilogue/To/Constantine the Great./That which was first Published being false printed/and surreptitious./—/Written by Mr. Dryden./—/
> London, Printed for J. Tonson, at the Judge's Head in Chancery-lane, 1684.

Tonson again attributed the epilogue to Dryden in *Miscellany Poems*, Part I, Third Edition, 1702, although he made no mention of Dryden in the first quarto edition of *Constantine the Great* (1684), of which he was one of the publishers. For such omission there is parallel. Dryden's authorship was stated in the "True Coppy" (1684), though overlooked in the quarto edition of the play (1684); Otway's authorship of the prologue to *Venice Preserved* was not repeated in 1682 after its announcement in 1681.

The significant variant readings of the epilogue published by Tebroc (1683) and that of the play (1684)[1] show that the epilogue in *Constantine the Great* (1684) is that of the "True Coppy" (1684), with minor variations in spelling, capitalization, and punctuation.

Dryden's very rare broadside epilogue, published by Tonson in 1684, was sold by Sotheby & Company to Mr. P. J. Dobell in June, 1939. Its text is reprinted in this book. To the left of "Written by Mr. Dryden," a manuscript note by Luttrell records a date: 14. Nov. 1683.

---

[1] The prologue printed in *Constantine the Great* (1684) shows no significant variations from the text of the folio half-sheet of 1683, but the epilogue differs in the following: l. 13, *to say* (1683), *saying* (1684); l. 28, *Sends* (1683), *Breeds* (1684); l. 29, *Treason Trimmers* (1683), *these Trimmers* (1684); l. 30, *they dare not Her, it wants Supply* (1683), *they cannot keep it in their eye* (1684); l. 36, *Mind* (1683), *Head* (1684); l. 37, *those* (1683), *these* (1684).

The
Prologue and Epilogue,
To The Last New Play;
Constantine the Great.

PROLOGUE, *Spoken by* Mr. Goodman:*

What think ye meant Wise Providence, when first
POETS were made? I'de tell you if I durst.
That 'twas in Contradiction to Heaven's Word,
That when its Spirit o're the Waters stir'd,
When it saw All, and said that All was good,   5
The Creature *POET* was not understood.
For were it worth the pains of Six long Days,   ⎤
To Mould Retailers of dull Third-Day-Plays,   ⎬
That starve out Three-score Years in Hopes of Bays.   ⎦
'Tis plain they ne're were of the First Creation,   10
But came by meer Equiv'cal Generation.
Like Rats in Ships, without Coition bred;
As hated too, as they are, and unfed.
Nature their Species sure must needs disown,
Scarce knowing *POETS*, less by *POETS* known.
Yet this Poor Thing so scorn'd, and set at nought,
Ye all pretend to, and would fain be thought.
Disabl'd wasting *Whore-Masters*, are not
Prouder to own the Brats they never got;
Then Fumbling Itching Rhimers of the Town,   20
T' Adopt some base Born Song that's not their own.
Spite of his State, my Lord sometimes Descends,
To please the Importunity of Friends.
The dullest He thought most for business fit,
'Twill Venture his bought Place, to Aim at Wit.   25
And though He sinks with His Imploys of State,
Till Common Sense forsake Him, He'l Translate.

* Concerning Goodman, see pp. 41–42 and Appendix C.

The *POET* and the *WHORE*, alike Complains
Of Trading Quality, that spoils their Gains;
The Lords will Write, and the Ladies will have
    Swains.   30
Therefore all you, who have Male Issue born,
Under the Starving Sign of *CAPRICORN;*
Prevent the Malice of their Stars in Time,
And warn them Early from the Sin of Rhime.
Tell 'em how *Spencer* starv'd, how *Cowley* mourn'd,   35
How *Butler's* Faith and Service was return'd;
And if such Warning they refuse to take,
This last Experiment, O Parents make!
With Hands behind them see the Offender ty'd,
The Parish Whip, and Beadle by his Side.   40
Then lead him to some Stall that does Expose
The Authors he loves most, there rub his Nose,
Till like a Spannel lasht, to know Command,
He by the due Correction understand,
To keep his Brains clean, and not foul the Land.   45
Till he against his Nature learn to strive,
And get the Knack of Dulness how to Thrive.

EPILOGUE.
Spoken by Mrs. Cook.*

Our *Hero's* Happy in the Plays Conclusion,
The Holy Rogue at last has met Confusion;
Tho' *Arrius* all along appear'd a Saint,
The last Act shew'd him a True Protestant:
Eusebius (for you know I Read Greek Authors)   5
Reports, That after all these Plots and Slaughters,
The Court of *CONSTANTINE* was full of Glory,
And every *TRIMMER* turn'd addressing *TORY:*
They Followed Him in Herds as they were Mad,
When *CAUSE* was King then all the World was Glad: 10

* Concerning Mrs. Cook, see p. 69 and Appendix C.

WHIGGS kept the Places they Possess'd before,
And most were in a Way of Getting more;
Which was as much as to say—*Gentlemen*,
Here's Power and Money to be ROGUES *agen.*
Indeed there were a sort of peaking Tools,   15
(Some call 'em Modest, but I call 'em Fools,
Men much more *Loyal*, though not half so *Loud*,)
But these Poor Devils were Cast *Behind* the Crowd.
For Bold Knaves Thrive without one Grain of Sense,
But Good Men Starve for want of Impudence.   20
Besides all these there were a sort of Wights,
I think my Authour calls 'em *Teckelites*:
Such hearty Rogues against the King and Laws,
They favour'd even a Forreign Rebell's Cause.
When their own Damn'd Design was quasht and aw'd, 25
At last they gave it their Good Word abroad;
As many a Man, who for a quiet life,
Sends out his Bastard, not to Nose his Wife:
Thus o're their Darling *Treason Trimmers* Cry,
And though they dare not Her, it wants Supply,   30
They Bind it Prentice to Count *TECKELEY*.
They believe not the last *PLOT*, may I be Curst,
If I believe, they e're believ'd the first.
No Wonder their own *PLOT*, no *Plot* they think,
The Man that makes it never Smells the STINK.   35
And now it comes into my Mind, I'le tell,
Why those Damn'd *Trimmers* love the *TURK* so well;
Th' Original *Trimmer*, tho' a Friend to no Man,
Yet in his heart Ador'd a pretty Woman:
He knew that *MAHOMET* laid up for Ever   40
Kind Black-Ey'd Rogues for ev'ry True Believer.
And which was more then Mortal Man e're Tasted,
One Pleasure that for Threescore Twelve-Months lasted:
To Turn for this may surely be Forgiven,
Who'd not be Circumcis'd for such a HEAVEN?   45

Printed for *C. Tebroc*, 1683.

A TRUE COPPY
Of The
EPILOGUE
To
CONSTANTINE the *GREAT*.
That which was first Published being false printed and
surreptitious.
Written by Mr. Dryden.

Our Hero's happy in the Plays Conclusion,
The holy Rogue at last has met Confusion:
Tho' *Arius* all along appear'd a Saint,
The last Act shew'd him a true Protestant.
Eusebius, (for you know I read Greek Authors,)   5
Reports, that after all these Plots and Slaughters,
The Court of *Constantine* was full of Glory,
And every *Trimmer* turn'd Addressing *Tory;*
They follow'd him in Heards as they were mad:
When *Clause* was King, then all the World was glad.   10
Whigs kept the Places they possest before,
And most were in a Way of getting more;
Which was much as saying, Gentlemen,
Here's Power and Money to be Rogues again.
Indeed there were a sort of peaking Tools,   15
Some call them Modest, but I call e'm Fools,
Men much more Loyal, tho' not half so loud;
But these poor Devils were cast behind the Croud.
For bold Knaves thrive without one grain of Sence,
But good men starve for want of Impudence.   20
Besides all these, there were a sort of Wights,
(I think my Author calls them *Teckelites;*)
Such hearty Rogues, against the King and Laws,
They favour'd even a Foreign Rebel's Cause.
When their own damn'd Design was quash'd and aw'd, 25
At least they gave it their good Word abroad.
As many a Man, who, for a quiet Life,

186

Breeds out his Bastard, not to nose his Wife;
Thus o're their Darling Plot, these *Trimmers* cry;
And tho' they cannot keep it in their Eye,   }30
They bind it Prentice to Count *Teckely*.
They believe not the last Plot, may I be curst,
If I believe they e're believ'd the first;
No wonder their own Plot, no Plot they think;
The Man that makes it, never smells the Stink.   35
And, now it comes into my Head, I'le tell
Why these damn'd *Trimmers* lov'd the *Turks* so well.
The Original *Trimmer*, tho' a Friend to no man,
Yet in his heart ador'd a pretty Woman:
He knew that *Mahomet* laid up for ever,   40
Kind black-eyed Rogues, for every true Believer:
And, which was more than mortal Man e're tasted,
One Pleasure that for threescore Twelve-months lasted:
To turn for this, may surely be forgiven:
Who'd not be circumcis'd for such a Heav'n!   45

London, Printed for *J. Tonson*, at the Judge's Head in *Chancery-lane*, 1684.

Prologue/To a New Play, Call'd,/
The Disappointment:/or,/The Mother
in Fashion./Spoken by Mr. Betterton./
Epilogue/By Another Hand./
London, / Printed for E. Lucy.
M.DC.LXXXIV.

Folio half-sheet; printed on both sides.
Imprint at bottom of p. 2.
The Henry E. Huntington Library.

For the biographical sketch of the author of the prologue,
John Dryden, see pp. 33–35.

The author of the epilogue, the Hon. John Stafford, may
be mentioned in Narcissus Luttrell's *A Brief Historical Relation
of State Affairs* (Oxford: At the University Press, 1857), I,
399: "Capt. Browns troop is given to lieutenant Vaughan,
and capt. Fairfaxe's to Mr. Stafford, son to the late lord
Stafford."

FOR SOUTHERNE'S THE DISAPPOINTMENT

Frequently, Southerne's plays were accompanied by
prologues and epilogues that came from other hands.[1] Dryden
was the first to lend support to Southerne's work, his prologue
and epilogue assisting the young dramatist's début as a playwright in *The Loyal Brother* of 1682. Southerne's second play,
The Disappointment, likewise leaned upon a prologue by the
Laureate while an epilogue of disputed authorship concluded
the performance. This epilogue, described in the folio half-
sheet as a piece "By Another Hand," is ascribed to the Hon.

[1] Dryden, John Stafford, Esq., Congreve, Charles Boyle, Esq., Colonel
Codrington, Fenton, Major Pack, Welsted, and George Jeffrys, Esq.

John Stafford,[1] although sometimes contained in Dryden's pieces. Saintsbury, when including the prologue in *The Works of Dryden*,[2] added a note on the epilogue:

> An epilogue to the same play has sometimes (though not by Scott) been assigned to Dryden. It will appear in the 'Doubtful Poems.'

This piece, beginning with the line:

> "You saw your wife was chaste, yet throughly tried,"

carried the following notation: "'An Epilogue' Date and occasion not known.—Ed."[3]

Concerning both prologue and epilogue, Genest remarked:

> . . . there are two lines in the Prologue and two in the Epilogue more than usually indecent—the Epilogue is a good one—but what is very odd, in the play is attributed to the Hon. John Stafford: and yet it is printed in Dryden's poems; but without being appropriated to any particular play.[4]

Southerne's plays often had female prologues and epilogues spoken by such glamorous actresses as Mrs. Barry and Mrs. Bracegirdle,[5] but the greatest actor of the day, Thomas

---

[1] See, for example, *The Poems of John Dryden*, ed. John Sargeaunt, Oxford University Press, 1929, p. 249, note on the Prologue to *The Disappointment*: "The Epilogue is printed in some editions as Dryden's. It was rightly rejected by Christie on the ground of its ascription in the collected edition of Southern's plays to the Hon John Stafford. It has escaped the notice of editors that the same ascription is made in the original edition of the play. The statement that the Prologue was spoken by Betterton is omitted by the editors."

[2] Ed. Scott, 1885, X, 291–303.

[3] Saintsbury-Scott, *op. cit.*, X, 421.

[4] *Op. cit.*, I, 419.

[5] Mrs. Barry's epilogues to *The Wives Excuse* (1692) and *The Fate of Capua* (1700) and her prologue to *The Maid's Prayer* (1693), Mrs. Bracegirdle's prologues to *Sir Anthony Love* (1691) and *The Fatal Marriage* (1694) and her epilogue to *The Maid's Last Prayer* (1693), Mrs. Botelar's epilogue to *Sir Anthony Love* (1691), Mrs. Verbruggen's epilogues to *The Fatal Marriage* (1694) and *Oronooko* (1699), and Miss Younger's epilogue to *Money the Mistress* (1726).

Betterton, repeated prologues for *The Disappointment* (1684) and *The Wives Excuse* (1692). Powell, Cibber, and Quin followed him in this service.[1]

The prologue and epilogue to *The Disappointment* are reprinted here from the folio half-sheet printed for E. Lucy in 1684. No notable variation from this original text was made in the first edition of the play, 1684. Today's interest in the two pieces depends, no doubt, upon the authorship and the position of *The Disappointment* in the development of a new problem drama that was sentimental and moral.

---

[1] Powell's prologue to *Oronooko* (1699), Cibber's prologue to *The Spartan Dame* (1719), and Quin's prologue to *Money the Mistress* (1726).

PROLOGUE
To a NEW PLAY, Call'd,
The Disappointment:
or,
The Mother in Fashion.
Spoken by Mr. Betterton.

How comes it, Gentlemen, that now aday's
When all of you so shrewdly judge of Plays,
Our Poets tax you still with want of Sence?
All Prologues treat you at your own Expence.
Sharp Citizens a wiser way can go;   5
They make you Fools, but never call you so.
They, in good Manners, seldom make a Slip,
But, Treat a Common Whore with Ladyship:
But here each sawcy Wit at Random writes,
And uses Ladies as he use's Knights.   10
Our Author, Young, and Grateful in his Nature,
Vow's, that from him no Nymph deserves a Satyr.
Nor will he ever Draw—I mean his Rhime,
Against the sweet Partaker of his Crime.
Nor is he yet so bold an Undertaker   15
To call MEN Fools, 'tis Railing at their MAKER.
Besides, he fears to split upon that Shelf;
He's young enough to be a FOPP himself.
And, if his Praise can bring you all A-bed,
He swears such hopeful Youth no Nation ever bred.   20
Your Nurses, we presume, in such a Case,   ⎫
Your Father chose, because he lik'd the Face; ⎬
And, often, they supply'd your Mothers place. ⎭
The Dry Nurse was your Mothers ancient Maid,
Who knew some former Slip she ne're betray'd.   25
Betwixt 'em both, for Milk and Sugar Candy,
Your sucking Bottles were well stor'd with Brandy.
Your Father to initiate your Discourse   ⎫
Meant to have taught you first to Swear and Curse; ⎬
But was prevented by each careful Nurse.   ⎭   30

For, leaving Dad and Mam, as Names too common,
They taught you certain parts of Man and Woman.
I pass your Schools, for there when first you came,
You wou'd be sure to learn the Latin name.
In Colledges you scorn'd their Art of thinking,   35
But learn'd all Moods and Figures of good Drinking:
Thence, come to Town you practise Play, to know
The Vertues of the High Dice, and the Low.
Each thinks himself a SHARPER most profound:
He cheats by Pence; is cheated by the Pound: 40
With these Perfections, and what else he Gleans, ⎫
The SPARK sets up for Love behind our Scenes;   ⎬
Hot in pursuit of Princesses and Queens.   ⎭
There, if they know their Man, with cunning Carriage,
Twenty to one but it concludes in Marriage.   45
He hires some Homely Room, Love's Fruits to gather,
And, Garret-high, Rebels against his Father.
But he once dead—
Brings her in Triumph, with her Portion down,
A Twillet, Dressing-Box, and Half a Crown.   50
Some Marry first, and then they fall to Scowring,
Which is, Refining Marriage into Whoring.
Our Women batten well on their good Nature,
All they can rap and rend for the dear Creature.
But while abroad so liberal the DOLT is,   55
Poor SPOUSE at Home as Ragged as a Colt is.
Last, some there are, who take their first Degrees
Of Lewdness, in our Middle Galleries:
The Doughty BULLIES enter Bloody Drunk,
Invade and grubble one another's PUNK: 60
They Caterwaul, and make a dismal Rout,
Call SONS of WHORES, and strike, but ne're lugg-out:
Thus while for *Paultry Punk* they roar and stickle,
They make it *Bawdier* than a CONVENTICLE.

EPILOGUE
By Another Hand.

You saw our Wife was Chaste, yet throughly try'd,
And, without doubt, y'are hugely edify'd;
For, like our Heroe, whom we shew'd to day,
You think no Woman true, but in a Play;
Love once did make a pretty kind of Show,   }   5
Esteem and Kindness in one Breast wou'd grow, }
But 'twas Heav'n knows how many years ago.   }
Now some small Chatt, and Guinney Expectation,
Gets all the pretty Creatures in the Nation:
In Comedy, your Little Selves you meet;   10
'Tis *Covent-Garden*, drawn in *Bridges-street*.
Smile on our Author then, if he has shown,
A jolly Nut-brown Bastard of your own.
Ah! Happy you, with Ease and with Delight,
Who act those Follies, Poets toil to write!   15
The sweating Muse does almost leave the Chace,
She puffs, and hardly keeps your *Protean* Vices pace.
Pinch you but in one Vice, away you fly
To some new Frisk of Contrariety.
You rowle like Snow-Balls, gathering as you run,   20
And get seven Dev'ls, when dispossess'd of one.
Your *Venus* once was a *Platonique* Queen,
Nothing of Love beside the Face was seen;
But every Inch of Her you now Uncase,
And clap a Vizard-Masque upon the Face.   25
For sins like these, the Zealous of the Land,
With Little Hair, and Little or no Band,
Declare how circulating Pestilences
Watch every Twenty Years, to snap Offences.
Saturn, even now, takes Doctoral Degrees,   30
Hee'l do your work this Summer, without Fees.
Let all the Boxes, *Phœbus*, find thy Grace,
And, ah, preserve thy Eighteen-penny Place!

But for the Pit Confounders, let 'em go,
And find as little Mercy as they show: 35
The Actors thus and thus, thy Poets pray;
For every Critick sav'd, thou damn'st a Play.

LONDON,
Printed for *E. Lucy*. M.DC.LXXXIV.

VolV.   Joe Haines Epilogue.   p.233.

British Museum

JOE HAYNES SPEAKING THE ASS-EPILOGUE

Prologue/To the Northern Lass.
By J. H./
Epilogue./Spoken by Mrs. Butler./
Printed for C. Corbet at the Oxford-
Arms in Warwick-lane.   1684.

Folio half-sheet; printed on both sides.
Imprint at bottom of p. 2.
British Museum.

JOSEPH HAYNES

Joseph Haynes (or Haines), player, attended the school of
St. Martin-in-the-Fields, London, and was sent to Queen's
College, Oxford, where he attracted the attention of Joseph
Williamson, a fellow of the College. Later, when made
secretary of state, Sir Joseph Williamson appointed Haynes
his Latin secretary. Dismissed for lack of discretion, Haynes
went to Cambridge and joined a company of comedians at
Stourbridge fair. By 1668 he was at the Theatre Royal, being
then a talented dancer. After the burning of the Theatre
Royal in Jan. 1671/2 Haynes was sent to Paris by Hart and
Killigrew to examine the machinery of French opera.

Popular in many parts, Haynes played in 1667 Jamy in
Lacy's *Sauny the Scott* (printed in 1698); in 1672, Benito in
Dryden's *The Assignation;* in 1674/5, Sparkish in Wycherley's
The Country Wife; in 1675, Visconti in Fane's *Love in the Dark;*
in 1676, the First Lord Plausible in Wycherley's *The Plain
Dealer;* in 1677, Gregory Dwindle in Leanerd's *The Country
Innocence,* Harlequin in Ravenscroft's *The Scaramouch,* and Sir
Simon Credulous in Chamberlayne's *Wits led by the Nose;* in
1677/8, Launce in D'Urfey's *Trick for Trick;* in 1678, Whiffler
in E. Howard's *The Man of New Market;* in 1684, Bullfinch in

Brome's *The Northern Lass;* in 1685, Bramble in Tate's *Cuckolds-Haven*, Hazard in D'Urfey's *A Common-wealth of Women;* in 1692, Depazzi in Shirley's *The Traytor* (reprint, 1692); in 1692/3, Captain Bluffe in Congreve's *The Old Bachelor;* in 1694, Gines de Passamonte in D'Urfey's *Don Quixote*, Part I; in 1696, Roger in Vanbrugh's *Aesop*, Syringe in Vanbrugh's *The Relapse;* in 1697, Rumour in Dennis' *Plot and No Plot;* in 1699, Clown in *Othello*, Pamphlet and Rigadoon in Farquhar's *Love and a Bottle*, and Tom Errand in Farquhar's *The Constant Couple;* in 1700, Doctor in Burnaby's *The Reformed Wife*. Famous also as a speaker of prologues and epilogues, Haynes appeared often as a stage-orator (Appendix C). At the same time, he was also a writer of verse and drollery.

Haynes' career was picturesque in detail. Arrests were not novelties for Joe, and witty pranks were almost the rule of his life. He turned Catholic in the reign of James II and made sport of his case. In his *Dramatic Miscellany*, III, 267, Davies repeats a story told by Quin about Lord Sunderland, who summoned Haynes and questioned him about his religious conversion. Haynes said the Virgin appeared to him while he was lying in his bed and commanded: "Arise, Joe!" "You lie, you rogue," said the earl; "if it had really been the Virgin herself, she would have said Joseph, if it had only been out of respect for her husband." A recantation Prologue records Haynes' views concerning conversion and reconversion.

Haynes died in Hart Street, in Long Acre, and was buried in the churchyard of St. Paul's, Covent Garden. *The Life of the Late Famous Comedian, Jo Hayns* was published in 1701. In this year there was an announcement of a benefit for a Mrs. Hains, appearing in *The Post Man* (May 1–3, 1701), *The Flying Post* (May 1–3, 1701), and *The Post Boy* (May 1–3, 1701).

PLAYHOUSE-WIT FOR NOVELTY

The sudden and surprising fusion of ideas known as wit was a prize sought with eager emulation in the days of Charles II, when elevated fancies titillated the society of the Restoration.

Joseph Haynes

Among the men who prided themselves upon some kind of wit in that age was a merry Tom Fool of the playhouse named Jo Haynes. His acting on the stage, writing and speaking clever verse, and tricking men of the streets amused England and the Continent from 1672 to 1700. Tricksy Haynes posed as the wittiest of men and refused to be kept in obscurity. As a player, he interpreted wit as the prating noise and laughter of a jovial man, the lying invention of a babbling courtier, the repartee of an airy court-wit, the conceit of a town-wit, and the pose and officious plotting of a fawning attendant. As a matter of fact, it was in the rightful territories of wit—namely, the contrivances of his own—that Jo Haynes proved himself a playhouse-wit. There he was often cast to play the manipulator, jealous of his fame and striving always to be Rex wherever he was.

Haynes showed a wit's impudence when composing verse and speaking and singing his own lines in the theatres. The extent of his activity as an author has not been defined; but from the extant broadsides up to 1700 in the libraries in England and the United States, the manuscripts in the British Museum, and more than three hundred miscellanies available in the libraries in England, I have culled twenty-one items that carry the name of Haynes as their author. These are satires, ballads, prologues and epilogues, and songs set to music.[1] At times, nice problems in attribution arise, however, when, for instance, the epilogue to Crowne's *The Ambitious Statesman*, spoken by Haynes, gets into print in *A Collection of State Poems* (1704) as a prologue written and spoken by Jo Haynes. Crowne made a complaint in the preface to his play in 1679 that his enemies were denying him the authorship of his epilogue:

> . . . Much is lost by Poetry; Time, Pains, and often Friends: Nothing is gotten but a little Reputation, and that some envious Enemies of ours will

---

[1] For the prologues and epilogues, see Appendix B. Information concerning other pieces will be given in a separate study of Haynes now in preparation.

rather fling to the Doggs than let us have it, witness the silly malice of some Adversaries of mine, who because my *Epilogue* had great success, wou'd let any thing rather than me be the Author; though I had succeeded aswel in the same kind in my *Epilogues* to both my *Jerusalems*, since my Enemies are such little creeping Creatures, as not to dare to look in the Face a good Play, but to bite at the Tayl, 'tis a shame to oppose 'em.

As composer and speaker of prologues and epilogues, Haynes enjoyed a flattering vogue. No other player's name was called so often as his in the occasional addresses of the theatre and in the writings that took satiric and journalistic note of the times.[1] Though a good actor and poet, he received highest praise for his prologues and epilogues, one opinion being that he was "more remarkable for the witty, tho' wicked, Pranks he play'd, and for his Prologues and Epilogues, than for Acting."[2] Wittiest of our speakers, he spoke his own verse as well as poems by Brown, Congreve, Duffett, D'Urfey, and Motteux; and in all his addresses[3] there is the vivid impress of the man who often spoke of himself,[4] put on mourning

---

[1] See, for example, Prologue to *The Rival Kings* (1677); Epilogue to Mrs. Behn's *Like Father, like Son* (1682); Robert Gould's *The Play-House. A Satyr* (1685); Prologue to Mountfort's *The Injur'd Lovers* (1687); D'Urfey's *New Poems* (1690); pp. 204–207; Langbaine's *English Dramatick Poets* (1691), p. 102; *The Reasons of Mr. Joseph Hains the Player's Conversion & Reconversion* (1691); Epilogue to Bancroft's *Henry II* (1693); Prologue to Dennis's *A Plot, and No Plot* (1697); *Familiar Letters*, Tom Brown to "My Lady" (1697), p. 194; Dryden's Epilogue to *The Pilgrim* (1700); *Letters from the Dead to the Living* (1702); *The Life of the Late Famous Comedian, Jo. Hayns* (1701); Tom Brown's *Dialogues of the Dead* (1702); "The Long Vacation Epilogue" in *Apollo's Feast* (1703); *Mr. Collier's Dissuasive from the Play-House* (1704), p. 30; *Memoirs Relating to the late Famous Mr. Tho. Brown* (1704), p. 8; "The Stage Vindicated" in the *Muses Mercury*, July, 1707.

[2] *A Brief Supplement to Colley Cibber, Esq; His Lives of the late Famous Actors and Actresses* (N.D.), p.20.

[3] Appendix C.

[4] "I'll boast 'twas I, Jo. Haynes, reform'd the Age," *Apollo's Feast* (1703), p. 162.

British Museum

MR. SHUTER, AS HE SPOKE THE EPILOGUE,
ON AN ASS

and promised to reform,[1] sang snatches, danced, made faces, and forsook his poet's text to speak his own wit, as a note in *Neglected Virtue* indicates:

> Here Mr. *Hains* made several pleasant Digressions, too long to be inserted; and to make place for 'em, omitted some Lines of this Epilogue.[2]

In 1677 this penchant for stage oratory brought Haynes the heartiest applause ever given an epilogue-speaker. He rode a donkey on to the stage and spoke the epilogue to Thomas Scott's *The Unhappy Kindness* (1677), beginning:

> Wherefore by th' Example of Fam'd Dogget, my Brother,
> To shew our Stage has Asses on't as well as t'other;
> Thus mounted I'm come . . .

The laughter and applause on this occasion were so great that Haynes was almost an hour speaking the lines.[3] No other novel epilogue inspired so many imitations beyond the middle of the eighteenth century. Its wit was good for more than one hundred years to come. And although other actors made frequent use of it, the genius that Haynes lent to its interpretation left so deep an impress that fifty-six years after he died when an engraver pictured Shuter riding an ass and speaking this epilogue, he forgot the author, Tom Brown, and wrote beneath the engraving:

> Mr. Shuter, one of his Majesty's Comedians, Drawn, as he spoke Joe Haynes's Epilogue, Riding an Ass.

Glancing backward, as well as forward, we may trace the history of this most popular stage novelty. From the end

---

[1] "Thus Cloath'd with shame, which is one step to Grace," *Apollo's Feast* (1703), p. 131.
[2] Motteux's Epilogue to *Neglected Virtue* (1696), by C. Hopkins.
[3] *British Theatre* (1752), p. 120.

of the sixteenth century, when the bear or "any other beast"
came forth running in the Introduction to *The Lamentable
Tragedy of Locrine* (1586, pr. 1595), to 1715, when Penkethman was still riding his long-eared mount to fame, were some
one hundred and twenty years during which London playgoers
saw prologues and epilogues draw their novelty from a small
theatrical menagerie of real or personated kind. By 1665 the
fashionable prologue was, according to Dryden,[1] one spoken
by "some ingenious Bird or Beast"; but the Laureate's words
speak more emphatically upon this point than evidence at
hand. Up to this date, 1665, I can point out one signal example:
the farcial prologue to *Ignoramus* (1614; 1662 at Court) with
a talking horse, who thrust himself "into the company of the
nobility" by speaking a prologue. Without failing to note
the claims of a lap-dog to chronological priority, since he
bowed his *humble Congé* to the pit in an epilogue to D'Urfey's
The Marriage Hater Match'd in January, 1691/2, we may say
the vogue of the animal-piece really began in Dorset Garden
with D'Urfey's *Don Quixote*, Part I, in 1694, when Dogget,
riding an ass, spoke the epilogue to which Haynes referred
in 1697. Dogget's lines were printed in *Apollo's Feast* (1703)
with Haynes named as the speaker, but it appears that this
epilogue to *Don Quixote*, Part I, or another earlier and similar,
was Dogget's.

The ass-epilogue was adopted by the master showman,
Penkethman, as his main vehicle and used with astonishing
frequency from 1702 through 1716. During this period
there were at least twenty-seven occasions when the epilogue-
speaker rode a mount, twenty-four of these being Penkethman's when he rode an ass, two being Pack's when he rode a
pad-nag, one being Spillar's when he rode an elephant. The
mount—particularly the ass—owed his popularity to Will
Penkethman, for his beast-epilogue was announced in play-
bills more often than any other epilogue. In fact, it appears
to have attained the distinction of being continued, with
modifications, in 1707 in a vocal "Epilogue after the Old

[1] Prologue, *The Indian Emperor*, c. April, 1665.

Joseph Haynes

English manner, Compiled and Spoken by the famous Singer Signior Pinkethmano, upon an Ass," burlesqued in an epilogue in 1708/9, and revived as a "new Epilogue" in 1711 and 1712. Penkethman appeared in his best-known after-piece at least fifteen times before he joined Bullock in a burlesque on the ass-epilogue at Cibber's *The Rival Fools* (1708/9) in Drury Lane, when Penkethman said:

"I'm better—with an Ass to back me,"

and Bullock, mounted on Penkethman—the famous rider of the ass, addressed the audience in these words:

And is't not just, that I shou'd now keep down,
The Ass that has so often rid the Town?

Before this farcical epilogue ended, Penkethman rode Bullock, and the two fools of the stage closed their trifling with the words:

"I'm an Ass as well as You."

Essentially comic, these epilogues accompanied comedies for the most part, though two tragedies and one opera accepted the services of the dull ass.[1] Other entertainers of less frequent use were the talking horse,[2] the pad-nag,[3] the elephant,[4] the lion,[5] the parrot,[6] and the dog[7]—many of them with stage-names announced to their audiences: Dony, Dapple, Bucephalus, and Dobbin, the Nimble Pad. Playwrights whose dramas were accompanied by these performers

[1] The tragedies: Scott's *The Unhappy Kindness*, 1697; Beaumont and Fletcher's *Bonduca*, 1716; the farcical opera: Mrs. Behn's *The Emperor of the Moon*, 1707/8.
[2] Prologue, Codrington's *Ignoramus* (1614; 1662 at Court).
[3] Epilogues to Mrs. Centlivre's *The Gamester*, 1704/5, and Vanbrugh's *The Confederacy*, 1705.
[4] "An Epilogue spoken by Mr. Pinkeman, upon the Back of an Elephant," *The Third Volume consisting of Poems on Divers Subjects*, by the Author of the *London Spy* (1706), pp. 347–350.
[5] Prologue, Farquhar's *The Recruiting Officer*, 1712.
[6] Epilogue, D'Urfey's *Wonders in the Sun*, 1706.
[7] Epilogue, D'Urfey's *The Marriage Hater Match'd*, 1691/2.

are Beaumont and Fletcher,[1] Behn,[2] Betterton,[3] Brome,[4] Centlivre,[5] Cibber,[6] Codrington,[7] Congreve,[8] Dryden,[9] D'Urfey,[10] Farquhar,[11] Ben Jonson,[12] Norris,[13] Ravenscroft,[14] Ruggle,[15] Scott,[16] Shadwell,[17] and Vanbrugh.[18] It appears that only D'Urfey and Scott intended animal-pieces for their plays, for in all other examples this particular novelty in epilogues accompanied revivals. With but two exceptions after 1660, the animal assisted the epilogue; and I have found only one announcement of an actor mounted upon an ass in a prologue before 1716. The animal-piece enjoyed considerable vogue as late as the nineteenth century, no doubt, because it was adopted by such popular comic actors as Dogget, Haynes, Penkethman, Pack, Cibber, Spillar, Shuter, and Liston.

To this ever-increasing vogue of novelty, Haynes gave more than a passing attention. He knew popularity in many modes, but he never enjoyed praise so enduring as that which came when he mounted an ass to speak an epilogue. Even the engraver made him immortal in the rôle, passing the spectacle

---

[1] *The Royal Merchant*, 1706; *Bonduca*, 1716.
[2] *The Emperor of the Moon*, 1707/8; *The Rover*, 1710.
[3] *The Amorous Widow*, 1711.
[4] *The Northern Lass*, 1705/6, 1706.
[5] *The Gamester*, 1704/5.
[6] *Love Makes a Man*, 1707, 1712.
[7] *Ignoramus*, 1614; 1662.
[8] *The Way of the World*, 1715.
[9] *An Evening's Love*, 1716.
[10] *The Marriage Hater Match'd*, 1691/2; *Don Quixote*, Part I, 1694; *Wonder in the Sun*, 1706.
[11] *The Recruiting Officer*, 1707; *The Stratagem*, 1708; *The Constant Couple*, 1716, 1752.
[12] *The Silent Woman*, 1709.
[13] *The Royal Merchant*, 1706.
[14] *The London Cuckolds*, 1702.
[15] With Codrington, *Ignoramus*, 1716.
[16] *The Unhappy Kindness*, 1697.
[17] *The Miser*, 1703; *The Lancashire Witches*, 1704; *The Squire of Alsatia*, 1704; *The Libertine*, 1709.
[18] *The Confederacy*, 1710.

on to posterity in Brown's *Works* (1702), IV, opposite p. 233. The ass, or another, seems to have worn its original regalia a number of years after Jo Haynes was dead, for in *The Royal Merchant* (1706) the epilogue is described thus: "Spoken by Mr. Pinkeman, mounted on an Ass; a long whig on the Ass's Head." It had no wig in 1752.

Playing in the theatre, writing verse, seeking always to be the manipulator in affairs whether his own or other men's, Haynes knew life to be a battle of wit. If he could not be a real wit, he would fain be a little wit or, at least, think himself one. Speaking upon the subject, he is here in the rôle of poet and actor in a rare broadside, the Prologue and Epilogue to the *Northern Lass*, 1684. In both pieces, says Genest,[1] "there are some good lines, but they must not be quoted."

[1] Vol. I, pp. 420–421.

PROLOGUE
To the *Northern Lass*. By *J. H.*

If any here, this Prologue, does cry down,
Henceforth I'le not allow one Wit i'th' Town:
As Houses haunted with ill Spirits, are
All Noise, and Lies, such, is our *Theatre*.
Ye talk of *Wits*, the Devil a *Wit* is here. 5
Wherefore to let you know
What Wit is not, I think can't be amiss,
For no man here, I'me sure, *knows* what it is.

First then,

Wit is no *Scarf* upon *Phantastick* Hips, 10
Nor an *affected Cringe*, t'approach the *Lips*.
'Tis not, *I gad*, *O Lord*, or, *let me die*,
Nor is it *Damme ye Son of a Whore, ye Lie*:
'Tis not to tell how lewd you were last Night,
What *Watches*, *Wenches*, *Windows* felt your spite; 15
Nor is it an abusive Epilogue,
Nor being Drunk, and cry, *more Wine ye Dog*:
'Tis not the *Pert*, *Dull*, *Nonsense*, e'ry day
Ye teaze the *Gallery Nymphs* with, who t'each Play,
Like *Weavers*, with unlawfull *Engines*, come 20
And manage *twenty Shuttles* with one *Loom*;
Whilst honest *labourers* that use but one,
For want of work, lie *still*, and are undone:
'Tis not your *Scholar*, *Trav'ler*, nor *Math'matician*,
Poet, nor *Player*, and faith 'tis no *Physician*: 25
Were I now *clapt* I were in a sweet *condition*.
'Tis none of these, that, singly, *Wit* can be,
But all in one man meeting's, *Wit*; *that's Me*.

Joseph Haynes

EPILOGUE.
Spoken by Mrs. Butler.

Gentlemen,
When this Old Play first came upon the Stage,
You see 'twas e'en like now, a Whoring Age.
And youre Forefathers, in those Grandame days,
Kind, much like you·for Wit, and Vertue praise.
Wherefore I mean t'advise you all to Night: 5
Give good attention, Sparks, and profit by't.
I've long since observ'd, with mighty grief of mind,
You're like my Knight, to Widows much inclin'd:
They're grown a common Vice, Match-maker sell 'em;
Ugly or Old some buy 'em, others steal 'em.   10
Consider by a Youth, well Made, well bred,
Much in his Veins, though little in his Head,
Shou'd quit Delights, yet hardly well enjoy'd,
Shou'd be so soon with Love's sweet Manna cloy'd,
And on that Naucious bit, a Widow, venter,   15
That rank *Egyptian* Flesh-pot with a Joynter.
A Widow! what's a Widow? Let me see,
Nothing so like a Sapless hollow Tree.
And thus the Parallel most aptly holds,
The Screech-Owl's in her Branches when she scolds. 20
She with much Mossy rottennesss o'regrown,
From her late Husband's and her own,
Who weds her lives a Prisoner in a Tomb,
Decay'd, disquiet, and I* smell his Doom.
Hee's haunted all the Day with Jealous Sprights,   25
And horrid, due Benevolence a Nights:
The poor endeav'ring Creature does his best,
Yet the foul Fiend, as greedy as before,
Still with unsatiate Fury, yells out more.

* In the edition of the play (1684) this is "I'le" while an imperfection
in the folio half-sheet leaves only "I" to be made out. There are no important
textual variations to make note of.

Which Curse light on you all for your deceiving,   30
While we poor Younlings are too much believing,
He who next wrongs a kind yielding Maid,
Too apt, by specious Oaths to be betray'd,
In recompence for Spoils so basely got,
That bottomless pit of Widow be his Lot.   35

Printed for C. Corbet *at the* Oxford-Arms *in* Warwick-lane. 1684.

The/Prologue/To/Mr. Lacy's New Play, Sir Hercules / Buffoon or the Poetical Esquire./—/Written by Tho. Durfey, Gent./—/Spoken by Mr. Haynes./—/

London,/Printed for Joseph Hindmarsh, Bookseller to / His Royal Highness, living/at the Black Bull in Cornhill. 1684.

Folio half-sheet; printed on both sides.
Imprint at bottom of p. 2.
British Museum.

The/Epilogue/To/Mr. Lacy's New Play, Sir Hercules/Buffoon, or the Poetical Esquire. / — / Wrote and Spoke by J. H. Com./—/

London,/Printed for Joseph Hindmarsh, Bookseller to / His Royal Highness, living/at the Black Bull in Cornhill. 1684.

Folio half-sheet; printed on both sides.
Imprint at bottom of p. 2.
British Museum.

For the biographical sketch of the author of the prologue, Thomas D'Urfey, see pp. 46–47.

For the biographical sketch of the author of the epilogue, Joseph Haynes, see pp. 195–196.

D'URFEY'S PIECES

D'Urfey and Haynes wrote the addresses that accompanied Lacy's *Sir Hercules Buffoon* when it was acted at Dorset Garden in 1684, and Haynes spoke both the prologue and the epilogue. It is not unusual to find these two men in close association, for Thomas D'Urfey was a composer of novel prologues and epilogues suited to the talents of Jo Haynes. In his plays and in *New Poems* (1690),[1] *Apollo's Feast* (1703),[2] and *Wit and Mirth* (1700,[3] Vol. IV, 1709;[4] Vols. I, II, III, V,[5] 1719), he published many of his pieces

[1] "A Prologue By way of Satyr, spoke before King Charles II. at New-Market," "Epilogue to the Opera of Dido and Aeneas, performed at Mr. Preist's Boarding-School at Chelsey; Spoken by the Lady Dorothy Burk," "Prologue spoken by Mr. Hains to Trapolin, or a Duke and no Duke," "An Epilogue intended for a late Comedy, and to be spoke by Mr. Monford, in a long Presbyterian Cloak," "Another Epilogue intended for the same," "Mr. Haines's Second Recantation: A Prologue intended to be spoken by him dress'd in a Turkish habit."

[2] Epilogue to the first part of *Don Quixote*, Prologue to *Sir Hercules Buffoon*, Jo Haynes's Reformation Prologue, spoken in black, Epilogue spoken by Underhill at the New Theatre in Puritanical habit, Prologue spoken to the University by Mumford, Epilogue by Mrs. Mumford, Epilogue spoken by Mr. Pinkeman, The last new Prologue and Epilogue spoken by the Famous Comedian William Pinkeman, The Long Vacation Epilogue spoken by Pinkeman, A Vacation Epilogue spoken by Pinkeman, Epilogue spoken by Mr. Pinkeman on an ass, Prologue spoken by Haynes (If any here this Prologue dare cry down), Epilogue spoken by Haynes.

[3] Prologue, by Sir John Falstaff.

[4] Prologue in the *Island Princess*, set and sung by Leveridge; Epilogue in the same, set by Clarke, and sung by Mrs. Lindsey and the boy.

[5] The first volume: Epilogue to the first part of *Don Quixote*, Prologue to the *Massacre of Paris* for Betterton, Epilogue for Crab and Gillian, Prologue to the *French Coquet*, An Epilogue; the second volume: Epilogue to *Henry II* intended for Rosamond, Prologue at the Opening of the playhouse spoken

which show the remarkable variety in his prologues and
epilogues. Music, dancing, scenes, animals, farce—such
materials he cast in the mould of a stage-address that went
before or after a play. The Prologue to his *Cinthia and Endimion*
(1697) shows just how novel his prologues did become very
early in London's acquaintance with these devices that were
already well known in the French theatre, and this break-
away from the homespun prelude continues, for example, in
his musical Prologue to *Wonders in the Sun* (1706). As a matter
of fact, there is proof that D'Urfey was fully aware of the
novelty that he was introducing into stage-orations, for he
had Bayes refer thus to "Prologue Rarities" in an introduction
to one of his pieces:

> Bayes. No, Sir, we never give these Prologue
> Rarities Name —— And yet I have one that would
> fit it rarely, rarely faith; why look'e, I could call
> it, *The Sham-Mississippi*: Or, *The Exchange-Alley-
> Sharpers*, Ha, ha, ha; but 'tis stinging at first, but
> igad they grow so powerful, that I dare not venture.[1]

D'Urfey wrote frequently for his own plays, but he also
assisted Lacy's *Sir Hercules Buffoon* (1684) with a Prologue,
Powell's *Alphonso King of Naples* (1691) with an Epilogue,
John Smyth's *Win her and Take her* (1691) with an Epilogue,
Shadwell's *The Rival Sisters* (1696) with a Prologue and an
Epilogue. There must have been a vogue for his lines since

by Young Powell, Epilogue for Mrs. Verbruggan, Prologue for Cave
Underhill, Prologue for the *Basset-Table* spoken by Pinkethman as a footman,
Prologue to the King at the Masque at Court, Prologue made to entertain
her Royal Highness at her coming to the play call'd *Ibrahim*, Prologue
spoken by a Comedian who lately left the Irish theatre, Epilogue for Mrs.
Lucas, A Prologue, An Epilogue for Mrs. Verbruggan, A Prologue for
Estcourt's Benefit Day; the third volume: A Prologue by Sir John Falstaff;
the fifth volume: Epilogue to the *Island Princess*, set by Clarke, sung by Mrs.
Lindsey and the boy; Prologue in the *Island Princess*, set and sung by
Leveridge. (Note that several pieces were published at an earlier date. I
have omitted editions that contained no new prologues and epilogues.)
   [1] Prologue's Introduction, "The Queens of Brentford," *New Operas*, 1721.

they were often used and since a "New oration by way of Prologue" from his pen was looked upon as a drawing-card in 1714:

For the Benefit of Mr. D'Urfey.
By Her Majesty's Company of Comedians.

At the Theatre-Royal in Drury-Lane, on Monday next, being the 7th of June, will be presented a Comedy call'd, The Richmond Heiress; or, A Woman once in the Right. And at the Desire of several Persons of Quality, and to Entertain them and others of his Friends, there will be a New Oration by way of Prologue, written and to be spoken by Mr. D'Urfey, part of it design'd for a New Comedy of his, call'd, A Wife worth a Kingdom.[1]

D'Urfey's prologue and Haynes' epilogue to Lacy's *Sir Hercules Buffoon* were brought out in folio half-sheet and in the quarto-edition of the play in 1684. The texts show only minor differences in spelling, capitalization, and punctuation.

[1] *The Daily Courant*, June 5, 1714. The announcement was made again on June 7.

The
PROLOGUE
To
Mr. Lacy's *New Play*, Sir HERCULES
BUFFOON *or the* Poetical Esquire
Written by THO. DURFEY, Gent.
Spoken by Mr. HAYNES.

Ye scribling Fops, (cry mercy if I wrong ye)
But without doubt, there be must some* among ye
Know, that fam'd *Lacy*, Ornament o'th' Stage,
That standard of true Comedy in our Age;
Wrote this new Play,   5
And if it takes not, all that we can say on't,
Is we have his Fiddle, not his Hands to play on't:
Against our Interest, he to do you right,   ⎫
Your Foes, the Poets, has abus'd to night;   ⎬
And made us like rude Birds our Nest Besh—te. ⎭ 10
We know,
If you would Write us Plays, they'd lose their ends, ⎫
Kind Parties still would make your pains amends; ⎬
For there's no Fop but has a world of friends: ⎭
Who will like *City-Whiggs* help one another,   15
And every noisie Fool cry up his Brother:
No more then rack for *Prologue* or for Song,
Such Trifles, to dull Quality belong;
Nor Lampoon Ladies, that your Virtues trust,
That Bask in the hot Malls Pulvillio dust;   20
Whose low hung Fringes, with Attractive Arts,
Sweep heaps of straws, 'mongst Crowds of Lovers
      Hearts;
Subjects like these will never get you Fame,   ⎫
Nor can you Write, if this be all your Aim;   ⎬
More than a Rogue can Sing that sets a Psalm. ⎭ 25

*MS.—correction reads "must be some."

But if like Wits you would the Town oblige,
Write a good Comedy on some fam'd Siege,
But not in Rhime, and if to please you mean,
Let *Luxemberg* be taken the first Scene;
Yet, now I think on't, choose another story,   30
Some Sparks that late went o're to hunt for Glory;
Have spoyl'd that jest, and ta'ne the Town before ye:
No wonder too, for who could stand their Rage,
Since they with *Conningsmark*-broad-Swords Ingage;
I fancy you'l turn Butchers the next Age: 35
For these new Weapons look that guard your Lives,
Like bloody *Cozen Germans* to their Knives:
I'le put a question t'ee, pray does the Writer
As times go, get most Credit, or the Fighter?
Wit is aplauded when with fancy dress't,   40
But to be knockt o'th'head's a cursed jest;
A fate in which your forward Fool miscarries,
No, 'tis much better, to ly sick at *Paris;*
Where he can Write, what the *French* King intends,
And storm a Town, in Letters to our Friends.   45
Another Inconvenience we must own,
There's many a Fool is by a Bullet known,
That once pass't for a Wit of high renown.
The proof of sence, lyes hid in safety, here;
But when the Scull is broke the Brains appear.   50
Ah Sirs! if you to the rough Wars should follow,
How many Pates like mine would be found hollow;
Faith then take my Advice, stick to *Apollo.*
Write, and be studious in Dramatick Rules,
For should our Poets sound your shallow Sculls,   55
You were undone for Wits, and we for Fools.

LONDON,
Printed for *Joseph Hindmarsh,* Bookseller to
His ROYAL HIGHNESS, living
at the *Black Bull* in *Cornhill.* 1684.

The
EPILOGUE
To
Mr. Lacy's *New Play*, Sir HERCULES
BUFFOON, *or the* Poetical Esquire.
Wrote and Spoke by *J. H.* Com.

Methinks (*Right Worthy* Friends) you seem to sit,
As if you had all ta'ne *Physick* in the *Pit;*
When the Play's done, your jaded Fancies pall;
After *Enjoyment*, thus 'tis with us all.
You are   5
Meer *Epicures* in thinking, and, in fine,
As difficult to please in Playes, as Wine:
You've no true *taste* of either, judge at randome,
And Cry—*De Gustibus non disputandum.*
One's for *Vin d'Hermitage*, Loves *Lofty* inditing;   } 10
Another *Old Hoc*, he a style that's biting;   }
Both hate *Champaign*, and *Damn* soft natural Writing. }
And some forsooth
Love *Rhenish* Wine and *Sugar; Playes* in *meeter*,
Like *Dead Wine*, swallowing *Nonsence, Rhimes* make *sweeter:* 15
There's one's for a Cup of *Nants*, and he, 'tis odds
Like Old *Buffoon*, loves Plays that *swinge* the *Gods.*
True *English* Topers Racy *Sack* ne're fail,
With such *Ben Johnsons Humming* Plays prevail;
Whil'st some at Tricks, and Grimace, only fleer;   } 20
To such, must *Noisy, Frothy Farce* appear;   }
These new Wits Relish, *small, smart,* Bottle Beer.   }
French Gouts, that mingle Water with their Wine,
Cry—*Ah de French Song Gosoun Dat is ver' fine.*
Who never Drink without a *Relishing* Bit,   25
Scapin methinks such *Sickly* tasts might hit;
Where we entertain each *Squeamish*, nicer Palat,
With *Sawce* of *Dances*, and with *Songs* for *Salat:*
Since then 'tis so hard to please, (with choicest Dyet)

Our *Guests*, wh'in wit and sence do daily *Ryot;*   30
Since Wit is Damn'd by those, whom *Wits* we call,
As *Love* that stands by *Love*, by *Love* does fall,
When Fools, both good and bad, like *Whores*, swallow all.
'I wish, for your sakes, the *Sham Wits* o'th' Nation
'Would take to some *honest*, some thriving *Vocation.*   35
'The Wit of our Feet you see every Night,
'Says more to our purpose than all you can Write.
'Since things are thus carried, a Wit's such a Tool,
'He that makes the best Plays, do's but best play the Fool.
    A *Dreaded* Fool's your *Bully*,   40
        A *Wealthy* Fool's your *Cit*,
    A *Contented* Fool's your *Cully*,
        But your *Fool* of *Fool's* your *Wit:*
They all Fool Cit of's *Wife*,
    He Fools them of their *Pelfe*,
But your Wit's so *damn'd* a Fool,
    He only Fools *himself.*
Oh! *Wits*, then face about to sence, Alas!
I know it by my *self*, a *Wit's* an *Ass;*
    For (like you) in my time,   50
    I've been *Foolish* in *Rhyme*,
But now, so repent the *Nonsensical* Crime;
I speak it in *tears*, which from me may seem *odly*,
Henceforth I'le grow wiser, (*Dam' Wit*) I'le be *Godly;*
That when by *New Grace* I have wip'd off *old staines*,   55
In time I may Pass, not for *Count*, but Sir *Haynes.*

LONDON,
Printed for *Joseph Hindmarsh*, Bookseller to
His ROYAL HIGHNESS, living
at the *Black Bull* in Cornhill. 1684.

The/Prologue/To the last new Play/
A Duke and no Duke./Spoken by
Mr. Jevon./
The / Epilogue, / Spoken by Mr.
Haines./
London, Printed by Geo. Croom,
in Thames-street, over against Bay-
nard's Castle, 1684.

Folio half-sheet; printed on both sides.
Imprint at bottom of p. 2.
British Museum.

THOMAS DUFFETT

The dramatist and poet, Thomas Duffett, was once a milliner
in the New Exchange, London. In 1673 he saw his first plays
performed: *The Spanish Rogue*, acted at L. I. F. *c.* June and
published in 1674, and *The Empress of Morocco*, acted at D. L.
c. December and published in 1674. For three years his pen
was active, giving the playhouses *The Mock Tempest* (D. L.
Nov. 1674), published in 1675; *Psyche Debauch'd* (D. L.
c. May 1675), published in 1678; and *Beauties Triumph*, a
masque presented by the scholars of Jeffery Banister and
James Hart at Chelsey, 1676. Duffett's works, in addition to
his plays, include a broadsheet ballad without date, *Amintor's
Lamentation*, and a volume of verse, *New Poems*, 1676. Thomas
Duffett's pen was for burlesque.

THE PROLOGUE AND EPILOGUE TO
    A DUKE AND NO DUKE

In 1684, Cockain's *Trappolin creduto principe* (1658) was

altered by Tate and acted at Drury Lane in November as
A Duke and No Duke. The prologue and epilogue spoken at
this time were printed in folio half-sheet by George Croom
in 1684 and included in the quarto edition of the play in
1685. The textual history of both pieces is of interest.

Unlike the prologue in the folio half-sheet (1684), that
in the quarto, *A Duke and No Duke* (1685), is accompanied
by an acknowledgment, "Written by a Friend of the Authors."
The text gives *your Fate* in line 22 where the half-sheet has
your Sail, but other variants are of a minor nature in punctuation and spelling. Genest, citing *Langbaine,* says the prologue
to Tate's play was written by Duffett for a revival.[1] The
epilogue exists in several texts that show notable variation.
The earliest version, appearing in Duffett's *New Poems* in 1676,
was entitled "Prologue to the Suppos'd Prince":

> *Trappolin* suppos'd a Prince this humor shows,
> All pleasures do depend upon suppose.
> We by a strong suppose, may have to do
> With Wine and Women, Wit and Mony too.
>
> Thus while you think a zealous Sisters eyes
> Are lifted up in pious extasies,
> In strong suppose all her Religion lies.
> The modest longing girl that dares not woo,
> Thus does enjoy her fame and pleasure too.
>
> He that sits next a pretty female, knows
> His hand trembles, and something comes and goes.
> He gazes, faints and dyes, why all this shows
> The pow'r and pleasure of a sweet suppose.
> Those that for garnish'd dishes keep adoe,
> May have as wholesome Fish well butter'd too,
> In a plain earthen pan for half the toil;
> But for suppose—for all's but—
> The bodys all one flesh, and yet, dear hearts,

---

[1] *Op. cit.,* I, 439–440.

Thomas Duffett

A mere suppose makes difference of parts.
All were design'd alike for our delight,
Yet we suppose it fit to lose our right,
And keep the sweetest both from touch and sight.
Let that suppose that leads us so astray,
As strongly further our supposing Play.
The Duke and *Trappolin* must both be thought
Transformed really, though they are not.
Suppose that strongly thence our mirth all flows,
Then we shall please you all—as we suppose.[1]

Eight years later the two opening lines were reshaped and expanded into a new discourse upon "Suppose" and published as the epilogue to *A Duke and No Duke.* This text in folio half-sheet was changed somewhat in 1685 when the quarto edition of the play gave the epilogue with variations.[2] In 1690 the three versions were mingled in a "Prologue spoken by Mr. Hains to Trapolin, or a Duke and no Duke," published in D'Urfey's *New Poems:*

> *Trapolin* suppos'd a Prince, this humour shows
> Strange Matters do depend upon suppose,
> You wh—res* may be thought Chast,
>
> *To the Eighteen penny Gallery.

---

[1] Pp. 82–83.

[2] l. 1, *Duke, This Action* (Q), *Duke, in this place* (F); l. 4, *Flatterers at* (Q), *Flattery at* (F); l. 5, *thought* (Q), *suppos'd* (F); *Pulling off his Periwig* (Q, stage-instruction omitted in F); l. 7, *their Noses* (Q), *nor Roses* (F); l. 11, *But ask his Wife, and she supposes not* (Q), *But Wife could tell that she supposes not* (F, l. 12); l. 12, *Mean time the Sot, whil'st he's a Cuckold made* (Q), *Whilst the dull Sot, whilst he's a Cuckold made* (F, l. 15); l. 13, *Supposes she's at Church praying for Trade* (Q), *Supposes she's at Church Praying for Trade* (F, l. 16); l. 19, *honest Hols* (Q), *Doctor Hobs* (F, l. 22); l. 21, *And found helping to her Sons and Daughters* (Q), *So found her helping to us Sons and daughters* (F, l. 24); l. 22, *so the Belly* (Q), *e're her Belly* (F, l. 25); l. 34, *Woodcocks in* (Q), *Wedlock in* (F, l. 37); l. 44, *But shall we by That suppose to get* (Q), *That we cannot suppose to get* (F, l. 47); l. 48, *But tho you are not satisfi'd, suppose it* (Q), *But if you think it Bad, pray Good suppose it* (F, l. 51).

217

You Criticks witty.†
And I that have been kept for being pretty,
Suppos'd a Beau, through the well govern'd City;
Fancy digested into strong Supposes,
Makes Cheeks fair, where no Lillies grow nor Roses,
And Women beautiful that want their Noses:
'Tis that and Nature all the World inspires,
Fancy's the Bellows, kindling up new Fires
When th'Fuel's gone, that should supply desires;
And Nature is the Parent we all know,
By whom like Plants, we fructifie and grow.
The Reverend Citizen sixty and above,
That by poor Inch of Candle barters Love;
Supposes, that his Son and Heir he got,
But ask his Wife, and she supposes not.
The Trees by *Rosamonds* Pond her Sins have known,
And the dear Leaves still stick upon her Gown;
Whilst the dull Sot, that's just a C—old made,
Supposes she's at Church, and praying for a Trade.
The Country Novice newly come to Town,
Doom'd by his Parents to a dagled Gown;
That wanting Grace, in Love most lewdly falls
With some hot Nymph in these unhallow'd Walls,
Supposes some bright Angel he has gotten,
Till finding by sad signs the Wh—re was rotten;
His sweating Study's chang'd to sweating Tubs,
And Doctor *Littleton*, for Doctor *Hobs*,
Pray tell me, who would marry here among ye,
(For Whoring ye all hate, I scorn to wrong ye,)
That did not first suppose his Wife a Maid,
And Virgin Pleasures blest the Marriage Bed;
Yet 'tis Opinion must your Peace secure,
For no Experiment can do't I'm sure;
In Paths of Love, no footsteps e'er were trac'd,

†To the Pit.[1]

[1] Pp. 88-91.

218

All you can do is to suppose her Chast;
For Women are of that deep subtle kind
The more you dive to know, the less you find,
Ah, Ladies, what strange Fate attends us Men, ⎫
For when we prudently would scape your gin, ⎬
Sweet Supposition draws the Woodcocks in: ⎭
In all Affairs 'tis so, the Lawyer bawls,
And with dam'd Noise and Nonsence plagues the Halls,
Supposing after seven years being a Drudge,
'Twill be his Fortune to be made a Judge:
The Parson too that prays against Ill Weathers,
That thumps the Cushion till he leaves no Feathers,
Would let his Flock, I fear, grow very lean,
Without a fat Suppose of being a Dean:
In every thing is some by End, but Wit,
And that has too much Virtue in't, to get;
Then for our sakes that want a lucky Hit,
Let kind Suppose, for once possess your Mind,
Think in that Charm all Pleasures are confin'd,
Tho you mislike the Farce, pray don't disclose it;
But if you are not satisfi'd,—Suppose it.

After the Restoration, writers of prologues and epilogues adopted the manner of the essay in the critical and editorial types; but though employing frequently the informal style of the conversationalist in discourses upon literary and social questions, they wrote very few stage-orations which resembled the familiar essay as it was practised later, for example, by Addison and Steele. In the rare moments when they did permit their thoughts to play upon a topic, they chose subjects that would introduce a virgin poet or afford playful comment upon some aspects of London society. In this latter group, which may be called informal stage-discourses, we place the epilogue to *A Duke and No Duke*, as a good example of a familiar essay for the playhouse on the subject *Suppose*.

The speakers whose names appear in the texts of the prologue and epilogue to Tate's *A Duke and No Duke* have been introduced. Jevon, well known in 1684 as dancer and actor and destined two years later to be a playwright with one play,[1] was a gay, popular actor when he spoke the prologue to *A Duke and No Duke* while his companion in drollery, Jo Haynes, delivered the epilogue.

[1] *The Devil of a Wife* (1686), prologue spoken by Jevon, epilogue spoken by Jevon and Mrs. Percyval.

The
PROLOGUE
To the last new Play
A Duke and no Duke.
Spoken by Mr. *Jevon.*

Gallants,
   Who would have thought to have seen so many here,
At such a Rambling season of the Year;
And what's more strange? all Well and Sound to the Eye,
Pray Gentlemen forgive me if I Lye.
I thought this Season to have turn'd *Physician,*   5
But now I see small hopes in that condition:
Yet how if I should hire a Black Flower'd *Jump,*
And plye at *Islington,* Doctor to *Sadlers Pump.*
But first let me Consult old *Erra Pater,*
And see what he advises in the Matter.   10
   Let's see————
Venus and *Mars,* I find in *Aries* are,
In the Ninth *House,* a Damn'd dry Bobbing Year.
The price of *Mutton,* will run high 'tis thought,
And Vizard *Masks* will fall to ten a Groat.   15
The *Moon's* in *Scorpio's House* or *Capricorns,*
Friends of the City govern well your *Hornes:*
Your Wives will have a mighty Trade this Quarter,
I find they'll never leave their Natural *Charter.*
For once take my Advice as a true Friend,   20
When they a Walk to the new *Wells* pretend,
If youl avoid your Sail, quick hasten after,
They use more wayes to Cool, than Drinking *Water.*

The
EPILOGUE,
Spoken by Mr. *Haines.*

Trapolin, suppos'd a *Duke*, in this place shows
Strange matters may depend on meer suppose.
One may suppose *Masks* chast lov'd Nonsense Witty,
No Flattery at *Court*, nor *Whig* i'th' *City*
I am by one i'th' World supposed Pretty.   5
Fantasie digested unto Storms supposes,   ⎫
Whereas you see no *Lillies* grow nor *Roses*.   ⎬
So *Masks* for Beauty pass that want their *Noses*. ⎭
The Reverend *Cityzen*, Sixty and above,
That by poor inch of *Candle* buys his Love   10
Supposes that his Son and Heir he Got,
But Wife could tell that she supposes not.
The Trees by *Rosamonds* Pond, her Sins have known,
And tell-Tale Leaves, still stick upon the Gown:
Whilst the dull Sot, whilst he's a *Cuckold* made,   15
Supposes she's at *Church* Praying for Trade.
The Country Squire newly come to Town,
By Parents doom'd to a Lawyers daggl'd Gown.
supposes some Bright *Angel* he has gotten
In our Lewd Gallary, till proving Rotten: 20
His Study soon he leaves for Sweating Tubs,
And *Cook* and *Littlton*, for Doctor *Hobs*.
Nor had Dull *Cit* sent Spouse to Drink the *Waters*,
So found her helping to us Sons and Daughters.
Had he suppos'd when e're her Belly Swells,   25
There must be something in't besides the *Wells*.
Ther's no Man there had Married I'me afraid,
Had he not first suppos'd his Wife a Maid:
For 'tis Opinion must our Peace secure,
For no Experiment can do't I'm sure.   30
In Paths of Love no Foot-steps e're were Trac'd,
All we can do is to suppose her Chast;

For Women are of that deep subtile kind,
The more we dive to Know, the less we find.
Ah Ladies! what strange Fate still Rules us Men?   35
For whil'st we Wisely would escape the *Gin*,
A kind suppose still draws the *Wedlock* in:
In all Affairs 'tis so, the Lawyers Baul,
And with damn'd Noise and Nonsense fill the *Hall*.
Supposing after Seven Years being a Drudge,   40
'Twill be his Fortune to be made a Judge.
The Parson too that Prays against ill Weathers
That thumps the Cushion till he leaves no *Feathers*.
woud let his Flock I fear grow very Lean,
Without suppose at least of being a *Dean*.   45
All things are helpt out by suppose, but Wit
That we cannot now suppose to get.
Unless a kind suppose your Minds possess,
For on that Charm depends our Play's Success.
Then tho you like it not, Sirs don't Disclose it,   50
But if you think it Bad, pray Good suppose it.

London, Printed by *Geo. Croom*, in *Thames-street*, over against *Baynard's Castle*, 1684.

The/Prologue/And/Epilogue/To the
New/Comedy,/Called,/Sir Courtly
Nice, or,/It Cannot be./
London, Printed for Tho. Benskin
at the Corner Shop in/Little-Lincolns-
Inn-Fields. 1685.

Folio half-sheet; printed on both sides.
Imprint at bottom of p. 2.
Harvard College Library.

For the biographical sketch of the author, John Crowne,
see p. 18.

THE PROLOGUE AND EPILOGUE TO
SIR COURTLY NICE

Crowne's best comedy, *Sir Courtly Nice*, drawn from
Augustin Moreto's *No puede esser*, was written at the command
of Charles II in 1685. Two months before its performance
England's patron-king of drama died, and the theatres were
closed until the twentieth of April in that year. Under James'
fair patronage Crowne's play was acted for the first time at
Drury Lane in May 1685 with a prologue and an epilogue
which mirrored popular opinion in political and social affairs.
Noting the nation's loss followed quickly by its new blessing,
the accession of Charles' brother, the prologue was a brief
document of sufficient interest to merit publication in folio
half-sheet. It was printed for Thomas Benskin in 1685 and
sold at his Corner Shop in Little-Lincolns-Inn-Fields. This
prologue, with the epilogue, is reprinted here from the
folio half-sheet in the Harvard College Library.

A comparison of texts shows the prologue in half-sheet and that in the first quarto-edition of the play to be almost the same,[1] but the original epilogue on the reverse of the half-sheet was not given out again, line for line, in the quarto. The epilogue that was published with *Sir Courtly Nice* in 1685 opened with fourteen lines that did not occur in the epilogue published separately:

> 'Tis a hard Case, an Audience now to please,
> For every Pallat's spoyl'd with some Disease.
> Poor Plays as fast as Women now decay,
> They'r seldom car'd for after the first day;
> How often have I heard true wit call'd stuff,
> By Men with nothing in their Brains but Snuff?
> Each Shante Spark, that can the Fashion hit,
> Place his Hat thus, role full Forsooths a Wit;
> And thinks his Cloaths allows him judge of it.
> The City Gallant, The Exchange being done,
> Takes Sword at Temple-Bar which Nice stuck on.
> Comes here and passes for a Beaugarzoon.
> Audacious Vizards too, so fast do grow,
> You hardly can the Virtuous from 'em know.

The epilogue in folio half-sheet, however, began with eight lines which were not used in the quarto text:

> To plead for Freedome in so free a time,
> May seem Impertinent, if not a Crime.
> The Circling Sea, gives Limits to our Shores,
> But nothing bounds our Rabble, Wives, or Whores.
> In Spite of all Indulgent Sway can do,
> Our Croud, their Lust of Faction will persue,
> And either Sex will to their Joys go on,
> Scorning all ills to Honour, Purse, or Bone.

---

[1] Aside from minor differences in spelling, capitalization, and punctuation, the folio half-sheet (F) and the quarto (Q) vary in l. 5, *worth* (F), *worths* (Q); l. 28, *have oft seen with* (F), *oft have seen what* (Q); l. 40, *doth* (F), *does* (Q); l. 41, *Vertues, Grac'd* (F), *Vertue's Grace;* l. 43, *our* (F) *the* (Q); l. 44, *this* (F), *that* (Q).

Beginning with the ninth line of the original edition of this epilogue (the folio half-sheet) and the fifteenth line of the text in the first edition of the play, we have the following variant readings:

l. 9 (F), *only*, l. 15 (Q), *likely;* l. 11 (F) *Proud Mother*, l. 17 (Q), *the Mother;* l. 14 (F), *Needle*, l. 20 (Q), *wheedle;* l. 17 (F), *Speak*, l. 23 (Q), *say;* l. 19 (F), *Net*, l. 25 (Q), *Nott;* ll. 21–22 (F), *Nay, we have gotten other Schools of late,/As Masquerades, and the Jews Chocolate*, not included in Q; ll. 27–36 (Q) not in F:

> But the Grand Randevouz is kept of late,
> Exact at Nine, hard by o're Chocolate,
> Sad fate, that all the Christian Youth o'th' Nation,
> Should be oblig'd to Jews for Procreation.
> Nay, what is worse, that's, if reports be true,
> Many a Christian Gallant there turns Jew;
> That is, so oft some rotten Strumpet plyes him,
> The Chirurgion's forc't at last to Circumcise him.
> Our Bridges-street is grown a Strumpet Fair,
> Where higling Bawds do Palmb their rotten Ware.

l. 23 (F), *a*, l. 37 (Q), *the;* l. 25 (F) not in Q: *Whose Coach and Bones comes Ratling to the Dores;* ll. 26–28 (F):

> Nearer he creeps, discharges some kind words,
> And off he carries streight the wounded Birds.
> Another Gallant waits in the great Room,

ll. 38–41 (Q):

> And from his tongue lets flye such charming Words,
> That strait he carrys off the wounded Birds.
> Another waits above in the great Room;

ll. 30–34 (F):

> And there with his own Face he Treats his Eyes;
> What need he see, he can Act Comedies?

There by four Glasses plac'd, as for the nonce,
Sir Sparkish Acts four Coxcombs all at once.
Our Galleries were finely us'd of late,

ll. 43–45 (Q):

There by three Glasses plac't the Affected Dunce,
Acts you Four Courtly-Nices all at once;
Our Gallerys too, were finely us'd of late;

ll. 38–39 (F) not in Q:

Both Pit and Gallery was a Strumpet Fair,
Where Higling Whores, Sold Rotten Pumpions dear,

ll. 49–52 (Q) not in F:

Our Plays it was impossible to hear,
The honest Country Men were forc't to swear:
Confound you, give your bawdy prating o're,
Or Zounds, I'le sling you i'the Pitt, you bawling
    Whore—

l. 41 (F), *it pleads,* l. 54 (Q), *is pleas'd;* l. 43 (F),
At once to Profit and Delight the Mind, l. 56 (Q). *As
well to profit, as delight the Mind.*

The
PROLOGUE
and
EPILOGUE
To the NEW
COMEDY,
called,
Sir Courtly Nice, or,
It Cannot be.

THE PROLOGUE.

What are the Charms by which these happy Isles,
Have gain'd Heavens brightest, and Eternal Smiles?
What Nation upon Earth besides our own,
But by a loss like ours had been undone?
Ten Ages scarce such Royal worth display,   5
As *England* Lost, and Found, in one strange day.
One hour in Sorrow and Confusion hurl'd,
And yet the next the Envy of the World.
Nay, we are Blest in Spite of us, 'tis known,
Heavens Choice for us, was better than our own.   10
To stop the Blessings that o'reflow this day,
What heaps of Rogues we pil'd up in the way?
We chose fit Tools against all good to strive,
The Sawciest, Lewdest Protestants alive.
They wou'd have form'd a Blessed Church indeed,   15
Upon a Turn-Coat Doctors Lying Creed;
To know if e're he took Degree is hard,
'Tis thought he'l have one in the *Palace-Yard*.
Plot-Swallowers sure, will Drink no more Stuff down,
From that foul Pitcher, when his Ears arc gone.   20
Let us Rely on Conscience, not on Cheats,
On Heavens Wisdom, not State-Juglers Feats.
How greatly Heaven has our loss supplied?
'Tis no small Vertue Heals a Wound so wide:

Nay, in so little time to Rear our Head,   25
To our own Wonder, and our Neighbours dread.
They see that Valour Crown'd with Regal Power,
They have oft seen with Lawrels Crown'd before.
Verse is too Narrow for so great a Name;
Far sounding Seas hourly repeat his Fame.   30
Our Neighbours Vanquish'd Fleets oft wafted o're,
His Name to theirs, and many a Trembling Shore.
And we may go by his great Conduct Lead,
As far in Fame as our Fore-Fathers did.
At Home, he milder ways to Glory chose;   35
God-like, by Patience, he Subdued his Foes:
Now they, and their Designs are Ruin'd all,
Beneath their fallen accurst Excluding Wall:
These are not all the Blessings of this Isle,
Heaven on our Nation in a Queen doth Smile,   40
Whose Vertues, Grac'd by Beauty, shine so bright,
All the Fair Sex to Vertue she'l Invite,
And all our Clouds turn to a Glorious day,   ⎫
By this Illustrious pairs United Ray,   ⎬
Who both Reform and Grace us by their Sway.   ⎭

The EPILOGUE.

  To plead for Freedome in so free a time,
May seem Impertinent, if not a Crime.
The Circling Sea, gives Limits to our Shores,
But nothing bounds our Rabble, Wives, or Whores.
In Spite of all Indulgent Sway can do,   5
Our Croud, their Lust of Faction will persue,
And either Sex will to their Joys go on,
Scorning all ills to Honour, Purse, or Bone.
Nay, Parents now, not only can endure
Their Childrens Faults, but which is worse, procure, 10
Of Old, Proud Mother, full of Parent Sway,
Kept Miss a Vassal to her work all day;

And to the Wooing Spark, Miss was not brought,
But some fine Golden thing, her Needle wrought.
Now you shall meet Young Lady and her Mother,   15
Rambling in *Hackney-Coaches*, Masqu'd together.
Yes, and to Speak the Truth, to work they go,
Fine work, but such as they will never show;
Except some Net to draw a Fool to Wed,
And then he finds Miss rare at work—a Bed.   20
Nay, we have gotten other Schools of late,
As *Masquerades*, and the *Jews Chocolate*.
There Fowler like, a watching Gallant pores,
Behind his Glove, to get a Shot at Whores,
Whose Coach and Bones comes Ratling to the   25
   Dores.
Nearer he creeps, discharges some kind words,
And off he carries streight the wounded Birds.
Another Gallant waits in the great Room,
Till a New Cargazon of Strumpets come;
And there with his own Face he Treats his Eyes;   30
What need he see, he can Act Comedies?
There by four Glasses plac'd, as for the nonce,
Sir Sparkish Acts four Coxcombs all at once.
Our Galleries were finely us'd of late,
Where Roosting Masques sate Cackling for a Mate;   35
They came not to see Plays, but Act their own,
And had throng'd Audiences when we had none:
Both Pit and Gallery was a Strumpet Fair,
Where Higling Whores, Sold Rotten Pumpions dear.
This Comedy throws all this Leudness down,   40
For Vertuous Liberty it pleads alone;
Promotes the Stage toth' ends at first design'd,
At once to Profit and Delight the Mind.

LONDON, *Printed for* Tho. Benskin *at the Corner Shop in* Little-Lincolns-Inn-Fields. 1685.

Prologue/To A/Commonwealth of Women, / Spoke by Mr. Haynes, / Habited like a Whig, Captain of the/ Scyth-men in the West, a Scythe in his/Hand./

Epilogue./

London, Printed for R. Bentley in Covent-Garden, and are to/be sold by R. Baldwin in Old-Baily Corner. 1685.

Folio half-sheet; printed on both sides.
Imprint at bottom of p. 2.
Bodleian Library.

For the biographical sketch of the author, Thomas D'Urfey, see pp. 46-47.

OLD AND NEW TYPES IN ONE

Armed prologues and epilogues were known to Elizabethan audiences when Marston and Jonson engaged in the War of the Theatres. Andrugio, who wore armour in Marston's *Antonio and Mellida*, spoke an epilogue likewise in armour, and gave a name to this particular kind of stage-oration:

> Gentlemen, though I remain an armed Epilogue,
> I stand not as a peremptory challenger of desert,
> either for him that composed the Comedy, or for us
> that acted it; but a most submissive suppliant
> for both.[1]

[1] Epilogue to Marston's *Antonio and Mellida* (1602).

With the *Poetaster* came Jonson's armed prologue and a further designation of the intent of addresses in this mode:

> If any muse why I salute the stage,
> An armed Prologue; know, 'tis a dangerous age:
> Wherein who writes, had need present his scenes
> Forty-fold proof against the conjuring means
> Of base detractors, and illiterate apes,
> That fill up rooms in fair and formal shapes.
> 'Gainst these, have we put on this forced defence.[1]

Then Shakespeare's armed prologue introduced *Troilus and Cressida* with:

> . . . and hither am I come
> A prologue arm'd, but not in confidence
> Of author's pen or actor's voice, but suited
> In like conditions as our argument,
> To tell you, fair beholders, that our play
> Leaps o'er the vaunt and firstlings of those broils.[2]

So the address that upheld the author and the players with a defiant challenge to the audience took a name that other dramatists remembered long after. An armed prologue, armed with Mercury's wand, introduced Randolph's *Aristippus* (1635). A constable who was not to be feared, though he came "thus arm'd" as a peace officer, spoke a prologue to Glapthorne's *Wit in a Constable* (1640). An Amazon with a battle-axe in her hand delivered an armed prologue and epilogue for H. Burnell's *Landgartha* (1641). A pedant spoke a prologue to Brome's *The City Wit* with a playful allusion to the arm'd prologue in these words: "You see I come unarm'd among you, *sine Virga aut Ferula*, without Rod or Ferular, which are the Pedants weapons."[3] Another unarmed prologue was Dryden's introducing *All for Love* when the poet announced

---

1 Prologue to Jonson's *Poetaster* (1602).
2 Prologue to Shakespeare's *Troilus and Cressida*.
3 Prologue to Brome's *The City Wit* (1653).

himself ready to fight unarmed, without his rime. With this group of stage-orations we place the prologue to *A Commonwealth of Women*, spoken by Haynes, scythe in hand:

> . . . ——And to share
> This dreadful Fate, You Critticks all prepare.
> For besides all my Scythians yet unseen,
> We've yet a Female Common-wealth within,
> Who strongly Arm'd, like Furies venture on,
> And if y'approach their Trenches once, y'are gone.

Historians of literary forms, treating the character as a sketch pencilled for readers, have neglected to note the portrait created for an audience, the personated character, let us say, which was spoken and enacted as prologue or epilogue in the English theatre of the seventeenth and eighteenth centuries. When scourging or anatomizing frailties in the style perfected by Ben Jonson, prologues and epilogues were especially hospitable to the character, which satirists and pamphleteers adopted rather generally in the seventeenth century. But while making room for expository portraiture, they were aware, let it be noted, of surrendering their distinctive traits as prologues and epilogues and invading a different form of literary expression, the satire and the character. From an examination of more than 1,600 plays that were published before the close of the first quarter of the eighteenth century, I have noted a type of stage-oratory that has received no consideration, though it suggests to the historian investigating the evolution of literary forms the theory that literary types are cannibalistic; it shows a form of discourse, the character of Theophrastus, for example, adapted to a new purpose by poets who thought, not of readers, but of audiences in pits and galleries; and it illustrates a form of seventeenth-century wit.

Indicative of the taste of the audience and the vogue of characters in the theatre is the frequency with which sketches of types appear in prologues and epilogues; therefore, an account of interspersed characters should preface a note on the stage-oration that is a single character-sketch spoken and

enacted, such as we have, for example, in the Prologue to
A Commonwealth of Women, 1685.

Gallants, wits, beaux, brisk fools, and critics were the jury
of the stage that sat for the portraits which appear in the
prologues and epilogues sharing indisputably in the traditions
of such writers as Overbury, Hall, and Earle. Men of fashion
inspired the greatest number, their dress being the subject of
at least fifty-six per cent. of the portraits, and their conduct
the occasion of no less than forty-two per cent. Six lines, for
example, defined the type:

> 'Tis your brisk fool that is your Man of Note;
> Yonder he goes, in the embroider'd Cote;
> Such wenching eyes, and hands so prone to ruffle;
> The gentile fling, the Trip and modish shuffle;
> Salt soul and flame, as gay as any Prince
> Thus Taggs and Silks, make up your Men of Sense.[1]

Wits, but more often pretenders to wit, were likewise
targets for the satirists who followed a precedent laid by the
master scourger[2] more than sixty years before characters were
popular additions to prologues and epilogues. Some of the
best examples of type-portraiture in stage-orations were
devoted to the delineation of the man of wit;[3] but the critics
also inspired the prologuing poets to write in this manner,
some heightening their satire with simile and metaphor after
D'Urfey's way in the prologue reprinted after this essay:

[1] Prologue to Lee's *The Tragedy of Nero* (1675).

[2] Ben Jonson, *Every Man out of His Humour* (1616), Induction, Asper's
lines:

> Well I will scourge those apes,
> And to these courteous eyes oppose a mirrour,
> As large as is the stage, whereon we act;
> Where we shall see the time's deformity
> Anatomiz'd in euerie nerue and sinnew,
> With constant courage, and contempt of feare.

[3] See, for example, the epilogues to Arrowsmith's *The Reformation* (1673),
Etherege's *The Man of Mode* (1676), and Otway's *The Souldiers Fortune* (1683).

Critticks, like Flyes, have several Species.
There's one that just has paid his grutch'd half-Crown,
Cries, Rot the Play, Pox on't, let's cry it down.
The censuring Spark wou'd fain seem Great and Witty,
Yet Whispers Politicks with Orange Betty;
She cracks his Philberds, whilst he, in her Ear,
Is Fighting o're again the Western War,
Bragging what numbers his sole Arm has kill'd,
Tho' the vain Fop perhaps was ne're i'th' Field.
    Thus Worm that snugs in Shell where it was bred,
    Is nothing to the Maggot in his head,
For Harmless Insect that those Nuts create
Is nothing to the Maggot of the Pate,
Now such a Fop as this wou'd I be at.

Less frequent subjects for this type of wit in prologues and epilogues were the author,[1] the young poet,[2] the lawyer,[3] the playhouse audience,[4] and certain abstractions personified in Fame,[5] Honesty,[6] and Vice.[7] Of course, in this last group we find the style more frequently marked by similes and metaphors adopted to animate the abstractions.

The personated, or dramatised, character, appearing in the Prologue to *A Commonwealth of Women*, represents a prologue-type that was never extensively adopted. It made its appearance for the sake of novelty, and it claims our attention as one of the new ways of wit which playwrights sought with the eagerness of the seeker of Eldorado. For the most familiar example one turns, of course, to the prologue to Shakespeare's *Henry the Fourth*, the Second Part, though the type appeared more frequently after the Restoration, when stage-orations took on a

---

[1] Epilogue, Dryden's *All for Love* (1678).
[2] Epilogue, John Dryden Junior's *The Husband His Own Cuckold* (1696).
[3] Prologue, Lee's *Theodosius* (1692).
[4] Prologue, Dryden's *The Spanish Fryar* (1681).
[5] Epilogue, Dryden's *The Conquest of Granada*, Part I (1672).
[6] Epilogue to *Honesty in Distress* (1708).
[7] Prologue, Granville's *The She-Gallants* (1696).

variety of shapes in response to the demand for the unusual. Our best pieces from seventeenth- and eighteenth-century drama are the prologues to D'Urfey's *The Bath* (1701), Mrs. Centlivre's *The Basset-Table* (1706), and Brown's *The Stage Beaux toss'd in a Blanket* (1704), and the epilogues to Ravenscroft's *The Italian Husband* (1698) and Gildon's *The Patriot* (1703).

Many prologue-writers were wits, and in the stage-orations just named they exhibited what one Sir Puppy in the Duchess of Newcastle's *A Piece of a Play* (1668) called "drolling and raillery wit." Masked as a jester, the speaker of the stage-oration was at liberty to rail at and abuse a man of fashion or any other particular person. And as he did so, he demonstrated, not gulling or libellous wit, but drolling wit at which the world was pleased to laugh.

The Epilogue to *A Commonwealth of Women* is one of a numerous class given to young actors. Some note has already been taken of the prologues and epilogues spoken by boys and girls,[1] though the vogue of these juvenile performances was just rising when the actress "not yet Thirteen" spoke her bold lines on topics native to most of the young actresses' epilogues. Up to 1695, a year in which the child's prologue and epilogue were most popular,[2] notable performances by young players were in the prologue and epilogue by a young boy playing Richard III, printed in Heywood's *Pleasant Dialogues* (1637); the prologue to *The Indian Queen*, by Dryden and Howard, in 1662; an epilogue to Carlell's *Heraclius* in 1663/4; epilogues to Mrs. Behn's *Abdelazer*, Otway's *The Orphan*, and *The Indian Emperor* as given in Duffett's *New Poems* (1676) in 1676; the prologue to Tate's *Brutus of Alba* in 1678; the epilogue to Settle's *The Heir*

---

[1] See pp. 81–83.

[2] In 1695 young actors spoke the epilogues to Banks' *Cyrus the Great*, Dilke's *Lover's Luck*, Powell's *Bonduca*, Settle's *Philaster;* and two spoke the prologue to D'Urfey's *Don Quixote*, Part III. In 1715 a similar vogue occurred when the child spoke prologues to revivals of *Jane Shore* and *The Stratagem*, a prologue to Charles Johnson's *Country Lasses*, and epilogues to revivals of *Bonduca* and *Don Carlos*.

of Morocco in 1682; and the epilogue to D'Urfey's *A Common-
wealth of Women* in 1685. The next thirty years saw a notable
increase in the vogue of juvenile addresses, interesting
examples in addition to those of 1695 already listed in note 2,
p. 236, being the epilogues to Powell's *Cornish Comedy* and Mrs.
Manley's *Royal Mischief* in 1696; the prologue to Settle's
World in the Moon and the epilogues to Dennis' *A Plot and No
Plot* and Mrs. Pix's *Deceiver Deceived* in 1697; the epilogue to
Crowne's *Caligula* in 1697/8; the epilogues to Motteux's
Island Princess and Phillips' *Revengeful Queen* in 1698; the
epilogue to Mrs. Pix's *Beau Defeated* in 1699/1700; the
epilogue to *The Pilgrim* in 1702 and 1703; the epilogue
to D'Urfey's *Wonders in the Sun* in 1706; a new prologue
to *The Lancashire Witches* and an epilogue to *The Fatal
Marriage* in 1710; the prologues and epilogues to *Orpheus's
Journey to Hell* and *Thyrsis* in 1711; and the epilogue to *The
Recruiting Officer* in 1712. Then came 1715 with a renewed
interest in the little-girl speaker and the child who acted
the Princess Elizabeth and spoke prologues and epilogues.
She was a part of the vogue of novelty and frequently an
addition to a performance of a revived play. Being given
epilogues in the main, the young actress and, rarely, the young
actor appeared in stage-addresses with some constancy from
1695 to 1700, every year witnessing at least one such performance, and four of these five seeing the actress a popular
figure in novel prologues and epilogues. More than a decade
before their greatest vogue, however, Shadwell had found
young girls nothing new in the extravagant pursuit of originality
in stage-oratory:

> Our Prologue-Wit grows flat: the Nap's worn off;
> And howsoe're We turn, and trim the Stuff,
> The Gloss is gone, that look'd at first so gaudy;
> 'Tis now no Jest to hear young Girls talk Baudy.[1]

The text of the prologue and epilogue in folio half-sheet

[1] "A Lenten Prologue refus'd by the Players."

237

(1685) and that of the prologue and epilogue in the quarto edition of D'Urfey's *A Commonwealth of Women* (1686) are very similar. Aside from the second, twelfth, and sixteenth lines of the prologue,[1] the variants are minor in both prologue and epilogue, being entirely in spelling, punctuation, and capitalization.

[1] L. 2, *the* (F), *you* (Q); l. 12, *paltry* (F), *City* (Q); l. 16, *bit with us* (F), *at our House* (Q).

PROLOGUE
To A
Commonwealth of Women,
Spoke by Mr. *Haynes*,
Habited like a WHIG, Captain of the Scyth-men in the
West, a Scythe in his Hand.

From the *West*, as Champion in defence of Wit,
I come, to mow the Critticks of the Pit,
Who think we've not improv'd what *Fletcher* Writ.
This Godly Weapon first invented was
By Whigs, to cut down Monarchy like Grass;   5
But I know better how to use these Tools,
And have reserv'd my Scythe to mow down Fools:
Yet o' my Conscience they wou'd sprout again,
And the *Herculean* Labour were in vain.
The Pit, like *Hydra's*, still wou'd yield supplies,   10
From one lop't Block-head, twenty more would rise.
A sort of paltry Critticks yonder sit,
For this destroying Engine not unfit,
Cuckolds were always Enemies to Wit;
   For Wit oft draws the Wife to leave her Spouse, 15
   To take a small refreshing bit with us.
Phantastick Tastes how hard it is to please!
Critticks, like Flyes, have several Species.
There's one that just has paid his grutch'd half-Crown,
Cries, Rot the Play, Pox on't, let's cry it down.   20
The censuring Spark wou'd fain seem Great and Witty,
Yet Whispers Politicks with Orange *Betty;*
She cracks his Philberds, whilst he, in her Ear,
Is Fighting o're again the Western War,
Bragging what numbers his sole Arm has kill'd,   25
Tho' the vain Fop perhaps was ne're i'th' Field.
   Thus Worm that snugs in Shell where it was bred,
   Is nothing to the Maggot in his head,
For Harmless Insect that those Nuts create

Is nothing to the Maggot of the Pate, 30
Now such a Fop as this wou'd I be at.
Another to compleat his daily Task,
Fluster'd with Claret, seizes on a Mask,
Hisses the Play, steals off with Punk i'th'dark,
He Damns the Poet, but she Claps the Spark. 35
I wonder if the Law cou'd doom one dead,
That now should lop off such a Fellow's Head!
It cannot be found Murther.—And to share
This dreadful Fate, You Critticks all prepare.
For besides all my Scythians yet unseen, 40
We've yet a Female Common-wealth within,
Who strongly Arm'd, like Furies venture on,
And if y'approach their Trenches once, y'are gone.

EPILOGUE.

How silly 'tis for one, not yet Thirteen,
To hope her first Essay should please you Men:
You cannot taste what such a Creature speaks;
Would she were three years older for your sakes;
Two handfuls taller, a Plump pretty Lass, 5
I doubt not then my Epilogue would pass.
But, as I am, for your Applause I sue,
Pray spare me for the Good that I may do.
Gallants, I better shall perform e're long,
Despise not a poor thing because she's young. 10
Twigs may be bent, Trees are too stubborn grown;
And th' Roses Bud is sweet as Roses blown.
In *China* (as I often have been told)
The Women marry at eleven years old:
Our Play-House is a kind of *China* too, 15
And nothing like the Stage to make me grow ;
For, tho' not Power, I have the Will to please,
And Will's a mighty help in such a Case.
We on this fruitful Soyl have Women seen,

That in few Months have grown as big agen.   20
Oh Jemminy ! what is the Cause of that ?
I wonder what they Eat to grow so Fat?
Wc young ones know not how that business is;
But for all that we may be allow'd to guess;
And I beginning now to chatter Sence,   25
Encourag'd, may divert a Twelve-month hence:
And therefore humbly thus I make Address,
Excuse Faults, and accept my Will to please;
But if you fail me, may you nevermore
Kiss Woman under (at the least) fourscore.   30

FINIS.

This may be Printed. *Aug.* 20. 1685. R.L.S.
LONDON, Printed for *R. Bentley* in *Covent-Garden,* and are to be sold by *R. Baldwin* in *Old-Baily* Corner. 1685.

Prologue / To the Opera. / — / By Mr. Dryden. /—/
Epilogue/—/To the Opera. By Mr. Dryden. /—/

Folio half-sheet; printed on both sides.
No imprint.
British Museum.

For the biographical sketch of the author, John Dryden, see pp. 33–35.

PROLOGUE AND EPILOGUE TO THE OPERA

The first prologue and epilogue to an opera to be printed in folio half-sheet was written by Dryden for his *Albion and Albanius*, an elaborate work of flattery intended to honour Charles II. The death of Charles, which occurred shortly before the opera was to be performed, necessitated Dryden's making some changes, Albanius, for example, being presented as James II. Thus modified to suit the day's condition, *Albion and Albanius* began on June 3, 1685, in Dorset Garden, with the prologue and epilogue which are reprinted here from a folio half-sheet without imprint, and which are included in the edition of the opera (fol. 1685; 4to 1691) with no important textual variation.

The prologue comments upon the vogue of opera and spectacle, confessing *Albion and Albanius* to be Dryden's reply to the taste of his age; and the epilogue considers the character of kings and calls upon the English to maintain their "native Character." On the thirteenth of June, news of the landing of Monmouth on the eleventh brought a quick end to this loyal performance of Dryden's, its promise of a long run ending with six nights.[1] Nevertheless, the prologue and epilogue in folio half-sheet made Dryden's praise of James II current at a time when the people heard much about their king's promise to maintain the government in Church and State, as established by law.[2]

Thus prologues and epilogues watched the times and noted fads. When the theatres were content to accept an innovation, the stage-orations left off commenting; but so long as matters called for change, or challenged a break with tradition, just so long prologues and epilogues bantered and argued for a reformation of taste. They were the historians and the critics of the playhouse.

[1] Nicoll, *op. cit.*, p. 148, n. 3 on p. 148.
[2] Genest, *op. cit.*, I, 438.

PROLOGUE
To the OPERA.
By Mr. Dryden.

Full twenty years and more, our lab'ring Stage
Has lost, on this incorrigible age:
Our Poets, the *John Ketches* of the Nation,
Have seem'd to lash yee, ev'n to excoriation:
But still no sign remains; which plainly notes,   5
You bore like Hero's, or you brib'd like *Oates*.
What can we do, when mimicking a Fop,
Like beating Nut-trees, makes a larger Crop?
Faith we'll e'en spare our pains: and to content you,
Will fairly leave you what your Maker meant you.   10
Satyre was once your Physick, Wit your Food;
One nourisht not, and t'other drew no Blood.
Wee now prescribe, like Doctors in despair,
The Diet your weak appetites can bear.
Since hearty Beef and Mutton will not do,   15
Here's Julep dance, Ptisan of Song and show:
Give you strong Sense, the Liquor is too heady;
You're come to farce, that's Asses milk, already.
Some hopeful Youths there are, of callow Wit,
Who one Day may be Men, if Heav'n think fit;   20
Sound may serve such, ere they to Sense are grown;
Like leading strings, till they can walk alone:
But yet to keep our Friends in count'nance, know,
The Wise *Italians* first invented show;
Thence, into *France* the Noble Pageant past;   25
'Tis *England's* Credit to be cozn'd last.
Freedom and Zeal have chous'd you o'er and o'er; ⎫
'Pray' give us leave to bubble you once more; ⎬
You never were so cheaply fool'd before. ⎭
Wee bring you change, to humour your Disease;   30
Change for the worse has ever us'd to please:
Then 'tis the mode of *France*, without whose Rules,

None must presume to set up here for Fools:
In *France*, the oldest Man is always young, ⎫
Sees *Opera's* daily, learns the Tunes so long, ⎬ 35
Till Foot, Hand, Head, keep time with ev'ry Song. ⎭
Each sings his part, echoing from Pit and Box,
With his hoarse Voice, half Harmony, half Pox.
Le plus grand Roy du Monde, is always ringing:
They show themselves good Subjects by their singing. 40
On that condition, set up every Throat;
You Whiggs may sing for you have chang'd your Note.
Cits and Citesses, raise a joyful strain,
'Tis a good Omen to begin a Reign:
Voices may help your Charter to restoring; 45
And get by singing, what you lost by roaring.

EPILOGUE
To the Opera. *By Mr*. Dryden.

After our *Aesop's* Fable, shown to day,
I come to give the Moral of the Play.
Feign'd Zeal, you saw, set out the speedier pace;
But, the last heat, *Plain Dealing* won the Race:
Plain Dealing for a Jewel has been known; 5
But ne'er till now the Jewel of a Crown.
When Heav'n made Man, to show the work Divine,
Truth was his Image, stampt upon the Coin:
And, when a King is to a God refin'd,
On all he says and does, he stamps his Mind: 10
This proves a Soul without allay, and pure;
Kings, like their Gold, should every touch endure.
To dare in Fields is Valour; but how few
Dare be so throughly Valiant to be true?
The Name of Great, let other Kings affect: 15
He's Great indeed, the Prince that is direct.
His Subjects know him now, and trust him more,

Than all their Kings, and all their Laws before.
What safety could their publick Acts afford?
Those he can break; but cannot break his Word.　20
So great a Trust to him alone was due;
Well have they trusted whom so well they knew.
The Saint, who walk'd on Waves, securely trod,
While he believ'd the beckning of his God;
But, when his Faith no longer bore him out,　25
Began to sink, as he began to doubt.
Let us our native Character maintain,
'Tis of our growth, to be sincerely plain.
'T' excel in Truth, we Loyally may strive;
Set Privilege against Prerogative:　30
He Plights his Faith; and we believe him just;
His Honour is to Promise, ours to Trust.
Thus *Britain's* Basis on a Word is laid,
As by a Word the World it self was made.

FINIS.

Prologue. Spoken by Mrs. Cook./ Epilogue by a Person of Quality. Spoken by Mrs. Barrey./ Printed for Charles Tebroc.

Folio half-sheet; printed on both sides.
Imprint at bottom of p. 2.
British Museum.

For the biographical sketch of the author of the prologue, Mrs. Aphra Behn, see pp. 92–93.

FOR VALENTINIAN

On 26 July 1680 John Wilmot, Earl of Rochester, died. His play, *Valentinian*, was acted at Drury Lane in February 1683/4, with Mrs. Behn's prologue for the first day spoken by Mrs. Cook, a prologue for the second day also spoken by Mrs. Cook, and an epilogue written by a Person of Quality and spoken by Mrs. Barry.

A folio half-sheet printed by Charles Tebroc, but without date, gives the first prologue under the title, "Prologue, spoken by Mrs. Cook," and the epilogue with the caption, "Epilogue by a Person of Quality. Spoken by Mrs. Barrey." A comparison of the texts with the prologue and epilogue published with the play in 1685 brings out several differences, scraps of information concerning authors and speakers being furnished by both the folio half-sheet and the quarto. The half-sheet does not name the prologue-writer, but it describes the author of the epilogue as a "Person of Quality." It names both speakers: Mrs. Cook having the prologue; Mrs. Barry, the epilogue. The quarto furnishes still more, with some variations from the text of the folio half-sheet. It reprints the first prologue under the caption, "Prologue spoken by Mrs. Cook the first Day. Written by Mrs. Behn," but omits the last lines:

> 'Twill please his Ghost even in th' Elizian shade,
> To find his Power has such a Conquest made.

Other variations in the text are less significant.[1] Two additional prologues appear: the prologue spoken by Mrs. Cook on the second day, and a prologue intended for Mrs. Barry. The epilogue shows minor departures[2] before concluding with:

> When left with the wild Emperor alone?
> I know in thought yee kindly bore a part,
> Each had her Valentinian in her heart,

whereas the folio half-sheet said in five lines:

> When left with the wild Emperor alone:
> I know your Tender Natures, did Partake,
> At least in Thought you suffer'd for my sake,
> And in my Rape bearing a friendly part,
> Each had her *Valentinian* in her Heart.

---

[1] L. 2, *Beauty* (F), *Beauties* (Q); l. 16, *like* (F), *likes* (Q); l. 27, *tiresome* (F), *tedious* (Q); l. 35, *Young* (F), *Great* (Q); l. 37, *his Heav'nly Muse* (F), *their heav'nly Notes* (Q); l. 43, *lady* (F), *Ladies* (Q); l. 45, *sighs* (F), *Praise* (Q); l. 46, *Wit* (F), *Death* (Q) . . . *Eyes* (F), *Life* (Q).

[2] L. 9, *A surly* (F), *Surly* (Q); l. 11, *Horn'd* (F), *headed* (Q); l. 17, *happen* (F), *hapned* (Q).

PROLOGUE.
Spoken by *Mrs. Cook*.

With that assurance we to day address,
As standar'd Beauty certain of success;
With careless Pride at once they charm and vex,
And scorn the little Censures of their Sex.
Sure of the unregarded Spoil, despise   5
The needless affectation of the Eyes.
The softening Languishment that faintly warms,
But trust alone to their resistless Charms.
So we secur'd by undisputed Witt,
Disdain the damning Malice of the Pitt.   10
Nor need false Art to set great Nature off,
Or studied tricks to force the Clap, and Laugh.
Ye Wou'd-be Criticks you are all undone,
For here's no Theam for you to work upon.
Faith, seem to talk to *Jenney*, I advise;   15
Of who, like who, and how Loves Markets rise:
Try these hard Times how to abate the Price,
Tell her how Cheap were Damzels on the Ice!
'Mongst City Wives and Daughters that came there,
How far a Guinny went at Blanket-fair!   20
Thus you may find some good Excuse for failing,
Of your beloved Exercise of railing;
That when friend cries,—how does the Play succeed,
Damme—I hardly minded, what they did.
We shall not your ill Nature please to Day,   25
With some fond Scriblers new uncertain Play,
Loose as vain Youth, and tiresome as dull Age,
Or Love and Honour, that o're-runs the Stage:
Fam'd and substantial Authours give this Treat,
And 'twill be solemn! Noble all, and Great!   30
Witt! sacred Witt, is all the buis'ness here,
Great *Fletcher!* and the Greater *Rochester!*
Now name the hardy Man one fault dares find,

In the vast work of two such *Heroe's* join'd.
None but Young *Strephon's* soft and powerfull Wit,   35
Durst undertake to mend what *Fletcher* writ.
Different his Heav'nly Muse, yet both agree,
To make an everlasting Harmony.
Listen ye Virgins to his Charming Song,
Eternal Musick dwelt upon his Tongue: 40
The Gods of Love and Witt inspir'd his Pen,
And Love and Beauty was his Glorious Theam;
Now Lady you may Celebrate his Name,
Without a Scandal on your spotless Fame:
With sighs his dear lov'd Memory pursue,   45
And pay his Wit, what to his Eyes was due,
'Twill please his Ghost even in th' Elizian shade,
To find his Power has such a Conquest made.

Epilogue by a Person of Quality. *Spoken
by Mrs.* Barrey.

'Tis well the Scene is laid remote from hence,
'Twould bring in Question else our Authors Sense.
Two Monstrous, things produc'd for this our Age;
And no where to be seen but on the Stage.
A Woman Ravisht and a great man wise,   5
Nay honest too without the Least disguise.
Another Character deserves great blame,
A Cuckold daring to revenge his shame:
A surly ill Natur'd Roman wanting wit, ⎫
Angry when all true Englishmen submit, ⎬   10
Witness the tameness of the well Horn'd Pit. ⎭
Tell me ye fair ones, pray now tell me why
For such a fault as this to bid me dye:
Should Husbands thus Command and Wives obey, ⎫
'Twoul'd spoil our Audience for the next New Play, ⎬   15
Too many wanting who are here to day. ⎭
For, I suppose if e're that happen to ye,

Aphra Behn

'Twas force prevail'd you said he would undoe ye.
Strugling, cry'd out, but all alas in Vain,
Like me you Underwent the Killing pain.   20
Did you not pity me, Lament each groan,
When left with the wild Emperor alone:
I know your tender Natures, did Partake,
At least in Thought you suffer'd for my sake,
And in my Rape bearing a friendly part,   25
Each had her *Valentinian* in her Heart.

Printed for *Charles Tebroc*.

Prologue / To the Injur'd Lovers,
Spoken by Mr. Mountfort. /
Epilogue/To the Injur'd Lovers,
Spoken by Mr. Jevon. /
London Printed for Sam. Manship
at the Black Bull in Cornhill, 1687.

Folio half-sheet; printed on both sides.
Imprint at bottom of p. 2.
Bodleian Library.

WILLIAM MOUNTFORT

The actor and dramatist, William Mountfort, was the son of Captain Mountfort, a gentleman of a good Staffordshire family. Joining the Dorset Garden Company in his youth, young Mumford, as he was known in 1678, played in Leanerd's *The Counterfeits*. In 1680 he was Jock in *The Revenge;* in 1682, the first Alphonso Corso in *The Duke of Guise*, and in 1684, Nonsense in *The Northern Lass*, Metellus Cimber in *Julius Cæsar*, Heartwell in *Dame Dobson*.

In 1685 Mountfort created the part of Sir Courtly Nice with such success that his fame grew steadily. The next year alone was an exception in Mountfort's record of taking some original character annually from 1684 to 1692, the year of his death. His chief rôles may be reviewed by the year: 1686, Tallboy in Brome's *Jovial Crew;* 1687, Don Charmante in Behn's *Emperor of the Moon*, Pymero in Tate's adaptation of Fletcher's *Island Princess;* 1688, Young Belfond in Shadwell's *Squire of Alsatia*, Lyonel in D'Urfey's *Fool's Preferment*, Dorenalus in his own *The Injur'd Lovers;* 1689, Wildish in Shadwell's *Bury Fair*, Young Wealthy in Carlile's *Fortune*

Hunters; 1690, King Charles IX in Lee's *Massacre of Paris*, Don Antonio in Dryden's *Don Sebastian*, Ricardo in J. Harris' *Mistakes*, Silvio in his own *The Successful Strangers;* 1691, Menaphon in Powell's *Treacherous Brothers*, Hormidas in Settle's *Distressed Innocence*, Valentine in Southerne's *Sir Anthony Love*, Sir William Rant in Shadwell's *Scowrers*, Bussy d'Ambois in D'Urfey's adaptation of Chapman's *Bussy d'Ambois*, Cesario in Powell's *Alphonso, King of Naples*, Jack Amorous in D'Urfey's *Love for Money;* first Lord Montacute in *Edward III* (attributed to Bancroft), Young Reveller in his own *Greenwich Park;* 1692, Sir Philip Freewit in D'Urfey's *Marriage-Hater Match'd*, Asdrubal in Crowne's *Regulus*, Friendall in Southerne's *Wives Excuse*, Cleanthes in Dryden's *Cleomenes*.

On 9 Dec. 1692 Mountfort was stabbed before his door in Howard Street, Strand, by Captain Richard Hill, assisted by Lord Mohun. Mountfort was buried in St. Clement Danes. His murderers went unpunished, Hill escaping, and Mohun winning an acquittal at his trial.

Mountfort's reputation as a playwright rests upon *The Life and Death of Dr. Faustus* (1697), acted at Dorset Garden in 1686; *The Injur'd Lovers* (1688), acted at Drury Lane c. March 1687/8; *The Successful Strangers* (1690), acted at Drury Lane c. June 1691; *Zelmane* (1705), acted at Lincoln's-Inn-Fields in 1705. His prologues and epilogues, which are named in the following essay, were spoken in the theatres and printed in the quarto editions of the plays and in *Poems on Affairs of State* (1703), I, 238.

THE PLAYWRIGHT SPEAKING

Reminding his listeners of Jo Haynes, and confessing himself likewise poet, player, and husband,[1] William Mountfort spoke the prologue to his own play, *The Injur'd*

[1] William Mountfort married Mrs. Susanna Peircivall on 2 July, 1686. *London Marriage Licences, 1521–1869*, ed. Joseph Foster, P. 950, cited by *D.N.B.*

Lovers, at Drury Lane in 1687/8. In name, as "Brother Mountfort," he was in their thoughts again when Jevon, speaking a novel epilogue adorned with tripping measures, sketched him as the anxious playwright waiting in the scene-room. Not many authors served as prologue-speakers, but a great number of stage-orators repeated lines about the authors of their plays. Ben Jonson's audiences were familiar with the expectant playwright sketched in lines that make a good pattern by which to cut such epilogues as Jevon's; they saw the harassed poet as Mirth described him, for example, when she looked into the tiring-house:

> . . . he doth sit like an unbraced drum, with
> one of his heads beaten out; for that you must note,
> a poet hath two heads as a drum has; one for making,
> the other repeating! and his repeating head is all to
> pieces; they may gather it up in the tiring-house; for
> he hath torn the book in a poetical fury, and put
> himself to silence in dead sack, which, were there
> no other vexation, were sufficient to make him the
> most miserable emblem of patience.[1]

Mountfort's vogue as a speaker of prologues and epilogues began after he had distinguished himself in the rôle of Sir Courtly Nice at Drury Lane in May 1685. The miscellanies[2] and the playbooks[3] show him much in demand from 1687,

[1] Part of the Induction introducing the Prologue, *Staple of News* (1625).

[2] Prologue spoken to the University, 1687, for which Atterbury made the following request of Tonson: ". . . pray do me the kindness to speak to Mr. Momford for a copy of the Oxford Prologue, which I have promised a Gentleman, but have here and there forgott a verse. I wrote to him according to your direction, but can hear nothing of him." For the letter see Malone's *The Critical and Miscellaneous Prose Works of John Dryden* (1800), I, pt. 1, p. 189; and for the prologue see *Apollo's Feast* (1703), p. 136. Epilogue intended for a late comedy, D'Urfey's *New Poems* (1690), pp. 112–114. Prologue spoken by Mountfort after he came from the Army, *State Poems* (1697), p. 238.

[3] Prologue spoken to the University (1687); Prologue to Mountfort's *The Injur'd Lovers* (c. March, 1687/8); Epilogue to D'Urfey's *The Fool's*

when he spoke a prologue to the University, until 1692, the year of his death. Appearing with another player in a prologue or an epilogue seems to have been a happy rôle of his, for he spoke with Mrs. Butler in the epilogue to D'Urfey's *Love for Money* in 1689, with Nokes and Lee in the epilogue to his *The Successful Strangers* in the same year, and with Mrs. Bracegirdle in the prologue to D'Urfey's *The Marriage-Hater Match'd* in 1691/2. In all his pieces one discovers even now opportunities for repartee that he must have made good use of since therein lay his rare talent.

But Mountfort did not finish with speaking prologues and epilogues; he wrote as well for his own plays and for other men's. The prologue to *King Edward the Third* (1691),[1] the epilogue spoken by Mrs. Knight to Settle's *The Distress'd Innocence* (1691), and the prologue spoken by Mrs. Knight and the epilogue spoken by Mrs. Butler for Powell's *The Treacherous Brothers* (1696) show Mountfort's skill as a writer of playhouse addresses.

The prologue and epilogue reprinted here from the rare folio half-sheet of 1687 in the Bodleian Library offer no important variations from those published with the play, *The Injur'd Lovers*, in 1688. They are interesting chiefly as typical compositions by handsome Will Mountfort, whose natural inclination to poetry was, by his own acknowledgment, born but not bred in him.[2]

Preferment (c. Apr., 1688); Prologue to Shadwell's *The Squire of Alsatia* (May, 1688); Prologue to Shadwell's *Bury Fair* (Apr., 1689); Prologue to Lee's *The Massacre of Paris* (Oct., 1689); Epilogue to D'Urfey's *Love for Money* (Dec., 1689) spoken with Mrs. Butler; Epilogue to Mountfort's *The Successful Strangers* (Dec., 1689) spoken with Lee and Nokes; Epilogue intended for a comedy, D'Urfey's *New Poems* (1690); Prologue to D'Urfey's *The Marriage-Hater Match'd* (Jan., 1691/2) spoken with Mrs. Bracegirdle; Prologue to Dryden's *Cleomenes* (Apr., 1692).

[1] This play is attributed to John Bancroft.
[2] Preface, *The Successful Strangers* (1690).

255

PROLOGUE

To the *Injur'd Lovers*, Spoken by Mr. *Mountfort*.

Jo' Hayns's Fate is now become my share,
For I'm a *Poet, Married*, and a *Player*:
The Greatest of these *Curses* is the *First*;
As for the latter *two*, I know the *worst*;
But how you mean to deal with me to Day,   5
Or how you'l *Massacre* my harmless Play,
I must confess distracts me every *Way*:
For I've not only *Criticks* in the Pit.
But even in the Upper Gallery they sit,
Knaves that will run down Mr. *Mountfort's* Wit;   10
I'm the Unlucky'st *Dogg* that ever Writ.
Some Care then must be taken, that may save
This *Dear*, my First Begotten, from the Grave:
Some Friends Advise, like Brother *Ben* declare,
By God 'tis Good, deny't the Slave that Dare.   15
Were I but sure 'twould *Take*, I'de do my best;
But to be Kick'd, you know, would spoil the Jest.
However I must still my Play maintain,
Damn it who will, *Damn me*, I'le Write again;
Clap down each thought, nay, more then I can think, 20
Ruin my Family in *Pen* and *Ink*.
And tho' my Heart should burst to see your spite,
True *Talboy* to the last I'le Cry and Write,
That's Certain.
Or since I am beset so by my *Foes*,   25
I beg your favours, Friends, *Brother Beaux;*
Joyn with the Ladies, to whose Power I bow,
Where I see Gentleness on every brow;
To whose Acuter Judgments I submit,
O! save me from the *Surlies* of the Pit: 30
Those Nauseous Wretches which have not the tast
Of Wit or Gallantry if Nicely Drest.

I never Writ till *Love* first touch'd my Brain,
And surely *Love* will now *Loves* Cause Maintain,
Besides my *Natural Love* to Write again.
Yet as you Please, *Ruin* or *Pity* bear,
Sir *Courtly* fears no Enemy so Fair:
Execute as you please Your Tyrant Will,
His Character's, *Your Humble Servant Still.*

35

EPILOGUE

To the *Injur'd Lovers*, Spoken by Mr. *Jevon.*

My Brother *Mountfort* in the Scene Room sits,
To hear the Censure of your sharp quick Wits:
Expecting a most dreadful Damning Doom;
My Third Day's past, but his Poor Soul's to come.
Encourage him, Faith Do, 'tis Charity.
Poets You know are Poor, and so are We:
Let this Tho, Give no Offence t' th' Brother Writers,
But if it does, there's few of 'em are *Fighters:*
Those that are so, he does exclude his *Pen,*
For like *Town Bully*, He would *Know* his *Men.*
He begs but one thing, be not so uncivil
To *Scan* his *Play*, for then 'twill be the *Devil;*
Not but he Dares stand by't, but to prevent Evil.
For Nice Sir *Courtly's* so well bred you know,
He would not question it, and pray don't you.
The *Plot* I'm sure is good, or if it be not, Fye,
Your *Chair-Men* now a-daies *Plot Tragedy.*
Pardon but this, and *I* will *Pawn* my Life;
His next shall match my *Devil of a Wife.*
We'l Grace it with the Imbellishment of *Song* and
  Dance
We'l have the *Monsieur* once again from *France,*
With's *Hoop* and *Glasses;* and when that's done,
He shall divert you with his *Riggadoone.* [*Dances
like him.*

5

10

15

20

257

Pluck up *de Petticoat* above *de Knee*,
To shew *de Fine Shooe-String*, and *de Dapper Thigh*, ⎫ 25
And not make one Blush, no *Begar*, not in one Lady. ⎭
With *Tawny Gullet*, *Face* as ugly too,
As a Fresh *Awkward Covent-Garden Beau*.
Hey de brave French-man *Mon foy* he can Fly
Home again he has into his own *Country*. 30
So fare him Well, of him no more, ⎫
But to the Poet, to him be kind, as I said before, ⎬
Else to stand by him every Man has Swore. ⎭
To *Salisbury-Court* we'l hurry the next Week,
Where not for *Whores*, but *Coaches* you may seek; 35
And more to *Plague You*, there shall be no Play,
But the *Emperor o' th' Moon* for every Day.

London Printed for *Sam. Manship* at the *Black Bull* in *Cornhill*, 1687.

Prologue/To the Squire of Alsatia.
Spoken by Mr. Mountfort./
Epilogue./Spoken by Mrs. Mount-
fort./
London, Printed for James Knapton,
at the Queens/Head in St. Pauls
Church-yard. 1688.

Folio half-sheet; printed on both sides.
Imprint at bottom of p. 2.
Bodleian Library.

For the biographical sketch of the author, Thomas Shadwell,
see pp. 154–155.

THE PROLOGUE AND EPILOGUE TO
SHADWELL'S THE SQUIRE OF ALSATIA

Shadwell's *The Squire of Alsatia* was acted at Drury Lane
in May 1688, with unusual success. For many years no comedy
had "filled the Theatre so long together."[1] Its thirteen-day run
without an interruption was momentous, the third day
earning for Shadwell £130 while many were turned away
from the full house.[2]

The prologue and epilogue to *The Squire of Alsatia*, reprinted
here from the folio half-sheet prepared for James Knapton in
1688, are the same as the prologue and epilogue included in
the play, which was printed also for Knapton in that year.
Speaking of wit in both pieces, Shadwell reviewed stage-

[1] Shadwell's Dedication to the Earl of Dorset, *The Squire of Alsatia*, 1688.
[2] Summers, *op. cit.*, p. 66.

fashions severely while his play showed forth as mùch of the "prodigious scarcity of Wit" as was to be found in those dramas which the playwright scorned. Jonson's chief disciple announced himself in the prologue:

> If all this stuff has not quite spoyl'd your taste,
> Pray let a Comedy once more be grac'd:
> Which does not Monsters represent, but Men,
> Conforming to the Rules of Master Ben.
> Our Author, ever having him in view,
> At humble distance would his steps pursue.
> He to correct, and to inform did write:
> If Poets aim at nought but to delight,
> Fidlers have to the Bays an equal right.

William Mountfort, who spoke the prologue, is already well known in these pages.[1] Mrs. Mountfort, who had the epilogue, was Mrs. Susanna Perceval before her marriage on 2 July 1686 to the famous creator of Sir Courtly Nice. From March 1685/6, when, as Mrs. Percyvale, she spoke with Jevon in the epilogue to his *The Devil of a Wife*, to the end of 1696, her name, as Mrs. Mountfort and later as Mrs. Verbruggen, appeared with epilogues and, occasionally, with prologues.[2] In 1689 a prologue was sent to Dryden for his *Don Sebastian*, proposing that it be spoken by Mrs. Mountfort dressed like an officer; the next year Mrs. Mountfort spoke the epilogue for Dryden's *Amphitryon*. Lines that she delivered were published in the editions of the plays and in such miscellanies as *Apollo's Feast* (1703)[3] and *Wit and Mirth* (1719).[4]

---

[1] See pp. 252–255.
[2] Appendix C, Mrs. Percyvale, Mrs. Mountfort, Mrs. Verbruggen.
[3] P. 137.
[4] Vol. II, p. 327 and p. 345.

PROLOGUE

To the *Squire of Alsatia*. Spoken by Mr. *Mountfort*.

How have we in the space of one poor Age,
Beheld the Rise and Downfal of the Stage!
When, with our King restor'd, it first arose,
They did each day some good old Play expose;
And then it flourish'd: Till, with Manna tir'd,   5
For wholesome Food ye nauseous Trash desir'd.
Then rose the whiffling Scribblers of those days,
Who since have liv'd to bury all their Plays;
And had their issue full as num'rous been
As *Priams*, they the Fate of all had seen.   10
    With what prodigious scarcity of Wit
Did the new Authors starve the hungry Pit?
Infected by the *French*, you must have Rhime,
Which long, to please the Ladies ears, did chime.
Soon after this came Ranting Fustian in,   15
And none but Plays upon the fret were seen:
Such Roaring Bombast stuff, which Fops would praise,
Tore our best Actors Lungs, cut short their days.
Some in small time did this distemper kill,   ⎫
And had the savage Authors gone on still,   ⎬ 20
Fustian had been a new Disease i'th' Bill.   ⎭
When Time, which all things trys, had laid Rhime dead,
The vile Usurper Farce reign'd in its stead.
Then came Machines, brought from a Neighbour Nation,
Oh how we suffer'd under Decoration!   25
If all this stuff has not quite spoyl'd your taste,
Pray let a Comedy once more be grac'd:
Which does not Monsters represent, but Men,
Conforming to the Rules of Master *Ben*.
Our Author, ever having him in view,   30
At humble distance would his steps pursue.
He to correct, and to inform did write: ⎫
If Poets aim at nought but to delight,   ⎬
Fidlers have to the Bays an equal right.   ⎭

Our Poet found your gentle Fathers kind,   35
And now some of his works your favour find.
He'll treat you still with somewhat that is new,
But whether good or bad, he leaves to you.
Baudy the nicest Ladies need not fear,
The quickest fancy shall extract none here.   40
We will not make 'em blush, by which is shown
How much their bought Red differs from their own.
No Fop no Beau shall just exceptions make,
None but abandon'd Knaves offence shall take:
Such Knaves as he industriously offends,   45
And should be very loth to have his Friends.
For you who bring good humour to the Play,
We'll do our best to make you laugh to day.

EPILOGUE.
Spoken by Mrs. *Mountfort*.

Ye mighty scowrers of these narrow Seas,
Who suffer not a Bark to sail in peace,
But with your Tire of Culverins ye roar,
Bring 'em by th' Lee, and Rummidge all their store;
Our Poet duck'd, and look'd as if half dead,   5
At every Shot that whistled o're his Head.
Frequent Engagements ne're could make him bold,
He sneak'd into a corner of the Hold.
Since he submits, pray ease him of his fear,   ⎤
And with a joynt Applause bid him appear,   ⎬   10
Good Criticks don't insult and domineer.   ⎦
He fears not Sparks, who with brisk dress and meen,
Come not to hear or see, but to be seen.
Each prunes himself, and with a languishing Eye,
Designs to kill a Lady by the by.   15
Let each fantastick ugly Beau and Shape,   ⎤
Little of Man, and very much of Ape,   ⎬
Admire himself, and let the Poet scape.   ⎦

Ladies, Your Anger most he apprehends, ⎫
And is grown past the Age of making Friends ⎬ 20
Of any of the Sex whom he offends. ⎭
No Princess frowns, no Hero rants and whines,
Nor is weak Sense embroyder'd with strong lines:
No Battels, Trumpets, Drums, not any dye;
No Mortal Wounds, to please your Cruelty; 25
Who like not any thing but Tragedy.
With fond, unnatural extravagancies,
Stolen from the silly Authors of Romances.
Let such the Chamber-maids diversion be,
Pray be you reconcil'd to Comedy. 30
For when we make you merry, you must own
You are much prettier than when you frown.
With charming smiles you use to conquer still,
The melancholly look's not apt to kill.
Our Poet begs you who adorn this Sphere, ⎫ 30
This Shining Circle, will not be severe. ⎬
Here no *Chit chat*, here no *Tea Tables* are. ⎭
The *Cant* he hopes will not be long unknown,
'Tis almost grown the language of the Town.
For Fops, who feel a wretched want of Wit, 40
Still set up something that may pass for it.
He begs that you will often grace his Play,
And lets you know *Munday's* his visiting day.

LONDON, Printed for *James Knapton*, at the *Queens Head* in St. *Paul's* Church-yard. 1688.

Mr. Haynes/His Recantation-Prologue/Upon his first Appearance on the/Stage/After His/Return from Rome:/
London,/Printed for Richard Baldwin, near the Black Bull/in the Old Baily, 1689.

Folio half-sheet; printed on both sides.
Imprint at bottom of p. 2.
Bodleian Library.

THOMAS BROWN

Tom Brown, born at Shifnal in Shropshire in 1663, received his education at Newport School and Christ Church, Oxford. He left the University without a degree and spent three years in school work at Kingston-on-Thames. His original intention of becoming a writer, however, led him to London, where he wrote translations, satirical poetry, and pamphlets.

Brown's satires distributed their venom, but took frequent note of Dryden in such pieces as *Reflections on the Hind and the Panther*, which was published with Matthew Clifford's *Four Letters on Dryden* (1687), *The Reasons of Mr. Bays' changing his religion* (1690), *The Reasons of the New Convert's taking the Oaths* (1690), and *The Reasons of Mr. Hains the Player's Conversion and Reconversion* (1691). Other examples of Brown's works are *The Weesils* (1691), *Wit for Money* (1691), *Novus Reformator Vopulans* (1691), *Lacedaemonian Mercury* (c. 1691), *The Salamancan Wedding* (1693), *A Collection of Miscellany Poems, Letters, &c.* (1699), *Commendatory Verses on the Author of the Two Arthurs* (1700), *Amusements Serious and Comical* (1700), *Letters from the Dead to the Living* (1702). His *Satyr upon the French King on the Peace of Reswick,* included in his *Works* (1707), led to his being imprisoned. For the theatre he wrote prologues and epilogues and two comedies, *Physic lies a-bleeding* (1697) and *The Stage-Beaux toss'd in a Blanket* (1704). Titles of still other writings, scattered and less significant, may be found in the *Dictionary of National Biography.*

Tom Brown died on 16 June 1704 and was buried in the cloisters of Westminster Abbey.

RECANTATION PROLOGUES

In the sprightly readiness with which he commented upon the events of the day, Jo Haynes was the clever wit of the playhouse without a peer. Yet the most interesting rôle that he played in this connection in the history of Dryden remains to be told. I refer to his Recantation Prologues: "Mr. Haynes His Recantation-Prologue upon his first Appearance on the Stage after his Return from Rome," spoken at a performance of the *Rehearsal* and printed in folio half-sheet in 1689; and "Mr. Haines's Second Recantation: A Prologue intended to be spoken by him dress'd in a Turkish habit," included in D'Urfey's *New Poems,* 1690. The single-sheet Prologue of 1689 in the Ashmolian Collection of the Bodleian Library is reprinted here, the text giving lines which do not occur in later versions.[1]

Both prologues glance at Dryden at a time when *The*

---

[1] In *The Fourth and Last Volume of the Works of Mr. Tho. Brown* (1719), for example, this Prologue has the title: "Jo. Haines in Penance: Or, his Recantation-Prologue, at his acting of Poet Bays in the Duke of Buckingham's Play call'd The Rehearsal. Spoken in a white Sheet, with a burning Taper in his Hand, upon his Admittance into the House after his Return from the Church of Rome." The chief variant readings are these: l. 1, *dislikt* (1689), *dislike* (1719); l. 6, *to's* (1689), *to his* (1719); l. 7, *owns his Crimes; that's leaving* (1689), *own my Crime, of leaving* (1719); l. 8, *His* (1689), *My* (1719); l. 9, *some go* (1689), *do go* (1719); l. 11, *from you to Rome* (1689), *from Rome to you* (1719); l. 12, *Renegate to* (1689), *Runagade for* (1719); l. 13, *Beau's* (1689), *Beau* (1719); l. 14, *Tyr'd, even with* (1689), *Ev'n tir'd with* (1719); *seek out* (1689), *seek for* (1719); l. 18, *Besides, when I left you* (1689),

Rehearsal was revived and eyes were turned upon the Laureate who had lost favour because of his adopted faith. In fact, Haynes's words must be taken for more than an allusion to the temper of the age when one reads a rare quarto in the Bodleian, having significance in relation to these prologues. I have reference to *The Reasons of Mr. Joseph Hains the Player's Conversion & Re-conversion* (1691), in which Haynes and Dryden discuss recantation. Haynes tells Bayes that he was converted to the Roman religion at Malta; and Bayes answers:

> And did the news then of my Conversion arrive to thee beyond Sea? Prithee let me know, what were the sentiments of your part of the World upon that occasion; for not to mince matters with you, every body here at home looked upon it as a Prodigy . . .
>
> *Hains.* Why to me, that was acquainted with thy Character, and the fickleness of thy Constitution,

Besides, I left ye (1719); l. 19, *you* (1689), *ye* (1719); l. 20, *Like most of you* (1689), *For I, like you* (1719); l. 21, *I early tackt about* (1689), *Did early tack about* (1719); l. 24, *for me* (1689), *to me* (1719); l. 25, *Drink, nor Roar, nor Swear* (1689), *roar, or rant, or swear* (1719); l. 26, *with Penance and with Prayer* (1689), *with Penitence and Prayer* (1719); l. 27, *went down* (1689), *relish'd* (1719); l. 28, *shou'd ha'the* (1689), *should have the* (1719); l. 29, *Ere* (1689), *Thus* (1719); ll. 30–31 in the broadside omitted from the later version:

> Never in all that time to break a Jest!
> Nor ever drink one *Bumper* to the *Best!*

l. 32, *'Twas very hard. Indeed th'* (1689), *'Tis very hard, indeed, th'* (1719); l. 33, *Did* (1689), *Should* (1719); l. 34, *Place* (1689), *Face* (1719); l. 35, *now, 'spite* (1689), *in spite* (1719); l. 38, *esteem me less, 'cause I did live* (1689), *despise me now because I've liv'd* (1719); l. 42, *To* (1689), *'Twas* (1719); l. 43, *For you, Pert Gallants, who are* (1689), *But you, kind Sirs! who here are* (1719); l. 45, *You'le ne'r damn Haynes* (1689), *Will never damn Jo. Haines* (1719); ll. 46–47 in the broadside omitted from the later version:

> For to make us of any, *Me* or *You,*
> Were such a *Miracle Rome* ne'r could do.

l. 49, *Being thus confess'd, and freed from Rome's Pollution* (1689), *B'ing thus confess'd, and free from all Pollution* (1719); l. 50, *I beg from your kind Hands, my Absolution. (Kneeling)* (1689), *I beg from your kind Hands my Absolution* (1719).

it passed for no Miracle I can assure thee. . . .

Bays. Why, I'faith, Mr. Hains, you and I have had the worst luck of any two Converts in the Universe. We cou'd get no body breathing to believe one syllable of our Conversation; as for yourself, though a Missionary from Heaven had come on purpose to attest the sincerity of your change, it had never passed: They remembered you palm'd a Count upon the *French* King formerly in your younger days, and so they concluded that from the same principle of mirth and diversion, you were resolved to palm a Convert upon the Pope and Cardinals in your Old Age.

Haynes then tells of his disappointment upon finding that nobody believed him sincere, that the King gave him no favour, and that not even a constable would arrest him when he told him he was a Papist:

Hains. Lord! thought I with my self, what a degenerate, profligate scandalous Age we do live in, that I cannot pass for a Papist, or at least for a reputed Papist?

In despair, he says he complained to a Justice who advised him to change his religion for two reasons:

Considering the present circumstances of affairs, says he, I am of opinion the Protestant Religion will serve you the best of any, and considering you are a Poet, Mr. Hains, I shall only make the use of two arguments to reduce you to it: The first is Interest, which a Poet ought always principally to mind; now the Protestant Religion, Mr. Hains, will qualifie you again for the Playhouse, or for the Guards, or for any other employment about the City. The second is the Fashion, which a Poet likewise ought to observe as religiously, as he does his Interest.

The Justice withdrew to let him consider; and shortly after, Jo says he confessed a reconversion and within a fortnight testified his reconversion in a prologue. Haynes refers here to his Second Recantation Prologue. Bayes concludes this dialogue in the following criticism of Haynes:

> Oh thou pusillanimous, abject, little creature!
> . . . how I despise and laugh at thee? You see I keep
> up my principles still; so farewell my Re-converted
> Comedian.

Thus the quarto on Haynes's Conversion or Reconversion shows his two prologues to be badgering Dryden in 1689 and 1690.

The Second Recantation-Prologue in D'Urfey's *New Poems*, 1690, ridicules the shifting faiths of the time, being most likely *à la mode* in the shadow still of 1688:

> My Reconversion, Sirs, you heard of late,
> I told you I was turn'd, but not to what,
> The Truth disguis'd for Cause best known to me;
> But now what really I am,—you see;
> In vain did *English* Education work,
> My Faith was fixt, I always was a Turk;
> Besides my rambling Steps ere I came home,
> *Constantinople* reach'd as well as *Rome*,
> And by the *Mufti*, who nice Virtue priz'd,
> For being so Circumspect, was Circumcis'd;
> 'Tis true, I did endeavor to refuse,
> That dam'd old silly Custom of the *Jews*,
> Because I was asham'd of being shown,
> I was too plump a Babe, and Infant too well grown;
> But they would finish what they had begun,
> So between *Turk* and *Jew* my Jobb was done;
> I wish the promis'd blessing may appear,
> I'm sure, I bought Religion plaguy dear;
> For to be free, I greater Danger ran
> Of being an Eunuch, than a Musselman;
> But Constancy takes in that Place,

Thomas Brown

I gain'd their Hearts, their chiefest Secrets saw,
We whor'd and got Drunk contrary to Law:
I had five Wives, thank the dear Prophet for it,
A Black, a Blew, a Brown, a Fair, a Carrot,
And by the way, 'tis worth your Observation
To note, the sollid Wisdom of the Nation:
Wives, are like Spannels there, and when ye marry
You need but whistle, Wife must fetch and carry,
A pretier Custom, if I understand,
Than 'tis in *England* here where they Command;
The Ladies here may without Scandal shew
Face, or white Bubbies, to each Ogling *Beau*;
But there close veil'd, not one kind Glance can fall,
She that once shews her Face, will shew ye all;
Wits there are too, but Poet there's but one,
A huge unweildy jarring Lute and Tunn,
That spite of all my Parts the Laurel won,
Not for his skill in Satyr, or in Lyricks,
Or for his humble Stile in lofty Panegyricks,
Or the rare Images that swell his Noddle,
His Patron's Wit, still as his own is us'd,
Yet never had a Friend, but he abus'd,
What is his own has neither Plot nor Soul,
Nor ever one good thought but what he stold;
Eating, not Writing, is his proper Function,
Supper's his Sacrament, his Extreme Unction;
Like Whores condemn'd, that free themselves from
     Chains;
But Poet Belly routed Poet *Haines*:
Missing this Post, I get into the Wars,
But finding quickly there's were real jars,
Not liking that robust Confusion there,
Sneak'd off in time, to get Commission here,
Well knowing that what ever wrongs are righting,
You *London* Blades, have wiser ways than fighting.[1]

[1] "Mr. Haines's Second Recantation: A Prologue intended to be spoken by him dress'd in a Turkish habit," D'Urfey's *New Poems* (1690), pp. 204–207.

While public affairs changed their colour after 1688, time-servers forgot their old faiths and parties to discover a new Sesame. The disinterested spectator's half-wicked pleasure and amusement at the sight of this confusion gleam occasionally in the day-to-day publications, in the prologues with their oblique glances at grave matters. In such season came a performance of *The Rehearsal*, badgering Dryden with a new relish shown even in the timely prologue spoken by Jo Haynes and printed in folio half-sheet as "Mr. Haynes His Recantation-Prologue Upon his first Appearance on the Stage after his Return from Rome." This rare text is reprinted here, with the kind permission of the Bodleian Library.

Mr. HAYNES
His Recantation-Prologue
Upon his first Appearance on the
STAGE
After His
RETURN from ROME:

As you dislikt the *Converts* of the Nation,
That went to *Rome*, and left your Congregation;
By the same Rule, pray, kindly entertain
Your *Penitent lost Sheep* return'd again:
For *Reconverted Haynes* (taught by the Age)   5
Is now come back to's *Primitive Church*—the *Stage*,
And owns his Crimes; that's leaving in the Lurch
His Mother Play-House, She's my Mother Church.
As Penitents some go from you to *Rome*,
A Penitent from *Rome* to you I come;   10
Tho' I, from you to *Rome*, did never go
As *Renegate* to Her, but *Spy* for you:
For seeing the *Beau's* and *Banterer's* every Day,
Tyr'd, even with themselves, in every Play,
I went to *Rome*, to seek out Fops more new,   ⎱   15
And more *Ridiculous* than *any of you*,   ⎰
A *Miracle* from *Rome* I thought might do.   ⎰
Besides, when I left you, ye all design'd for *Rome*,
But seeing you *came not over*—*I came home*,
Like *most of you*, finding my self mistaken,   20
I *early tackt about to save my Bacon*.
        Pox on't,
At *Rome*, a *Godly Part* they made me Play,
A damn'd unnatural one for me you'l say,
They wou'd not let me Drink, nor Roar, nor   25
        Swear,   ⎱
But fob'd me off with *Penance* and with Prayer;   ⎰
Guess how that *Penance* went down with a *Player*.   ⎰
That ever any *Player* shou'd ha'the *Face*

Ere to pretend to such a thing as *Grace!*
Never in all that time to break a *Jest!*   30
Nor ever drink one *Bumper* to the *Best!*
'Twas very hard. Indeed th' *Italian Nation*
Did put this *Phiz* a little out of Fashion:
But *yielding Nature*, and this *Tempting Place*
Confirms me *Flesh and Blood* now, 'spite of *Grace;*   35
Therefore Dear Loving *Sisters* of the *Pit*,
Again, your *Brother Renegade* admit;
And don't esteem me less, 'cause I did live
Where *Sawcy Boys* claim your Prerogative.
    No Sisters, no,   40
I ne'r turn'd *Heretick*—in Love at least
To *Decent Whoring* kept my Thoughts still *Chast*.
For you, *Pert* Gallants, who are daily known ⎫
To love all *Whores*—But her of *Babylon*.   ⎬
You'le ne'r damn *Haynes* for his *Religion;*   ⎭   45
For to make us of any, *Me* or *You*,
Were such a *Miracle Rome* ne'r could do.
    Well Sirs,
Being thus *confess'd*, and freed from *Rome's Pollution*,
I beg from your *kind Hands*, my *Absolution*. (*Kneeling*)   50

LONDON,
Printed for *Richard Baldwin*, near the *Black Bull* in the *Old Baily*, 1689.

The / Prolouge / To / King William
& Queen Mary, / At a Play Acted
before Their Majesties at / Whitehall,
on Friday the 15th of November
1689. /—/ Written by N. Tate. /—/
Licensed, / Novemb. 16. 1689. J.
Fraser. /—/
London, / Printed for F. Saunders,
at the Blue Anchor in the Lower
Walk of the / New Exchange, and
Published by R. Baldwin in the Old
Baily, 1689.

Folio half-sheet; printed on both sides.
Imprint at bottom of p. 2.
Bibliotheca Lindesiana.

NAHUM TATE

Nahum Tate (1652–1715) was a minor poet, collaborator,
and translator. After graduation as B.A. from Trinity College,
Dublin, in 1672, he published a volume of poems in London
but soon turned to drama. His plays, many of which were
adaptations, follow with dates of performance and publication:
Brutus of Alba (c. July 1678, 1678), *The Loyal General* (c.
Dec. 1679, 1680), *The History of King Richard the Second*
(c. Dec. 1680, 1681 and in 1691 as *The Sicilian Usurper*),
The History of King Lear (c. March 1681, 1681), *The Ingratitude
of a Common-wealth* (c. Dec. 1681, 1682), *A Duke and No*

Duke (Nov. 1684, 1685), *Cuckolds-Haven* (c. May 1685, 1685), *The Island Princess* (April 1687, 1687), *Injur'd Love* . . . design'd to be Acted at the Theatre Royal (1707).

Among Tate's collaborators were Dryden, with whom he wrote the second part of *Absalom and Achitophel* (1682), and Nicholas Brady, with whom he prepared in 1696 *New Version of the Psalms*.

Upon the death of Shadwell, Tate became poet laureate, 24 December 1692, and held office until his death, 12 August 1715. He was also historiographer-royal after 1702.

THE PROLOGUE TO
KING WILLIAM AND QUEEN MARY

From the Right Honourable Lord Balniel's Bibliotheca Lindesiana comes a very rare occasional address to Royalty:

> The/Prolouge [*sic*]/To/King William & Queen Mary/At a Play Acted before Their Majesties at/ Whitehall, on Friday the 15th of November 1689./—/Written by N. Tate./—/

The play presented upon the occasion for which this prologue was written was Brome's *The Jovial Crew*, acted at Whitehall on the fifteenth of November, 1689[1]. Green bays probably covered the stage when the stage-orator, speaking for the "Muses Tribe" and hesitating to detain the Monarch long, implored an "Hour of Thanks" in forty-five lines that closed with a prayer:

> The Muses once were Sacred, give 'em leave,
> One Vote for Britain's Welfare to conceive;
> They Sum Their Wishes up, in one short Pray'r,
> (Join all True Hearts) Long Live the ROYAL PAIR.

A warrant bearing the date, 15 November 1689, ordered

[1] Nicoll, *op. cit.*, p. 314, lists among the plays at Whitehall Brome's *The Jovial Crew*, Nov. 15, 1689. . . . £. 20.

"Greene bayes" to cover the stage at Whitehall for a play to be acted there "on Friday next."[1]

The Prologue to King William and Queen Mary shows Tate's laudatory style and voices sentiment that was expressed outside the playhouse as well. In *A Continuation of the Secret History of White-Hall* (1688–1696), by D. Jones, King William is "our King Hero-like Fighting our Battels abroad." The author adds:

> . . . (and pray think it not a small thing, for *England* has not enjoy'd such a Blessing these Hundred and fifty years; and it has scarce ever been well with us, when our Kings did not go in and out before our People) and our Queen, as wisely and gently Swaying the Scepter at Home, to the Gladning of all our Hearts; and in all Her excellent Comportment, choosing to Rule in the hope and Affections, rather than the Fears of Her People.[2]

Again, we see how the language of the theatre neither runs before nor lags behind the fashions of the moment.

[1] L. C. 5/149, p. 318.
[2] P. 391. The book was published in London, 1697.

The
PROLOUGE
To
King William & Queen Mary,
At a Play Acted before Their Majesties at
Whitehall, *on* Friday *the* 15th *of* November 1689.
Written by N. Tate.

While BRITAIN'S State Her Monarch does support,
Protects Her Liberties, adorns Her Court,
Confirms Her Laws; the Muses Tribe would wrong
The Publick Int'rest to detain him long.
Yet, with His grateful Subjects they implore
Their Hour of Thanks,—even Them He did Restore.
To Them and Their Lov'd Swains did safety bring,
Permits Their Flocks to Feed, and Them to Sing.
No Lambs shall now for Foreign Altars bleed,
The Flock, The Fleece, the Shepherds too are freed.
He Scorn'd all Danger, for Fair BRITAIN'S Aid,
(To Roman Zeal, a ready Victim laid,)
And with His Peril, sav'd the helpless Maid.
BELGIA, that next Devoted was to Fall,
Did for the same Advent'rous Courage call,
He Fac'd our Common Fears—
Outbrav'd both Seas and Foes, to rescue all!
So HERCULES, when Monsters did infest,
Commenc'd His Toils to give the Nations rest.
Such Pious Valour justly is Ador'd,
And well may different Tongues, that had implor'd,
His Guardian-Aid, consent to call him Lord.
Fortune and Chance, elsewhere may shew their Powers,
Give Kingdoms Lords, but Providence gives Ours!
Our kind Restorer first, who, to maintain
Our rescu'd Freedom, Condescends to Reign.
For ALBION'S Wounds a Sov'raign Balm decreed,
But Heav'n not sent Him, 'till the utmost Need,

To make its Champion Priz'd, and let Him lay
Engagements, such as we cou'd nere Repay.
His Fames vast only Price was his before,
MARIA'S Charms— —Empire cou'd add no more,
Nature in Her exhausted all its store.
What we conferr, on Us descends again,
Who wait the ripening Blessings of his Reign:
SATURNIAN Days revolve, of former Crimes,
If any Seeds molest our Halcyon Times,
And Rouze our MARS, on him lies all the Care,
Defence and Freedom nere were bought too Dear.
He only Arms to make our Dangers cease,
His Wars are Glorious, for his End is Peace.
The Muses once were Sacred, give 'em leave,
One Vote for BRITAIN'S Welfare to conceive;
They Sum Their Wishes up, in one short Pray'r,
(Join all True Hearts) Long Live the ROYAL PAIR.

FINIS.

LICENSED,
Novemb. 16. 1689. J. Fraser.

London,
Printed for *F. Saunders*, at the *Blue Anchor* in the Lower Walk of the *New Exchange*, and Published by *R. Baldwin* in the *Old Baily*, 1689.

The/Prologue and Epilogue to the/ History of Bacon in Virginia./—/ Written by Mr. Dryden./—/Prologue./Spoken by a Woman./ Epilogue./Spoken by a Woman./ London: Printed for Jacob Tonson, at the Judges Head in Chancery-Lane,/near Fleetstreet, 1689.

Folio: 4 pages.
Imprint at bottom of p. 4.
Bodleian Library.

For the biographical sketch of the author, John Dryden, see pp. 33–35.

DRYDEN'S PROLOGUE TO MRS. BEHN'S THE WIDOW RANTER OR, THE HISTORY OF BACON IN VIRGINIA

Though Dryden's long-lost Prologue and Epilogue to Mrs. Behn's *The Widow Ranter or, The History of Bacon in Virginia* (Bodleian: Ashmole. G. 15) were reprinted in 1930,[1] we have with us still the Dryden-Shadwell-Behn prologue-puzzle. Why was Dryden's prologue to Shadwell's *A True Widow* (1679) published in Mrs. Behn's *The Widow Ranter* (1690) when Dryden's prologue and epilogue to Mrs. Behn's play had been licensed and entered in the Stationer's Register:

[1] Roswell G. Ham, "Some Uncollected Verse of John Dryden," *London Mercury*, March, 1930, pp. 421–426.

Jacob Tonson   entered . . . booke or coppy under
the hand of Master Wardn Parkhurst
entituled The prologue and eppilogue to *The History of Bacon in
Virginia*, written by Mr. Dryden.
Lycensed Novr the 20th 1689 by
J. Fraser,

and published as "The Prologue and Epilogue to the History
of Bacon in Virginia. Written by Mr. Dryden" in 1689?

The facts known to us may be summarized briefly. In 1679
Knapton published Shadwell's *A True Widow* with a prologue
by Dryden. Ten years later, the twentieth of November, 1689,
Tonson received a licence for "The prologue and eppilogue
to *The History of Bacon in Virginia*, written by Mr. Dryden."
In the same year Knapton brought out *A True Widow* (1689)
with the prologue and epilogue of 1679, and in 1690 he
published Mrs. Behn's posthumous play, *The Widow Ranter
or, The History of Bacon in Virginia*, with the prologue by
Dryden that he published with Shadwell's *A True Widow* in
1679 and 1689. But we find that neither the prologue nor the
epilogue in Knapton's publication was like the prologue and
epilogue written by Dryden for Mrs. Behn's play and licensed
in 1689. Strange procedure! The discovery of the Dryden
items in the Bodleian proves that there were a prologue and
an epilogue by Dryden in print when Knapton achieved this
riddle for scholars, acting apparently upon a principle that
Bayes confessed to some time before:

> . . . I have made a Prologue and an Epilogue,
> which may both serve for either: that is, the
> Prologue for the Epilogue, or the Epilogue for the
> Prologue: (do you mark?) nay they may both serve
> too, I Gad, for any other Play as well as this.
> (*The Rehearsal*, 1687, I, i.).

In this connection, it may be observed that the character
of the numerous prologues and epilogues of this period, their

279

customary indifference to the matter of the drama, encouraged the practice of attaching old prologues and epilogues to new plays, though, of course, there was precedent for such action in plays before 1660.[1] D'Urfey, several times guilty, robbed himself of an epilogue which he used as a prologue to *The Injured Princess*, calling down upon his head the abuse of Langbaine, who was reminded of Dryden at the moment:

> In this Play he is not content with robbing Shakespeare, but tops upon the Audience an old Epilogue to the *Fool turn'd Critick*, for a new Prologue to this Play. So that what Mr. Clifford said of Mr. Dryden is more justly applicable to our Author. 'That he is a strange unconscionable Thief, that is not content to steal from others, but robbs his poor wretched Self too.' (*An Account of the English Dramatick Poets*, 1691, p. 182.)

Passing from this matter to other topics, we may remind the reader of such instances as the prologue to Orrery's *Mr. Anthony* and D'Urfey's *The Fool turn'd Critick*, the prologue to *The Double Marriage* (*Covent Garden Drollery*) as the epilogue to *The Widow Ranter* and later as the prologue to *Abdelazer*,[2] and the epilogue to Mrs. Pix's *Czar of Muscovy* and Lee's *Lucius Junius Brutus*.

Much of the speculation offered for the double use of

---

[1] Note, for example, the following: Thomas Heywood's *The Royal King and the Loyal Subject* (1637), closing with "The Epilogue to the Reader," and James Shirley's *The Martyr'd Souldier* (1638), in which the Epilogue to Heywood's play is printed under the title "To the Reader of this Play now come in Print." After this piece, taken from Heywood's *The Royal King and the Loyal Subject*, an Epilogue to *The Martyr'd Souldier* is given. The Prologue for Blackfriars introducing John Lyly's *Sapho and Phao* (1584; in *Sixe Court Comedies*, 1632) is reproduced, with the exception of the last sentence, as the Prologue to Beaumont and Fletcher's *The Knight of the Burning Pestle* (1635). The Prologue to William Rowley's *All's Lost by Lust* (1633) appears in Thomas Dekker's *The Wonder of a Kingdom* (1636).

[2] Noted, also, by Mr. Percy J. Dobell in *John Dryden. Bibliographical Memoranda*, 1922.

Dryden's prologue (particularly the surmise as to differences between Shadwell and Dryden) has taken too little account of the evidence in the Stationer's Register, to the effect that Dryden wrote a prologue and an epilogue for *The History of Bacon in Virginia*. The first tenable explanation that I know, in fact, was made by Mr. Percy J. Dobell when he reviewed this problem in his *John Dryden. Bibliographical Memoranda* (1922). Mr. Dobell suggested that Tonson may have refused to surrender Dryden's prologue and epilogue for *The History of Bacon in Virginia* to Knapton and that Knapton may, thereupon, have appropriated for his publication of Mrs. Behn's play the prologue which he had already printed with Shadwell's *A True Widow*. From his broad acquaintance with bibliographical problems in this period, Professor R. H. Griffith, of the University of Texas, writes me that he, too, believes that we see here the result of copyright ownership, Tonson and Knapton being "rivals at the time for belles-lettres publication." Professor Griffith cites a quarrel of 1690 between Tonson and Thomas Bennett over a book by Waller, involving Atterbury as an editor. Knapton, using Gildon as an editor, published Mrs. Behn's play; but Tonson preserved his rights in the prologue and epilogue securely, for even his posterity was slow discovering these folio pages. In 1922 Mr. Dobell expressed the hope that some manuscript or broadside, escaping the fate of prologue-ephemerae, might tell what Dryden said for Mrs. Behn's posthumous play. And all the while—in fact, since 1890[1]—this disputed item appeared under Dryden in the Bodleian Catalogue.

It will be noted that both the prologue and the epilogue were spoken by women, an assignment in the theatre which may be looked upon as a veiled courtesy to the deceased playwright, but which was more likely an acquiescence in the seventeenth-century custom of employing female prologues and epilogues.

No poet enjoyed prestige comparable to Dryden's in the

[1] According to E. J. Parsons, Assistant Librarian, the Bodleian Library, Oxford.

John Dryden

business of recommending other men's plays. The Laureate was sought after by young aspiring playwrights, and he was a highly esteemed recommender of plays when Knapton made double use of his prologue to Shadwell's *A True Widow* and Tonson secured a licence for "The Prologue and Epilogue to the History of Bacon in Virginia."

THE
PROLOGUE and EPILOGUE to the
History of BACON in *Virginia*.
Written by Mr. Dryden.

PROLOGUE.
Spoken by a Woman.

Plays you will have; and to supply your Store,
Our Poets trade to ev'ry Foreign Shore:
This is the Product of *Virginian* Ground,
And to the Port of *Covent-Garden* bound.
Our Cargo is, or should at least, be Wit: 5
Bless us from you damn'd Pyrates of the Pit:
And Vizard-Masks, those dreadful Apparitions; ⎫
She-Privateers, of Venomous Conditions,   ⎬
That clap us oft aboard with *French* Commissions. ⎭
You Sparks, we hope, will wish us happy Trading;   10
For you have Ventures in our Vessel's Lading;
And tho you touch at this or t'other Nation;
Yet sure *Virginia* is your dear Plantation.
Expect no polish'd Scenes of Love shou'd rise
From the rude Growth of *Indian* Colonies.   15
Instead of Courtship, and a tedious pother, ⎫
They only tip the Wink at one another;   ⎬
Nay often the whole Nation, pig together. ⎭
You Civil *Beaus*, when you pursue the Game, ⎫
With manners mince the meaning of—that same: ⎬ 20
But ev'ry part has there its proper Name. ⎭
Good Heav'ns defend me, who am yet unbroken
From living there, where such Bug-words are spoken:
Yet surely, Sirs, it does good Stomachs show,
To talk so savour'ly of what they do.   25
But were I Bound to that broad speaking land,
What e're they said, I would not understand,
But innocently, with a Ladies Grace,

Wou'd learn to whisk my Fan about my Face.
However, to secure you, let me swear,   30
That no such base *Mundungus* Stuff is here.
We bring you of the best the Soyl affords:
Buy it for once, and take it on our Words.
You wou'd not think a Countrey-Girl the worse,
If clean and wholsome, tho her Linnen's course.   35
Such are our Scenes; and I dare boldly say,
You may laugh less at a far better Play.
The Story's true; the Fact not long a-go;
The *Hero* of our Stage was *English* too:
And bate him one small frailty of Rebelling,   40
As brave as e're was born at *Iniskelling*.

EPILOGUE.
Spoken by a Woman.

By this time you have lik'd, or damn'd our Plot;
Which tho I know, my Epilogue knows not:
For if it cou'd foretel, I shou'd not fail,
In decent wise, to thank you, or to rail.
But he who sent me here, is positive,   5
This Farce of Government is sure to thrive;
Farce is a Food as proper for your lips,
As for *Green-Sickness*, crumpt Tobacco-pipes.
Besides, the Author's dead, and here you sit,
Like the Infernal Judges of the Pit: 10
Be merciful; for 'tis in you this day,
To save or damn her Soul; and that's her Play.
She who so well cou'd Love's kind Passion paint,
We piously believe, must be a Saint:
Men are but Bunglers, when they wou'd express   15
The sweets of Love, the dying tenderness;
But Women, by their own abundance, measure,
And when they write, have deeper sense of Pleasure.
Yet tho her Pen did to the Mark arrive,

'Twas common Praise, to please you, when alive;   20
But of no other Woman, you have read,
Except this one, to please you, now she's dead.
'Tis like the Fate of Bees, whose golden pains,
Themselves extinguish'd, in their Hive remains.
Or in plain terms to speak, before we go,   25
What you young Gallants, by experience, know,
This is an Orphan Child; a bouncing Boy,
'Tis late to lay him out, or to destroy.
Leave your Dog-tricks, to lie and to forswear,
Pay *you* for Nursing, and we'll keep him here.   30

Licens'd, *Nov.* 20. 1689. *J. F.*

FINIS.

LONDON:
Printed for *Jacob Tonson*, at the *Judges Head* in *Chancery-lane*, near *Fleetstreet*,
1689.

The Prologue and Epilogue to the New/Comedy, called, The English Fryer, Or,/The Town Sparks./—/ Licensed, March 17. 1689.   J. F./—/ The Prologue./ The Epilogue./ London, Printed for John Amery ; and published by Randal Taylor. 1690.

Folio half-sheet; printed on both sides.
Imprint at bottom of p. 2.
British Museum.

For the biographical sketch of the author, John Crowne, see p. 18.

THE PROLOGUE AND EPILOGUE TO THE ENGLISH FRYER

Political harangue fails to enliven the Prologue and Epilogue to Crowne's *The English Fryer*, spoken probably in March, 1689/90. The hot temper that is familiar in stage-orations of this kind was chilled by such recent events as the flight of Tory James and the success of the Whigs. In an atmosphere of political timidity, Crowne attempted to interest his audience in stale talk about the Tories, the church, and the French. There is a hint of weariness in his lines, for Crowne's success as a playwright was looking forward to a decline. His *The English Fryer* (1690) gives the same Prologue and Epilogue with only slight textual differences, the chief variants being in the Prologue, l. 18, "And strive to have it acted o'er agen" of the folio half-sheet, as compared with "And fain wou'd have it Acted o'er agen," and l. 27, "those who" of the half-sheet, as compared with "they who."

The PROLOGUE *and* EPILOGUE *to the New* COMEDY,
called, The English Fryer, *Or*, The Town Sparks.

LICENSED, March 17. 1689. J. F.

The PROLOGUE.

Heaven to the Muses well may Coyn deny;
Pleasures attend on 'em, no Gold can buy.
Our Poet even in Poetry is poor,
Yet he so charming finds his little Store,
All *England* seems to him, less rich than he;   5
For he's content,—which *England* ne'er will be.
All Sects and Parties lend him Stuff for Plays,
And his Delight, though not his Fortune, raise.
Goods borrowed thus, he does not long retain,
But on the Stage, brings Fools and Knaves again   10
To those that lent 'em, that they may have Use,
Profit and Pleasure of their own produce.
To Day, he does not make bold, a Farce to show,
Priests made, and acted here, some Months ago.
They turn'd to Farce, the Court, the Church, the   15
   Laws;
It met a while, some Fortune and Applause.
Now sure the Wits, that did assist it then,
And strive to have it acted o'er agen,
Will like it on the Stage; 'tis cheapest here.
Priests are good Actors, but they're cursed dear;   20
And will, if they return, have greater Pay;
With Reason!—Oh! They lost a hopeful Play.
Truth is, if ever Priests return, they come
With all the Hunger, Rage, Revenge of *Rome*:
And therefore we had best no longer jar;   25
We shall agree too late, when in the Snare.
Nay, those who once serv'd Priests, and still promote

France, Teague, and *Jesuite,* in their secret Vote:
And are so mad, they'd give up *Englands* Glory,
Only to keep, the wretched Name of *Tory;*　　30
Had better quit their Plots, and cheaply sit,
To see us act the Product o' their Wit.

The EPILOGUE.

Priests have the Keys of Heaven and Hell they boast;
No doubt to both, they let in many a Ghost:
But we, to Day, have Ranting *Sparks* display'd,
Can Damn themselves, without the Churches Aid;
Who count it Glorious to Drink, Whore and Swear,　　5
And rather would be catch'd at Rapes, than Prayer.
But Hect'ring Heaven, they will not trust it far;
Therefore our Play-House is their Seat of War.
And they encounter without Wit, or Fear,
Dang'rous French Forces in Lewd Vizards here.　　10
Our *Hero's* once in *France* great Fame did gain;
Our Masques give *France* revenge, and spoil the strain.
The Masques, no doubt, are Pensioners of *France;*
'Tis Treason now, French Interest to advance;
And French Commodities are all by Law　　15
Doom'd to be burnt: Then you, Bold Masques,
　　withdraw,
Or else the *Custom-House* will seize you all,
And make our House to the *Prize-Office* fall.
To revive English Virtue, drive away
Folly and Vice, is aim'd at by this Play.　　20
To Friends of *England* this must well appear;
And such, no doubt, is every Creature here.

ADVERTISEMENT.

A True and Impartial Account of the most Material

John Crowne

Passages in *Ireland* since *Decemb*. 1688. With a particular Relation of the late Forces of *London-Derry*. Taken from the Notes of a Gentleman who was Eye-Witness to most of the Actions mentioned therein during his risiding there; and now, being in *England*, publisht the same for the further Satisfaction of this Nation. To which is added, A Description, and an Exact Map of *London-Derry*, as he took it upon the place. Price 6*d*. Licensed and Entred according to Order. Printed for *John Amery* at the Peacock against St. *Dunstan's* Church in *Fleetstreet*. Sold by *Randal Taylor* at Stationers-Hall.

London, Printed for *John Amery*; and published by *Randal Taylor*. 1690.

289

A/Prologue/Spoken By/Mrs. Brace-girdle,/At The/Entertainment of Love for Love.

Folio half-sheet.
No imprint.
Victoria and Albert Museum.

A PROLOGUE INTENDED FOR
MRS. BRACEGIRDLE

Having quit Drury Lane, Betterton and his players in revolt opened a new playhouse in Lincoln's Inn Fields on the last day of April 1695. Their first performance was *Love for Love*, the brilliant success that made Congreve famous and gained him a share in the house.

A prologue for this occasion was printed in folio half-sheet with the title, "A Prologue Spoken By Mrs. Bracegirdle, At The Entertainment of Love for Love," but without imprint. A comparison of the text of this sheet in the Foster Collection of the Victoria and Albert Museum with that published in the play in 1695 discovers only minor differences in punctuation, spelling, and capitalization; but the information furnished in the captions is contradictory. The quarto says, "A Prologue for the opening of the new Play-House, propos'd to be spoken by Mrs. Bracegirdle in Man's Cloaths. Sent from an unknown Hand," although the half-sheet says, "Spoken by Mrs. Brace-girdle." According to the edition of the play, a prologue was spoken by Betterton, beginning,

"The Husbandman in vain renews his Toil,"

and an epilogue was given by Mrs. Bracegirdle, opening with "Sure Providence at first, design'd this Place."[1] Congreve's

1 Mrs. Bracegirdle always acted in Congreve's plays. For her prologues and epilogues, see Appendix C.

Dedication in *Love for Love* (1695) observes other variants to be found in the printed text but does not make mention of the prologue:

> . . . Here are some Lines in the Print, (and which your Lordship read before this Play was Acted) that were omitted on the Stage; and particularly one whole Scene in the Third Act. . . .

A
Prologue
Spoken By
Mrs. Bracegirdle,
At The
Entertainment of Love *for* Love.

Custom, which every where bears mighty Sway,
Brings me to Act the Orator to Day:
But Woman, you will say, are ill at Speeches,
'Tis true, and therefore I appear in Breeches:
Not for Example to you City-Wives,   5
That by Prescription's settled for your Lives.
Was it for Gain the Husband first consented?
O yes, their Gains are mightily augmented:
And yet, methinks, it must have cost some   *Making Horns*
   Strife: *with her Hands*
                                                           over her Head.
A Passive Husband, and an Active Wife!   10
'Tis aukward, very aukward, by my Life.
But to my Speech. Assemblies of all Nations
Still are suppos'd to open with Orations:
Mine shall begin, to shew our Obligations.
To you, our Benefactors, lowly Bowing,   15
Whose Favours have prevented our Undoing;
A long *Egyptian* Bondage we endur'd,
'Till Freedom, by your Justice, we procur'd:
Our Taskmasters were grown such very *Jews*,
We must at length have Play'd in Wooden Shoos,   20
Had not your Bounty taught us to refuse.
Freedom's of *English* Growth, I think, alone;
What for lost *English* Freedom can attone?
A Free-born Player loaths to be compell'd;
Our Rulers Tyranniz'd, and We Rebell'd.   25
Freedom! The Wise Man's Wish, the Poor Mans Wealth?
Which you, and I, and most of us enjoy by Stealth;

The Soul of Pleasure, and the Sweet of Life,　⎫
The Woman's Charter, Widow, Maid or Wife,　⎬
This they'd have cancell'd, and thence grew the ⎭
    Strife.　　　　　　　　　　　　　　　　30
But you, perhaps, wou'd have me here confess
How we obtain'd the Favour;—Can't you guess?
Why then I'll tell you, (for I hate a Lie)
By Brib'ry, errant Brib'ry, let me die:
I was their Agent, but by *Jove* I swear,　　⎫　35
No honourable Member had a share,　　　　⎬
Tho' young and able Members bid me Fair:　⎭
I chose a wiser way to make you willing,
Which has not cost the House a single Shilling;
Now you suspect at least I went a Billing.　　40
You see I'm Young, and to that Air of Youth,
Some will add Beauty, and a little Truth;
These pow'rful Charms, improv'd by pow'rful Arts,
Prevail'd to captivate your op'ning Hearts.
Thus furnish'd, I preferr'd my poor Petition,　45
And brib'd ye to commiserate our Condition:
I laugh'd, and sigh'd, and sung, and leer'd upon ye,
With roguish loving Looks, and that way won you:
The Young Men kiss'd me, and the Old I kiss'd,
And luringly I led them as I list.　　　　　　50
The Ladies in meer Pity took our Parts,
Pity's the Darling Passion of their Hearts.
Thus Bribing, or thus Brib'd, fear no Disgraces;
For thus you may take Bribes, and keep your Places.

FINIS.

MUSICAL PROLOGUES AND EPILOGUES

The Englishman's delight in the songs and airs of his drama fostered many novelties which have never been brought together in a brief summary. Yet if we are to understand the theatre which the past has given to our present, we cannot ignore even the bits in which some actor entertained with music. Research in dramatic collections abroad, newspapers, printed and manuscript music, and more than 1,600 plays printed before opera was an established institution in London impresses one with the force of popular taste that nurtured, as a legitimate part of English drama, the musical prologue and epilogue, which were sometimes sung and sometimes spoken to the accompaniment of strings, flutes, and oboes. Music was the most agreeable of all the theatre's excursions into the new.

Prologues and epilogues were not always mere introductions and conclusions spoken by a stage-orator, hat in hand. Before 1660, as already pointed out,[1] the vocal prologue and epilogue had been tried, and prologues had been spoken with instrumental adornment. After the Restoration, English poets mindful of Italian opera and the French *comédie-ballet* undertook serious imitations and burlesques, composing prologues and epilogues in the form of solos, duets, and choruses, ballads, songs, and snatches—all showing the playwright's impulse to draw into his play the current matters of popular interest. These pieces had their greatest vogue after 1697, when they were used with comedies most frequently, though also with tragedies, operas, pastorals, and masques. Entertainers in this mode were Harris and Sandford, Jevon, Leveridge, Haynes, Mrs. Bracegirdle, Cibber, Penkethman, and Mrs. Lindsey. Of all the types in vogue the most signally novel were vocal burlesques and spoken pieces with snatches introduced from popular songs. None other than the playhouse-epicure, Pepys, called one of these novelties "extra-

[1] See pp. 19–22.

ordinary" when he heard Harris and Sandford, acting as street ballad-singers, sing the epilogue to D'Avenant's *The Man's the Master*. The fashion continued in prologues by Crowne, Settle aided by Clarke, and Motteux assisted by Holcomb, Clarke, and Mrs. Lindsey. And, as we should expect, the new mode inspired humorous rejoinders while newspapers carried such advertisements as this:

> . . . the last new Vocal Epilogue, compos'd and perform'd by the famous Signior Cibberini, after the newest English, French, Dutch, and Italian Manner.[1]

Snatches of song crept into prologues and epilogues with the new rage for foreign singers and Italian opera. In 1685/6 the actor, Jevon, having referred to the vogue of opera, the possibility of using catcalls like "Hoboys to fill up a Chorus," sang in his prologue to *The Devil of a Wife* these words from a popular song:

> "*A Cadmeus Pur Qua, Pur Qua, Meme vou.*"

No doubt, this clever turn won him laughter and applause, for he was reminding his audience of a favourite of theirs in Quinault's *Cadmus et Hermiòne*:

> Ah! Cadmus, pourquoi m'aimex-vous?
> Pourquoi vouloir chercher une mort trop certaine?
> Eh! que peut la valeur humaine
> Contre le Dieu Mars en courroux?
> Voyes en quels perils votre amour nous entraine?
> J'aurois mieux aime votre haine:
> Ah! Cadmus, pourquoi m'aimex-vous?

Other stage-orators who imitated Jevon's trick of singing

---

[1] *The Daily Courant*, Jan. 1, 1708. On Jan. 10, 1708, this advertisement appeared with the reference to the Dutch manner omitted. The Prologue to Colley Cibber's *The Rival Fools* (1709) probably referred to the popularity of Cibber's rôle in these lines:

> But if their humble Jests should fail to win ye,
> We beg some Grace for Signior Cibberini.

bits of popular songs were Miss Dennis Chock, in the epilogue to Settle's *The World in the Moon;* Jo Haynes, in an epilogue to Farquhar's *Love and a Bottle;* and Mrs. Bracegirdle, in an epilogue designed for Mrs. Centlivre's *A Platonick Lady*.[1] This last-mentioned example is particularly interesting since Mrs. Bracegirdle's song was the line, "These Eyes are made so killing, &c.," from a popular song by Mrs. Lindsey in the opera, *Camilla*, performed for the first time in 1706:

> These Eyes are made so killing,
> That all who look must dye.
> To Art I'm nothing owing;
> From Art I nothing want:
> Despise the help of Paint.
> 'Tis Musick but to hear me;
> 'Tis fatal to come near me,
> And Death is in my Eye.

This same song will turn the student to Pope's lines in *The Rape of the Lock:*

> A mournful glance Sir Fopling upwards cast,
> 'Those eyes are made so killing'—was his last.

Mention should be made also of the vogue of group-singing, the chorus, evidenced by the works of Duffett, Crowne, Motteux, and D'Urfey. Duffett's epilogue to *The Empress of Morocco* contained songs set to such old tunes as "A Boat, a boat," a popular loyal ballad in the reign of Charles II, which was known to many in the audience as "Here's a health unto his Majesty"; and "John Dory," an old song that furnished the tune for "I cannot eat but little meat," which was sung in *Gammer Gurton's Needle.* The introduction to Motteux's *The Loves of Mars & Venus,* on the other hand, answered seriously the demand of the audience for a prologue novelty. Erato, Thalia, and Terpsicore, with their attendants, sang in solo

---

[1] This kind of entertainment has not been studied in relation to theatrical music.

and chorus to the accompaniment of trumpets, kettle-drums, violins, flutes, and hautboys. Set to music by Finger, some of the songs were accompanied by the symphony; others by only flutes and violins. The device, which is certainly a novel one in the history of prologues and epilogues, shows the influence of the French *ballet de cour* and the opera. Motteux undoubtedly knew the operatic introductions of Quinault, and he had before him the example of Crowne's prologue to *Calisto*. The prologue to D'Urfey's *Wonders in the Sun* is in the same tradition.

Among the novelties of the seventeenth and eighteenth centuries there was not one more often used than music. Leveridge, Clarke, Eccles, Finger, Freeman, Mrs. Lindsey, Holcomb, Jevon, Haynes, Cibber, Penkethman, Purcell, and many others answered the demand that their audiences made for musical entertainment. Playwrights, often "o'er Head and Ears, in Song," struggling to set out what they thought would best garnish the dish, turned to such musical inventions as the prologues and epilogues reproduced in this volume. Considerable account was taken of such pieces, and it was not a decade before Granville wrote to the vice-Chamberlain upon hearing that his *British Enchanters* was to be put on without singing and dancing and described the proposal as "a design to murder the Child of my Brain."[1]

[1] The James Winston Theatrical Collection, p. 51, British Museum, Ad. MS. 38, 607.

The/Songs/in The/Indian Queen :/ As it is now Compos'd into an/ Opera./—/By Mr. Henry Purcell,/ Composer in Ordinary to his Majesty./ And one of the Organists of his Majesty's Chapel-Royal./Orn./

London,/Printed for J. Heptinstall ; and are to be sold by John May, at his Shop under/St. Dunstan's Church: And for John Hudgbutt at Tho. Dring's, Bookseller, at the/Harrow at Clifford's-lane-end in Fleetstreet. 1695.

British Museum

For the biographical sketch of the author, John Dryden, see pp. 33–35.

THE PROLOGUE TO THE INDIAN QUEEN

The words of Dryden's prologue to *The Indian Queen* (1663) were set to music under the caption "A Song in the first Act, Sung by Mr. Freeman" and included in Purcell's *The Songs in The Indian Queen: As it is now Compos'd into an Opera* (1695). According to the publishers in their lines to "Mr. Henry Purcell" in 1695, the year of the composer's death, the score

British Museum

PROLOGUE TO THE INDIAN QUEEN

and original draft of music for *The Indian Queen* were found and printed at once to save Purcell's "Jewel of very great Value" from imperfect publication in a common ballad. Mr. Willard Thorp in *Songs from the Restoration Theatre*, pp. 89–93, reviews Purcell's gift to the stage, pointing out that from 1680 to 1695 Henry Purcell composed music for fifty-four productions and showed a rare talent for dramatic music.

Single / Songs, / and / Dialogues, / in / The Musical Play/of/Mars & Venus./ Perform'd with the Anatomist, or/ the Sham Doctor./—/Set to Musick by Mr. Finger, and Mr. John Eccles./ —/

London,/Printed by J. Heptinstall, for the Authors, and Sold by John Hare/Musical Instrument Seller, at the Golden Viol in St. Paul's Church-/ Yard, and at his Shop in Freeman's-Yard in Cornhill. And by John/ Welch Musical Instrument-maker in Ordinary to His Majesty, at the/ Golden Harp and Hautboy in Catha-rine-street against Somerset-house/ Water-gate in the Strand. 1697.

British Museum

PETER ANTHONY MOTTEUX

Peter Anthony Motteux, translator and dramatist, was born on 18 February 1660 at Rouen, Normandy. Probably the son

British Museum

PROLOGUE TO THE LOVES OF MARS AND VENUS

of a merchant, Antoine le Motteux, he had an East India warehouse in London after 1685, the year of his arrival in England. In 1692 and 1693 he edited the *Gentleman's Journal*, and thereafter he was frequently engaged in writing.

Motteux's works, listed in the *Dictionary of National Biography*, include prefatory verses written with Tate and others for Gildon's satire on Dunton in the *History of the Athenian Society*, Boileau's *Ode sur la Prise de Namur. Avec une Parodie de la mesme Ode par le Sieur P. Motteux* in 1693; a translation of Rabelais (books I to III) with others, 1693/4, the remainder coming in 1708; *Maria, Translation of St. Olon's Present State of the Empire of Morocco, Words for a Musical Entertainment on the taking of Namur* in 1695; *Love's a Jest* in 1696; *The Novelty* and *The Loves of Mars & Venus* in 1697; *Beauty in Distress* in 1698; *The Island Princess, The Four Seasons,* and the epilogue to H. Smith's *The Princess of Parma* in 1699; *Acis and Galatea* in 1701, *Britain's Happiness* in 1704, *Arsinoe, The Amorous Miser,* and the epilogue to Vanbrugh's *The Mistake* in 1705, *The Temple of Love* in 1706, *Thomyris* and *Farewell Folly* in 1707, *Love's Triumph* in 1708, and a translation of *Don Quixote,* with the assistance of Ozell and others, and *A Poem in Praise of Tea* in 1712.

From 1703 to 1711 Motteux was a clerk in the foreign office of the post office. In 1718, seven years after his place there was given to another, he died on his birthday and was buried at St. Andrew Undershaft on 25 February 1718.

PROLOGUE TO THE LOVES OF MARS & VENUS

The vocal prologue to Motteux's *The Loves of Mars & Venus* (1697) was set by Godfrey Finger and published with the music in *Single Songs, and Dialogues, in The Musical Play of Mars & Venus. Perform'd with The Anatomist, or The Sham Doctor. Set to Musick by Mr. Finger, and Mr. John Eccles* (1697). According to the stage-directions in the play, the actors were seated during a musical entertainment. Then followed a conversation, in which the Wife told the Doctor: "This is not all: This is but the Prologue to what follows; you must hear the rest." The overture was described as "A Symphony of Trumpets, Kettle-Drums, Violins and Hautbois." Certainly, Finger's setting of the prologue gave Mrs. Hudson room to show her vocal talent when the play opened at Little Lincoln's Inn Fields, probably in March 1697.

The Prologue, in the Island-Princess Set and Sung by / Mr. Leveridge and exactly engrav'd by Tho: Cross.

Folio half-sheet, printed on both sides.
New York Public Library.

The Epilogue in the Island-Princess Set by Mr. Clarke Sung/by Mrs. Lindsey and the Boy, and exactly engrav'd by Tho Cross.

Folio half-sheet, printed on one side.
Chetham's Library, Manchester.

For the biographical sketch of the author, Peter A. Motteux, see pp. 300–301.

THE PROLOGUE AND EPILOGUE TO THE ISLAND PRINCESS

Motteux thanked Daniel Purcell, Jeremiah Clarke, and Richard Leveridge for their contribution to the success of his *The Island Princess*,[1] acted probably in December, 1698, at Drury Lane. Their supplying the Musical Part was assuredly no little aid to the playwright of whom some thought :

> Motteux and D'Urfey are for nothing fit,
> But to supply with songs their want of wit.

[1] "To the Reader," *The Island Princess*, 1689.

Had not the Island Princess been adorn'd
With tunes and pompous scenes, she had been scorn'd.[1]

The Prologue, set by Leveridge, who had a gift for compositions of this kind, was likewise sung by him. His magnificent bass voice, managed with unadorned English artlessness,[2] delighted the audience in three stanzas that were confessedly an attempt at novelty in prologues; for this second prologue was introduced by one that explained:

. . . since for hum'rous Prologues most you long,
Before this Play we'll have a Ballad sung.

Leveridge's name was also in play-bills announcing prologues that were calculated to attract men who liked the unusual.[3]

Clarke set the epilogue, which was sung by Mrs. Lindsey and a popular entertainer, the "Boy," identified by Mr. Thorp as Jemmy Bowen, whose trills and shakes won him much favour.[4] This epilogue is reproduced from a broadside in the Halliwell Collection in Chetham's Library at Manchester.[5]

---

[1] Genest, II, 164.

[2] Willard Thorp, *Songs of the Restoration Theatre*, Princeton: The University Press, 1934, p. 121.

[3] See F. Latreille's copies in Ad. MS. 32, 249: Jan. 2, 1706, A New Prologue and a dialogue performed by Leveridge and others, *The Recruiting Officer*; July 19, 1711, A New Prologue set and sung by Leveridge and Mrs. Lindsey, *The Loves of Baldo and Media*.

[4] *Op. cit.*, pp. 119–120.

[5] Mr. Thorp, *op. cit.*, p. 124, says: "The words do not correspond to the printed epilogue, spoken by Pinkethman (quartos of 1699 and 1701). It may have been introduced at the conclusion of the interlude, which place it will fit logically."

British Museum

THE PROLOGUE TO THE ISLAND / PRINCESS

EPILOGUE TO THE ISLAND PRINCESS

Prologue,/Design'd for the last new
Farce,/Call'd,/The Fool's Expecta-
tion: Or, The Wheel of Fortune./
Acted at the Theatre Royal in Dorset
Gardens./Epilogue/By Fortune./
London: Printed in the Year, 1698.

Folio half-sheet.
Printed on one side; two columns.
Imprint at bottom of p. 1.
British Museum.

PROLOGUE AND EPILOGUE DESIGN'D FOR THE LAST NEW FARCE

The last examples in this work direct attention to dis-
integrating forces. At the close of the seventeenth century,
the theatre showed hospitality not only to music and spectacle,
but also to farce, as we see now in the Prologue and Epilogue
design'd for *The Fool's Expectation: or, The Wheel of Fortune.*

By 1698, London audiences relished the comedies that were
influenced by French or Italian actors, the antics of players
like Haynes and Jevon, the farcical dramas from Ravenscroft's
pillaging of foreign sources, and numerous plays of similar
fashion, including the last new farce at the Theatre Royal in
Dorset Garden, for which were designed the prologue and
epilogue reprinted in this work. The performance for which
these orations were intended is not recorded by Genest or
by Mr. Nicoll. Almost one hundred years later there was a
Wheel of Fortune acted in Drury Lane.[1]

Among the poets scorned by this broadside for writing

[1] Feb. 28, 1795.

305

whatever was marketable was Elkanah Settle, who descended to drolls and ballads after 1688. In 1691, he became City Poet. His *Triumphs of London* (1691) and four pageants with the same title (1692–1695) and his *Glory's Resurrection* (1698) concluded his career. Fortune in the epilogue to *The Fool's Expectation* took note of these pieces by the City Laureate:

> But the irrevocable Prize is gone,
> Which so devoutly all attend upon.
> Which cou'd I but recall, I wou'd bestow it,
> Upon the City Laureat, our Poet;
> Who has so much, and so divinely Writ,
> Yet never was suspected for a Wit.
> Of Slavish sense he still disdains the Yoke,
> And Apes the Nonsense, *Thou*, and *Woden* spoke;
> Still haughty Bombast rumbles in each line,
> Like that which does in London's Triumphs shine,
> For which next venture, he shall be so trim,
> Scarce shall his *Pageants* dare to rival him.

PROLOGUE,

Design'd for the last new FARCE,
CALL'D,

The Fool's Expectation: Or, *The Wheel of Fortune.*
Acted at the Theatre Royal in *Dorset Gardens.*

You're welcome, Gentlemen, I'm glad to see,
That Knaves, and Fools, so lovingly agree.
Here our *Advent'rers*, and *Projectors*, met,
In Crowds together undistinguish'd sweat.
See how each huggs his Cully like a Brother.   5
They match like *Tickets* cut from one another.
For *Knave* and *Fool's* so like, in all but heart,
You'd swear, that one was 'tother's Counterpart.
  This throng'd Appearance rids me of my Fear
Of a lean Harvest this untoward Year.   10
By *Neal*, and *Speed*, you've been so often bit,
I was afraid our *Project* wou'd not hit.
But, Heaven be prais'd! Ours is a Fertile Soil,
The forward Crop outshoots our busiest toil.
Henceforth we'l fear no Dearth, or Reformation 15
Of *Fools*, the Glory of the *English* Nation,
Pure *Sterling-Fools*, that *Wit* and *Caution* hate,
Whose pride 'tis to be dull, and obstinate.
  As *Flanders* was your Nursery for *Bullies*,
So *Projects* are Hot-beds that force up *Cullies;* 20
And *Lott'ries* are a Spot, that manag'd right,
Raises vast Crops, like Mushromes, in a Night.
By often paring, and reducing low,
Like Vines, by pruning, they more fruitful grow.
  I laugh to see so many Thousands round,   25
Gaping for *Pen'worths* of a *Thousand Pound;*
Not one, that has a single Ticket got,
Wou'd be contented with a meaner Lot.
Each huggs himself on his imagin'd Luck,
And Grins to think how the *bilkt Fools* will look. 30

So Fops, that laugh at Matrimony, wed,
That hiss'd their Neighbour, when he shar'd his Bed,
They own the Sex all naught, but *one*, and *Fate*,
Each thinks, reserves that *one* to be his *Mate*.
Faith, let the Frolick here for once go round,   35
Let each Man think he has the *Thousand Pound*.
For this Conceipt will be, when all is o're,
As justly grounded, as his hopes before.
　　But, comfort Friends, let no One here relent,
You've no great reason to be penitent.   40
For if your *Stars* ordain'd you *Fools*, the *Fates*
Have made you so at very easy Rates.
All those, that heretofore with *Neal* have traded,
In *Bank*, *East-India Stock*, and *Projects* waded,
Have paid excessive Fines, to raise their Gains,   45
And Summs advanc'd to shew a want of Brains.
The *Quality*, and *Rich*, might use those Tools,
None cou'd afford, but they to be their *Fools*.
But our *Projector*, that consults your ease,
Contriv'd to shew *you* here for *Pence* apiece.   50
Tho' *Fortune's* favours be to most deny'd,
He hopes you will be all well satisfy'd;
Nor grudge his *Gains*, whatever they appear,
Which are but *Five and Twenty Hundred* clear.
For in all *Sights* this Maxim still obtains,   55
That he, that shews the Monster, sweeps the Gains.

London: Printed in the Year, 1698.

EPILOGUE
BY FORTUNE.

From Immemorial Time the Fierce, and Bold,
Rash, Giddy, thoughtless *Fools* my Favour hold.
They plead Prescription, and shou'd I withdraw,
Wou'd prosecute their claim at *Common-Law*.

And *Chanc'ry* in their Favour would decree,   5
Their Title's questionless in Equity.
For *Fortune* must provide for want of Sense;
Fools are a Rent-charge upon Providence.
For *Wit*, and *Parts* a Portion are from Heaven,
And unto Mortals for Subsistance given;   10
And those, in whom those luckless gifts One meets,
Are left to shift, and live upon their *Wits*.
    Know therefore all, it has been long decreed,
That *Wit* shou'd never, where I rule, succeed.
If any such among this crow'd appear,   15
Let 'em withdraw, they have no business here.
    Thousands I see, that all expect my Graces,
Blanks in their hands, and *Benefits* in their Faces.
But if I'm forc'd to bilk their Expectation,
'Tis, I protest, sore against Inclination.   20
The *First Rate Fools* this time my Coffers drain,
But soon I hope, my *Wheel* will fill again.
Let the unlucky bring next time this Face,
And it shall be his Warrant for success.
For of this Crowd, not One's within my Sight,   25
But by his *Phiz* shou'd be my Favourite.
    Here's *Justice* blinking with her Trinkets too,
To give a Colour to what I shall do.
But comfort Friends! I say it to her Face,
She has no right to meddle in this Place.   30
She wou'd give Wealth, and pow'r to Worth, and Merit,
As if One Man should all Heav'n's Gifts inherit.
But she shall ne'r prevail to injure Fools,
Or Fetter me with her damn'd formal Rules.
Fortune, like Women, is to Merit coy;   35
Coxcombs are priviledg'd, and may enjoy.
Shou'd we caress ill manner'd, surly Brutes,
That rail, and call us Whores, and Prostitutes?
That challenge all our Bounties as their due,
And loath old Favours, only charm'd with new?   40
No! We must Fools our trusty Slaves advance;

None thrive, like Altars rais'd by Ignorance.
   But the irrevocable Prize is gone,
Which so devoutly all attend upon.
Which cou'd I but recall, I wou'd bestow it,   45
Upon the City Laureat, our Poet;
Who has so much, and so divinely Writ,
Yet never was suspected for a Wit.
Of Slavish sense he still disdains the Yoke,
And Apes the Nonsense, *Thou*, and *Woden* spoke;   50
Stiff haughty Bombast rumbles in each line,
Like that which does in *London's Triumphs* shine,
For which next venture, he shall be so trim,
Scarce shall his *Pageants* dare to rival him.

London: Printed in the Year, 1698.

APPENDICES: A, B, C, D, E.

ABBREVIATIONS

D. G.: Duke's Theatre in Dorset Garden.
D. L.: Theatre Royal in Drury Lane.
L. I. F.: Duke's Theatre in Lincoln's Inn Fields.
T. R.: Theatre Royal in Vere Street or in Bridges Street.

APPENDIX A

PROLOGUES AND EPILOGUES IN SEPARATE PUBLICATION
(1642–1872)

The / Prologue / and / Epilogue / To / A Comedie, / Presented, / At the Entertainment of the Prince His/Highnesse, by the Schollers of Trinity Col-/ledge in Cambridge, in March last,/1641./—/By Francis Cole./—/ London:/Printed for James Calvin, 1642.

The/Prologue/To His/Majesty/At the first Play presented at the Cock-pit in/Whitehall,/Being part of that Noble Entertainment which Their Maiesties received Novemb. 19./from his Grace the Duke of Albemarle./ London, Printed for G. Bedell and T. Collins, at the/Middle-Temple Gate in Fleet-street. 1660.

Prologue/To The/Reviv'd/Alchemist.
The/Prologue/To/Calistho,/With The/Chorus's/Between The/Acts./—/ Orn./—/London,/Printed in the Year MDCLXXV.

The/Prologue/To/Pastor Fido./Spoken by Mr. Edward Lambert.
The Epilogue./Writ by/Mr. Drey-/den, Spoke/before His/Majesty/at Oxford,/March 19./1680.
London, Printed for Rich. Royston.
The/Epilogue/Spoken to the King at the opening the/Play-House at Oxford on Saturday last./Being March the Nineteenth 1681.

A Prologue spoken at Mithridates King of/Pontus, the First Play Acted at the Theatre/Royal this Year, 1681./
Epilogue./
London, Printed for J. Sturton.

A/Prologue/To a New Play, called/The Royallist./
The Epilogue, spoken by Mr. Underhill.

Prologue./By Mr. Otway to his Play call'd Venice preserv'd, or the Plot/discover'd. Acted at his Royal Highness the Duke of/Yorks Theatre, the 9th of February, 1681./
Epilogue./
London, Printed for A. Green. 1681.

Prologue/To a New Play, called/Venice Preserv'd;/or/The Plot Dis-cover'd./At the Duke's Theatre; Spoken by Mr. Smith./
Epilogue/To the Same./Spoken by Mr. Betterton./
London, Printed for A. Banks. 1682.

313

A/Prologue/Written by Mr. Dryden, to a New Play,/call'd, The Loyal Brother, &c./
The Epilogue by the same Hand;/Spoken by Mrs. Sarah Cook./
London, Printed for J. Tonson.

The/Prologue/To the City Heiress,/Or, Sir Timothy Treatall./—/ Written by Tho. Otway. Spoken by Mrs. Barry./
Epilogue./—/Written by a Person of Quality. Spoken by Mrs. Butler./
London, Printed for J. Tonson, at the Judge's Head in Chancery-lane, 1682.

A Prologue by Mr. Settle to his/New Play, called The Emperor of Morocco, with the Life/of Gayland. Acted at the Theatre Royal, the 11th. of/March, 1682./
The Epilogue Spoken by Mrs. Coysh's/Girl, as Cupid./
London:/Printed for A. Banks.

Prologue to a New Play, called Anna/Bullen, Acted at the Duke's House./
Epilogue to the same./
London: Printed for Allen Banks. 1682.

A/Prologue/By Mrs. Behn to her New Play,/called/Like Father, like Son,/or the/Mistaken Brothers,/Spoken by Mrs. Butler./
Epilogue spoken by Mr. Gevan./
London, Printed for J. V. 1682.

Prologue/To His Royal Highness,/Upon His first appearance at the Duke's Theatre/since his Return from Scotland./—/Written by Mr. Dryden. Spoken by Mr. Smith./—/
London, Printed for J. Tonson.

The/Epilogue./Written by Mr. Otway to his Play call'd Ve-/nice Preserv'd, or a Plot Discover'd; spo-/ken upon his Royal Highness the Duke of York's/coming to the Theatre, Friday, April 21./1682./
Printed for Joseph Hindmarsh at the Black Bull in Cornhill, 1682.

Prologue/To/The Dutchess,/On Her Return from/Scotland./—/Written by Mr. Dryden./—/
Printed for Jacob Tonson at the Judge's Head in/Chancery-lane near Fleetstreet. 1682.

Epilogue/To/Her Royal Highness,/On Her Return from/Scotland./—/ Written by Mr. Otway./—/
Printed for Jacob Tonson, at the Judge's Head in Chancery-lane, 1682.

To the/Duke/On His/Return./—/Written by Nat. Lee./—/
Printed for J. Tonson, at the Judge's Head in Chancery-lane, 1682.

The/Prologue/Spoken by Mr. Powel./at Oxford, July the tenth. 1682./
The/Epilogue/Spoken by Mrs. Moyle./at Oxford July the 18th. 1682.

Appendix A

Prologue to Romulus,/Spoken by Mrs. Butler./—/Written by Mrs. Behn./—/
Epilogue to the Same,/Spoken by the Lady Slingsby./
London: Printed by Nath. Thompson, 1682.

Prologue./To The/King and Queen,/At The/Opening/of/Their Theatre. /—/Spoken by Mr. Batterton: Written by Mr. Dryden./—/
Epilogue./—/Spoken by Mr. Smith: Written by the same Authour./—/
London,/Printed for Jacob Tonson, at the Judge's Head in/Chancery-lane. 1683.

Prologue,/To The/Duke of Guise./—/Written by Mr. Dryden: Spoken by Mr. Smith./—/
Epilogue./—/Written by the same Authour: Spoken by Mrs. Cooke./
Another/Epilogue/Intended to have been Spoken to the/Play, before it was forbidden,/last Summer./—/Written by Mr. Dryden./—/
London,/Printed for Jacob Tonson, at the Judge's Head in Chancery-lane. 1683.

A/Lenten Prologue/Refus'd by the/Players.

The/Prologue and Epilogue/To The/City Politicks./The Prologue spoken by Mr. Smith./
The Epilogue spoken by Mr. Lee in the Character/of Bartaline the Old Lawyer./
London: Printed for Tho. Benskins in St. Brides Churchyard, 1683.

Prologue to Dame Dobson the Cunning Woman./Spoken by Mrs. Currer./
Epilogue to the Same!/Spoken by Mr. Jevorn./
London: Printed for Jo. Hindmarsh, Bookseller to his Royal Highness, at the/Black Bull in Cornhil, 1683.

The/Prologue and Epilogue,/To The Last New Play;/Constantine the Great./—/Prologue. Spoken by Mr. Goodman:/
Epilogue./Spoken by Mrs. Cook,/
Printed for C. Tebroc, 1683.

A True Coppy/Of The/Epilogue/To/Constantine the Great./That which was first Published being false printed/and surreptitious./—/Written by Mr. Dryden./—/
London, Printed for J. Tonson, at the Judge's Head in Chancery-lane, 1684.

Prologue/To a New Play, Call'd,/The Disappointment:/or,/The Mother in Fashion./Spoken by Mr. Betterton./
Epilogue/By Another Hand./
London,/Printed for E. Lucy. M.DC.LXXXIV.

Prologue/To the Northern Lass. By J. H./
Epilogue./Spoken by Mrs. Butler./
Printed for C. Corbet at the Oxford-Arms in Warwick-lane. 1684.

Appendix A

The/Prologue/To/Mr. Lacy's New Play, Sir Hercules/Buffoon or the Poetical Esquire./—/ Written by Tho. Durfey, Gent./—/Spoken by Mr. Haynes./—/
London,/Printed for Joseph Hindmarsh, Bookseller to/His Royal Highness, living/at the Black Bull in Cornhill. 1684.

The/Epilogue/To Mr. Lacy's New Play, Sir Hercules/Buffoon, or the Poetical Esquire./—/Wrote and Spoke by J. H. Com./—/
London,/Printed for Joseph Hindmarsh, Bookseller to/His Royal Highness, living/at the Black Bull in Cornhill. 1684.

The/Prologue/To the last new Play/A Duke and no Duke./Spoken by Mr. Jevon./
The/Epilogue,/Spoken by Mr. Haines./
London, Printed by Geo. Croom, in Thames-street, over against Baynard's Castle, 1684.

The/Prologue/And/Epilogue/To the New/Comedy,/Called,/Sir Courtly Nice, or,/It Cannot be./
London, Printed for Tho. Benskin at the Corner Shop in/Little-Lincolns-Inn-Fields. 1685.

Prologue/To A/Commonwealth of Women,/Spoke by Mr. Haynes,/ Habited like a Whig, Captain of the/Scyth-men in the West, a Scythe in his/Hand./
Epilogue./
London, Printed for R. Bentley in Covent-Garden, and are to/be sold by R. Baldwin in Old-Baily Corner. 1685.

Prologue/To the Opera./—/By Mr. Dryden./—/
Epilogue/—/To the Opera. By Mr. Dryden./—/

Prologue. Spoken by Mrs. Cook./
Epilogue by a Person of Quality. Spoken by Mrs. Barrey./
Printed for Charles Tebroc.

Prologue/To the Injur'd Lovers, Spoken by Mr. Mountfort./
Epilogue/To the Injur'd Lovers, Spoken by Mr. Jevon./
London Printed for Sam. Manship at the Black Bull in Cornhill, 1687.

Prologue/To the Squire of Alsatia. Spoken by Mr. Mountfort./
Epilogue./Spoken by Mrs. Mountfort./
London, Printed for James Knapton, at the Queens/Head in St. Pauls Church-yard. 1688.

Mr. Haynes/His Recantation-Prologue/Upon his first Appearance on the/ Stage/After His/Return from Rome:/
London,/Printed for Richard Baldwin, near the Black Bull/in the Old Baily, 1689.

The/Prologue and Epilogue to the/History of Bacon in Virginia./—/ Written by Mr. Dryden./—/Prologue./Spoken by a Woman./

Epilogue./Spoken by a Woman./
London: Printed for Jacob Tonson, at the Judges Head in Chancery-Lane,/near Fleetstreet, 1689.

The/Prolouge [*sic*]/To/King William & Queen Mary,/At a Play Acted
before Their Majesties at/Whitehall, on Friday the 15th of November 1689./
Written by N. Tate./
Licensed,/Novemb. 16. 1689. J. Fraser./
London,/Printed for F. Saunders, at the Blue Anchor in the Lower Walk
of the/New Exchange, and Published by R. Baldwin in the Old Baily, 1689.

The Prologue and Epilogue to the New/Comedy, called, The English
Fryer, Or,/The Town Sparks./—/Licensed, March 17. 1689. J. F./—/The
Prologue./
The Epilogue./
London, Printed for John Amery; and published by Randal Taylor. 1690.

A/Prologue/Spoken By/Mrs. Bracegirdle,/At The/Entertainment of
Love for Love.

The/Songs/in The/Indian Queen:/As it is now Compos'd into an/Opera./
—/By Mr. Henry Purcell,/Composer in Ordinary to his Majesty./And one of
the Organists of his Majesty's Chapel-Royal./Orn./
London,/Printed for J. Heptinstall; and are to be sold by John May,
at his Shop under/St. Dunstan's Church: And for John Hudgbutt at Tho.
Dring's, Bookseller, at the/Harrow at Clifford's-lane-end in Fleetstreet.
1695.

Single/Songs,/and/Dialogues,/in/The Musical Play/of/Mars & Venus./
Perform'd with the Anatomist, or/The Sham Doctor./—/Set to Musick by
Mr. Finger, and Mr. John Eccles./—/
London,/Printed by J. Heptinstall, for the Authors, and sold by John
Hare/Musical Instrument Seller, at the Golden Viol in St. Paul's Church-/
Yard, and at his Shop in Freeman's-Yard in Cornhill. And by John/Welch
Musical Instrument-maker in Ordinary to His Majesty, at the/Golden Harp
and Hautboy in Catharine-street against Somerset-house/Water-Gate in
the Strand. 1697.

The Prologue, in the Island-Princess Set and Sung by/Mr. Leveridge and
exactly engrav'd by Tho: Cross.
The Epilogue in the Island-Princess Set by Mr. Clarke Sung/by Mrs. Lindsey
and the Boy, and exactly engrav'd by Tho Cross.

Prologue,/Design'd for the last new Farce,/Call'd,/The Fool's Expecta-
tion: Or, The Wheel of Fortune./Acted at the Theatre Royal in Dorset
Gardens./Epilogue/By Fortune./
London: Printed in the Year, 1698.

The last new Prologue and Epilogue/spoken by the Famous Commedian
Mr./William Pinkeman, touching on the/Humours of the Age./Prologue./

Appendix A

Epilogue./
London Printed, and are to be sold/by John Nutt near Stationers-Hall.

A/Prologue,/Sent to Mr. Row [sic],/To his new Play, call'd, The Fair Pe-/nitent. Design'd to be Spoken by Mr./Betterton; but refus'd./—/—/Est & in Obscoenos deflexa Tragoedia Risus. Ovid.

The Last/New Prologues and Epilogues,/Relating to the/Life/Of the/ Observator/and the/Death of the Royal-Oak Lottery,/As they were Spoken at the New Theatre in Little Lin-/coln's Inn Eilds [sic];/With what was then Left-out./—/Publish'd in Opposition to some Spurious Copies/that have crept Abroad./—/—/London Printed, and sold by J. Nutt near Stationers-Hall. 1703.

The/Prologue,/By Way of Dialogue;/Between Heraclitus Ridens, the Obser-/vator, and his Country-Man./—/Spoken by Mr. Powel, Mr. Booth, and Mr. Pack./—/

The/Prologue,/on the/Death of the Royal-Oak Lottery./—/Spoken by Mr. Powell./—/
The/Epilogue./Upon The/Observator./—/Spoken by Mr. Powell./—/ Finis.

A/Prologue/To The/University of Oxford./Spoken by Mr. Betterton.

A/Prefatory/Prologue,/By way of Introduction,/To one Spoken by Mr. Betterton/at Oxford, on Monday/the 5th of July./Spoken by Mr. Mills at the/Theatre-Royal in Drury-Lane,/on Friday the 16th of July,/1703. (Prologue by Betterton and Epilogue by Mills included in this quarto)

The Players turn'd Academicks:/or, A/Description/(In Merry Metre)/ Of their Translation from the Theatre in Little/Lincolns-Inn-Fields, to the Tennis-Court in/Oxford./With a/Preface/Relating to the Proceedings of/ the University the last Act: As also the/Wadhamite Prologue that was spoken there,/with a Prologue and Epilogue, by way of/Answer to it, at the Theatre Royal./—/London:/Printed in the Year MDCCIII.

Prologue/For The/Musick,/Spoken on Tuesday, January the/4th, 1703./ Epilogue/To The/Ladies./
Finis./Printed for J. Tonson, 1704.

Prologue,/Spoken At/Court/Before The/Queen,/On Her Majesty's Birth-day, 1703/4./
Finis./London: Printed for Jacob Tonson. 1704.

The/Prologue and Epilogue/To the Last/New Play of the Albion Queens, or, the/Death of Mary Queen of Scotland./Printed as they were written, but not permitted to be spoken./—/
Sold by J. Nutt, near Stationers-Hall. 1704.

Prologue/To The/Court;/On the Queen's Birth-Day, 1704./
London: Printed for J. Tonson, 1705.

Appendix A

Prologue/Spoken at the First Opening of the/Queen's New Theatre in/ the Hay-Market./

The Opening Prologue Paraphras'd in a Familiar/Stile, for the better Conception of the True Meaning, and/for the Particular Use of Mr. Jer. Collier./
London:/Printed, and Sold by B. Bragg, in Ave-Mary-Lane. 1705.

Prologue/To The/University of Oxford./Written by Mr. Steel, and Spoken by Mr. Wilks./
London, Printed for Bernard Lintott at the Cross-Keys next/Nando's Coffee-House near Temple-Bar. 1706.

Epilogue/Spoken by Mrs. Barry,/April the 7th, 1709./At a Representation of/Love for Love:/For/The Benefit of Mr. Betterton/at His leaving the Stage./—/—/London,/Printed for E. Sanger at the Post-House at the/ Middle Temple-Gate, and E. Curll at the/Peacock without Temple-Bar, 1709./Price 2d.

A/Prologue/For the 4th of November, 1711./Being the/Anniversary for the Birth-Day/Of the Late/K. William,/of/Glorious and Immortal Memory. /—/Written by Dr. Garth./—/Printed in the year, 1711.

The Prologue to the University of Oxford./Written by Mr. Tickell./ Spoken by Mr. Cibber./
—/Printed for J. Tonson, at Shakespear's-Head, over against Catherine-street in/the Strand. 1713.

The/Prologue/at the/Opening of The Theatre-Royal, the Day after/His Majesty's Publick Entry./
Spoken by Mr. Wilks./
Finis./
Printed for J. Tonson in the Strand. 1714./(Price Two Pence.)

An/Epilogue/Recommending/The Cause of Liberty/To The/Beauties/ of/Great Britain./Spoken by Mrs. Oldfield,/At the/Theatre-Royal./—/—/ Printed in the year M.DCC.XVI.

A/Lash for the Laureat:/or an/Address/By Way of Satyr;/Most Humbly Inscrib'd to the/Unparallel'd Mr. Rowe,/On Occasion of a late Insolent/ Prologue/To The/Non-Juror./—/A Tool of Theirs supplies both Town and Stage/with just materials for Satyrick Rage./
—/London:/Printed for J. Morphew near Stationers-Hall. MDCCXVIII./ Price Six-Pence.

(Prologue,/Written by N. Rowe, Esq.)

Prologue/Spoke at the/Theatre-Royal/In/Behalf of the Poor Weavers of the City/of Dublin, April, 1st. 1720./—/By Mr. Elrington./—/
Dublin: Printed by J. Carson.

319

Appendix A

Prologue/To The/Orphan./Represented by some of the West-minster-Scholars at/Hickford's Dancing-Room, the 2d of February, 1720./Spoken by the Lord Duplin,/Who acted Cordelio./
London:/Printed for Jacob Tonson, at Shakespear's-Head over-against/ Katharine-Street in the Strand. MDCCXX.

A/Prologue/To the/Town,/as it was Spoken at the/Theatre in Little Lincoln's-Inn-Fields./Written by Mr. Welsted./With an Epilogue on the same Occasion,/By Sir Richard Steele./—/London,/Printed: And sold by J. Brotherton and W. Meadows, in Corn-/hill, J. Roberts in Warwick Lane, A. Dodd without Tem-/ple-Bar, W. Lewis in Covent-Garden, and J. Graves in St./James's Street. 1721. [Price 4 Pence.]

A/Prologue/To the/Conscious Lovers:/Spoken the 7th. of this Instant March, 1722./By the Ghost of Sir Fopling Flutter./On/Occasion of it's being Play'd at the Request of the Young/Gentlemen of the College, Dublin./
Printed by J. Carson in Coghils-Court in Dame-street, MDCCXXIII.

A New/Epilogue/To The/Conscious Lovers:/—/Spoken by Mrs. Knap. May the 13th. 1724./—/
—/Dublin Printed by J. Carson in Coghill's Court Dames-street. MDCCXXIV.

A New/Prologue,/On the/Anniversary of his Majesty K. George./—/ Spoke by Mr. Griffith./—/
Dublin: Printed by J: Carson in Coghill's Court, Dames-street. 1725.

A/Prologue,/Spoken by Mr. Elrington, on the 22d of April, being the Birth-Day of his Excellency the Lord Car-/teret./Written by C. C./ Epilogue,/Spoken by Mr. Griffith, who Play'd the part of Ben./By the same./
—/Dublin: Printed by Pressick Rider and Thomas Harbin, at the General-/ Post-Office Printing-House in the Exchange on Cork-Hill, 1725.

A/Prologue/For His Majesty's Birth-Day, May 28th, 1725./To be Spoken at the Play-House./—/Written by J. T. Lately one of His Majesty's Servants;/and Dedicated to his Excellency the Lord Carteret./—/
—/Dublin: Printed in the year 1725.

A/Prologue,/And an/Epilogue./And/Songs,/Spoken and Sung/To the Antient and Rt. Worshipful/ Society of Free-Masons, at the/Theatre-Royal, on Thursday Novem-/ber the 29th, 1733, being Mr./Griffith's Benefit./—/ Orn./—/Dublin:/Printed by Geo. Faulkner, in Essex-Street,/opposite to the Bridge, MDCCXXIV.

A *Catalogue of Old and Rare Books.* No. 288. Pickering & Chatt LTD., p. 60/

339 A PARODY ON POPE'S PROLOGUE TO CATO. Address'd to The Late Mr. Henry Bridges, etc. (c. 1740) Folio, Broadside Poem, Scarce.

Appendix A

Prologue/and/Epilogue,/Spoken at the Opening of the/Theatre/in/ Drury-Lane 1747./London:/Printed by E. Cave at St. John's Gate; sold by/Cooper in Pater-noster-Row, and R. Dodsley/Pall-Mall. M,DCC,XLVII. (Price 6d.)

An Occasional/Prologue/and/Epilogue/To/Othello,/As it was acted at the/Theatre-Royal in Drury-Lane,/On Thursday the 7th of March 1751,/ By Persons of Distinction for their Diversion./—/Written by/Christopher Smart, A. M./Fellow of Pembroke-Hall, in the University of Cambridge./ —/The Second Edition./—/London:/Printed for the Author; and sold by Thomas Carnan,/at Mr. Newbery's, at the Bible and Sun in St. Paul's/ Church-yard.

A/Prologue/on/Comic Poetry,/And an/Epilogue/On the/Comic Charac- ters of Women,/as spoke at the Theatre Royal in Covent-Garden,/with a/ Pastoral Dialogue/As performed at the same Theatre:/To which is prefixed an/Ode/To/John Rich, Esq;/—/London:/Printed, and sold, by J. Purser, in Red-Lion Court Fleetstreet,/and at the Pamphlet Shops in London and Westminster. 1753./(Price One Shilling.)

Prologue to the Cozeners,/Spoken by Mr. Foote,/Written by Mr. Garrick.
The/Rejected Prologue./By/W. H./Melbourne:/Clarson, Massina, & Co., Printers,/72 Little Collins Street East./1872.

APPENDIX B

AUTHORS*

BEAUMONT, FRANCIS: "Prologues, Epilogues, and Songs to severall Plaies, written by Mr. Francis Beaumont and Fletcher" in *Poems*, by Francis Beaumont, Printed for Laurence Blaiklock, 1653—Prologue and Epilogue to each of the following: *The Mad Lover, The Spanish Curate, The French Lawyer, The Custome of the Country, The Noble Gentleman, The Captaine, The Coxcomb, The False One, The Chances, The Loyall Subject, The Lovers Progresse, The Passionate Mad-Man, The Tamer Tamed, The Martiall Maid, The Faire Maid of the Inne;* Another Prologue and Epilogue to *The Custome of the Country;* Prologue to *Loves Pilgrimage*.

BEHN, MRS. APHRA: Prologue and Epilogue to Mrs. Behn's *Like Father, like Son*, broadside, 1682; Prologue and Epilogue to *Romulus and Hersilia*, broadside, 1682; Anon., *Romulus and Hersilia*, 1683; Epilogue, Thomas Randolph, *The Jealous Lovers*, 1682, in Mrs. Behn's *Miscellany*, 1685; Prologue, John Wilmot, *Valentinian*, 1685, and *Poems*, 1696.

BLOMER: Prologue spoken to the Ladies before the Music Act at Cambridge, 1698; epilogue; *A New Miscellany of Original Poems*, 1701, pp. 183–187, 187–190.

BROWN, THOMAS: Prologue to a Music Speech in the Theatre at Oxford (printed before an epilogue, by Dryden, published in broadside in 1680), *The Third Volume of the Works of Mr. Thomas Brown*, 1708, pp. 94–95; Prologue spoken to the University of Oxford, 1683, and Epilogue, *A Collection of Miscellany Poems*, by Thomas Brown, 1699, pp. 61–65; "Mr. Haynes His Recantation-Prologue upon his first Appearance on the Stage after his Return from Rome," folio half-sheet, 1689; Epilogue to Thomas Scott's *The Unhappy Kindness* (1697), authorship attributed to Haynes in the play, but assigned to Brown in Brown's *Works*, 1702, IV, 233.

CAREY, ANTHONY: See Falkland, fifth Viscount.

CHEEK, THOMAS: Prologue to Abel Boyer's *Achilles* (1700), performed in 1699.

CHETTLE, HENRY: Prologue and Epilogue to be used at Court, 1602, *Henslowe's Diary*, ed. W. W. Greg, 1904, p. 173.

---

* In addition to writing prologues and epilogues that they published with their own plays, these poets wrote prologues and epilogues for other dramatists and shared thereby in the very popular occupation of recommending other men's plays. Exclusive of pieces printed in their own dramas, the items listed here represent the poets' works published in folio half-sheets, other playwrights' plays, and miscellanies. Prologues and epilogues for their own plays printed only in editions of these plays are not named.

Appendix B

CIBBER, COLLEY: Prologue to Mrs. Behn's *Abdelazer* for a performance by the Patentees in April, 1695; Cibber's *Apology* (1826), pp. 114–115.

CLARKE, JEREMIAH: Set the epilogue to P. A. Motteux's *The Island Princess* (1699) and the second prologue to Elkanah Settle's *New World in the Moon* (1697).

CODRINGTON, COLONEL CHRISTOPHER: Epilogue, John Dennis, *Iphigenia* (1700), performed in 1699. In the eighteenth century, at the first turning, Codrington wrote the epilogue to Southerne's *The Fate of Capua* (1700), and his epilogue was in *A Collection of Poems* (1701).

CONGREVE, WILLIAM: Prologue, George Powell, *A Very Good Wife* (1693); Prologue to the Queen, *Annual Miscellany* (1694); Prologue, Charles Hopkins, *Pyrrhus King of Epirus* (1695); Prologue, John Dryden, Junior, *Husband His Own Cuckold* (1696).

DAVENANT, SIR WILLIAM: *Madagascar, with other Poems*, containing Prologue to Fletcher's *The Woman Hater*, Epilogue to *Love and Honor*, Epilogue to a Vacation Play; *Poems on Several Occasions* (1672) in *Works* (1673), containing Prologue to the *Unfortunate Lovers*, Epilogue, Prologue to the *Wits*, Epilogue, Prologue sung at the presentation of the *Faithful Shepherdess*, Prologue for the Temple, Epilogue to the King at Whitehall for the *Siege of Rhodes*, Epilogue to the *Villain*.

DEKKER, THOMAS: Prologue, *Ponesciones Pillet*, January, 1601, *Henslowe's Diary*, ed. W. W. Greg, 1904, p. 153.

DENHAM, SIR JOHN: Prologue to His Majesty at the first play presented at the Cock-pit in Whitehall, folio half-sheet, 1660.

DENNIS, John: Prologue, John Oldmixon, *Amintas* (1698).

DERING, SIR EDWARD: Epilogue, Mrs. Catherine Philips, *Pompey* (1663).

DILLON, WENTWORTH: Prologue spoken to the Duke of York in Edinburgh; Epilogue to *Alexander the Great* when acted at Dublin; Prologue, Mrs. Catherine Philips, *Pompey* (1663).

DOGGETT, Thomas: Prologue, Thomas Wright, *The Female Virtuoso's* (1693).

DRYDEN, JOHN: Prologue and Epilogue to *The Tempest* (1670), written with Sir William Davenant; Prologue after the Fire, *Covent Garden Drollery* (1672), *Miscellanies* (1692); Prologue, Lodowick Carlell, *Arviragus and Philicia Revived*, *Miscellanies* (1684); Prologue for the Women, *Miscellanies* (1684); Prologue and Epilogue to *The Silent Woman* at Oxford, *Miscellanies* (1684); Prologue and Epilogue at the Opening of the New House, March 26, 1674, *Miscellanies* (1684); Prologue and Epilogue to the University of Oxford, 1674, *Miscellanies* (1684); Epilogue intended for *Calisto* at Court, *Miscellanies* (1684); Epilogue, George Etherege, *The Man of Mode* (1676); Prologue, Charles Davenant, *Circe* (1677), two versions; Epilogue, Nathaniel Lee, *Mithridates* (1678); Prologue, Thomas Shadwell, *The True Widow* (1678), and Mrs. Aphra Behn, *The Widow Ranter* (1690); Prologue, Lee, *Cæsar Borgia* (1680); Prologue at Oxford, Lee, *Sophonisba*, and *Miscellany*

323

Appendix B

Poems (1684); Prologue, Nahum Tate, *The Loyal General* (1680); Epilogue, Charles Saunders, *Tamerlane the Great* (1681); A Prologue, *Miscellanies* (1693); Prologue and Epilogue, Lee, *The Princess of Cleves* (1681); First Prologue to the University of Oxford, 1681, *Miscellanies* (1693); Second Prologue to the University of Oxford, 1681, *Miscellany Poems* (1684); Prologue to the University of Oxford, *Miscellany Poems* (1684); Epilogue, John Banks, *The Unhappy Favourite* (1682); Prologue to His Royal Highness upon his First Appearance at the Duke's House since his Return from Scotland, folio half-sheet, 1682; Prologue to the Duchess on her Return from Scotland, folio half-sheet, 1682; Prologue and Epilogue, Thomas Southerne, *The Loyal Brother* (1682); Prologue and Epilogue to the King and Queen at the Opening of the Two Companies in 1682, folio half-sheet, 1683; Epilogue, Lee, *Constantine the Great* (1684); Prologue, Southern, *Disappointment* (1684); Prologue, Fletcher's *The Prophetess* made into an opera (1690); Prologue, Joseph Harris, *The Mistakes* (1690); Epilogue, John Bancroft, *Henry II* (1693); Epilogue, John Dryden, Junior, *The Husband His Own Cuckold* (1696); Prologue and Epilogue, Dryden's Benefit, March 25, 1700.

DUFFET, THOMAS: Epilogue to the *Shoomaker's a Gentleman*, Prologue to a Play acted privately, Prologue and Epilogue to a Play acted privately, Prologue and Epilogue to *Every Man out of his Humour* revived in 1675, Prologue to the *Mistaken Husband*, Epilogue to the *Mall or Modish Lovers*, Prologue in the Vacation, Prologue to the *Suppos'd Prince*, Prologue and Epilogue to the *Armenian Queen*, Epilogue by a Woman, Prologue to the *Indian Emperor*, spoken by Mr. Poel, and Epilogue to the same, spoken by a Girl, Prologue and Epilogue to *Psyche Debauch'd*—published in *New Poems, Songs, Prologues and Epilogues* (1676), pp. 60, 65–96.

DUKE, MR., OF CAMBRIDGE: Prologue, Nathaniel Lee, *Lucius Junius Brutus* (1681); Epilogue, Thomas Otway, *The Atheist* (1684).

D'URFEY, THOMAS: Prologue, John Lacy, *Sir Hercules Buffoon*, folio half-sheet, 1684; *New Poems* (1690), containing a Prologue by way of Satyr, spoken before King Charles II at New-Market, Epilogue to *Dido and Aeneas*, spoken by the Lady Dorothy Burk at Mr. Preist's Boarding-School, Prologue spoken by Hains to Trapolin, Epilogue intended for a late comedy and to be spoken by Monford, another Epilogue intended for the same, Mr. Haines' Second Recantation: a Prologue intended to be spoken by him; Epilogue, George Powell, *Alphonso King of Naples* (1691); Epilogue, John Smyth, *Win her and take Her* (1691); Prologue, Thomas Shadwell, *The Volunteers* (1693); Prologue and Epilogue, Robert Gould, *The Rival Sisters* (1696).

ETHEREGE, SIR GEORGE: Epilogue to *Every Man in his Humour, A Collection of Poems* (1672), mostly by Etherege, says Langbaine, MS. notes in

Appendix B

Dramatick Poets in the Bodleian, Malone 129 (1691), p. 290; Epilogue to *Tartuffe* in *Poems on Several Occasions* (1672), Langbaine, *op. cit.*, p. 367; Prologue spoken at the opening of the Duke's new playhouse, *A Collection of Poems* (1672).

FALKLAND, FIFTH VISCOUNT: Prologue, Thomas Otway, *The Souldiers Fortune* (1683); Malone mentions a Prologue intended for *The Old Bachelor*, 1692/3, Edmond Malone, *The Critical and Miscellaneous Prose Works of John Dryden* (1800), I, 224.

FINGER, GODFREY: Set the Prologue to Peter A. Motteux's *The Loves of Mars and Venus* (1697).

GLAPTHORN, HENRY: *Poems* (1639), containing Prologue to a revived Vacation play and Prologue for Ezekiel Fen at his first acting a man's part, pp. 26–28.

GOULD, ROBERT: Prologue design'd for a Play of mine, *Poems Chiefly consisting of Satyrs and Satyrical Epistles* (1689), pp. 53–54.

HARMAN: Prologue, Mrs. Catherine Trotter, *The Fatal Friendship* (1698).

HAYNES, JOSEPH: Epilogue to the University of Oxford, 1677; Prologue to the *Northern Lass*, folio half-sheet, 1684, used again in *Love without Interest* (1699); Epilogue, John Lacy, *Sir Hercules Buffoon*, folio half-sheet, 1684; Original Epilogue, John Banks, *Island Queens* (B.M. 144. g. 3, a new and altered edition, with an Epilogue, by Jo. Haynes, that is unlike that in a quarto of 1704, the title of the altered play being *Albion Queens*); Prologue, George Powell, *Alphonso King of Naples* (1691); Epilogue, Powell, *The Cornish Comedy* (1696); Epilogue, Thomas Scott, *The Unhappy Kindness* (1697), said to be Brown's in *The Works of Thos. Brown* (1702), IV, 313; Epilogue, Edward Ravenscroft, *The Italian Husband* (1698); Prologue and Epilogue, George Farquhar, *Love and a Bottle* (1699); Prologue in *The Life of the Late Famous Comedian, Jo. Hayns* (1701), pp. 39–40; Epilogue writ and spoke by Haynes in Mourning, *Apollo's Feast* (1703), p. 151; Epilogue wrote and Spoke by Haynes, *Apollo's Feast* (1703), p. 162.

HEYWOOD, THOMAS: *Pleasant Dialogues and Drammas* (1637), containing among the "divers Speeches" the following: A speech spoken to their two excellent Majesties at the first play played by the Queenes Servants in the new Theatre at Whitehall, To the King and Queen upon a New-yeares day at night, Epilogue spoken by the same Janus, Prologue spoken before the King, Epilogue, Another spoken at Whitehall, Epilogue, Prologue spoken to their Majesties at Hampton Court, Epilogue, Prologue spoken to their Majesties at Hampton Court, Epilogue, Prologue spoken to their Majesties at Whitehall, Epilogue, Prologue spoken to their Majesties upon like occasion, Epilogue, Prologue spoken to the King and Queen at the second acting of *Cupids Mistress*, Prologue honoring the King's birthday, Epilogue, Prologue spoken to his Majesty upon a New yeares day at night, Another spoken at Court, Epilogue, Prologue spoken at a play in the house of the Earl of Dover, Epilogue, Prologue to the Earl of Dover, Epilogue, Prologue and Epilogue for a young witty lad playing the part of Richard III, Prologue to the play of Queen Elizabeth revived at the Cockpit, Epilogue, Prologue upon his Majesty's last birth-night, Epilogue, Lines spoken to the Palsgrave at his coming, pp. 232–251.

HIGGONS, BEVILL: Epilogue, George Granville, *Heroick Love* (1698).

HODGSON: Prologue, Mrs. Mary Pix, *The False Friend* (1699).

HORDEN, HILDEBRAND: Prologue, Charles Hopkins, *Neglected Virtue* (1696).

JONSON, BEN: Prologue and Epilogue to *Henry VIII* written in part by Jonson, according to Dr. Johnson and Dr. Farmer (Davies, *Dramatic Miscellanies*, III, 67).

JORDAN, THOMAS: *A Rosary of Rarities* (1659), pp. 12–24, containing Prologue to the King, Epilogue to the King, Prologue to the King on August 16, 1660, Prologue to a Play called the Florentine Ladies, Epilogue on New Year's Day at Night, Prologue to *Love hath found his eyes*, Epilogue spoken by Cupid, Epilogue to those that would rise out of the Pit at the Red-Bull in the last scene (June 23, 1660), Prologue to the *Tamer Tam'd* (June 24, 1660), Epilogue spoken by the Tamer, a Woman, Prologue to introduce the first woman to act on the stage, Epilogue, Prologue to the *Poor Mans Comfort* (May 28, 1661); the same pieces in *A Nursery of Novelties* (N.D.) and in *Royal Arbour* (1664); *Wit and Drollery* (1661), containing a Bull Prologue, Another Prologue, An Epilogue upon the honest Lawyer, pp. 236–237.

LEVERIDGE, RICHARD: Set the Prologue to Peter A. Motteux's *The Island Princess* (1699).

LOVELACE, RICHARD: *Lucasta* (1649), containing a Prologue to the Scholars and an Epilogue, pp. 75–79.

LUMLEY, LORD: First Prologue for *The Empress of Morocco* at Court, 1660 or 1670 (F. C. Brown, *Elkanah Settle*, p. 11). See Mulgrave.

M., E.: Prologue, Robert Dareborne, *The Poor-Mans Comfort* (1655).

MIDDLETON, THOMAS: Prologue and Epilogue to be spoken at Court, 1602, *Henslowe's Diary*, ed. W. W. Greg, 1904, p. 172.

MOTTEUX, PETER A.: Epilogue, *She Ventures and He Wins* (1696), by a Young Lady; Prologue and Epilogue, Mrs. Mary Pix, *The Innocent Mistress* (1697); Prologue to the Royal Highness, Second Prologue, Epilogue, Edward Ravenscroft, *The Anatomist* (1697); Epilogue, Henry Smith, *The Princess of Parma* (1699).

MOUNTFORT, WILLIAM: Prologue, John Bancroft, *King Edward III* (1691), Epilogue, Elkanah Settle, *Distress'd Innocence* (1691); Prologue and Epilogue, George Powell, *The Treacherous Brothers* (1696).

MULGRAVE: First Prologue at Court, Elkanah Settle, *The Empress of Morocco* (1673). See Lumley.

OTWAY, THOMAS: Prologue and Epilogue in folio half-sheet to his *Venice*

Appendix B

Preserved, 1681, again the folio half-sheet Prologue to *Venice Preserved* in 1682; Prologue, Mrs. Aphra Behn, *The City Heiress* (1682), Epilogue to her Royal Highness upon her Return from Scotland, folio half-sheet, 1682; Epilogue to his Royal Highness upon his First Appearance at the Duke's House since His Return from Scotland, folio half-sheet, 1682; Prologue, Nathaniel Lee, *Constantine the Great*, folio half-sheet, 1683.

RAVENSCROFT, EDWARD: Epilogue, Mrs. Aphra Behn, *The Debauchee* (1677); Epilogue, Mrs. Behn, *The Town-Fopp* (1677); Epilogue, John Bancroft, *The Tragedy of Sertorius* (1679); Epilogue, William Whitaker, *The Conspiracy* (1680).

RAYNSFORD, SIR GEORGE: Prologue, Nahum Tate, *The Ingratitude of a Common-Wealth* (1682).

SACKVILLE, CHARLES: Epilogue, Molière, *Tartuffe* (1670); Epilogue, Jonson, *Every Man in his Humour* (revived between 1663 and 1682, Genest, I, 343).

ST. JOHN, HENRY: Prologue, Roger Boyle, *Altemira* (1702), acted first as *The General* in 1664; Prologue, George Granville, *Heroick Love* (1698).

SCROOP, SIR CAR: Prologue, Sir George Etherege, *The Man of Moda* (1676); Prologue, Nathaniel Lee, *The Rival Queens* (1677).

SETTLE, ELKANAH: Prologue to the Oxford Scholars at the Act there, 1671, signed J. S. and conjectured to be E.S. (Elkanah Settle), Bodleian, MS. Eng. Poet. e 4, p. 176; Prologue written by Settle to *Cambyses* at Oxford, 1672, and recited by Betterton, Bodleian, MS. Eng. Poet. e 4, p. 177; Roswell Gray Ham, *Otway and Lee* (1931), p. 2 and p. 221; Epilogue, Edward Ravenscroft, *The Careless Lovers* (1673).

SEDLEY, SIR CHARLES: Prologue, Thomas Shadwell, *Epsom Wells* (1673); Prologue, Henry Higden, *The Wary Widdow* (1693); Prologue, *Poems on Affairs of State*, Part III (1698).

SHADWELL, THOMAS: Epilogue, Laurence Maidwell, *The Loving Enemies* (1680); A Lenten Prologue refus'd by the Players, 1682, folio half-sheet; Epilogue, Dr. Brady, *The Rape* (1692).

SHEERS, SIR HENRY: Prologue, John Dryden, *Don Sebastian* (1690); The Strowlers Prologue at Cambridge, British Museum MS. Eg. 2623, pp. 58–59.

SHIPMAN, THOMAS: *Carolina* (1683), containing A Prologue for a Company of Players leaving London for York, 1670; Epilogue; pp. 130–132; Prologue spoken by Ant. Eyre, 1677; pp. 190–191; Prologue to *Henry the third of France* at the Royal Theatre, by Hart, 1678; pp. 206–208; Epilogue by a woman to the same; pp. 208–209.

SHIRLEY, JAMES: *Narcissus* (1646), containing a Prologue to Mr. Fletcher's Play in Ireland; a Prologue to the Alchimist Acted there; a Prologue there to the Irish Gent.; a Prologue to a Play there; Call'd, *No Wit to a Womans*, Prologue to another of Master Fletcher's Playes there; Prologue to a Play there; Call'd, *the Toy*; a Prologue to another

Appendix B

Play there; To a Play there, called *the Generall*; To his own Comedy there, called *Rosania*, or *Loves Victory*; Prologue to his Comedy at the Cock-pit, called the *Coronation*, Presented in the person of a Lady; Prologue to his Comedy of the *Changes*; Epilogue; Prologue at the Globe to his Comedy call'd *The Doubtfull Heire*; Epilogue to the same play there; Prologue to his Play called the *Brothers*; Epilogue in the person of Don Pedro; Prologue to his Tragedy call'd the *Cardinall*; pp. 35–46, 147—159.

STAFFORD, JOHN, ESQ.: Epilogue, Thomas Southerne, *The Disappointment* (1684). When published in folio half-sheet with the Prologue, this Epilogue was said to be "by another Hand." It is included by Saintsbury in the "Doubtful Poems" of Dryden, *The Works of John Dryden*, ed. Scott and Saintsbury, X, 421, with variation from the original text.

SUCKLING, SIR JOHN: *The Last Remains of Sr John Suckling* (1659), containing a Prologue of the Author's to a Masque at Witten, p. 37.

TATE, NAHUM: Prologue to King William and Queen Mary, at a play acted at Whitehall, November 15, 1689, *Term Catalogue*, II, 313, May, 1690; Prologue to *London Cuckolds*, acted at Hull, November, 1683, printed in *Poems on Several Occasions*, by W.C. (1684), assigned to Tate by Genest, I, 440; Epilogue, Joseph Harris, *The Mistakes* (1691).

TATHAM, JOHN: *The Fancies Theatre* (1640), containing a Prologue spoken upon removing of the late Fortune Players to the Bull; *Ostella* (1650), containing a Prologue spoken at the Cock-pit, at the coming of the Red-Bull Players thither, a Prologue spoken at the Red-Bull to a Play called the *Whisperer, or what you please*.

TROTTE, Nicholas: Introduction to Certaine Devices and shewes presented to her Majestie by the Gentlemen of Grayes-Inne at her Highnesse Court in Greenwich, February 28, thirtieth year of her Maiesties most happy Raigne. 1587.

UNDERHILL, CAVE: Prologue, John Smyth, *Win her and Take her* (1691).

W., P.: Prologue to *The Mistaken Husband* (1675) in *New Songs and Poems* (1677), MS. note in Langbaine, *Dramatick Poets* (Bodleian, Malone. 129), p. 167.

WYCHERLEY, WILLIAM: Prologue written at the author's request and designed to be spoken, Mrs. Catherine Trotter, *Agnes de Castro* (1696).

APPENDIX C

SPEAKERS OF PROLOGUES AND EPILOGUES

ADAMS: 2. Witch in epilogue, Thomas Duffett, *The Empress of Morocco* (1674), D.L. *c.* Dec. 1673.

ALLEYN, RICHARD: Prologue and epilogue, *Frederick and Basilea*, 1597. See Nungezer's *Dictionary of Actors*.

ALLISON, MRS. MARIA: Prologue, Anon., *The Triumphs of Virtue* (1697), D.L. *c.* 1696/7; epilogue, John Dennis, *A Plot and no Plot* (1697), D.L. May 1697; epilogue, Charles Gildon, *The Roman Brides Revenge* (1697), D.L. 1697.

ANGEL, EDWARD: Prologue, Roger Boyle, Earl of Orrery, *Tryphon* (1669), L.I.F. Dec. 1668; first prologue with Underhill and Nokes, Hon. Edward Howard, *The Womens Conquest* (1671), L.I.F. *c.* Nov. 1670; epilogue with Mrs. Long, John Crowne, *Juliana* (1671), L.I.F. *c.* August 1671.

ARIELL, LITTLE MRS.: Epilogue by a friend, Mrs. Aphra Behn, *Abdelazer* (1677), D.G. *c.* April 1676; epilogue, Thomas Otway, *Don Carlos* (1676), D.G. June 1676.

AYLIFF, MRS.: Prologue with others, Peter A. Motteux, *The Loves of Mars & Venus* (1697), L.I.F. *c.* March 1697.

BAKER, MRS.: Epilogue, Hon. Edward Howard, *The Man of Newmarket* (1678), D.L. *c.* April 1678.

BARRY, MRS. ELIZABETH: Epilogue, Thomas Otway, *Friendship in Fashion* (1678), D.G. April 1678; epilogue, John Leanerd, *The Counterfeits* (1679), D.G. May 1678; epilogue, Mrs. Aphra Behn, *The Young King* (1683), D.G. *c.* June 1679; prologue with Lee and Nokes, Thomas D'Urfey, *The Virtuous Wife* (1680), D.G. *c.* Sept. 1679; epilogue, Thomas Otway, *Caius Marius* (1680), D.G. *c.* Sept. 1679; epilogue, Thomas Shadwell, *The Woman Captain* (1680), D.G. *c.* Sept. 1679; epilogue, Laurence Maidwell, *The Loving Enemies* (1680), D.G. *c.* Oct. 1679; epilogue, Nahum Tate, *The Loyal General* (1680), D.G. *c.* Dec. 1679; epilogue, Mrs. Aphra Behn, *The Second Part of the Rover* (1681), D.G. Feb. or April 1680; epilogue, Nathaniel Lee, *Lucius Junius Brutus* (1681), D.G. Dec. 1680; prologue, epilogue with others, Edward Ravenscroft, *The London Cuckolds* (1682), D.G. Nov. 1681; epilogue with Leigh, Thomas Shadwell, *The Lancashire Witches* (1682), D.G. *c.* Sept. 1681; epilogue, Nahum Tate, *King Lear* (1681), D.G. *c.* March 1681; prologue, Mrs. Aphra Behn, *The City-Heiress* (1682), D.G. *c.* March 1681/2; epilogue, Mrs. Behn, *The False Count* (1682), D.G. *c.* Sept. 1682; prologue intended, John Wilmot, Earl of Rochester, *Valentinian* (1685), D.L. Feb. 1683/4;

Appendix C

epilogue to *Valentinian* at the same time; epilogue, Thomas Southerne, *The Wives Excuse* (1692), D.L. Dec. 1691; prologue, Southerne, *The Maid's Last Prayer* (1693), D.L. Jan. 1692/3; epilogue, William Congreve, *The Old Batchelour* (1693), D.L. Jan. 1692/3; prologue, Thomas Doggett, *The Country-Wake* (1696), L.I.F. c. May 1696; epilogue, D'Urfey, *The Intrigues at Versailles* (1697), L.I.F. c. Feb. 1696/7; prologue, Ravenscroft, *The Anatomist* (1697), L.I.F. c. March 1697; epilogue, Mrs. Catherine Trotter, *The Fatal Friendship* (1698), L.I.F. 1698; epilogue, Southerne, *The Fate of Capua* (1700), L.I.F. 1700. Mrs. Barry continued her stage-orations in the eighteenth century.

BEAUMONT, JOSEPH: Prologue with Nicholas Coleman, *Apollo Shroving Composed for the Schollars of the Free-schools of Hadleigh in Suffolke and acted by them on Shrove-tuesday*, Feb. 6, 1626; epilogue to the same.

BETTERTON, MRS. MARY: Epilogue, Samuel Pordage, *The Siege of Babylon* (1678), D.G. c. Sept. 1677.

BETTERTON, THOMAS: Epilogue, Thomas Porter, *The Villain* (1663), L.I.F. Oct. 1662; prologue, Sir Samuel Tuke, *The Adventures of Five Hours* (1663), L.I.F. Jan. 1662/3; prologue, Roger Boyle, Earl of Orrery, *Altemira* (1702), L.I.F. Sept. 1664; prologue, *Cambyses* at Oxford, 1672; prologue, Sir George Etherege, *The Man of Mode* (1676), D.G. March 1675/6; prologue, Mrs. Aphra Behn, *Sir Patient Fancy* (1678), D.G. Jan. 1677/8; prologue, John Dryden, *Troilus and Cressida* (1679), D.G. c. April 1679; prologue, Thomas Otway, *Caius Marius* (1680), D.G. c. Sept. 1679; epilogue, Otway, *Venice Preserved* (1682), D.G. Feb. 1681/2; prologue to the King and Queen by Dryden, Nov. 1682; prologue, Thomas Southerne, *The Disappointment* (1684), D.L. c. April 1684; epilogue, Mrs. Behn, *The Luckey Chance* (1687), D.L. c. April 1686; prologue, Nathaniel Lee, *The Massacre of Paris* (1690), D.L. Oct. 1689; prologue, Dryden, *King Arthur* (1691), D.G. c. May 1691; prologue, Southerne, *The Wives Excuse* (1692), D.L. Dec. 1691; prologue, Dr. Brady, *The Rape* (1692), D.L. Feb. 1691/2; prologue, Dryden, *Love Triumphant* (1694), D.L. c. Dec. 1693; prologue, Thomas D'Urfey, *Don Quixote* Part I (1694), D.G. c. May 1694; prologue, William Congreve, *Love for Love* (1695), L.I.F. April 1695; prologue, George Granville, Lord Lansdowne, *The She-Gallants* (1696), L.I.F. Dec. 1695; epilogue, Thomas Doggett, *The Country-Wake* (1696), L.I.F. c. May 1696; prologue, Mrs. Manley, *The Royal Mischief* (1696), L.I.F. c. April 1696; Congreve's prologue to John Dryden, jun.'s *Husband His Own Cuckold* (1696), L.I.F., Feb. 1696; prologue, Congreve, *The Mourning Bride* (1697), L.I.F. 1697; second prologue, Edward Ravenscroft, *The Anatomist* (1697), L.I.F. c. March 1697; prologue, Charles Hopkins, *Boadicea* (1697), L.I.F. 1697; prologue, Mrs. Mary Pix, *Queen Catharine* (1698), L.I.F. c.

Appendix C

Sept. 1698; prologue, Congreve, *The Way of the World* (1700), L.I.F. March 1699/1700; prologue, Charles Gildon, *Measure for Measure* (1700), L.I.F. *c.* 1699; prologue, Nicholas Rowe, *The Ambitious Step-mother* (1700), the old L.I.F. *c.* Dec. 1700. Betterton spoke prologues and epilogues frequently in the eighteenth century.

BOUTELI, MRS.: Epilogue, John Corye, *The Generous Enemies* (1672), T.R. *c.* Aug. 1671; prologue, Thomas Duffett, *The Spanish Rogue* (1674), L.I.F. *c.* June 1673.

BOWEN, WILLIAM: Prologue (with Bright and Williams), Joseph Harris, *The Mistakes* (1691), D.L. *c.* Dec. 1690; epilogue, Edward Ravenscroft, *The Canterbury Guests* (1695), D.L. Sept. 1694; prologue and epilogue, Peter A. Motteux, *Love's a Jest* (1696), the epilogue being with Underhill and Gipsy, L.I.F. *c.* Sept. 1696; epilogue, Ravenscroft, *The Anatomist* (1697), L.I.F. *c.* March 1697; prologue, Motteux, *The Novelty* (1697), L.I.F. *c.* June 1697; prologue, Mrs. Mary Pix, *The Deceiver Deceived* (1698), L.I.F. *c.* Dec. 1697; prologue, Mrs. Catherine Trotter, *Fatal Friendship* (1698), L.I.F. 1698; prologue (extempore), Motteux, *Beauty in Distress* (1698), L.I.F. *c.* April 1698; prologue, Thomas Dilke, *The Pretenders* (1698), L.I.F. *c.* May 1698; epilogue, *The Unnatural Mother* (1698), by a Young Lady, L.I.F. *c.* Aug. 1697.

BOWMAN, MRS.: Prologue, Anon., *She Ventures and He Wins* (1696), L.I.F. *c.* 1695/6; epilogue, Joseph Harris, *The City Bride* (1696), L.I.F. *c.* Jan. 1696; epilogue, Charles Hopkins, *Boadicea* (1697), L.I.F. 1697; epilogue, Edward Ravenscroft, *The Italian Husband* (1698), L.I.F. 1697; prologue, Mrs. Mary Pix, *The Beau Defeated* (1700), the old L.I.F. March 1699/1700. Mrs. Bowman spoke prologues and epilogues in the eighteenth century.

BRACEGIRDLE, MRS. ANNE: Prologue, William Mountfort, *The Successful Strangers* (1690), D.L. *c.* Dec. 1689; prologue, Thomas Shadwell, *The Amorous Bigotte* (1690), D.L. *c.* March 1689/90; prologue, Thomas Southerne, *Sir Anthony Love* (1691), D.L. *c.* Dec. 1690; epilogue, John Bancroft, *King Edward III* (1691), D.L. *c.* Dec. 1690; prologue, John Dryden, *Amphitryon* (1690), D.L. April 1690; epilogue, Dryden, *King Arthur* (1691), D.G. *c.* May 1691; prologue (with Mountfort), Thomas D'Urfey, *The Marriage-Hater Match'd* (1692), D.L. Jan. 1691/2; epilogue, Dr. Brady, *The Rape* (1692), D.L. Feb. 1691/2; epilogue, Bancroft, *Henry II* (1693), D.L. Nov. 1692; prologue, Shadwell, *The Volunteers* (1693), D.L. Nov. 1692; epilogue, Dryden, *Cleomenes* (1692), D.L. April 1692; prologue, William Congreve, *The Old Batchelor* (1693), D.L. Jan. 1692/3; epilogue, Southerne, *The Maid's Last Prayer* (1693), D.L. Jan. 1692/3; prologue, Congreve, *The Double Dealer* (1694), D.L. Oct. 1693; prologue, Southerne, *The Fatal Marriage* (1694), D.L. Feb. 1693/4; epilogue, John Dryden

Appendix C

Jr., *The Husband His Own Cuckold* (1696), L.I.F. 1695/6; epilogue, George Granville, *The She-Gallants* (1696), L.I.F. *c.* Dec. 1695; prologue and epilogue, Congreve, *Love for Love* (1695), L.I.F. April 1695; epilogue, Congreve, *The Mourning Bride* (1697), L.I.F. 1697; prologue, Sir John Vanbrugh, *The Provok'd Wife* (1697), L.I.F. May 1697; epilogue, Peter A. Motteux, *Beauty in Distress* (1698), L.I.F. *c.* April 1698; epilogue, Henry Smith, *The Princess of Parma* (1699), L.I.F. *c.* Jan. 1699. Mrs. Bracegirdle continued to please in prologues and epilogues after 1700.

BRADSHAW, MRS.: Epilogue, Mrs. Manley, *The Royal Mischief* (1696), L.I.F. *c.* April 1696; epilogue, Mrs. Mary Pix, *The Deceiver Deceived* (1698), L.I.F. *c.* Dec. 1697. Mrs. Bradshaw spoke prologues and epilogues after 1700.

BRIGHT: Prologue (with Bowen and Williams), Joseph Harris, *The Mistakes* (1691), D.L. *c.* Dec. 1690.

BURBAGE, RICHARD: Epilogue (with William Ostler), Ben Jonson, *The Alchemist*, 1610, winter; epilogue, William Shakespeare, *The Tempest*, 1611, winter. See Thomas W. Baldwin, *The Organization and Personnel of the Shakespearean Company* (1927).

BURK, LADY DOROTHY: Epilogue to the Opera of Dido and Aeneas, *New Poems*, by D'Urfey, 1690.

BUTLER, MRS. CHARLOTTE: Prologue, John Crowne, *Calisto* (1675), Court, 1675; epilogue, Mrs. Aphra Behn, *The City-Heiress* (1682), D.G. *c.* March 1681/2; prologue, Mrs. Behn, *Like Father like Son*, 1682; prologue, Anon., *Romulus and Hersilia* (1683), D.G. *c.* Aug. 1682; epilogue, Richard Brome, *The Northern Lass*, 1684; epilogue (with Mountfort), Thomas D'Urfey, *Love for Money* (1691), D.L. *c.* Dec. 1689; epilogue (with Mountfort), George Powell, *The Treacherous Brothers* (1690), D.L. *c.* Dec. 1689; prologue, Thomas Shadwell, *The Amorous Bigotte* (1690), D.L. *c.* March 1689/90; epilogue, Thomas Southerne, *Sir Anthony Love* (1691), D.L. *c.* Dec. 1690; epilogue, Joseph Harris, *The Mistakes* (1691), D.L. *c.* Dec. 1690; epilogue, John Smyth, *Win her and Take her* (1691), D.L. 1691; epilogue (with lap-dog), D'Urfey, *The Marriage-Hater Match'd* (1692), D.L. Jan. 1691/2.

CAMPIAN, MISS: Epilogue, Thomas D'Urfey, *The Famous History of the Rise and Fall of Massaniello* (1699), D.L. *c.* May 1699.

CHAUNDLER: Prologue, Hausted's *The Rival Friends* (1632), with the name "Chaundler" written in the margin of the copy in the British Museum. The play was presented at Cambridge.

CHOCK, MISS DENNIE: Epilogue, George Powell, *Bonduca* (1696), D.L. *c.* Sept. 1695; epilogue, Powell, *The Cornish Comedy* (1696), D.G. 1696; epilogue, Elkanah Settle, *The World in the Moon* (1697), D.G. May 1697; prologue (with Powell and Miss Cross), Charles Gildon,

Appendix C

Phæton (1698), D.L. 1698; epilogue, William Philips, *The Revengeful Queen* (1698), D.L. 1698.

CIBBER, COLLEY: Epilogue, Sir John Vanbrugh, *The Relapse* (1697), D.L. Dec. 1696; epilogue, Thomas D'Urfey, *The Campaigners* (1698), D.L. *c.* Nov. 1698; prologue and epilogue, John Dryden, *The Pilgrim*, 1700. The majority of Cibber's pieces were spoken after 1700.

CLARKE: Prologue, John Leanerd, *The Country Innocence* (1677), D.L. *c.* April 1677; prologue, Hon. Edward Howard, *The Man of Newmarket* (1678), D.L. *c.* April 1678.

CLUN: Epilogue, Beaumont and Fletcher, *The Humorous Lieutenant*, T.R. April 8, 1663.

COLEMAN: Prologue with Joseph Beaumont, *Apollo Shroving Composed for the Schollars of the Free-schools of Hadleigh in Suffolke and acted by them on Shrove-tuesday*, Feb. 6, 1626.

COOK, MRS. SARAH: Prologue, John Leanerd, *The Rambling Justice* (1678), D.L. *c.* March 1677/78; epilogue, Nahum Tate, *The History of King Richard the Second* (1681), D.L. *c.* Dec. 1680; epilogue, John Dryden, *The Duke of Guise* (1683), D.L. Nov. 1682; epilogue, Nathaniel Lee, *Constantine the Great* (1684), D.L. *c.* Dec. 1683; prologue and prologue for second day, John Wilmot, Earl of Rochester, *Valentinian* (1685), D.L. Feb. 1683/4; epilogue, Mrs. Aphra Behn, *The Emperor of the Moon* (1687), D.G. *c.* March 1686/7; epilogue to the University of Oxford, *Poems on Affairs of State*, Part III, 1698.

CORY, MRS.: Epilogue, William Wycherley, *The Plain Dealer* (1677), D.L. Dec. 1676.

COX, MRS.: Epilogue, Nathaniel Lee, *Sophonisba* (1676) at its first acting at Oxford; D.L. April 1675; epilogue, Lee, *Mithridates King of Pontus*, folio half-sheet of 1681, D.L. *c.* March 1677/8.

COX, ROBERT: Prologue written by the Butler of a college and quoted in part by Francis Kirkman, *The Wits* (1673), Preface.

CROSBY: Epilogue, Anon., *The Counterfeit Bridegroom* (1677), D.G. *c.* Sept. 1677.

CROSS, MRS.: Prologue, Thomas Scott, *The Mock-Marriage* (1696), D.G. *c.* Oct. 1695; prologue (with Horden), Thomas D'Urfey, *The Comical History of Don Quixote*, Part III (1696), D.G.? *c.* Nov. 1695; prologue, Mrs. Mary Pix, *Ibrahim* (1696), D.L. 1696; prologue to entertain the Queen at *Ibrahim*, printed in D'Urfey's *Wit and Mirth* (1719), II, 339–340; epilogue, Colley Cibber, *Woman's Wit* (1697), D.L. *c.* Dec. 1696; prologue, Sir John Vanbrugh, *The Relapse* (1697), D.L. Dec. 1696; prologue (with Powell and Miss Chock), Charles Gildon, *Phæton* (1698), D.L. 1698; epilogue, William Walker, *Victorious Love* (1698), D.L. 1698. Mrs. Cross's name appears with prologues and epilogues after 1700.

Appendix C

CUNDALL, HENRY: Epilogue, William Shakespeare, *All's Well that Ends Well*, 1607, summer.

CURRER, MRS. ELIZABETH: Prologue, Anon., *The Counterfeit Bridegroom* (1677), D.G. *c.* Sept. 1677; epilogue, Thomas D'Urfey, *Squire Oldsapp* (1679), D.G. *c.* June 1678; prologue, Mrs. Aphra Behn, *The Feign'd Curtizans* (1679), D.G. *c.* March 1678/9; epilogue, Nahum Tate, *The Loyal General* (1680), *c.* Dec. 1679; epilogue (with others), Edward Ravenscroft, *The London Cuckolds* (1682), D.G. Nov. 1681; prologue, Ravenscroft, *Dame Dobson* (1684), folio half-sheet of 1683, D.G. 1683.

DAVIS, MARY: River Thames in prologue (with others), John Crowne, *Calisto* (1675), Court, 1675.

DOGGET, Thomas: Prologue, Thomas D'Urfey, *The Richmond Heiress* (1693), D.L. *c.* Feb. 1692/3; prologue, Thomas Wright, *The Female Virtuoso's* (1693), D.G. April 1693; epilogue, John Crowne, *The Married Beau* (1694), D.L. *c.* Jan. 1694; epilogue, D'Urfey, *Don Quixote*, Part I (1694), D.G. *c.* May 1694; epilogue, A Young Lady, *She Ventures and He Wins* (1696), L.I.F. *c.* 1695/6; epilogue, D'Urfey, *Cinthia and Endimion* (1697), D.L. *c.* Sept. 1697. Dogget spoke prologues and epilogues after 1700.

ESTCOURT, RICHARD: Epilogue spoken upon Lord Sydney's leaving Ireland, 1693; *Poems on Affairs of State*, Part III (1698), pp. 187–188. Estcourt spoke prologues and epilogues after 1700.

EYRE, ANTONY, ESQ.: Prologue to the Huffer, 1677, spoken "by Ant. Eyre Esquire, and directed to the right Honourable, the Lady Roos, when he acted Almanzor in the Granada, at Belvoir"; Thomas Shipman, *Carolina: Or, Loyal Poems* (1683), pp. 190–191.

FEN, EZEKIEL: Prologue for his first acting a man's part, Henry Glapthorne, *Poems* (1639), p. 28.

FORD: America in the prologue (with others), John Crowne, *Calisto* (1675), Court, 1675.

GIBBS, MRS. ANN: Epilogue, Thomas Rawlins, *Tom Essence* (1677), D.G. *c.* Sept. 1676.

GOODMAN, CARDELL or CARDONELL: Thunder in Epilogue (with others), Thomas Duffett, *The Empress of Morocco* (1674), D.L. *c.* Dec. 1673; epilogue (with Mrs. Cox), Nathaniel Lee, *Mithridates* (1678), D.L. *c.* March 1677/8; prologue, Lee, *Constantine the Great* (1684), D.L. *c.* Dec. 1683.

GWINN, NELL: Epilogue, Thomas Porter, The *Villain* (1663), L.I.F. Oct. 1662; prologue (with Mrs. Knepp), Sir Robert Howard, *The Great Favourite* (1668), T.R. Feb. 1667/8; prologue and epilogue, Ben Jonson, *Catiline's Conspiracy* (1674), T.R. Dec. 1668; epilogue, John Dryden, *Tyrannick Love* (1670), T.R. *c.* April 1669; prologue, Dryden, *The Conquest of Granada*, Part I (1672), T.R. *c.* Dec. 1670;

prologue, Beaumont and Fletcher, *The Knight of the Burning Pestle*, revived (before 1671), Genest, *op. cit.*, I, 348; epilogue, Mrs. Aphra Behn, *Sir Patient Fancy* (1678), D.G. Jan. 1677/8; prologue, John Banks, *The Destruction of Troy* (1679), D.G. *c.* Nov. 1678.

HAINES (HAYNES), JOSEPH: Prologue, John Dryden, *The Assignation* (1673), L.I.F. *c.* Nov. 1672, Genest, *op. cit.*, I, 127; prologue, Nathaniel Lee, *Nero* (1675), D.L. May 1674; prologue, Thomas Duffett, *The Mock-Tempest* (1675), D.L. Nov. 1674; prologue, Ben Jonson, *Every Man out of his Humour*, July, 1675, Duffett, *New Poems* (1676), pp.72–75; epilogue, Sir Francis Fane, *Love in the Dark* (1675), D.L. May 1675; prologue, Duffett, *Psyche Debauch'd* (1678), D.L. *c.* May 1675; epilogue, Lee, *Gloriana* (1676), D.L. Jan. 1675/6; epilogue to Oxford, 1677; prologue, intended for Dr. William Chamberlayne's *Wits led by the Nose* (1678), D.L. *c.* Sept. 1677; prologue, Thomas D'Urfey, *Trick for Trick* (1678), D.L. *c.* March 1677/8; induction (with others), Edward Howard, *The Man of Newmarket* (1678), D.L. *c.* April 1678; epilogue, John Crowne, *The Ambitious Statesman* (1679), D.L. *c.* March 1678/9; prologue and epilogue, John Lacy, *Sir Hercules Buffoon* (1684), D.G. *c.* Sept. 1684; prologue and epilogue, Nahum Tate, *A Duke and no Duke* (1685), D.L. Nov. 1684; prologue, Richard Brome, *The Northern Lass*, revived, 1684; original epilogue intended for the *Island Queens*, 1684; prologue, D'Urfey, *A Common-Wealth of Women* (1686), D.L. *c.* Sept. 1685; prologue after the Vacation, Edward Ravenscroft, *Titus Andronicus* (1687), D.L. *c.* April 1686; prologue, William Mountfort, *The Injur'd Lovers* (1688), D.L. *c.* March 1687/8; Recantation prologue for *The Rehearsal*, 1689, Tom Brown's *Works* (1719), IV, 320–321; Second Recantation prologue, intended to be spoken, D'Urfey's *New Poems* (1690), pp. 204–207; prologue, George Powell, *A Very Good Wife* (1693), D.L. March 1692/3; epilogue, D'Urfey, *Don Quixote*, Part I (1694), D.G. *c.* May 1694; epilogue, Charles Hopkins, *The Neglected Virtue* (1696), D.L. 1696; epilogue, Dr. James Drake, *The Sham Lawyer* (1697), D.L. *c.* Sept. 1696; epilogue, Thomas Scott, *The Unhappy Kindness* (1697), D.L. 1697; prologue, John Dennis, *A Plot, and no Plot* (1697), D.L. May 1697; epilogue, George Farquhar, *Love and a Bottle* (1699), D.L. 1699; prologue, William Penkethman, *Love without Interest* (1699); epilogue, Mrs. Susanna Centlivre, *The Perjur'd Husband* (1700), Sept. 1700. Haines died the next year.

HARPE: Hero of the Sea in prologue (with others), John Crowne, *Calisto* (1675), Court 1675.

HARRIS, JOSEPH: Epilogue (with Sandford), Sir William Davenant, *The Man's the Master* (1669), L.I.F. March 26, 1668; epilogue, Nevil Payne, *The Fatal Jealousie* (1673), D.G. Aug. 1672; epilogue (with others), Thomas Duffett, *The Empress of Morocco* (1674), D.L. *c.* Dec. 1673;

Appendix C

epilogue, Nathaniel Lee, *Nero* (1675), D.L. May 1674; prologue, Thomas Otway, *Alcibiades* (1675), D.G. Sept. 1675.

HART, CHARLES: Prologue, John Dryden, *Marriage A-la-mode* (1673), L.I.F. *c.* May 1672; prologue, Lodowick Carlell, *Arviragus*, revived, 1672, Dryden's lines printed in *Miscellany Poems* (1684), pp. 281–283; prologue to the University of Oxford, 1674, by Dryden, *Miscellany Poems* (1684), pp. 267–269; Dryden's prologue and epilogue at the acting of the *Silent Woman* at Oxford, *Miscellany Poems* (1684), pp. 263–267; prologue, William Wycherley, *The Country-Wife* (1675), D.L. Jan. 1674/5; prologue as Europe (with others), John Crowne, *Calisto* (1675), Court 1675; prologue, Wycherley, *The Plain-Dealer* (1677), D.L. Dec. 1676.

HODGSON, JOHN: Prologue, Thomas Dilke, *The Lover's Luck* (1696), L.I.F. *c.* Dec. 1695; prologue, Dilke, *The City Lady* (1697), L.I.F. *c.* Jan. 1696/7.

HODGSON, MRS.: Prologue (with others), Peter A. Motteux, *The Loves of Mars & Venus* (1697), L.I.F. *c.* March 1697.

HORDEN, HILDEBRAND: Prologue, Robert Gould, *The Rival Sisters* (1696), D.L. *c.* Oct. 1695; prologue, Thomas D'Urfey, *Don Quixote*, Part III (1696), D.G.? *c.* Nov. 1695; prologue, Elkanah Settle, *Philaster* (1695), D.L. *c.* Dec. 1695; prologue, Charles Hopkins, *The Neglected Virtue* (1696), D.L. 1696; prologue, Richard Norton, *Pausanias* (1696), D.L. 1696; prologue, Mrs. Manley, *The Lost Lover* (1696), D.L. *c.* April 1696; epilogue, Mrs. Aphra Behn, *The Younger Brother* (1696), D.L. *c.* Dec. 1696.

HOWARD, LADY ELIZABETH: First prologue at Court, Elkanah Settle, *The Empress of Morocco* (1673), Court, *c.* 1671; second prologue at Court, *The Empress of Morocco* (1673), *c.* 1671.

HOWARD, MISS: Epilogue, Thomas Dilke, *The Lover's Luck* (1696), L.I.F. *c.* Dec. 1695; epilogue, Dilke, *The City Lady* (1697), L.I.F. *c.* Jan. 1696/7.

HUDSON, MRS.: Prologue (with others), Peter A. Motteux, *The Loves of Mars & Venus* (1697), L.I.F. *c.* March 1697.

JEVON, THOMAS: Epilogue, Mrs. Aphra Behn, *Like Father, like Son*, D.G. March 1682; epilogue, Edward Ravenscroft, *Dame Dobson* (1684), D.G. *c.* Sept. 1683; prologue, Nahum Tate, *A Duke and no Duke* (1685), D.L. Nov. 1684; prologue, epilogue (with Mrs. Percyvale), Thomas Jevon, *The Devil of a Wife* (1686), D.G. March 1685/6; prologue, Mrs. Behn, *The Luckey Chance* (1687), D.L. *c.* April 1686; prologue (with Stentor), Mrs. Behn, *The Emperor of the Moon* (1687), D.G. *c.* March 1686/7; epilogue, William Mountfort, *The Injur'd Lovers* (1688), D.L. *c.* March 1687/8; prologue, Thomas D'Urfey, *A Fool's Preferment* (1688), D.G. *c.* April 1688.

KEW: Lightning in epilogue, Thomas Duffett, *The Empress of Morocco* (1674),

Appendix C

D.L. c. Dec. 1673. See other performers: Powel, Harris, Lyddal, Goodman, Adams.

KNEPP, MRS.: Prologue (with Nell Gwynn), Sir Robert Howard, *The Great Favourite* (1668), T. R. Feb. 1667/8; epilogue, Thomas Duffett, *The Spanish Rogue* (1674), L.I.F. c. June 1673.

KNIGHT, MRS. MARY: Peace in prologue (with others), John Crowne, *Calisto* (1675), Court, 1675; prologue, George Powell, *The Treacherous Brothers* (1690), D.L. c. Dec. 1689; epilogue, Elkanah Settle, *The Distress'd Innocence* (1691), D.L. c. Oct. 1690; epilogue, Powell, *Alphonso King of Naples* (1691), D.L. c. Dec. 1690; epilogue, Powell, *A Very Good Wife* (1693), D.L. March 1692/3; prologue, Elkanah Settle, *The Ambitious Slave* (1694), D.L. c. Oct. 1693/4; epilogue, Thomas Scott, *The Mock-Marriage* (1696), D.G. c. Oct. 1695.

L., MRS. P.: *Olympus*, 1675, "Spoken by Mrs. P.L. to the right honourable the Lord and Lady Roos, at Belvoir, before a Play; she standing up, as rising from the dead," Thomas Shipman, *Carolina: Or, Loyal Poems* (1683), pp. 157–160.

LACY, JOHN: First epilogue, Sir Robert Howard, *The Vestal Virgin* (1665), T.R. c. 1664; prologue, John Lacy, *The Old Troop* (1672), T.R. c. 1665; epilogue, Peter Belon, *The Mock-Duellist* (1675), D.L. c. May 1675.

LAMBERT, Edward: Prologue, Elkanah Settle, *Pastor Fido* (1677), D.G. c. Dec. 1676.

LASSELLS, MRS.: Epilogue, Henry Higden, *The Wary Widdow* (1693), D.L. Feb. 1692/3.

LEE, MRS. MARY: Epilogue, Elkanah Settle, *Love and Revenge* (1675), D.G. Nov. 1674; epilogue (with Smith), Settle, *The Conquest of China* (1676), D.G. May 1675; epilogue, Thomas Otway, *Alcibiades* (1675), D.G. Sept. 1675; epilogue, Thomas D'Urfey, *Madam Fickle* (1697), D.G. Nov. 1676; epilogue, Otway, *The Cheats of Scapin* (1677), D.G. c. Dec. 1676; epilogue, Otway, *Titus and Berenice* (1677), D.G. c. Dec. 1676; prologue, Anon., *The Constant Nymph* (1678), D.G. c. July 1677; epilogue, Anon., *Romulus and Hersilia* (1683), D.G. c. Aug. 1682; prologue, Anon., *Mr. Turbulent* (1682), D.G. c. Jan. 1682. See Lady Slingsby.

LEE, ANTHONY: Epilogue, Thomas D'Urfey, *A Fond Husband* (1677), D.G. May 1676; epilogue, Thomas Porter, *The French Conqueror* (1678), D.G. c. July 1677; prologue, Thomas Shadwell, *The Woman-Captain* (1680), D.G. c. Sept. 1679; prologue (with Nokes and Mrs. Barrer), D'Urfey, *The Virtuous Wife* (1680), D.G. c. Sept. 1679; epilogue (with Mrs. Barry), Shadwell, *The Lancashire Witches* (1681), D.G. c. Sept. 1681; epilogue (with Mrs. Currer, Mrs. Barry, Mrs. Petty, Smith, Nokes, Underhill), Edward Ravenscroft, *The London Cuckolds* (1682), D.G. c. Nov. 1681; epilogue (with two Gentlemen), John

Appendix C

Crowne, *The City Politiques* (1683), D.L. Jan. 1682/3; epilogue, Nahum Tate, *A Duke and no Duke* (1685), D.L. Nov. 1684; epilogue (with Nokes and Mountfort), William Mountfort, *The Successful Straingers* (1690), D.L. c. Dec. 1689.

LEVERIDGE, RICHARD: Prologue, Peter A. Motteux, *The Island Princess* (1698), D.L. c. Dec. 1698. Pieces were assigned to Leveridge after 1700.

LINDSEY, MRS.: Epilogue (sung with the Boy), Peter A. Motteux, *The Island Princess* (1698), D.L. c. Dec. 1698.

LONG, MRS.: Epilogue (with Angel), John Crowne, *Juliana* (1671), L.I.F. c. Aug. 1671.

LYDDAL: Third Witch in epilogue (with others), Thomas Duffett, *The Empress of Morocco* (1674), D.L. c. Dec. 1673.

MACKAREL, BETTY: Prologue (with Haynes), Thomas Duffett, *The Mock-Tempest* (1675), D.L. Nov. 1674. See note on the name in M. Summers, *The Restoration Theatre*, p. 151.

MARMYON, SHAKERLEY: Prologue (with the Critic), Shakerley Marmyon, *A Fine Companion* (1633).

MARSH, JR.: Africa in prologue (with others), John Crowne, *Calisto* (1675), Court, 1675.

MARSHALL, MRS.: Prologue, Thomas Killigrew, *The Parson's Wedding* (1664), T.R. Oct. 1664; prologue and epilogue, Beaumont and Fletcher, *Philaster* revived, T.R. 1673, Genest, *op. cit.*, I, 146; epilogue, John Crowne, *The Destruction of Jerusalem*, II (1677), D.L. Jan. 1676/7; epilogue to Oxford, written by Dryden, *Miscellany Poems* (1684), pp. 275–277 (Compare with lines for Mrs. Boutell in the same volume, pp. 269–271).

MEDBOURNE, MATTHEW: Epilogue, Matthew Medbourne, *Tartuffe* (1670), T.R. c. April 1670. MS. note in Langbaine, *Dramatick Poets* (Bodleian, Malone. 129), p. 367.

MILLS, JOHN: Epilogue, George Powell, *The Imposture Defeated* (1698), D.L. c. Sept. 1697; epilogue, Charles Gildon, *Phaëton* (1698), D.L. 1698. The majority of Mills' pieces were spoken after 1700.

MODERS, MADAM (alias MARY CARLETON): Epilogue, *The German Princess* (probably the same as *The Witty Combat*, 1663), L.I.F. April 15, 1664. See Genest, *op. cit.*, I, 52.

MOHUN, MAJOR MICHAEL: Epilogue, Ben Jonson, *The Silent Woman* revived, T.R. June 1, 1664. See Genest, *op. cit.*, I, 56; epilogue, Jonson, T.R. Jan. 14, 1665 (Genest, *op. cit.*, I, 56); prologue, John Dryden, *The Conquest of Granada*, II (1672), T.R. Jan. 1670/1; epilogue, William Wycherley, *Love in a Wood* (1672), T.R. c. April 1671; prologue, Anon., *The Amorous Old Woman* (1674), D.L. c. March 1674; epilogue, Thomas D'Urfey, *Trick for Trick* (1678), D.L. c.

March 1677/8; prologue, John Banks, *The Unhappy Favourite* (1682), D.L. c. Sept. 1681.

MONMOUTH: Prologue, Mrs. Catherine Phillips and Sir John Denham, *Horace* (1667), Whitehall, 1667/8.

MOOR, MRS.: Epilogue, Thomas Dilke, *The Pretenders* (1698), L.I.F. c. May 1698. Pieces were assigned to Mrs. Moor after 1700.

MOUNTFORT, MRS. SUSANNA (*nee* PERCYVAL): Epilogue, Thomas Shadwell, *The Squire of Alsatia* (1688), D.L. May 1688; prologue proposed, John Dryden, *Don Sebastian* (1690), D.L. Dec. 1689; epilogue, Dryden, *Amphitryon* (1690), D.L. April 1690; epilogue, Thomas Wright, *The Female Vertuoso's* (1693), D.G. April 1693; epilogue, William Congreve, *The Double Dealer* (1694), D.L. Oct. 1693; epilogue, Thomas Southerne, *The Fatal Marriage* (1694), D.L. Feb. 1693/4; epilogue, Thomas D'Urfey, *Don Quixote*, III (1696), D.G.? c. Nov. 1695; epilogue, Southerne, *Oronooko* (1696), D.L. c. Nov. 1695; epilogue, Mrs. Catherine Trotter, *Agnes de Castro* (1696), D.L. c. Dec. 1695; epilogue, Richard Norton, *Pausanias* (1696), D.L. 1696; epilogue, Mrs. Mary Pix, *The Spanish Wives* (1696), D.L. c. Sept. 1696; prologue for the third day, Sir John Vanbrugh, *The Relapse* (1697), D.L. Dec. 1696. See Mrs. Percyval and Mrs. Verbruggen.

MOUNTFORT, WILLIAM: Prologue to the University, 1687, *Apollo's Feast* (1703), p. 136; prologue, William Mountfort, *The Injur'd Lovers* (1688), D.L. c. March 1687/8; epilogue, Thomas D'Urfey, *A Fool's Preferment* (1688), D.G. c. April 1688; prologue, Thomas Shadwell, *The Squire of Alsatia* (1688), D.L. May 1688; prologue, Shadwell, *Bury Fair* (1689), D.L. April 1689; prologue, Nathaniel Lee, *Massacre of Paris* (1690), D.L. Oct. 1689; epilogue (with Mrs. Butler), D'Urfey, *Love for Money* (1691), D.L. c. Dec. 1689; epilogue (with Nokes and Lee), Mountfort, *The Successful Straingers* (1690), D.L. Dec. 1689; epilogue intended for a late comedy, Thomas Duffett, *New Poems* (1690), pp. 112–114; prologue (with Mrs. Bracegirdle), D'Urfey, *The Marriage-Hater Match'd* (1692), D.L. Jan. 1691/2; prologue, John Dryden, *Cleomenes* (1692), D.L. April 1692.

MOYLE, MRS.: Epilogue at Oxford, July 18, 1682, folio half-sheet, 1682.

MYNNS: Gypsy in epilogue (with others), Peter A. Motteux, *Love's a Jest* (1696), L.I.F. c. Sept. 1696.

NOKES, JAMES: Prologue (with Angel), Roger Boyle, Earl of Orrery, *Tryphon* (1669), L.I.F. Dec. 1668; first prologue (with Underhill and Angel), Hon. Edward Howard, *The Womens Conquest* (1671), L.I.F. c. Nov. 1670; epilogue, John Dryden, *The Kind Keeper* (1680), D.G. March 1677/8; prologue, Thomas D'Urfey, *Squire Oldsapp* (1679), D.G. c. June 1678; epilogue, D'Urfey, *The Virtuous Wife* (1680), D.G. c. Sept. 1679; epilogue (with others), Edward Ravenscroft, *The London*

Appendix C

Cuckolds (1682), D.G. Nov. 1681; epilogue (with Lee and Mountfort) Mountfort, *The Successful Straingers* (1690), D.L. *c.* Dec. 1689.

NORRIS, HENRY: Epilogue, Abel Boyer, *Achilles* (1700), D.L. *c.* Dec. 1699 Norris spoke prologues and epilogues after 1700.

PENKETHMAN, WILLIAM: Prologue, Mrs. Mary Pix, *The Spanish Wive.* (1697), D.L. *c.* Sept. 1696; prologue, Thomas D'Urfey, *The Campaigners* (1698), D.L. *c.* Nov. 1698; prologue, D'Urfey, *The Famous History of the Rise and Fall of Massaniello*, I (1700), D.L. *c.* May 1699; epilogue, Peter A. Motteux, *The Island Princess* (1701), D.L. *c.* Dec. 1698. Penkethman spoke many prologues and epilogues after 1700.

PERCYVAL, MRS. SUSANNA: Epilogue (with Jevon), Thomas Jevon, *The Devil of a Wife* (1686), D.G. March 1685/6. See Mrs. Susanna Mountfort and Mrs. Verbruggen for the pieces spoken after this date.

PERRIN, MRS.: Prologue (with others), Peter A. Motteux, *The Loves of Mars & Venus* (1697), L.I.F. *c.* March 1697.

PETTY, MRS.: Epilogue (with Smith, Leigh, Nokes, Underhill, Mrs. Currer, Mrs. Barry), Edward Ravenscroft, *The London Cuckolds* (1682), D.G. Nov. 1681.

POEL: Prologue to the *Indian Emperor*, Thomas Duffett, *New Poems* (1676), pp. 89–91.

POLLARD, THOMAS: Epilogue, Beaumont and Fletcher, *The Humorous Lieutenant*, *c.* May 1619. See Baldwin, *op. cit.* Epilogue, James Shirley, *The Cardinal*, lic. Nov. 25, 1641. See Baldwin, *op. cit.*

POPE, THOMAS: Prologue (with Cundall), Ben Jonson, *Every Man out of His Humour*, Baldwin, *op. cit.*, as Quince, a prologue in *A Midsummer Night's Dream.*

PORTER, MRS.: Prologue, George Powell, *Bonduca* (1696), D.L. *c.* Sept. 1695; epilogue, Francis Manning, *The Generous Choice* (1700), L.I.F. *c.* Feb. 1699/1700. Mrs. Porter spoke prologues and epilogues after 1700.

POWELL, the ELDER: Epilogue, Thomas Duffett, *The Empress of Morocco* (1674), D.L. *c.* Dec. 1673 (as Hecate with others); prologue to *The Indian Emperor*, spoken by Poel, in Duffett's *New Poems* (1676), pp. 89–91; epilogue, John Leanerd, *The Rambling Justice* (1678), D.L. *c.* March 1677/8; Prologue at Oxford, printed in folio half-sheet, July 10, 1682.

POWELL, the YOUNGER: George Powell was first heard of as a player in 1687, according to the *Dictionary of National Biography*. All prologues and epilogues carrying the name "Powel" after this date are listed here: Epilogue, Nathaniel Lee, *The Massacre of Paris* (1690), D.L. Oct. 1689; prologue, John Bancroft, *Edward the Third* (1691), D.L. *c.* Dec. 1690; prologue, George Powel, *Alphonso King of Naples* (1691), D.L. *c.* Dec. 1690; prologue, Thomas D'Urfey, *Don Quixote*, Part II (1694), D.G. *c.* May 1694; prologue by Colley Cibber, Mrs. Aphra Behn,

Appendix C

Abdelazer (1677), acted by Patentees in April 1695; prologue, Thomas Southerne, *Oronooko* (1696), D.L. *c.* Nov. 1695; second prologue, Mrs. Catherine Trotter, *Agnes de Castro* (1696), D.L. *c.* Dec. 1695; prologue, Mrs. Aphra Behn, *The Younger Brother* (1696), D.L. *c.* Dec. 1696; prologue, George Powell, *The Imposture Defeated* (1698), D.L. *c.* Sept. 1697; prologue, Anon., *Fatal Discovery* (1698), D.L. *c.* March 1697/8; prologue, John Crowne, *Caligula* (1698), D.L. *c.* March 1697/8; prologue (with Mrs. Cross and Miss Chock), Charles Gildon, *Phæton* (1698), D.L. 1698; prologue (first part), Peter A. Motteux, *The Island Princess* (1699), D.L. *c.* Dec. 1698; prologue, George Farquhar, *Love and a Bottle* (1699), D.L. 1699; prologue, Abel Boyer, *Achilles* (1700), D.L. *c.* Dec. 1699; epilogue designed for Powel for *Love without Interest* (1699). Powel continued to speak prologues and epilogues after 1700.

PRICE, JOSEPH: Prologue, Sir William Davenant, *The Rivals* (1668), acted at L.I.F. before Sept. 1664, according to Downes (p. 33) and Genest (I, 55).

PRINCE, MRS.: Epilogue, Peter A. Motteux, *Novelty* (1697), L.I.F. *c.* June 1697. Mrs. Prince was a prologue-epilogue speaker after 1700.

RICHARDS, JOHN: Epilogue, *The Constant Nymph* (1678), by a Person of Quality, D.G. *c.* July 1677; epilogue in folio half-sheet, Mrs. Behn, *Like Father, like Son*, 1682 (spoken with Mr. Gevan).

RICHARDSON: Asia (with others) in prologue to John Crowne's *Calisto* (1675), Court, 1675.

ROCHE, MRS.: Prologue, Nathaniel Lee, *Gloriana* (1676), D.L. Jan. 1675/6.

ROGERS, MRS.: Epilogue, Elkanah Settle, *The Ambitious Slave* (1694), D.L. Feb. 1693/4; epilogue, Anon., *The Triumphs of Virtue* (1697), D.L. *c.* 1696/7; epilogue (with Penkethman), Peter A. Motteux, *The Island Princess* (1699), D.L. *c.* Dec. 1698; epilogue, Thomas D'Urfey, *The Famous History of the Rise and Fall of Massaniello*, Part I (1700), D.L. *c.* May 1699.

SANDFORD, SAMUEL: Epilogue (with Harris), Sir William Davenant, *The Man's the Master* (1669), L.I.F. March 1667/8. Genest, I, 85.

SCUDAMORE: Epilogue, Mrs. Mary Pix, *The Innocent Mistress* (1697), L.I.F. *c.* Sept. 1697.

SHATTERIL: Prologue (with Haynes), Hon. Edward Howard, *The Man of Newmarket* (1678), D.L. *c.* April 1678.

SLINGSBY, LADY: Epilogue, Anon., *Romulus and Hersilia* (1682), D.G. Aug. 1682; prologue, Anon., *Mr. Turbulent* (1682), reissued as *The Factious Citizen*, with same prologue, in 1685, D.G. *c.* Jan. 1682. See Mrs. Mary Lee.

SMITH, WILLIAM: Epilogue, Sir Samuel Tuke, *The Adventures of Five Hours* (1663), L.I.F. Jan. 1662/3; prologue, Nevil Payne, *The Fatal Jealousie* (1673), D.G. Aug. 1672; epilogue, Arrowsmith, *The Reformation*

Appendix C

(1673), D.G. *c.* Sept. 1673; epilogue, spoken with Mrs. Lee, Elkanah Settle, *The Conquest of China* (1676), D.G. May 1675; epilogue by Dryden, George Etherege, *The Man of Mode* (1676), D.G. March 1675/6; prologue, Thomas D'Urfey, *Madam Fickle* (1677), D.G. Nov. 1676; prologue, Samuel Pordage, *The Siege of Babylon* (1678), D.G. *c.* Sept. 1677; prologue, Thomas Otway, *Friendship in Fashion* (1678), D.G. April 1678; epilogue, Mrs. Aphra Behn, *The Feign'd Curtizans* (1679), D.G. *c.* March 1678/9; prologue, Mrs. Behn, *The Rover,* Part II (1681), D.G. Feb. or April 1680; epilogue, Edward Ravenscroft, *The London Cuckolds* (1682), D.G. Nov. 1681; prologue, Thomas Otway, *Venice Preserved* (1682), D.G. Feb. 1681/2; prologue, Mrs. Behn, *The False Count* (1682), D.G. *c.* Sept. 1682; prologue by Dryden, Otway, *Venice Preserved* performed upon his Royal Highness' return from Scotland, D.G. April 21, 1682; prologue, Dryden and Lee, *The Duke of Guise* (1683), D.L. Nov. 1682; prologue, John Crowne, *The City Politiques* (1683), D.L. Jan. 1682/3; epilogue, by Dryden, To the King and Queen at the Opening of their Theatre, Nov. 16, 1682, printed in 1683.

SPENCER, MRS.: Epilogue, Samuel Pordage, *Herod and Mariamne* (1673), L.I.F. Oct. 1673.

TEMPLE, MRS.: Epilogue, *Brutus of Alba,* published by G. Powell (1697), D.G. *c.* Oct. 1696.

THURMOND: Prologue, Joseph Harris, *The City Bride* (1696), L.I.F. *c.* Jan. 1696.

TOOLEY, NICHOLAS: As Puck sang words concluding *A Midsummer Night's Dream,* summer, 1694, Baldwin, *op. cit.*

TURNER: Genius of England in prologue to Crowne's *Calisto* (1675), Court, 1675.

UNDERHILL, CAVE: Epilogue, Abraham Cowley, *The Cutter of Coleman Street* (1663), L.I.F. Dec. 16, 1661; song-epilogue, *Twelfth Night,* L.I.F. May 28, 1663; epilogue, Thomas Shadwell, *The Libertine* (1676), D.G. June 1675; prologue, Thomas Otway, *Titus and Berenice* (1677), D.G. *c.* Dec. 1676; epilogue, John Dryden, *Troilus and Cressida* (1679), D.G. April 1679; epilogue, Thomas D'Urfey, *The Royalist* (1682), D.G. Jan. 1681/2; epilogue, Anon., *Mr. Turbulent* (1682), reissued with this epilogue as *The Factious Citizen* (1685), D.G. *c.* Jan. 1682; epilogue (with Bowen and Gypsy), Peter A. Motteux, *Love's a Jest* (1696), L.I.F. *c.* Sept. 1696.

VERBRUGGEN, JOHN: Epilogue, Robert Gould, *The Rival Sisters* (1696), D.L. *c.* Oct. 1695; prologue to a Young Lady's *The Unnatural Mother* (1698), L.I.F. *c.* Aug. 1697; prologue, Mrs. Mary Pix, *The Innocent Mistress* (1697), L.I.F. *c.* Sept. 1697; epilogue design'd for Mr. Verbruggen to Mrs. Pix's *The Deceiver Deceived* (1698), L.I.F. *c.* Dec. 1697; prologue, Thomas Scott, *The Unhappy Kindness* (1697), D.L.

Appendix C

1697; prologue, John Dennis, *Iphigenia* (1700), L.I.F. 1699. Verbruggen spoke prologues and epilogues after 1700.

VERBRUGGEN, MRS. (See Mrs. Mountfort): Epilogue, Thomas Southerne, *The Fatal Marriage* (1694), D.L. Feb. 1693/4; epilogue, Thomas D'Urfey, *Don Quixote*, Part III (1696), D.G.? *c.* Nov. 1695; epilogue, Southerne, *Oronooko* (1696), *c.* Nov. 1695; epilogue, Catherine Trotter, *Agnes de Castro* (1696), D.L. *c.* Dec. 1695; epilogue, Richard Norton, *Pausanias* (1696), D.L. 1696; epilogue, Mrs. Mary Pix, *The Spanish Wives* (1696), D.L. *c.* Sept. 1696; prologue for the third day, Sir John Vanbrugh, *The Relapse* (1697), D.L. Dec. 1696.

WENTWORTH, LADY HENRIETTA MARIA: Epilogue to *Calisto* (*Miscellany Poems*, 1684), intended for Lady Henrietta Maria Wentworth.

WILLIAMS, JOSEPH: Prologue by Dryden, spoken with Bowen and Bright, Joseph Harris, *The Mistakes* (1691), D.L. *c.* Dec. 1690.

343

APPENDIX D

SEVENTEENTH-CENTURY
MISCELLANIES CONTAINING PROLOGUES AND
EPILOGUES

Pleasant Dialogues and Drammas, Selected out of Lucian, Erasmus, Textor, Ovid, &c. . . . With sundry Emblems extracted from the most elegant Iacobus Catsius. . . . With divers Speeches (upon severall occasions) spoken to their most Excellent Majesties . . . London, 1637.

Poems, By Henry Glapthorn. London, 1639.

The Fancies Theatre. By John Tatham Gent. . . . London, 1640.

Narcissus, Or, The Self-Lover. By James Shirley. London, 1646.

Lucasta. . . . By Richard Lovelace. London, 1649.

Ostella: Or the Faction of Love and Beauty Reconcil'd. By I. T. Gent. London, 1650.

Poems: By Francis Beaumont, Gent. London, 1652/3.

Wit Restor'd in severall Select Poems not formerly publish't. London, 1658.

The Last Remains of Sr John Suckling. . . . London, 1659.

A Rosary of Rarities Planted In a Garden of Poetry . . . By Tho. Jordan. . . . London, N. D.

Wit and Drollery . . . By Sir J. M. Ja. S. Sir W. D. J. D. and the most refined Wits of the Age. London, 1661.

A Nursery of Novelties. . . . By Tho. Jordan. London, N. D.

The Works of Mr Abraham Cowley. London, 1668.

A Collection of Poems . . . Printed for Hobart Kemp . . . 1672. See Hugh Macdonald, *John Dryden* (Oxford Press, 1939), p. 97, n. 4.

Covent Garden Drollery. . . . London, 1672.

Madagascar, With other Poems. By Sr William D'Avenant. London, 1672.

Poems on Several Occasions, Never before Printed. London, 1672.

Westminster-Drollery, The Second Part . . . 1672.

London Drollery: Or, The Wits Academy . . . By W. N. London, 1673.

New Poems, Songs, Prologues and Epilogues. Never before Printed. Written by Thomas Duffett. . . . London, 1676.

Appendix D

New Songs, and Poems, A-la-mode both at Court, and Theatres, Now Extant Never Before Printed . . . by P W Gent. London, 1677.

Carolina: Or, Loyal Poems. By Tho. Shipman. London, 1683.

Poems on Several Occasions, By W. C. London, 1684.

Miscellany Poems. . . . London, Printed for Jacob Tonson, 1684.

Poems Written On several Occasions, By N. Tate. London, 1684.

Miscellany, Being a Collection of Poems. . . . London: Printed for J. Hindmarsh, 1685.

Sylvae: or, the Second Part of Poetical Miscellanies. . . . London, 1685.

Poems Chiefly consisting of Satyrs and Satyrical Epistles. By Robert Gould. . . . London and Westminster, 1689.

New Poems, Consisting of Satyrs, Elegies, and Odes: Together with a Choice Collection Of the Newest Court Songs . . . All Written by Mr. D'Urfey. London, 1690.

Examen Poeticum: Being The Third Part of Miscellany Poems. . . . London: Printed by R. E. for Jacob Tonson, 1693.

The Works of Mr. Abraham Cowley. . . . London, 1693.

The Annual Miscellany; for The Year 1694. . . . London, 1694.

Poems, (&c.) On Several Occasions: With Valentinian. . . . Written By the Right Honourable John Late Earl of Rochester. London, 1696.

State-Poems: Continued From the time of O. Cromwel, to this present Year 1697. Written by the Greatest Wits of the Age. . . . London, 1697.

Poems on Affairs of State. The Second Part. . . . London, 1697.

Poems on Affairs of State. . . . Part III. . . . London, 1698.

A Collection of Miscellany Poems, Letters, &c. By Mr. Brown, &c. . . . London, 1699.

APPENDIX E

BOOKSELLERS AND PRINTERS

INDEX TO THE FIRST LINES

Index to the First Lines

GENERAL INDEX

General Index

General Index

General Index

General Index

355

General Index

General Index

357

General Index

UNIVERSITY LIBRARY NOTTINGHAM

358